Facts About Canada, Its Provinces and Territories

Facts About Canada, Its Provinces and Territories

JEAN WEIHS

Illustrations by Cameron Riddle

H.W. Wilson Company
1995

Library of Congress Cataloging-in-Publication Data

Weihs, Jean Riddle.
    Facts about Canada, its provinces and territories / Jean Weihs.
      p. cm.
    Includes bibliographical references and index.
    ISBN 0-8242-0864-1
    1. Canada–Miscellanea.   I. Title.
F1008.W44   1994
971—dc20   94-23275
                                             CIP

Printed in the United States of America

Contents

Introduction

The focus of this book is the provinces and territories that make up Canada rather than Canada as a whole. This has been done because an adequate number of sources describing the social and economic framework of the Canadian federation are available while there is a dearth of handy information about the provinces and territories. The brief section on Canada does provide some basic background information with which to set the provinces and territories in a wider context.

The geographic, economic, cultural, and social information included in every chapter is intended to provide a general picture of each province and territory. This information may be used also to provide answers to specific questions. The bibliography at the end of each chapter directs the reader to sources of further information.

Figures from the 1991 census data are the basis for the demographic statistics used in this book. While population figures for later years have been published, these have not been included in this book because they are estimates. Where information relates to other dates, this is indicated. In other sections, also, statistical data are for 1991 unless otherwise indicated.

Much of the information has been supplied by agencies of the provinces and territories. Their methods of presenting information has often differed, resulting in what may appear as inconsistencies within the book, e.g., the categorization of roads. Measurements, temperatures, etc., are those given in official sources and may also be inconsistent, e.g., some provinces and territories report the size of provincial parks in hectares, others in square kilometres. A translation into non-metric measurements and into degrees Fahrenheit is given in parentheses. When a province has provided measurements in non-metric terms, these have been translated into metric figures. Measurements have been rounded off to the indicated decimal.

The following notes apply to certain sections and subsections of the text.

Geography and Climate

Major Rivers.   There is no agreed definition about what constitutes a major river. Various departments of Canadian government agencies use different factors in making their determination: length, mean annual discharge at outlet, size of drainage areas, and the historical importance of the waterway. When a province has not named its major rivers, the author has selected those rivers that appear to be major because of their length or importance.

Parks and Historic Sites

Ramsar Sites.   Wetlands, the home for a large and diverse array of plants and animals, make an important contribution to the world's life-support systems. These wetlands are imperilled by many factors, such as urban growth and hydroelectric development.

An international convention, "The Convention on Wetlands of International Importance Especially as Waterfowl Habitat" or more commonly "The Ramsar Convention" was drafted by representatives of eighteen countries and came into force on December 21, 1975. Many more countries have joined the convention since that time. Canada signed the convention in 1981. Wetlands occupy about 14% of Canada's total area and they contain 15% of the world's fresh water. Canada has designated 31 Ramsar sites covering about 13 million ha. (50,200 sq. mi.), the largest area of any member nation.

Unesco Biosphere Reserves. Unesco defines a biosphere reserve as an area that "is a good example of some of the ways in which conservation objectives can be balanced with development". It describes a reserve's main functions as "conservation of important biological systems; demonstration of the practicability of sustainable development; and provision of opportunities to integrate research, monitoring, education and training in conservation and the sustainable use of resources". Biosphere reserves differ from national and provincial parks and reserves in that they include areas of managed or transformed landscapes together with protected areas of undisturbed land. There are six biosphere reserves in Canada; it is estimated that nine more are needed to represent the biogeographic diversity of Canada.

Demography

Cities and Towns. In the 1991 census Statistics Canada defined a census metropolitan area (CMA) as "a very large urban area, together with adjacent and rural areas which have a high degree of economic and social integration with that urban area. A CMA is delineated around an urban area (called urbanized core and having a population of at least 100,000 based on the previous census). Once an area becomes a CMA, it is retained in the program even if its population subsequently declines".

The definition for a census agglomerate (CA) differs from CMA only in the population size of the area, which must be at least 10,000 based on the previous census but less than 100,000.

A census subdivision (CSD) is defined as "the general term applying to municipalities (as determined by provincial legislation) or their equivalent, e.g., Indian reserves, Indian settlements and unorganized territories".

For each province all CMAs and cities or towns with more than 10,000 population to a maximum of ten centres have been listed. For Ontario, the most populous province, all ten population centres are CMAs, while for Prince Edward Island, the smallest province, only two of the centres have more than 10,000 residents. The acronym CMA or CA beside the population indicates that the figure includes the surrounding area. In the sparsely populated Northwest Territories and Yukon Territory only the capital cities are ranked as CAs although no surrounding agglomeration is part of their total population. In these instances, all towns have been given in CSD rank.

Finances

Financial statements are based on information supplied by provinces and territories and the designations used by them have been maintained. The breakdown into sources and revenues and function of expenditures has been selected to reflect major activities only.

Economy

The latest revised data available at the time of writing have been used to present significant economic indicators and activities. If the same reporting year had been used throughout, more recent information provided by some provinces and territories could not have been included.

Statistics Canada defines factor cost as representing "the costs of the factors of production".

Export data have been supplied by Statistics Canada, the provinces, and the territories. In some instances the data apply to merchandising trade only.

Culture and Education

Performing Arts. When a province or territory has not indicated its major companies and events, the selection has been made based on a variety of factors, including the number of years the company or event has been in operation, its international or national importance, and its significance to the province or territory.

Sources of Information

The author appreciates the time taken by the staff of government and other organizations to answer questions which, in many cases, required extensive work. These organizations are listed by the names under which they provided information. Subsequent government reorganization may have changed names or functions.

Alberta Aboriginal Affairs
Alberta Community Development
    Arts and Cultural Industries Branch
    Historic Sites and Archive Services
Alberta Economic Development and Tourism
Alberta Environmental Protection
    Alberta Parks Service
    Information Resource Management
    Surface Water Monitoring Branch, River Forecast Centre
Alberta Federal and Intergovernmental Affairs
Alberta Labour
    Employment Standards Branch
Alberta Legislative Assembly
    Public Information Branch
Alberta Native Affairs
Alberta Registries, Motor Vehicles
Arctic College
British Columbia Archives and Records Service
British Columbia Chief Electoral Office
British Columbia Ministry of the Environment
    British Columbia Geographic Names Office
    British Columbia Parks
British Columbia Ministry of Small Business, Tourism and Culture
    Cultural Services Branch
    Heritage Properties Branch
British Columbia Ministry of Transportation and Highways
    Motor Vehicle Branch
British Columbia Office of the Premier
Bureau de Québec, Toronto Office
Canada. Energy, Mines and Resources Canada
    Canada Centre for Mapping, National Atlas Information Service

Canada. Environment Canada
 Atmospheric Environment Service
 Ecosystem Sciences and Evaluation Directorate, Surveys and Information
  Branch
 Canadian Parks Service
 Canadian Wildlife Service

Canada. Industry, Trade, and Technology Canada

Canadian Commission for Unesco

City of Saint John (New Brunswick)
 Intergovernmental Affairs

City of Toronto (Ontario) Information Services

Communications New Brunswick

Communications Québec

Elections Alberta

Elections Manitoba

Fredericton (New Brunswick) Tourism Department

Greater Saint John (New Brunswick) Economic Development Commission

Manitoba Arts Council

Manitoba Citizen's Inquiry Service

Manitoba Culture, Heritage and Citizenship
 Historic Resources Branch

Manitoba Executive Council Protocol Office

Manitoba Finance
 Comptroller's Office
 Federal-Provincial Relations and Research

Manitoba French Language Service Secretariat

Manitoba Highways and Transportation
 Driver and Vehicle Licensing

Manitoba Industry, Trade and Tourism
 Business Library

Manitoba Labour
 Employment Standards

Manitoba Natural Resources
 Parks and Natural Areas

Municipality of Metropolitan Toronto, Access Metro

National Capital Commission

Native Council of Nova Scotia

New Brunswick Department of Economic Development and Tourism

New Brunswick Department of Transportation
 Planning Branch

New Brunswick Inquiries

New Brunswick, Office of the Premier

New Brunswick Statistics Agency

New Brunswick Tourism

Newfoundland and Labrador Department of Finance
Newfoundland and Labrador Department of Tourism and Culture
Newfoundland and Labrador, Office of the Premier
Newfoundland Information Service
Newfoundland Legislative Library
Northwest Territories Department of Education, Culture and Employment
    Culture and Heritage Division Library
Northwest Territories Department of Economic Development and Tourism
Northwest Territories Department of Public Works and Services
Northwest Territories Department of Renewable Resources
    Conservation Education
Northwest Territories Department of Transportation
Northwest Territories Intergovernmental and Aboriginal Affairs
Northwest Territories Legislative Assembly
    Research and Information
Northwest Territories, Office of the Government Leader
Northwest Territories Official Languages
Nova Scotia Department of Economic Development
    Statistics Branch
Nova Scotia Department of Finance
Nova Scotia Department of Supply and Services
    Information and Communications Branch
Nova Scotia Department of Tourism and Culture
Nova Scotia Department of Transportation and Communications
Nova Scotia Information Service
Ontario Cancer Institute, Princess Margaret Hospital Library
Ontario Citizens Inquiry Bureau
Ontario. Delegation of Ontario, Paris, France
Ontario Ministry of Agriculture and Food
Ontario Ministry of Colleges and Universities
Ontario Ministry of Culture and Communications
Ontario Ministry of Economic Development
    Trade Promotion Branch
Ontario Ministry of Environment and Energy
Ontario Ministry of Natural Resources
Ontario Ministry of Northern Development and Mines
Ontario Ministry of Transportation
Ontario, Office of the Premier
Ontario, Office of the Chief Electoral Officer
Ontario Travel
Prince Edward Island Department of Economic Development and Tourism
Prince Edward Island Department of Education and Human Resources

Prince Edward Island Department of the Environment
  Water Resources Division
Prince Edward Island Department of Transportation and Public Works
  Highway Safety Division
  Vehicle Registration Section
Prince Edward Island, Office of the Premier
Saskatchewan Economic Development
Saskatchewan Finance
Saskatchewan Legislative Library
Statistics Canada
Tourism British Columbia
Tourism Saskatchewan
Tourisme Québec, Toronto Office
Travel Manitoba
Yukon Territory Bureau of Statistics
Yukon Territory Department of Community and Transportation Services
  Motor Vehicle Branch
Yukon Territory Executive Council Office Inquiry Centre
Yukon Tourism
  Arts Branch

Abbreviations

B.C.	British Columbia
BNA	British North America Act 1867
C	Celsius
CA	census agglomerate
CCF	Co-operative Commonwealth Federation
cm.	centimetre(s)
CMA	census metropolitan area
comp.; comps.	compiler; compilers
CSD	census subdivision
cu.	cubic
ed.; eds.	editor, edited; editors
E.E.C.	European Economic Community
F	Fahrenheit
FLQ	Front de liberation du Québec
ft.	foot, feet
g.	gram(s)
gal.	gallon(s)
G.D.P.	gross domestic product
ha.	hectare(s)
hr.	hour(s)
kg.	kilogram(s)
km.	kilometre(s)
kPa	kilopascal(s)
kph	kilometres per hour
l.	litre(s)
lb.	pound(s)
m.	metre(s)
mi.	mile(s)
min.	minute(s)
mm.	millimetre(s)
mph	miles per hour
N.B.	New Brunswick

N.W.T.	Northwest Territories
oz.	ounce(s)
P.E.I.	Prince Edward Island
pop.	population
RCMP	Royal Canadian Mounted Police
rev.	revised
sq.	square
U.K.	United Kingdom
USSR	Union of Soviet Socialist Republics
UTC	coordinated universal time

CANADA

Canada occupies the northern part of the North American continent. It extends north-south for 4,346 km. (2,701 mi.) from Cape Columbia on Ellesmere Island in the Northwest Territories to Middle Island in Lake Ontario; east-west for 5,514 km. (3,426 mi.) from Cape Spear in Newfoundland to the Yukon-Alaskan border. It is bordered by the United States in the south and northwest, the polar regions in the north, and by the Atlantic and Pacific Oceans in the east and west.

Name The name Canada is derived from the Huron-Iroquois word "Kanata", meaning a "village" or "settlement". Jacques Cartier is reported to have encountered the word when some Indian youths directed him to the village of Stadacona, on the site of present-day Quebec City. The word soon came to mean "the province of Canada".

Flag A red flag containing a white square with a maple leaf in the centre, adopted by Parliament on February 15, 1965. Prior to its adoption, Canada did not have a national flag and the red ensign, a British maritime flag, was in general use as a flag of Canada.

Coat of Arms The arms of Canada contain the arms of England, France, Ireland, and Scotland denoting the founding peoples. Beneath the four quarters is a white field with a sprig of three maple leaves, originally green, but changed to red in 1957. The arms were proclaimed by George V on November 21, 1921.

Motto *A Mari Usque ad Mare* (From sea to sea).

Emblems Maple leaf; the Beaver (*Castor canadensis*).

Confederation Canada as a country came into being on July 1, 1867 as a result of the British North America Act, 1867 (BNA) passed by the British Parliament. Four provinces, Ontario, Quebec, Nova Scotia, and New Brunswick, made up the original Dominion of Canada. In 1870 the Hudson's Bay Company surrendered to the crown large territories in its possession from which the remaining provinces and territories were in time created. Manitoba entered Confederation in 1870, British Columbia in 1871, Prince Edward Island in 1873, Saskatchewan and Alberta in 1905, and Newfoundland in 1949. Yukon Territory was created in 1898, and Northwest Territories in its present form in 1905, both by acts of the Canadian Parliament.

Official Languages English and French.

Capital City Ottawa is situated in eastern Ontario on the Ottawa River. The name probably derives from an Indian tribe of the same name, which meant 'to trade'. A campsite established by John By in 1826 to serve the construction of the Rideau Canal eventually grew into By-town. In 1855 Bytown became a city re-named Ottawa. The city was selected by Queen Victoria as the capital of the Province of Canada in 1857 and was named the capital of the newly created Dominion of Canada in 1867.

Provinces and Territories The ten provinces, listed from east to west, are:
  Newfoundland
  Prince Edward Island
  Nova Scotia
  New Brunswick
  Quebec
  Ontario
  Manitoba
  Saskatchewan
  Alberta
  British Columbia

The two territories in existence in 1994, listed from east to west, are:
  Northwest Territories
  Yukon Territory

A new territory, Nunavut, with a mainly Inuit population, is being carved out of Northwest Territories and is scheduled to come into formal existence in 1999.

Public Statutory Holidays In addition to Sundays, and any other day specially proclaimed as a holiday by the Governor General of Canada, the following are public statutory holidays.

Name	Date
New Year's Day	January 1
Good Friday	Varies
Easter Monday	Varies
Victoria Day	Monday preceding May 25
Canada Day	July 1
Labour Day	First Monday in September
Thanksgiving Day	Second Monday in October
Remembrance Day	November 11
Christmas Day	December 25
Boxing Day	December 26

When July 1 falls on a Sunday, July 2 is observed as Canada Day.
In addition, some provinces have provincial public holidays.

Geography and Climate

Geography Canada is a country of widely different landscapes, including vast, fertile prairies, an estimated two million fresh water lakes, tall mountain ranges, boreal forests, and huge tracts of tundra. Canada has the longest coastline of any country in the world, almost 244,000 km. (151,600 mi.), with shorelines on three oceans and many coastal islands.

Area Canada comprises a total of 9,970,610 sq. km. (3,849,650 sq. mi.), of which 92.4% is land and the rest fresh water. Canada is the second largest country in the world. With the exception of the prairie areas, Canada has abundant fresh water resources, and can claim 9% of the world's renewable water supply.

Drainage Basins
Pacific
  1,010,300 sq. km. (390,080 sq. mi.)
Arctic
  3,576,900 sq. km. (1,381,040 sq. mi.)
Hudson Bay
  3,797,300 sq. km. (1,466,140 sq. mi.)
Atlantic
  1,559,900 sq. km. (602,280 sq. mi.)
Gulf of Mexico
  26,200 sq. km. (10,120 sq.mi.)

Climate The Canadian climate varies considerably from region to region. In the north temperatures are above freezing only a few months each year. Most Canadians, however, live in a 300 km. (180 mi.)

wide stretch along the southern border, where spring, summer, and fall bring warm temperatures for up to eight months of the year.

Major Weather Systems Within Canada

West Coast: Cool and fairly dry in summer, mild, cloudy, and wet in winter.

Prairies: Continental climate with long, cold winters, hot summers, little precipitation.

Great Lakes/St. Lawrence: Humid, cold winters, hot summers, ample precipitation.

Atlantic Canada: Humid continental climate in the interior, maritime in coastal areas.

Boreal Forest: Long, cold winters, considerable periods of summer.

High Arctic: Long, cold winters, only a few months with temperatures above freezing.

Time Zones There are six time zones in Canada, and they are listed here from east to west with the time difference from coordinated universal time (UTC), which, until recently, was known as Greenwich mean time:

Newfoundland Standard Time: $3^{1}/_{2}$ hours behind UTC

Atlantic Standard Time: 4 hours behind UTC

Eastern Standard Time: 5 hours behind UTC

Central Standard Time: 6 hours behind UTC

Mountain Standard Time: 7 hours behind UTC

Pacific Standard Time: 8 hours behind UTC

Daylight Saving Time (throughout Canada except Saskatchewan): Forward one hour on the first Sunday in April; back one hour the last Sunday in October.

Demography

Population: 27,296,859

Historical population data

1981	24,343,181
1971	21,568,311
1961	18,238,247
1951	14,009,429
1941	11,506,655
1921	8,787,949
1901	5,371,315
1881	4,324,810
1861	3,229,633

Newfoundland's population is included for the first time in 1951.

Population Density: 3.0 persons per sq. km. (7.7 per sq. mi.)

Number of Dwellings: 10,079,442

Population Characteristics:
  urban: 20,907,135; 76.6%
  rural: 6,389,724; 23.4%

19 and under: 7,561,190; 27.7%
65 and over: 3,169,970; 11.6%
average income for full-time employment 15 years and over (1990): $30,274; men $34,921; women $22,799
average life expectancy at birth: men 74.0 years; women 80.6 years
live birth rate: 411,910; 15.2 per 1000
deaths: 191,700; 7.2 per 1000
marriages: 188,660; 7.0 per 1000
divorces: 77,031; 2.82 per 1000
immigration: 224,550

Quality of Life In 1992 and 1994 the United Nations Human Development Report placed Canada first among 160 nations on its quality-of-life human development index. Indicators of life expectancy, educational attainment, and income are combined to produce this index.

Government and Politics, 1867–

Canada is a federal state combining, in the words of its first Prime Minister, Sir John A. Macdonald, "A general government and legislature for general purposes with local government and legislatures for local purposes." The federation came into existence with the British North America Act 1867 (BNA).

The BNA, which functioned as Canada's constitution, defined the respective jurisdictions of the federal and provincial governments as follows:

Federal jurisdiction: defence, external relations, criminal law, money and banking, transportation, citizenship, Indian affairs.

Provincial jurisdiction: education, health and welfare, civil law, natural resources, local government.

Joint federal and provincial jurisdiction: agriculture, immigration.

Federal jurisdiction prevails in areas not specifically assigned under the Act.

As originally enacted, the BNA made no provision for its own amendment other than through action by the British Parliament. Not until the Constitution Act 1982 was there a procedure for amending the basic laws of Canada. The 1982 act contains the Canadian Charter of Rights and Freedoms and renamed the British North America Act 1867 the Constitution Act 1867.

Responsible Government Canada has adopted the British system of responsible government in which the executive, or cabinet, is part of Parliament and responsible to Parliament and must retain the confidence of the House of Commons in order to remain in power. The Parliament consists of the Queen, the Senate, and the House of Commons.

The Queen The Queen is the head of state and symbolically executive power is vested in her. The present Queen, Elizabeth II, in addition to being Queen of Canada, is also Queen of other Commonwealth countries and the head of the Commonwealth. She is represented federally by the Governor General and in each province by Lieutenant-Governors who are appointed by her on the advice of the Prime Minister of Canada. Canada has had six sovereigns since Confederation: Victoria, Edward VII, George V, Edward VIII, George VI, and Elizabeth II.

Governor General The Governor General is appointed by the Queen on the recommendation of the Prime Minister of Canada and is the representative of the Queen in Canada acting on her behalf almost exclusively except on special occasions when the Queen herself is in Canada. It is the Governor General who, acting on the advice of the Prime Minister, summons and dissolves Parliament, gives royal assent to legislation passed by Parliament, and calls upon the leader of the largest party in the House of Commons to form a government. There are only a very limited number of occasions when the Governor General can act on his own initiative. One example is when the government is defeated in the House of Commons on a vote of confidence. Then, it is the Governor General's decision either to ask the leader of the largest opposition party to form a government or to dissolve the House and call a general election.

Until 1952 Governor Generals were drawn mainly from the British aristocracy. Since then, however, they have all been Canadians.

Governor Generals of Canada	Term
Charles Stanley, 4th Viscount Monck	1867–1869
John Young, Baron Lisgar	1869–1872
Frederick Temple Blackwood, 1st Marquess of Dufferin and Ava	1872–1878
John Douglas Sutherland Campbell, Marquess of Lorne	1878–1883
Henry Charles Keith Petty-Fitzmaurice, 5th Marquess of Lansdowne	1883–1888
Frederick Arthur Stanley, Baron Stanley of Preston, 16th Earl of Derby	1888–1893
John Campbell Gordon, 1st Marquess of Aberdeen and Temair	1893–1898

continued	
Gilbert John Murray Kynynmond Elliot, 4th Earl of Minto	1898–1904
Albert Henry George Grey, 4th Earl Grey	1904–1911
Arthur William Patrick Albert, 1st Duke of Connaught and Strath earn	1911–1916
Victor Christian William Cavendish, 9th Duke of Devonshire	1916–1921
Julian Hedworth George, Viscount Byng of Vimy	1921–1926
Freeman Freeman-Thomas, 1st Marquess of Willingdon	1926–1931
Vere Brabazon Ponsonby, 9th Earl of Bessborough	1931–1935
John Buchan, 1st Baron Tweedsmuir	1935–1940
Alexander Augustus Frederick William Alfred George Cambridge, Earl of Athlone	1940–1946
Harold Rupert Leofric George Alexander, 1st Earl Alexander of Tunis	1946–1952
Charles Vincent Massey	1952–1959
Georges-Philéas Vanier	1959–1967
Daniel Roland Michener	1967–1974
Jules Léger	1974–1979
Edward Richard Schreyer	1979–1984
Jeanne-Mathilde Sauvé	1984–1990
Ramon John Hnatyshyn	1990–

Senate Senators are selected by the Prime Minister and on his recommendation appointed by the Governor General. They serve until they reach the age of 75 years (until 1965 senators served for life). The Senate usually has 104 members although there is a provision for the appointment of an additional four or eight members. Appointments are made on a provincial and regional basis: 24 members from among the Atlantic provinces, 24 each from Ontario and Quebec, and 24 from among the western provinces.

Every piece of federal legislation must be passed by the Senate. The Senate has the power to amend or reject legislation originating from the House of Commons although it has exercised the right of rejection only cautiously and rarely. Except for bills involving public expenditure and taxation, the Senate may also initiate legislation. The Senate is regarded generally as the chamber of sober second thought and as a guardian of provincial and regional rights and concerns. The Speaker of the Senate is named by the Governor General, but as always, on the advice of the Prime Minister.

House of Commons The House of Commons is the major legislative body. Since 1983 its membership has been set at 295, each member representing a constituen-cy. The number of constituencies can change after each federal election to reflect population changes in the country. The Speaker of the House is elected by the members of the House of Commons following a general election.

Political Parties Political parties play an essential role in the Canadian parliamentary system. Originally there were two main parties, the Liberals and the Conservatives. The formation in 1932 of the Cooperative Commonwealth Federation, now the New Democratic Party, put an end to two-party rule and created the basis for what has now become a multiparty system. In 1994 five parties had seats in the House of Commons.

Prime Minister The leader of the largest party in the House of Commons is asked by the Governor General to form a government and assume the position of Prime Minister. If the government is later defeated on a vote of confidence, the Governor General may dissolve the House and call a new election or ask the leader of the opposition, the next largest party in the House, to form a government. The new government must then call the House into session and be able to muster a majority to pass legislation and the fiscal measures required to operate the government. The Prime Minister has the power to appoint ministers, privy councilors, provincial administrators, the Speaker of the Senate, chief justices, senators, and senior public servants, but he exercises this power by recommending appointments to the Governor General, who officially makes them.

Prime Ministers of Canada/Party/Term

John Alexander Macdonald
  (Conservative, 1867–1873)
Alexander Mackenzie
  (Liberal, 1873–1878)
John Alexander Macdonald
  (Conservative, 1878–1891)
John Joseph Caldwell Abbott
  (Conservative, 1891–1892)
John Sparrow David Thompson
  (Conservative, 1892–1894)
John Mackenzie Bowell
  (Conservative, 1894–1896)
Charles Tupper
  (Conservative, 1896)
Wilfrid Laurier
  (Liberal, 1896–1911)
Robert Laird Borden
  (Conservative, 1911–1917)
Robert Laird Borden
  (Unionist, 1917–1920)
Arthur Meighen
  (Coalition, 1920–1921)
William Lyon Mackenzie King
  (Liberal, 1921–1926)
Arthur Meighen
  (Conservative, 1926)
William Lyon Mackenzie King
  (Liberal, 1926–1930)
Richard Bedford Bennett
  (Conservative, 1930–1935)
William Lyon Mackenzie King
  (Liberal, 1935–1948)
Louis Stephen St. Laurent
  (Liberal, 1948–1957)
John George Diefenbaker
  (Conservative, 1957–1963)
Lester Bowles Pearson
  (Liberal, 1963–1968)
Pierre Elliott Trudeau
  (Liberal, 1968–1979)
Charles Joseph Clark
  (Conservative, 1979–1980)

Pierre Elliott Trudeau
  (Liberal, 1980–1984)
John Napier Turner
  (Liberal, 1984)
Martin Brian Mulroney
  (Conservative, 1984–1993)
Kim Campbell
  (Conservative, 1993)
Joseph-Jacques Jean Chretien
  (Liberal, 1993–   )

Cabinet The Cabinet exercising executive power consists generally of ministers in charge of government departments. Members of the Cabinet are appointed by the Prime Minister usually from his own party and serve at his pleasure. As a result, the Prime Minister's power far exceeds that of other members of the Cabinet. Cabinet members are expected to conform to the policies of the government and thus maintain cabinet solidarity. All members of the Cabinet must be members of the Queen's Privy Council for Canada.

Privy Council Privy councilors are appointed by the Governor General on the advice of the Prime Minister and serve for life. In addition to present and former cabinet members, the present and former chief justices, past speakers of the House of Commons and Senate, and other prominent Canadians are also appointed. The function of the Privy Council is purely ceremonial and is called into session on rare and special occasions. The full Privy Council has never met and its operative role is exercised by the Cabinet.

Elections There is no set time for elections, but they are held when the Governor General, acting on the advice of the Prime Minister, dissolves the House of Commons. However, elections must be held at least every five years. If the government is defeated in the House of Commons on a major issue or on a vote of confidence, convention requires the government to resign or the Prime Minister to advise the Governor General to dissolve the House and call an election.

Provincial, Territorial, and Local Governments

Lieutenant-Governor On the advice of the Prime Minister, the Governor General appoints a Lieutenant-Governor for each province to act as the Queen's representative in provincial matters. A Lieutenant-Governor acts on the advice of his provincial premier and all bills passed by the provincial legislature must receive royal assent by the Lieutenant-Governor. The last time royal assent was refused was in 1945 in Prince Edward Island. In this instance, the Lieutenant-Governor of Prince Edward Island refused to sign the legislation—an amendment to the Prohibition Act altering the grounds for the legal possession of liquor—because the provincial cabinet was split on the issue.

Legislative Assembly The legislature of each province consists of a Lieutenant-Governor and a unicameral legislative assembly. In areas of provincial jurisdiction the legislative assembly fulfills a role similar to that of the House of Commons federally. All legislation must be passed there to become law. Elections must be held at least every five years but the legislature may be dissolved earlier by the Lieutenant-Governor on the advice of the Premier under circumstances similar to those prevailing federally.

Premier The Lieutenant-Governor calls upon the leader of the largest party to form a ministry, which remains in office as long as it retains the confidence of the legislative assembly. The Premier appoints a cabinet with ministers to head provincial government departments, usually from members of his party elected to the legislature. Ministers remain in office at the Premier's pleasure.

Territorial Government Territorial governments are creations of the federal government; they have no basis in the Constitution and their powers and structures are established and defined by Parliament. Territorial government consists of a legislative assembly and a Commissioner. The Commissioner reports to the federal Minister of Indian Affairs and Northern Development whose function is in some respects similar to that of a Lieutenant-Governor. An executive council made up of members of the territorial legislative assembly fulfills a role similar to that of a provincial cabinet within the limits established by federal statutes.

Local Governments Local governments, comprising municipalities and metropolitan and regional governments, are created by provincial or territorial governments. Powers assigned to local governments vary but may include jurisdiction over police, fire prevention and fighting, public health, social services, local transportation, and recreation. Infrastructure—for example, roads, water supply, and sewers—may also fall within local government jurisdiction.

Aboriginal Self Government The aboriginal peoples of Canada have long sought to achieve self government. The federal government has recently been engaged in negotiations with native organizations toward not only settlements of land claims but also the establishment of native self government. The Royal Commission on Aboriginal People, created in 1991, is expected to issue its report sometime in 1994.

Courts

Federal Courts The Constitution provides authority for Parliament to create a general court of appeal and other courts to further the administration of justice in Canada. Under this authority Parliament has created the Supreme Court of Canada, the Federal Court of Canada, the Court Martial Appeal Court of Canada, and the Tax Court of Canada.

Supreme Court of Canada The Supreme Court of Canada is the highest court of appeal in Canada for all civil, criminal, and constitutional cases. For an appeal to be heard, in most cases, the court must agree beforehand to hear it, although appeal is a right in some instances. The Supreme Court is made up of a Chief Justice and eight associate puisne judges, three of them from Quebec. Judges are appointed by the Governor General on the recommendation of the Prime Minister. The Government of Canada may refer important questions concerning the Constitution and the powers of Parliament or provincial legislatures to the Supreme Court for interpretation.

Federal Court of Canada The Federal Court of Canada consists of a Trial Divi-sion and the Federal Court of Appeal. It has jurisdiction in claims against the Crown, claims by the Crown, and miscellaneous cases involving the Crown.

Administration The administration of justice within their own borders is the responsibility of the provinces. Provinces exercise that responsibility generally by establishing courts of appeal, superior (supreme or trial) courts, county courts, and provincial courts. Territories have similar responsibility for the administration of justice, although the federal Attorney General retains responsibility for criminal prosecutions and for proceedings involving federal statutes. Judges are appointed and paid by the federal or provincial governments and hold office during "good behaviour" and can be removed only by an act of Parliament or the provincial legislature.

Finances

A statement of the federal government's revenues and expenditures for the years 1992/93 and 1991/92 is shown below in millions of dollars. The financial year runs from April 1 to March 31 of the year following.

	Actual 1992/93	Actual 1991/92
Revenue		
Taxation	109,777	103,776
Health and social insurance levies	18,575	15,462
Sales of goods and services	4,212	3,501
Return on investments	6,238	6,556
Other	2,316	2,033
Total revenue for the year	141,118	131,327
Expenditures		
General services	8,156	7,933
Protection of persons and property	15,706	14,788
Transportation and communication	3,577	3,364
Health	7,599	7,674
Social services	57,065	55,216
Education	4,468	4,445
Resource conservation and industrial development	6,911	6,917
Labour employment and immigration	2,442	2,080
Housing	2,090	1,911
Foreign affairs and international assistance	3,747	3,434

Transfer to other government	10,010	9,915
Other	8,319	5,762
Interest on debt	39,928	41,366
Total expenditures for the year	170,019	164,807
Deficit for the year	28,900	33,480

Economy

Gross Domestic Product (1992) $601,309 million (in current dollars at factor cost).

Distribution of Gross Domestic Product (1990)

Manufacturing	17.9%
Finance, insurance, real estate	7.6%
Construction	6.9%
Government services	6.8%
Retail trade	6.1%
Educational services	5.6%
Wholesale trade	5.4%
Health services	4.4%
Transportation, storage	3.9%
Mining	3.7%
Other utilities	3.0%
Agriculture	1.9%
Logging	0.6%
Fishing and trapping	0.2%

Value of Manufacturing Shipments $277,824 million

Farm Cash Receipts $21,415 million

Employment (seasonally adjusted) 12,291,000; participation rate: 65.7%

Unemployment (seasonally adjusted) 1,433,000; per capita: 10.4%

Exports Canada's merchandising export in 1992 amounted to $162,596 million.

Largest trading partner: United States; more than 75% of Canada's export is shipped to the United States.

Other important export areas (1986): Pacific Rim 9%, E.E.C. 7%

ALBERTA

Alberta, the most westerly of the Prairie Provinces, is bordered on the west by the province of British Columbia; on the north by the Northwest Territories; on the east by the province of Saskatchewan; and on the south by the state of Montana.

Name   Province of Alberta. Chosen to honor Princess Louise Caroline Alberta, daughter of Queen Victoria and wife of the Marquis of Lorne, Governor General of Canada, 1878–1883. *Previous names:* part of Rupert's Land (1670–1870); part of the North-West Territories (1870–1905); from 1882–1905 divided into the provisional district of Alberta in the south and the provisional district of Athabasca in the north.

Flag   Ultramarine blue background with the provincial shield in the centre. Proclaimed on June 1, 1968.

Coat of Arms   The top portion of the shield has the red cross of St. George on a white background; in the bottom portion are a field of wheat, the prairie, and rolling hills in front of the Rocky Mountains. The shield is supported on the left by a golden lion and on the right by a prong-horn antelope. Above the shield is a helm with a silver and gold wreath upon which rests a beaver with a royal crown on its back. In the compartment below the shield wild roses grow from a grassy mound and around a scroll with the provincial motto. The coat of arms was granted by King Edward VII on May

30, 1907, the crest and supporters by Queen Elizabeth II on July 13, 1980.

Motto   *Fortis et Liber* (Strong and free).

Emblems
Bird   great horned owl (*Budo virginianus*)
Colors   blue and gold
Flower   wild rose (*Rosa acicularis*)
Mammal   Rocky Mountain big horn sheep (*Ovis Canadensis Canadensis*)
Stone   petrified wood
Tartan   green, gold, blue, pink, and black
Tree   lodgepole pine (*Pinus contorta var. latifolia*)

Date of Entry into Confederation   September 1, 1905.

Official Language   English.

Capital City   Edmonton, situated on the North Saskatchewan River near the geographic centre of the province, the most northerly of Canada's major cities; population 616,741, CMA population 839,924. Fort Edmonton was founded in 1795 by the Hudson's Bay Company and named by George Sutherland, its builder, for Edmonton (now part of London, England), the birthplace of his clerk, John Pruden. Edmonton was incorporated as a town in 1892 and as a city on November 7, 1904. It was designated as the capital of the Province of Alberta in 1905.

Provincial Holidays   In addition to national statutory holidays (see page 2), Alberta residents celebrate Alberta Family Day (the third Monday in February) and Alberta Heritage Day (the first Monday in August).

Geography and Climate

Geography   Alberta has one of the most varied landscapes in Canada, with the Rocky Mountains and their foothills on its western border, gently rolling open prairie in the southeast, a central parkland, a boreal forest region in the north, and badlands in the Red Deer River valley. Except for the mountain regions and the northeast corner, which is part of the Canadian shield, Alberta's soil is arable.

Area   661,190 sq. km. (255,287 sq. mi.); 6.6% of Canada. *Rank:* 4th among the provinces, 5th among the provinces and territories.

Inland Water   16,800 sq. km. (6,487 sq. mi.), includes several thousand lakes. Largest lake wholly in Alberta: Lake Claire 1,168 sq. km. (451 sq. mi.), size varies due to flow control being at times larger or smaller than Lesser Slave Lake.

Elevations   Highest point: Mount Columbia 3,747 m. (12,293 ft.). Lowest point: Salt River at the border of Northwest Territories 183 m. (600 ft.).

Major Rivers (* indicates a designated Canadian Heritage River): *Athabasca, Battle, Beaver, Bow, Hay, Milk, *North Saskatchewan, Oldman, Peace, Pembina, Red Deer, Slave, Smoky, South Saskatchewan, Wabasca.

Climate   Alberta has a continental climate and is the warmest and driest of the Prairie Provinces with short, cool summers and long, cold winters that can be suddenly warmed by Chinook winds.

Western Alberta, in the Rocky Mountains' rain shadow, has low precipitation. The average daily mean temperature in January in Edmonton is −16.5 °C (2.3°F); in Calgary −11.8°C (11.8°F); in July in Edmonton 15.8°C (60.4°F); in Calgary 16.4°C (61.5°F). The lowest recorded temperature in Alberta: −61.1°C (−78°F) at Fort Vermillion on January 11, 1911; the highest recorded temperature 43.3°C (110°F) at Fort Macleod on July 18, 1941.

Average annual precipitation in Edmonton, 466.1 mm. (18.4 in.); in Calgary, 423 mm. (16.7 in.). Average annual snowfall in Edmonton, 135.7 cm. (53.4 in.); in Calgary, 152.5 cm. (60 in.). Greatest recorded snowfall over five consecutive days: 169.2 cm. (66.6 in.) at Columbia Ice Fields, November 15, 1946; greatest recorded annual snowfall: 1,066 cm. (419.7 in.) at Columbia Ice Fields in winter 1973/4.

Alberta holds several Canadian weather records: sunniest year, 2,785 hours of sunshine, at Manyberries in 1976; sunniest town under 10,000 population, 2,490 hours average at Coronation; more average annual sunny days, 330 at Vauxhall; lowest relative humidity, 6% at Calgary on March 22, 1968; city with the most number of days without measurable precipitation, 271 at Medicine Hat; most extreme temperature change in one hour: from −19°C (−2.2°F) to 22°F (71.6°F) at Pincher Creek on January 27, 1962, caused by a Chinook.

Time Zone   Mountain.

Parks and Historic Sites

In this section, the following designations are used: * indicates the area is, or part of it is, a Unesco World Heritage; ** indicates the area is, or part of it is, a Ramsar site; *** indicates the area is, or part of it is, a Unesco Biosphere Reserve.

National Parks Located In Alberta

Park	Location	Size
*Banff	Banff	6,641 sq. km. (2,564 sq. mi.)
Elk Island	Fort Saskatchewan	194 sq. km. (75 sq. mi.)
*Jasper	Jasper	10,878 sq. km. (4,200 sq. mi.)
***Waterton Lakes	southwest corner	505 sq. km. (195 sq. mi.)
*/**Wood Buffalo	N.W.T./Alberta border two-thirds in Alberta	44,807 sq. km. (17,300 sq. mi.)

Provincial Parks There are 313 legislated provincial sites covering 2.2% of Alberta's area: 123 natural areas, 1 wilderness park, 3 wilderness areas, 2 wildlife sanctuaries, 65 provincial parks, 14 ecology reserves, 78 recreation areas, 2 conservation areas, 7 provincial game bird sanctuaries, 2 habitat development areas, 10 forest land-use zones, and 6 historic reserve-natural sites. The largest parks are:

Park	Location	Type	Size
Willmore	Grand Cache	wilderness park	4597 sq. km. (1,775 sq. mi.)
Peter Lougheed	Kananaskis	provincial park	501 sq. km. (193 sq. mi.)
White Goat	near Banff	wilderness area	445 sq. km. (172 sq. mi.)
Lakeland Lake	near Rich	recreation	443 sq. km. (171 sq. mi.)
Siffleur	near Banff	wilderness area	412 sq. km. (159 sq. mi.)
Cypress Hills	Elkwater	provincial park	204 sq. km. (79 sq. mi.)
Ghost River	near Banff	wilderness area	153 sq. km. area (59 sq. mi.)
Lakeland	near Lac La Biche	provincial park	147 sq. km. (57 sq. mi.)
Cooking Lake	near Blackfoot	recreation	97 sq. km. (37 sq. mi.)
Notikewin	near Hotchkiss	provincial park	97 sq. km. (37 sq. mi.)

Dinosaur Provincial Park, a smaller park in the Red Deer River Valley, is a Unesco World Heritage Site. Alberta also has 4 national bird sanctuaries, 4 national wildlife areas and 3 Ramsar sites plus one shared with Northwest Territories.

Major National Historic Sites and Parks in Alberta

Banff Museum, Banff
Cave and Basin, Banff
Rocky Mountain House, Rocky Mountain House
Village of Sterling, Sterling
Yellowhead Pass, Yellowhead Pass

In addition, there are a large number of historic sites in Alberta administered by the province, municipalities, or organizations. The major sites are:

Brooks Aqueduct Historic Site, near Brooks
Cochrane Ranche Provincial Historic Site, near Cochrane
Fort George/Buckingham House Provincial Historic Site, near Elk Point
*Head-Smashed-In Bison Jump, near Fort Macleod
Leitch Collieries Provincial Historic Site, Crowsnest Pass
Ukrainian Cultural Heritage Village, near Edmonton
Victoria Settlement, near Smoky Lake

Demography

All figures relating to Alberta population and dwellings are 1991 data and do not include the population on 11 Indian reserves that did not cooperate in the 1991 census. Indian and Northern Affairs Canada's 1989 figures suggest that there are between 7,000 and 8,000 residents on these reserves.

Alberta Population: 2,545,553; 9.3% of national; *rank* 4th

Historical population data

1981	2,237,725
1971	1,627,875
1961	1,331,944
1951	939,501
1941	796,169
1921	588,454
1901	73,022

Population Density: 4.0 per sq. km. (10.3 per sq. mi.)

Number of Dwellings: 914,720

Indian Reserves (1989): 42 bands on 92 reserves and 13 Indian settlements

Population Characteristics:
urban: 2,030,893; 79.8%
rural: 514,660; 20.2%
19 and under: 779,035; 30.6%
65 and over: 230,550; 9.0%
average income for full-time employment 15 years and over (1990): $33,325; men $38,389; women $25,037
average life expectancy at birth (1987): men 73.6 years; women 80 years
live birth rate: 42,776; 16.8 per 1000 (highest in Canada)
deaths: 14,451; 5.7 per 1000
marriages: 18,612; 7.3 per 1000 (highest in Canada)
divorces: 8,389; 3.3 per 1000 (highest in Canada)

Largest Cities (for definitions of CMA and CA, see page viii)

Name	Population	Dwellings	National Pop. Rank
Edmonton	839,924 (CMA)	307,345	5
Calgary	754,033 (CMA)	276,973	6
Lethbridge	60,974 (CA)	23,403	45
Red Deer	58,134 (CA)	21,490	49
Medicine Hat	52,681 (CA)	20,117	52
Fort McMurray	49,204 (CA)	15,949	55
Grande Prairie	28,271	9,910	86
Grand Centre	24,265 (CA)	8,004	92
Lloydminster	17,283	6,575	107
(part in Alberta)	10,042		
Camrose	13,420	5,257	123

Government and Politics, 1905–

A description of the division of powers between the federal and provincial governments will be found on page 4.

Lieutenant-Governor The Lieutenant-Governor is the nominal head of the Alberta government, and is appointed by the Governor General of Canada on the rec-

ommendation of the Prime Minister of Canada. (A description of the duties of lieutenant-governors is found on page 7.)

Lieutenant-Governors of Alberta	*Term*
George Hedley Vicars Bulyea	1905–1915

Robert George Brett	1915–1925
William Egbert	1925–1931
William Legh Walsh	1931–1936
Philip Carteret Hill Primrose	1936–1937
John Campbell Bowen	1937–1950
John James Bowlen	1950–1959
John Percy Page	1959–1965
John Walter Grant MacEwan	1965–1974
Ralph Garvin Steinhauer	1974–1979
Francis Charles Lynch-Staunton	1979–1985
Wilma Helen Hunley	1985–1991
Thomas Gordon Towers	1991–

Legislative Assembly The Legislative Assembly of Alberta consists of 83 members elected by popular vote, each member representing a constituency; term of office: up to 5 years as long as the party in power maintains the confidence of the Legislative Assembly; remuneration (1993): $38,335 + $19,167.50 tax-free expense allowance, additional amounts for special appointments; qualifications for members: must be a Canadian citizen, at least 18 years of age on polling day, ordinarily resident in Alberta continuously for six months immediately preceding polling day, not a member of the Senate or House of Commons of Canada, and not legally disqualified. (A description of the duties of provincial legislatures are found on page 7.)

Qualifications for Alberta Voters in Provincial Elections A voter must be a Canadian citizen, at least 18 years of age, ordinarily resident in Alberta six months prior to the enumeration date, ordinarily resident in the electoral division and subdivision, and not legally disqualified.

Premier Nominally appointed by the Lieutenant-Governor of Alberta, the Premier is generally the leader of the party with the majority of seats in the Legislative Assembly. (A description of the responsibilities of provincial premiers is found on page 7.)

Premiers of Alberta/Party/Term
Alexander Cameron Rutherford
  (Liberal, 1905–1910)
Arthur Lewis Sifton
  (Liberal, 1910–1917)
Charles Stewart
  (Liberal, 1917–1921)
Herbert Greenfield
  (United Farmers of Alberta, 1921–1925)
John Edward Brownlee
  (United Farmers of Alberta, 1925–1934)
Richard Gavin Reid
  (United Farmers of Alberta, 1934–1935)
William Aberhart
  (Social Credit, 1935–1943)
Ernest Charles Manning
  (Social Credit, 1943–1968)
Harry Edwin Strom
  (Social Credit, 1968–1971)
Peter Lougheed
  (Conservative, 1971–1986)
Donald Ross Getty
  (Conservative, 1986–1992)
Ralph Klein
  (Conservative, 1992–   )

Cabinet The Cabinet consists of ministers appointed by the Premier, usually from elected members of the majority party in the Legislative Assembly. Cabinet ministers serve at the Premier's pleasure; each minister usually heads a government department.

Government Departments The following telephone numbers may be used to obtain general information from the departments.

Advanced Education and Career Development   (403)422-4488
Agriculture, Food and Rural Development   (403)427-2727
Community Development
  (403)427-6530
Economic Development and Tourism
  (403)422-9494
Education
  (403)427-7219
Energy
  (403)427-7425

Environmental Protection
(403)944-0313
Family and Social Services
(403)427-2734
Federal and Intergovernmental Affairs
(403)427-2611
Health
(403)427-0259
Justice
(403)427-2745
Labour
(403)427-2723
Municipal Affairs
(403)427-2732

Public Works, Supply and Services
(403)427-7988
Transportation and Utilities
(403)427-2731
Treasury
(403)427-3035

Alberta Representation in Federal Government
House of Commons: 26 members
Senate: 6 members

Finances

A consolidated statement of Alberta's revenue and expenditures for the years 1992/93 and 1991/92 is shown below in millions of dollars. The financial year runs from April 1 to March 31 of the year following.

	Actual 1992/93	Actual 1991/92
Revenue		
Taxation	4,695	5,016
Payments from Government of Canada	2,384	2,086
Non-renewable resource revenue	2,183	2,022
Investment income	1,621	2,155
Fees, permits, and licences	1,027	935
Other	1,314	627
Total revenue for the year	13,224	12,841
Expenditures		
Health	4,336	4,098
Education	3,125	2,960
Social services	1,880	1,746
Agriculture and economic development	1,718	1,700
Regional planning and development	849	881
Protection of persons and property	841	939
Interest on debt	1,109	1,067
Other	2,045	1,914
Total expenditures for the year	15,903	15,305
Deficit for the year	2,679	2,464

Not included in the above statement: Valuation adjustments, pensions, and other provisions.

Economy

Alberta has Canada's largest deposits of oil and natural gas, and 70% of the country's known coal deposits are located in the province. Alberta is second to Saskatchewan in area of farmland and wheat production, and second to Ontario in farm income. It is Canada's chief producer of beef cattle and feed grains. The beautiful scenery in the Rocky Mountains makes tourism a significant economic factor. Calgary is the financial centre of western Canada and the headquarters of Canada's oil and gas industry. In recent years Calgary has become the third largest head office location in Canada, after Toronto and Montreal.

Major Industries Principal industries include agriculture, beef ranching, oil and gas, and manufacturing. Manufacturing is closely related to the agriculture and petroleum industries, e.g., petrochemicals, meat packing; Alberta has the fourth largest manufacturing sector in Canada.

Gross Domestic Product (1992) $68,217 million (in current dollars at factor cost); % of national G.D.P.: 11.3%; *rank:* 4th

Distribution of gross domestic product (1992)

Services	21.43%
Finance	18.50%
Mining	16.30%
Trade	10.34%
Manufacturing	8.50%
Transportation	7.10%
Public administration	5.80%

Construction	4.60%
Utilities	3.80%
Agriculture	3.30%
Forestry	0.30%

Value of Manufacturing Shipments $19,279 million

Farm Cash Receipts $4,204 million

Employment (seasonally adjusted) 1,246,000; participation rate: 72.5%

Unemployment (seasonally adjusted) 124,000; per capita: 9.1%

Minimum Wage $5.00, general minimum; $4.50 under 18 (1993)

Exports Alberta's total exports in 1992 amounted to $19.4 billion, 11.1% of total Canadian exports; *rank:* 3rd. Mining—specifically oil, gas, and coal—accounted for 54% of total exports, manufactured goods for 24.2%, and agricultural and related products for 11.8%.
Largest trading partner: United States, 76.5% of Alberta's total exports
Other important markets: Japan 6.1%; China 3.1%; former USSR 2.0%; and South Korea 1.6%
Major export commodities: Oil, gas, and sulphur, 51.3%; chemicals and chemical products, 7.9%; wheat, 6.9%; live cattle 2.6%

History

ca. 10–9,000 B.C.	Evidence of the Clovis Paleo-Indian culture near Edmonton.
ca. 7,000 B.C.	Evidence of trading in northern Alberta.
ca. 17th century	Beaver, Blackfoot, Blood, Gros Ventre, Sarcee, and Slavey peoples inhabit present-day Alberta.
1670	*May 2* Hudson's Bay Company is formed and granted trade rights over all territory draining into Hudson Bay; the territory is named Rupert's Land.
1754	Anthony Henday, a Hudson's Bay Company employee, becomes the first white man to see what is now Alberta, and on *October 17* the first known European to view the Rocky Mountains (near present-day Innisfail).
1778	Peter Pond becomes the first white man to see the Athabasca River and establishes the first fur trading post in the region on Lake Athabasca, for the North West Company. He finds pools of a pitch-like substance nearby.

1790–1793	Explorer Peter Fidler surveys from Lake Athabasca to the foothills of the Rocky Mountains.
1795	Hudson's Bay Company establishes Fort Edmonton on the banks of the North Saskatchewan River.
1799	David Thompson and Duncan McGillivray, fur taders and explorers, journey up the Bow River past present-day Calgary.
1802	Thompson explores from mouth of Lesser Slave River to Peace River.
1806	Thompson sets out to explore passes through the Rocky Mountains west from the Athabasca and Saskatchewan rivers.
1807	Blood Indians destroy Fort Edmonton.
1811	William Henry builds Henry House, the first permanent habitation at present day Jasper.
1818	*October 20* Convention of 1818 between the United States and Britain sets the southern boundary of the Hudson's Bay Company territory at the 49th parallel from the Lake of the Woods to the Rocky Mountains.
1819	Fort Edmonton is rebuilt as a larger post.
1830	Fort Edmonton is rebuilt on the present site of the Alberta legislative buildings.
1840	*October 18* Robert Terrill Rundle, a Methodist minister, arrives in Fort Edmonton to become the first missionary and the first resident cleric in present-day Alberta.
1857	Palliser Expedition sent to assess Rupert's Land's potential reports a fertile belt and deposits of coal and minerals.
1861	Father Albert Lacombe, an Oblate missionary, founds St. Albert.
1868	Plague of grasshoppers causes crop failure.
1869	*November 19* Hudson's Bay Company transfers Rupert's Land to British Crown.
	Establishment of Fort Whoop-Up by American merchants to trade illicit guns and whiskey is a major factor in the formation of the North-West Mounted Police.
1870s	Permanent settlements develop outside Fort Edmonton.
1870	*Fall* Battle between Cree and Assiniboine Indians and the Peigan Indians near Fort Whoop-Up leaves some 300 dead.
1872	Dominion Lands Act (federal government) grants 65 ha. (161 acres) of free land to each settler family.
	First coal mining in Alberta takes place in Lethbridge.
1873	*May* Canadian and American wolf hunters massacre 36 Assiniboines at Cypress Hills.
1874	North-West Mounted Police establishes the first Alberta post at Fort Macleod.
1875	North-West Mounted Police founds Fort Calgary.
	North-West Territories Act provides for a lieutenant-governor and legislature operating from the territorial capital in Battleford, Saskatchewan.
1876	Headquarters of North-West Mounted Police are moved to Fort Macleod.
	Treaty with Cree covers lands in central Alberta.
1877	*September 22* Crowfoot, chief of the Blackfoot Indians, signs a treaty at Blackfoot Crossing, cedes lands between Cypress Hills and Rocky Mountains to Canada, and leads his people to a reserve near Calgary. Other treaties with Sarcee and Stoney cover lands in southern Alberta.
	November 20 Edmonton receives telegraph service.
	North-West Territories Act amendment gives equal status to French and English.

1880	*December 6* First newspaper in Alberta, the *Edmonton Bulletin*, is published.
1882	*May 8* North-West Territories (Prairie section) is divided into four provisional districts: Athabasca in northern part of present-day Alberta, Alberta in the southern part, and two in Saskatchewan.
1883	*August 11* Canadian Pacific Railway reaches Fort Calgary, opening up area for settlement. Railway engineers lay out a town site.
	Canadian Pacific Railway crew finds first natural gas in Alberta while drilling for water near Medicine Hat.
1884	*Spring* The first dinosaur skull found in Canada is discovered by Joseph Tyrrell in the Alberta badlands.
	Calgary is incorporated as a town, the first in Alberta.
	North-West Territories School Ordinance establishes a dual Protestant-Catholic system.
1885	*May 14* Thomas Bland Strange leading the Alberta Field Force leaves Edmonton to fight against the North-West Rebellion. (See also Saskatchewan history on page 204.)
	November First Canadian national park, the Cave and Basin Hot Springs, is established at Banff.
1887	*January 6* First union in Alberta, the Brotherhood of Locomotive Firemen, Cascade Lodge, no. 342, is formed.
1888	Federal government establishes a Territorial Assembly with 23 elected members and 3 nonvoting legal advisors with substantial federal control.
1889	Jacob Lion Diamond, the first Jewish settler in Alberta, arrives in Calgary.
1890	Petroleum is discovered along the Athabasca River.
1891	*July 27* Calgary and Edmonton Railway is completed.
	Territorial legislature discards the official use of French.
	Legislative Assembly is made totally elective.
1893	*September 16* Calgary becomes the first city to be incorporated in Alberta.
1896–1914	Large numbers of immigrants arrive from Ontario, the United States, Great Britain, and Europe.
1897	*July 14* Canadian Pacific Railway begins construction of the Crowsnest Pass to southeastern British Columbia.
	Responsible government granted to North-West Territories, but without control of public lands and natural resources or a wide tax base.
	Edmonton becomes supply base for Klondike gold rush.
1899	Treaty with Indians covers lands in northern Alberta.
1901	*July 10* Hailstones, 8 cm. (3.2 in.) and 140 g. (5 oz.), ruin almost every roof in Edmonton.
1903	*April 29* The most disastrous rockfall in Canada, a 74 million-ton slide from Turtle Mountain near Frank kills more than 70 people and buries houses and farms in its 1.6 km. (1 mi.) spread across the valley.
	July Barr colonists, originally led from England by Reverend Isaac Barr, found Lloydminster.
1904	*March* Three-day blizzard with 100 kph. (62 mph.) winds drops 30 cm. (12 in.) snow in southern Prairies; 5 trains snowbound between Winnipeg and Calgary.
1905	*September 1* Alberta becomes a province of Canada.
	November 24 Canadian Northern Railway reaches Edmonton.
	One provincial education system with local provision for dissenting religious minorities is established.
1906	*March 15* First legislature of the Province of Alberta opens at the Thistle Rink in Edmonton.

	May 8 University of Alberta is founded in Edmonton.
	Chipewayan and Cree of Alberta and Northern Saskatchewan sign a treaty covering 220,150 sq. km. (85,000 sq. mi.)
1907–1914	Grand Trunk Pacific Railway builds line from Edmonton to British Columbia coast.
1907	*February 11* Supreme Court of Alberta is established.
	Marquis wheat, a fast-maturing variety well suited to the Prairies, is developed.
	Free Libraries Act is passed.
1908	*March* Alberta government buys telephone company and sets up telephone service as a public utility.
1910	*December 10* Explosion in Bellevue coal mine near Frank kills 35.
1911	Dower Act protects a wife's right to a one-third share of her husband's property.
1912	*September 12* First Calgary Stampede opens.
	September 13 Alberta legislative building opens officially.
	Edmonton and Strathcona are amalgamated.
	Oldest currently operating theatre in Alberta, the Empress Theatre, opens in Fort Macleod.
1913	Calgary Stock Exchange is founded. (Name changed to Alberta Stock Exchange in 1974).
	Alberta farmers organize the Alberta Farmers' Co-operative Elevator Company.
1914	*May* First major gas and oil field in Alberta is discovered.
	June 19 Worst Canadian coal mine disaster occurs in the Hillcrest explosion when 189 are killed.
1915	*July 21* Plebiscite brings prohibition to Alberta, becoming effective *July 1, 1916*.
1916	*April 19* Women are granted the right to vote in provincial elections.
1917	*March 1* Alberta provincial police take over law enforcement from Royal North-West Mounted Police.
1919	*August 7* E.C. Hoy makes the first airplane flight across the Rocky Mountains, from Vancouver to Lethbridge.
1920	*October 25* Albertans vote in a plebiscite to retain prohibition.
1922	12,000 coal miners in Alberta and British Columbia go on strike.
1923	*November 5* Prohibition ends as Alberta votes for government control of liquor effective in 1924.
	United Farmers' of Alberta form the Albert Wheat Pool to sell wheat at stable prices.
	Alberta's first oil refinery opens in Calgary.
1929	*October 18* Judicial Committee of the Privy Council of Great Britain rules that "the word persons includes members of the male and female sex" after the petition of five Alberta women has been rejected by the Supreme Court of Canada.
1930s	Agricultural depression caused by low world wheat prices and severe drought afflicts Alberta.
1930	*October 1* Federal government transfers control of natural resources to Alberta.
1932	*June 1* Royal Canadian Mounted Police absorbs the Alberta provincial police.
	Co-operative Commonwealth Federation is founded in Calgary.
	First provincial park is established at Aspen Beach.
1942	Building of the Alaska Highway brings growth to Edmonton as a transportation and supply base.

1947	*January* Oil sand deposits are found beneath the banks of the Athabasca River. *February 13* Imperial Oil Company strikes oil at Leduc, ushering in Alberta's modern era of prosperity.
1948	Mackenzie Highway opens from Grimshaw to Hay River, Northwest Territories.
1950	First regional planning organization in Canada is formed in Edmonton.
1953	*October 15* Trans Mountain oil pipeline is completed from Edmonton to Vancouver.
1957	Provincial Social Credit government pays $22.00 to each resident over 21.
1958	*February 1* James Gladstone, a member of the Blood tribe, becomes the first Indian appointed to the Senate of Canada.
1960	*December 3* Edmonton International Airport opens.
1961	Worst drought year of the century.
1962	*April 2* Albert Government Telephones and CN Telecommunications open a microwave system between Peace River and Hay River, Northwest Territories. *September 3* TransCanada Highway from St. John's, Newfoundland, to Victoria opens in Rogers Pass ceremony, 7,821 km. (4,860 mi.).
1963	*June 29* One hundred twelve cm. (44.1 in.) snow falls at Livingstone Ranger Station in southwestern Alberta.
1964	Alberta licenses Sun Oil Company to begin work on the Great Canadian Oil Sands plant at Fort McMurray; plant begins operation *September 30, 1967.* *December 15* Edmonton International Airport experiences −35.6°C (−32.1°F) and 55 km. (34.2 mi.) per hour winds, a windchill factor of −69°C (−92.2°F)
1967	Extensive drought in the Prairies. *April 6* George Brinton McClellan becomes Alberta's ombudsman, the first ombudsman in Canada.
1969	*May 28* Alberta Resources Railway from Grande Prairie to Solomon is opened. *July* Alberta enters the federal medicare scheme. *August 4* Some of the largest hailstones ever observed in the Edmonton area cause $17 million damage.
1970s	Rise in world price for oil causes Alberta boom.
1971	*July* Alberta legal age of majority is lowered to 18.
1972	*November 15* Alberta passes a provincial Bill of Rights.
1973	*October 2* Ruptured gas main near Red Lakes causes evacuation of 500.
1974	*April 30* Ralph Garvin Steinhauer becomes Lieutenant-Governor of Alberta, the first Indian to hold this position in Canada.
1976	*Spring* Alberta Heritage Savings Trust Fund is established to invest revenues from sale of oil and natural gas. First International Ombudsman Conference is held in Edmonton.
1977	Southern Alberta experiences severe drought.
1978	Edmonton opens a light rapid transit system, the first medium-size Canadian city to do so.
1979–1980	Poor wheat and pasture years.
1980	Federal government imposes National Energy Program on Alberta.
1981	*March 1* Alberta limits oil production in opposition to federal government's energy policy. Federal government imposes compensation charge of $0.75 per barrel to help pay for oil imports necessitated by cutback. *July 28* Fifteen-minute hailstorm causes more than $100 million damage, a record in Canada for insurance claims due to hailstones. *September 1* Federal and Alberta governments reach agreement about oil pricing and division of revenues.

1982	*April 30* Alsands Project in northern Alberta collapses when several companies withdraw support.
1983	*September 20* Esso Resources Canada Ltd., the Alberta and federal governments agree to participate in the Cold Lake oil sands project.
1984	*January 7* Release of dangerous gases from a train wreck causes evacuation of 800 in Medicine Hat.
1985	*September* Canadian Commercial Bank in Edmonton and Northlands Bank in Calgary, the first Canadian banks to fail in 62 years, cause Canada's worst banking crisis.
1986	*February 8* Via Rail passenger train collides with freight train near Hinton killing 26.
	North Saskatchewan River rises 7.6 m. (24.9 ft.), causing 900 in Edmonton to flee.
	Sharp decline in international petroleum prices ends Calgary's boom.
1987	*July 31* Tornado in Edmonton leaves 27 dead, 250 injured, and 400 homeless, the worst natural disaster in 30 years.
1988	*February 13–28* Winter Olympic Games are held in the Calgary area.
	Drought and low wheat prices affect the Alberta economy.
	October 22 Lubicon Indian band and Alberta agree on land and mineral rights.
1989	*March 2* First test over Canada of a United States cruise missile using Stealth technology is successfully completed between Beaufort Sea and Primrose Lake testing ranges near Cold Lake.
	October 16 Stanley Waters wins Canada's first election for a seat in the Senate of Canada.
1990	Supreme Court reprimands Alberta for the violation of the rights of Edmonton francophones to control their education and facilities. These rights were to be secured dependent on the size of the minority and the government's financial resources.
1992	*March 13* Catherine Anne Fraser is appointed Chief Justice of Alberta, the first Canadian woman to hold a top provincial judicial position.
1993	Oil exploration revives.

Culture and Education

Performing Arts Alberta has 8 major and 52 smaller performing companies. A selection are:

Alberta Ballet Company, Edmonton	(403)245-4222
Alberta Theatre Projects, Calgary	(403)294-7475
Calgary Opera Association, Calgary	(403)262-7286
Calgary Philharmonic Orchestra, Calgary	(403)294-7420
Citadel Theatre, Edmonton	(403)425-1820
Edmonton Opera Association, Edmonton	(403)424-4040
Edmonton Symphony Orchestra, Edmonton	(403)428-1108
Lunch Box Theatre, Calgary (One-act plays;	
Canada's longest running noontime theatre)	(403)265-4292
Theatre Calgary, Calgary	(403)294-7440

Festivals Alberta has 52 festivals. Among the best known are:

Calgary Exhibition and Stampede, Calgary (July)	(403)261-0101	1-800-661-1260
Calgary Winter Festival, Calgary (February)	(403)268-2688	

Edmonton Folk Festival, Edmonton (August)	(403)429-1899
Edmonton Heritage Days Festival, Edmonton (July/August)	(403)433-3378
Fringe Theatre Festival, Edmonton (August) (Largest annual fringe festival of alternate theatre in North America)	(403)448-9000
·International Jazz Festival, Edmonton (June/July)	(403)432-7166
International Native Arts Festival, Calgary (August)	(403)233-0022

Provincial Museums and Galleries The following are major Alberta institutions.

Alberta Science Centre/Centennial Planetarium, Calgary
Edmonton Art Gallery, Edmonton
Edmonton Space and Science Centre, Edmonton
Glenbow-Alberta Institute, Calgary
Provincial Museum of Alberta, Edmonton
Reynolds-Alberta Museum, Wetaskin
Royal Tyrrell Museum, Drumheller
Whyte Museum of the Canadian Rockies, Banff

Universities and Colleges
Athabasca University, Athabasca
Augustana University College, Camrose
King's College, Edmonton
University of Alberta, Edmonton
University of Calgary, Calgary
University of Lethbridge, Lethbridge

Colleges and Institutes (* indicates additional campuses in other centres)
Alberta College of Art, Calgary
Fairview College, Calgary
Grande Prairie Regional College, Grande Prairie
Grant MacEwen Community College, Edmonton*
Keyano College, Fort McMurray
Lakeland College, Vermilion
Lethbridge Community College, Lethbridge
Medicine Hat College, Medicine Hat
Mount Royal College, Calgary
Northern Alberta Institute of Technology, Edmonton
Olds College, Olds
Red Deer College, Red Deer
Southern Alberta Institute of Technology, Calgary

Miscellaneous Educational Institutions
Banff Centre for the Arts and Centre for Management, Banff

Motor Vehicle Use

Motor Vehicles Registered for Use in Alberta: 1,878,709

Drivers Licensed by Alberta: 1,918,098. Minimum driving age: 16

Roads Primary highways: 13,643 km. (8,478 mi.); secondary highways: 15,123 km. (9,397 mi.); gravel roads: 126,700 km. (78,730 mi.); bridges located in the province: 12,720

Speed Limits Primary highways: 100 kph (62 mph); urban: 50 kph (31 mph)

First, Biggest, and Best

World's largest shopping centre: West Edmonton Mall, 483,080 sq. m. (5.2 million sq. ft.) on a 49 ha. (121 acre) site, contains over 800 stores and services and over 10 major department stores
World's largest indoor amusement park: West Edmonton Mall

World's largest car park: 30,000 car capacity at West Edmonton Mall
World's largest fenced single wheat field: 14,000 ha. (35,000 acres), southwest of Lethbridge, in 1951
World's most northerly grain growing area: Peace River region in northwest Alberta
Western hemisphere's largest park: Wood Buffalo National Park 44,800 sq. km. (17,297 sq. mi.), two thirds of it in Alberta
North America's longest stretch of urban parkland: Edmonton, 7,400 ha. (18,285 acres) including 26 km. (16 mi.) paved paths and 25 km. (16 mi.) nature trails
World's largest producer of elemental sulphur from hydrocarbon sources
World's largest single reserve of oil: Athabasca tar sands with an estimated reserve of 900 billion barrels, more than one-half world's proven reserves
World's largest source of bitumen: Alberta has 50% of world's total
World's largest discovery of dinosaur bones: Alberta badlands
North America's first all-new light rapid transit service: Edmonton, 1978
North America's first commercial cellular mobile telephone system: Alberta Government Telephones, July 1983
North America's first international music festival: Edmonton, 1908
World's first International Ombudsman Conference: Edmonton, 1976
World's first international ombudsman institute: University of Alberta, 1978
North America's first ombudsman: George Brinton McClellan, ombudsman of Alberta, April 6, 1967
British Empire's first woman magistrate: Emily Gowan Murphy appointed a police magistrate in Edmonton, 1916
British Empire's first woman elected to a legislature: Louise McKinney, June 1917

Sources of Information About Alberta

Alberta Public Affairs Bureau: 10909 Jasper Avenue, Edmonton, Alta. T5J 3L9 (403)427-2754
Alberta Economic Development and Tourism: 10155 102 Street, 4th floor, Edmonton, Alta. T5J 4L6 (403)427-4321, 800-667-6501 (Alberta), 800-661-8888 (general)
Alberta Government Publications Services: 11510 Kingsway Avenue, Edmonton, Alta. T5G 0X5 (403)427-4952

Books About Alberta: A Selected List

Reference Guides

Acorn, John. *Butterflies of Alberta* (1993).
Alberta. Chief Electoral Office. *A Report on Alberta Elections, 1905–1982* (1983).
Alberta Genealogical Society, Edmonton Branch. *Genealogical Resources in the Edmonton Area: A Helpful Guide* (1985).
Artibise, Alan F.J. *Western Canada Since 1870: A Select Bibliography and Guide* (1978).
Baker, Suzanne Devonshire. *Artists of Alberta* (1980).
Bolton, Ken and others. *The Albertans* (1981).

Budd, A.C. *Budd's Flora of the Canadian Prairie Provinces* (rev. and enl. by J. Looman and K.F. Best, 1987).
Byfield, Ted (ed.). *The Atlas of Alberta* (1984).
Canada. Atmospheric Environment Service. *Canadian Climate Normals, 1961–1990: Prairie Provinces* (1993).
Canada. Energy, Mines and Resources Canada. *Gazetteer of Canada: Alberta* (3rd ed. 1988).
Clifford, Hugh F. *Aquatic Invertebrates of Alberta: An Illustrated Guide* (1991).

Cormack, Robert G.H. *Wildflowers of Alberta* (new ed. 1977).

Dew, Ian F. *Bibliography of Materials Relating to Southern Alberta Published to 1970* (1975).

Dryden, Jean E. (ed.). *Voices of Alberta: A Survey of Oral History Completed to 1980* (1981).

Dzikowski, Peter and Richard T. Heywood. *Agroclimatic Atlas of Alberta* (1990).

Fryer, Harold. *Stops of Interest in Alberta: Wildrose Country*, 2 vols. (1976–1978).

Gilroy, Doug. *Prairie Birds in Color* (rev. and expanded ed. 1976).

Hauff, Donna von. *Alberta's Parks: Our Legacy* (1992).

Holmgren, Eric J. and Patricia M. Holmgren. *Over 2000 Place Names in Alberta* (3rd ed. 1976).

Karamitsanis, Aphrodite. *Place Names of Alberta*, 4 vols. (1990).

Klivokiotis, P. and R.B. Thomson. *The Climate of Calgary* (1986).

Krotki, Joanna E. *Local Histories of Alberta: An Annotated Bibliography* (1980).

Lemieux, Victoria and David Leonard. *Tracing Your Ancestors in Alberta: Guide to Sources of Genealogical Interest in Alberta's Archives and Research Centres* (1992).

Mitchell, Patricia and Ellie Prepas (eds.). *The Atlas of Alberta Lakes* (1990).

Moss, E.H. *The Flora of Alberta: A Manual of Flowering Plants, Conifers, Ferns and Fern Allies Found Growing Without Cultivation in the Province of Alberta* (2nd ed. rev. by John G. Parker, 1983).

Nelson, Joseph S. and Martin J. Paetz. *The Fishes of Alberta* (2nd ed. 1992).

Olson, Rod. *The Climate of Edmonton* (1985).

Owram, Douglas R. *The Formation of Alberta: A Documentary History* (1979).

Peel, Bruce (comp.). *A Bibliography of the Prairie Provinces to 1953, With Bibliographical Index* (2nd ed. 1973).

Russell, Anthony P. and Aaron M. Bauer. *The Amphibians and Reptiles of Alberta: A Field Guide and Primer of Boreal Herpetology* (1993).

Salt, W. Ray and Jim R. Salt. *The Birds of Alberta: With Their Ranges in Saskatchewan & Manitoba* (1976).

Semenchuk, Glen P. (ed.). *The Atlas of Breeding Birds of Alberta* (1992).

Spalding, David A.E. (ed.). *A Nature Guide to Alberta* (1980).

Stelfox, J. Brad (ed.). *Hoofed Mammals of Alberta: The Complete Reference for Naturalists, Sport Hunters, Scientists, Students and Wildlife Managers* (1993).

Strathearn, Gloria M. *Alberta, 1954–1979: A Provincial Bibliography* (1982).

———. *Alberta Newspapers, 1880–1982: An Historical Directory* (1988).

Thomas, Lewis G. (ed.). *The Prairie West to 1905: A Canadian Sourcebook* (1975).

Vance, Fenton R., J.R. Jowsey, and J.S. McLean. *Wildflowers Across the Prairies* (rev. and expanded 1984).

Warkentin, John (ed.). *The Western Interior of Canada: A Record of Geographical Discovery, 1612–1917* (1964).

Nonfiction Sources

Angus, Terry (ed.). *The Prairie Experience* (1975).

Babcock, D.R. *Alexander Cameron Babcock: A Gentleman of Strathcona* (1989).

Barr, B.M. and P.J. Smith. *Environment and Economy: Essays on the Human Geography of Alberta* (1984).

Basque, Garnet (ed.). *Frontier Days in Alberta* (1992).

Berton, Pierre. *The Promised Land: Settling the West, 1896–1914* (1984, rpt. 1990).

Bickerstreth, J. Burgon. *The Land of Open Doors: Being Letters From Western Canada, 1911–13* (1976). An Anglican missionary in Northern Alberta.

Blower, James. *Gold Rush: A Pictorial Look at the Part Edmonton Played in the Gold Era of the 1890s* (1971).

Brado, Ed. *Cattle Kingdom: Early Ranching in Alberta* (1984).

Breen, David H. *The Canadian Prairie West and the Ranching Frontier, 1874–1924* (1983).

Broadfoot, Barry. *The Pioneer Years, 1895–1914: Memories of the Settlers Who Opened the West* (1976).

Bryan, Liz. *The Buffalo People: Prehistoric Archaeology on the Canadian Plains* (1991).

Burnet, Jean R. *Next-Year Country: A Study of Rural Social Organization in Alberta* (1951, rpt. 1978).

Byfield, Ted (ed.). *The Birth of a Province* (1992).

Byrne, T.C. *Alberta's Revolutionary Leaders* (1991).

Calf Robe, Ben. *Siksika: A Blackfoot Legacy* (1979).

Cavanaugh, Cathy and Randi Warne (eds.). *Standing on New Ground: Women in Alberta* (1993).

Colley, Kate Brightly. *While Rivers Flow: Stories of Early Alberta* (1970).

Cunningham, Dave. *Making Do: A Prairie Memory Guide* (1982).

——— and David Sternthal. *Alberta Album: The Living Past* (1985).

Dempsey, Hugh A. *Crowfoot: Chief of the Blackfeet* (1972, rpt. 1988).

———. *Indian Tribes of Alberta* (2nd ed. 1986).

———. *Red Crow: Warrior Chief* (1980).

——— (ed.). *The Best From Alberta History* (1981).

Destrube, Maurice. *Pioneering in Alberta: Medical Doctor's Story* (ed. by James E. Hendrickson, 1981).

Dolphin, Frank. *The Alberta Legislature: A Celebration* (1987).

Eggleston, Wilfrid. *Homestead on the Range* (1982).

Elliott, David R. and Iris Miller. *Bible Bill: A Biography of William Aberhart* (1987).

Finkel, Alvin. *The Social Credit Phenomenon in Alberta* (1989).

Foggo, Cheryl. *Pourin' Down the Rain* (1990). A memoir about growing up black in Calgary in the 1960s and 1970s.

Foran, Max. *City Makers: Calgarians After the Frontier* (1987).

—— and Heather MacEwan Foran. *Calgary, Canada's Frontier Metropolis: An Illustrated History* (1982).

Francis, R. Douglas and Howard Palmer (eds.). *The Prairie West: Historical Readings* (2nd ed. 1992).

Frideres, J.S. and R. Gibbins (eds.). *Alberta into the 21st Century* (1993).

Friesen, Gerald. *The Canadian Prairies: A History* (1984).

Gilpin, John F. *Edmonton, Gateway to the North: An Illustrated History* (1984).

Grant, Ted and Andy Russell. *Men of the Saddle: Working Cowboys of Canada* (1978).

Gray, James H. *Boomtime: Peopling the Canadian Prairies* (1979).

——. *Booze: The Impact of Whiskey on the Prairie West* (1972).

——. *Red Lights on the Prairies* (1971, rpt. 1986).

——. *R.B. Bennett: The Calgary Years* (1991).

——. *The Roar of the Twenties* (1975, rpt. 1982).

——. *The Winter Years: The Depression on the Prairies* (1966, rpt. 1990).

Halvorson, Marilyn. *To Everything a Season: A Year in Alberta Ranch Country* (1991).

Harrison, Dick. *The Struggle for a Canadian Prairie Fiction* (1977).

Higinbotham, John D. *When the West Was Young: Historical Reminiscences of the Early Canadian West* (1933, rpt. 1978).

Hopkins, Monica. *Letters From a Lady Rancher* (1982). Written in 1909–1911 to a friend in Australia.

Hungry Wolf, Adolf. *The Blood People: A Division of the Blackfoot Confederacy: An Illustrated Interpretation of the Old Ways* (1977).

Hungry Wolf, Beverly. *The Ways of My Grandmothers* (1980).

Hustak, Allan. *Peter Lougheed: A Biography* (1979).

Irving, John A. *The Social Credit Movement in Alberta* (1959).

Jones, David C. *Empire of Dust: Settling and Abandoning the Prairie Dry Belt* (1987).

Kroetsch, Robert. *Alberta* (1993).

Lamb, James B. *Jingo* (1992). Biography of Thomas Bland Strange, founder of the Alberta Field Force.

Macdonald, R.H. *Grant MacEwan, No Ordinary Man* (1979).

MacEwan, Grant. *Calgary Cavalcade, From Fort to Fortune* (1975).

——. *Grant MacEwan's Journals* (ed. by Max Foran, 1986).

——. *Poking Into Politics* (1966).

MacGregor, James G. *Edmonton: A History* (2nd ed. 1975).

——. *Edmonton Trader: The Story of John A. McDougall* (1963).

——. *A History of Alberta* (rev. ed. 1981).

Macpherson, C.B. *Democracy in Alberta: Social Credit and the Party System* (2nd ed. 1962).

Mallory, J.R. *Social Credit and the Federal Power in Canada* (1954, rpt. 1976).

Mann, W.E. *Sect, Culture and Church in Alberta* (1955).

Mansell, Robert L. and Michael B. Percy. *Strength in Adversity: A Study of the Alberta Economy* (1990).

Mardon, Ernest G. and Austin A. Mardon. *The Followers of Moses: The United Farmers of Alberta* (1992).

Masson, Jack with Edd LeSage. *Alberta's Local Governments and Their Politics* (1985).

McCourt, Edward. *Buckskin Brigadier: The Story of the Alberta Field Force* (1959).

Melnyk, Brian P. *Calgary Builds: The Emergence of an Urban Landscape, 1905–1914* (1985).

Mitchell, Elizabeth B. *In Western Canada Before the War: Impressions of Early Twentieth Century Prairie Communities* (1915, rpt. 1981).

Mountain Horse, Mike. *My People, The Bloods* (1979).

Nelson, Ferne. *Barefoot on the Prairie: Memories of Life on a Prairie Homestead* (1989).

Nevitt, R.B. *A Winter at Fort Macleod* (ed. by Hugh A. Dempsey, 1974).

Nikiforuk, Andrew. *Running on Empty: Alberta After the Boom* (1987).

Palmer, Howard. *Land of the Second Choice: A History of Ethnic Groups in Southern Alberta* (1972).

——. *Patterns of Prejudice: A History of Nativism in Alberta* (1982).

—— with Tamara Palmer. *Alberta: A New History* (1990).

—— (eds.). *Peoples of Alberta: Portraits of Cultural Diversity* (1985).

—— and Don Smith (eds.). *The New Provinces: Alberta and Saskatchewan, 1905–1980* (1980).

Patterson, R.M. *The Buffalo Head* (1961).

Peach, Jack. *Days Gone By: Jack Peach on Calgary's Past* (1993).

Person, Dennis and Carin Routledge. *Edmonton: Portrait of a City* (1981).

Pocklington, T.C. *The Government and Politics of the Alberta Metis Settlements* (1991).

Pratt, Larry (ed.). *Socialism and Democracy in Alberta: Essays in Honour of Grant Notley* (1986).

Richards, John and Larry Pratt. *Prairie Capitalism: Power and Influence in the New West* (1979).

Ring, Dan. *The Urban Years* (1993).

Roe, Frank Gilbert. *Getting the Know-How: Homesteading and Railroading in Early Alberta* (1982).

Russell, Andy. *The Canadian Cowboy: Stories of Cows, Cowboys, and Cayuses* (1993). Most of these stories are about Alberta cowboys.

——. *The Life of a River* (1987). The Oldman River is depicted.

——. *Memoirs of a Mountain Man* (1984).

Silverman, Elaine Lesbau. *The Last Best West: Women on the Alberta Frontier, 1880–1930* (1984).

Smith, David E. *The Regional Decline of a National Party: Liberals on the Prairies* (1981).

Snow, John. *These Mountains Are Our Sacred Places: The Story of the Stoney Indians* (1977).

Swainson, Donald (ed.). *Historical Essays on the Prairie Provinces* (1970).

Thomas, Lewis G. *The Liberal Party in Alberta: A History of Politics in the Province of Alberta, 1905–1921* (1959).

——. *Rancher's Legacy: Alberta Essays* (rpt. 1986).

Thomas, Lewis H. *William Aberhart and Social Credit in Alberta* (1977).

Trottier, Alice, Kenneth J. Munro, and Gratien Allaire (eds.). *Glimpses of the Franco-Albertan Past: Recollections and Studies* (1980).

Tupper, Allan and Roger Gibbins (eds.). *Government and Politics in Alberta* (1992).

Tyman, John Langton. *By Sector, Township and Range: Studies in Prairie Settlement* (1972).

Ward, Tom. *Cowtown: An Album of Early Calgary* (1975).

Wetherell, Donald G. with Irene R.A. Kmet. *Homes in Alberta: Building, Trends, and Design, 1870–1967* (1991).

——. *Useful Pleasures: The Shaping of Leisure in Alberta, 1896–1945* (1990).

Wiebe, Rudy. *Alberta, a Celebration: Stories* (1979).

Wood, David G. *The Lougheed Legacy* (1984).

Alberta in Literature

* denotes a winner of a Governor General's Literary Award.

Alford, Edna. *A Sleep Full of Dreams* (1981). A Calgary home for aged women is the setting for ten stories.

Allen, Ralph. *Peace River Country* (1958). A Saskatchewan mother with her two children seeks refuge in Peace River from an alcoholic husband.

Bell, Wade. *The North Saskatchewan River Book* (1976). A collection of short stories, vignettes, and anecdotes.

Bugnet, Georges. *The Forest* (1976). Two urban French citizens try to settle in Northern Alberta.

Byfield, Jacques. *Forever 33* (1982). An amusing story set in an Alberta town during the depression.

Carpenter, David (ed.). *Wild Rose Country: Stories From Alberta* (1977).

Chalmers, John W. (ed.). *The Alberta Diamond Jubilee Anthology* (1979).

Clark, D.M. *Wild Rose* (1982). In the 1950s an Alberta bible college student comes in conflict with authority.

Cullen, Michael. *Goodnight, Sammy Wong* (1982). Humourous novel set in Lethbridge.

Dagg, Mel. *The Women on the Bridge* (1992). Historical fiction about the Frog Lake Massacre.

Forrester, Helen. *The Latchkey Kid* (1971, rpt. 1985). A young man in a small Alberta town gets revenge for his neglected childhood by writing a best-seller.

Forrie, Allan, Patrick O'Rourke, and Glen Sorestad (eds.). *The Last Map is the Heart: An Anthology of Western Canadian Fiction* (1989).

Fraser, Frances. *The Bear Who Stole the Chinook: Tales From the Blackfoot* (1959, rpt. 1990).

Frey, Cecelia. *Breakaway* (1974). A homesteading family in northern Alberta in the 1930s is seen through the eyes of a young girl.

——. *The Love Song of Romeo Paquette* (1990). Episodes in the life of a retired Edmonton widower.

Gard, Robert E. *Johnny Chinook: Tall Tales and True from the Canadian West* (1967).

Gillese, John Patrick (ed.). *Chinook Arch: A Centennial Anthology of Alberta Writing* (2nd ed. 1968).

Glass, Joanna M. *Reflections on a Mountain Summer* (1974). Memories of a wealthy mother's affair with a forestry worker.

Haley, Susan. *Getting Married in Buffalo Jump* (1987). A teacher and farm owner struggles with conflicting emotions when her uneducated, immigrant, attractive farm worker proposes a practical marriage.

Harker, Herbert. *Goldenrod* (1972). A tale about an unsuccessful ranch hand.

Heath, Caroline (ed.). *Double Bond: An Anthology of Prairie Women's Fiction* (1984).

Huser, Glen. *Grace Lake* (1990). After a heart attack a man returns to a summer camp on an Alberta lake.

Huston, Mervyn J. *Gophers Don't Pay Taxes* (1981). Humourous stories about a young lawyer in an Alberta farming community.

Huston, Nancy. *Plainsong* (1993). An Alberta man constricted by physical realities is given a second chance by an affair with a native artist.

Joudry, Patricia. *The Selena Tree* (1980). A romantic saga spanning four generations in a small Alberta town.

King, Thomas. *Medicine River* (1989); *Green Grass, Running Water* (1993). Satires concerning relations between natives and whites in a small Alberta town.

Kinsella, W.P. *Dance Me Outside* (1977); *The Fencepost Chronicles* (1978); *Born Indian* (1981); *The Moccasin Telegraph and Other Stories* (1983). These humourous tales about Cree Indians on an Alberta reserve poke fun at white society.

——. *Box Social: A Novel* (1991). Set in rural northern Alberta after the depression.

Konrad, Anne. *The Blue Jar* (1985). Short stories about a Russian immigrant family in northern Alberta in the 1940s and 1950s.

Kroetsch, Robert. *Gone Indian* (1973, rpt. 1981). Humour and fantasy combine in this novel about a winter festival near Edmonton and a man's doomed quest.

——. **The Studhorse Man* (1970, rpt. 1988). A man searches Alberta for a suitable mate for his stallion.

——. *The Words of My Roaring* (1966, 1977 rpt.). To win an election an undertaker promises rain to drought-stricken farmers.

McCourt, Edward. *Music at the Close* (1947, rpt. 1966). A boy in rural Alberta grows up between the two world wars.

Mitchell, Ken (ed.). *Horizon: Writings of the Canadian Prairies* (1977).

Mitchell, W.O. *The Kite* (1962, rpt. 1983); *The Vanishing Point* (1973); *Roses Are Difficult Here: A Novel* (1990); *For Art's Sake: A Novel* (1992). Humorous novels set in Alberta.

Morritt, Hope. *Bohunk Road* (1987). Fiction set in Edmonton and Whitehorse, Yukon Territory.

Moser, Marie. *Counterpoint* (1987). Three generations of women in a French-Canadian family in western Canada are remembered when the granddaughter makes a pilgrimage to her inherited property in Alberta.

O'Hagen, Howard. *The School-Marm Tree: A Novel* (1977). A girl dreams of leaving a dismal Alberta railroad town.

Oliva, Peter. *Drowning in Darkness* (1993). A woman from southern Italy longs to escape a coal mining community in the Crowsnest Pass.

Powe, Bruce Allen. *The Aberhart Summer* (1983). A man explores his friend's 1935 suicide.

Radford, Tom and Harry Savage (eds.). *The Best of Alberta* (1987).

Ravvin, Norman. *Cafe des Westens* (1991). Conflict between a Calgary father and son.

Ryga, George. *Ballad of a Stonepicker: A Novel* (rev ed. 1976). A story of two brothers in the 1940s and 1950s, one staying on the family farm, the other pursuing higher education.

——. *Hungry Hills* (1963, rpt. 1977). A novel of survival in the foothills of Alberta.

Silvester, Reg. *Wishbone* (1990). Seven linked stories and a novella tell about a family of hotel keepers in small-town Alberta.

Stenson, Fred. *Lonesome Hero* (1974). Comic novel about young people in a southern Alberta farm community who are reluctant to face life.

—— (ed.). *Alberta Bound: Thirty Stories by Alberta Writers* (1986).

—— (ed.). *The Road Home: New Stories by Alberta Writers* (1992).

Summers, Merna. *The Skating Party* (1974); *Calling Home: New Stories* (1982). Stories about rural and small-town Alberta.

Van der Mark, Christine. *In Due Season* (1947, rpt. 1979). The difficult life on a northern Alberta farm in the 1930s causes a woman to alienate family and neighbours.

——. *Honey on the Rock* (1966). A story of the tensions created in a Brethren of Christ community in southern Alberta.

Van Herk, Aritha. *Judith: A Novel* (1978, 1984 rpt.). A young urban woman becomes a pig farmer.

——. *Places Far From Ellesmere: A Geografictione: Explorations on Site* (1990). Fiction based on the author's youth in Alberta.

—— (ed.). *Alberta Rebound: Thirty More Stories By Alberta Writers* (1990).

—— (ed.). *Boundless Alberta* (1993). Anthology.

Walker, Ella May. *Fortress North* (1947). Historical fiction set in Edmonton.

Wex, Michael. *Schlepping the Exile* (1993). A comic novel about growing up Jewish in Coalbanks.

Wiebe, Rudy. *The Angel of the Tar Sands and Other Stories* (1982).

—— (comp.). *Getting Here: Stories* (1977). Seven stories by Alberta women.

Yip, Yuen Chung. *The Tears of Chinese Immigrants* (1990). Married Chinese immigrants in Lethbridge in the 1950s.

BRITISH COLUMBIA

British Columbia, located between the Rocky Mountains and the Pacific Ocean, is bordered on the west by the state of Alaska and the Pacific Ocean; on the north by Yukon Territory and Northwest Territories; on the east by the province of Alberta; and on the south by the states of Washington, Idaho, and Montana. It is the only Canadian province that shares two land borders with the United States.

Name Province of British Columbia. Chosen by Queen Victoria and officially proclaimed on August 2, 1858. *Previous name:* central highland region called New Caledonia (1806–1858).

Flag The upper third consists of a Union Jack with an antique gold crown in the center. In the lower two-thirds a golden half-sun is superimposed on blue wavy lines on a white background. Proclaimed by Order-in-Council on June 20, 1960.

Coat of Arms The shield is similar to the flag and is supported by a wapiti stag at left and a bighorn sheep ram at right. Above the shield is a wreathed helm upon which rests a lion, garlanded with dogwood, standing on a crown. In the compartment below the shield dogwood entwines a scroll with the provincial motto. The shield was granted by Edward VII on March 31, 1906, the complete coat of arms by Elizabeth II on October 15, 1987.

Motto *Splendor Sine Occasu* (Splendor without diminishment).

Emblems
Bird Stellar's jay (*Cyanocitta stelleri*)
Flower Pacific dogwood (*Cornus nuttallii*)

Mineral jade
Tartan blue, green, white, and gold on a red background
Tree western red cedar (*Thuja plicata donn*)

Date of Entry into Confederation July 20, 1871.

Official Language English.

Capital City Victoria, situated on the southeastern tip of Vancouver Island; population 71,228, CMA population 287,897. The site was selected on March 15, 1843, by James Douglas partly to strengthen British claims to Vancouver Island and partly to build a Hudson's Bay Company post, Fort Camosum, which was renamed Fort Victoria on December 12, 1843, in honour of the Queen. It was incorporated on August 2, 1862, and became the capital of the colony of British Columbia on April 2, 1868 (before the colonies were amalgamated, Victoria was the capital of the Vancouver Island colony and New Westminster the capital of the mainland colony).

Provincial Holidays In addition to national statutory holidays (see page 2), British Columbia residents celebrate British Columbia Day (the first Monday in August).

Geography Except for open plains in the northeast corner, British Columbia is part of the North American Cordillera with four parallel north-south mountain ranges separated by parallel valleys and plateaus. Vancouver Island, one of many coastal islands, is the largest island on the west coast of North America. The tallest and broadest trees in Canada are found in the extensive forests that cover 55% of British Columbia. While only 2% of the land is used for agriculture, these pockets of fertile soil are extremely productive.

Area 948,596 sq. km. (366,255 sq. mi.); 9.5% of Canada. *Rank:* 3rd among the provinces, 4th among the provinces and territories.

Inland Water 18,068 sq. km. (6,976 sq. mi.), includes 7,800 officially named lakes (only 60–70% of lakes in British Columbia have been named officially). Largest lake: Williston Lake 1,772 sq. km. (684 sq. mi.).

Elevations Highest point: Mount Fairweather 4,663 m. (15,299 ft.). Lowest point: coast, sea level.

Major Rivers (* indicates a designated Canadian Heritage River): *Alsek, Columbia, Fraser, Iskut, *Kicking Horse, Kootenay, Liard, Nass, Nechako, Peace, Skeena, Stikine, Taku, Thompson, Wannock.

Climate British Columbia has three major climate regions. The coast has a maritime climate with abundant rainfall, the most temperate climate in Canada. The average daily mean temperature in January in Victoria is 4.1 °C (39.4°F); in July 15.4°C (59.7°F). The interior region has mainly a continental climate with considerable variation in winter. The average daily mean temperature in January in Kamloops is −6.1°C (43.0°F); in July 20.8°C (69.4°F). The northeast corner has a more extreme continental climate. The average daily mean temperature in January in Fort Nelson is −23.8 °C (−10.8°F);

in July 16.6°C (61.9°F). The lowest recorded temperature in British Columbia: −58.9°C (−74.0°F) at Smith River on January 31, 1947; the highest recorded temperature 44.4°C (111.9°F) at Lilloet, Lytton, and Chinook Cove on July 16, 1941.

Average annual precipitation in Prince Rupert, 2,523.2 mm. (99.3 in.); in Vancouver, 1,112.6 mm. (43.8 in.); in Kamloops, 265.2 mm. (10.4 in.). Average annual snowfall in Prince Rupert, 151.7 cm. (59.7 in.); in Vancouver, 60.4 cm. (23.8 in.); in Kamloops, 91.5 cm. (36.0 in.).

British Columbia holds many Canadian weather records including all the records for precipitation and snowfall: greatest annual precipitation, 8,122.4 mm. (319.8 in.) at Henderson Lake in 1931; greatest precipitation in one month, 2,235.5 mm. (88.0 in.) at Swanson Bay in November 1917; greatest precipitation in 24 hours, 489.4 mm. (19.3 in.) at Ucluelet Brymor Mines on October 6, 1967; greatest snowfall in a single season, 2,446.9 cm. (963.3 in.) at Mount Copeland in winter 1971/2; greatest snowfall in one month, 535.9 cm. (211.0 in.) at Haines Apps No. 2 in December 1959; greatest snowfall over five consecutive days, 246.2 cm. (96.9 in.) at Kitimat January 14, 1974; greatest snowfall in one day, 118.1 cm. (46.5 in.) at Lakelse Lake January 17, 1974; greatest average annual snowfall, 1,433 cm. (564.2 in.) at Glacier, Mount Fidelity; greatest depth of accumulated snow on the ground, 483 cm. (190.2 in.) at Whistler on March 31, 1974.

Prince Rupert is the Canadian city with the least average annual sunshine: 985 hours; while Kamloops has the highest average daytime temperature during June, July, and August: 27.2°F (81.0°C); Vancouver has the highest average annual temperature: 9.9°C (49.8°F); Victoria has the lowest average annual snowfall: 47 cm. (18.5 in.).

Time Zones Most of the province is in the Pacific time zone; eastern British Columbia is in the Mountain time zone.

PARKS AND HISTORIC SITES

In this section * indicates the area is, or part of it is, a Unesco World Heritage Site.

National Parks Located in British Columbia

Park	Location	Size
Glacier	near Revelstoke	1,349 sq. km. (521 sq. mi.)
Kootenay	Radium Hot Springs	1,406 sq. km. (543 sq. mi.)
*Gwaii Haanas	Queen Charlotte Islands	1,740 sq. km. (672 sq. mi.)
Mount Revelstoke	Columbia Mountains	260 sq. km. (100 sq. mi.)
Pacific Rim	Ucluelet	500 sq. km. (193 sq. mi.)
*Yoho	Field	1,313 sq. km. (507 sq. mi.)

Provincial Parks There are 370 provincial parks, 36 recreation areas, 1 wilderness conservancy, and 131 ecological reserves covering 6,730,870 ha. (25,988 sq. mi.), 7% of British Columbia's area. The largest parks are:

Park	District	Type	Size
Tweedsmuir	Skeena	park	9,609 sq. km. (3,710 sq. mi.)
Tatshenshini-Alsek	Skeena	park	9,580 sq. km. (3,699 sq. mi.)
Spatsizi Plateau	Skeena	park	6,082 sq. km. (2,348 sq. mi.)
Wells Gray	Thompson River	park	5,158 sq. km. (1,992 sq. mi.)
Ts'yl-os	Cariboo	park	2,332 sq. km. (900 sq. mi.)
Atlin	Skeena	park	2,327 sq. km. (898 sq. mi.)
Mount Edziza	Skeena	park	2,287 sq. km. (883 sq. mi.)
*Mount Robson	Prince George	park	2,195 sq. km. (847 sq. mi.)
Stikine River	Skeena	recreation	2,170 sq. km. (838 sq. mi.)
Strathcona	Strathcona	park	2,119 sq. km. (818 sq. mi.)

British Columbia also has 7 national bird sanctuaries, 5 national wildlife areas, and 1 Ramsar site.

Major National Historic Sites and Parks in British Columbia

Fort Langley, Fort Langley
Fort Rodd Hill, Victoria
Fort St. James, Fort St. James
Gulf of Georgia Cannery, Steveston
Kitwanga Fort, Kitwanga
Ninstints, Queen Charlotte Islands
St. Roch, Vancouver Maritime Museum

In addition, there are many parks and historic sites administered by the province, municipalities, or organizations. The major sites are:

Barkerville Historic Town, Barkerville
Cottonwood House Historic Park, east of Quesnel
Doukhobor Historic Village, Castlegar
Fort McLeod Historic Park, south of Mackenzie
Fort Steele Heritage Town, Fort Steele
Morden Colliery Historic Park, south of Nanaimo
Seton Portage Historic Park, west of Lillooet

Demography

All figures relating to British Columbia population and dwellings are 1991 data and do not include the population on 18 Indian reserves that did not cooperate in the 1991 census.

British Columbia Population: 3,282,061; 12.0% of national; *rank* 3rd

Historical population data
1981	2,744,465
1971	2,184,620
1961	1,629,082
1951	1,165,210
1941	817,861
1921	524,582
1901	178,657
1881	49,459
1861	51,524

Population Density: 3.5 per sq. km. (9.5 per sq. mi.)

Number of Dwellings: 1,251,414

Indian Reserves: 196 bands on 468 reserves

Population Characteristics:
urban: 2,640,139; 80.4%
rural: 641,922; 19.6%
19 and under: 873,970; 26.6%
65 and over: 422,015; 12.9%
average income for full-time employment 15 years and over (1990): $34,866; men $40,200; women $26,170
average life expectancy at birth (1987): men 74.1 years (highest in Canada); women 80.3 years (highest in Canada)
live birth rate: 45,612; 13.9 per 1000
deaths: 23,977; 7.5 per 1000
marriages: 23,691; 7.2 per 1000
divorces: 10,369; 3.16 per 1000

Largest Cities *(for definitions of CMA and CA, see page viii)*

Name	Population	Dwellings	National Pop. Rank
Vancouver	1,602,502 (CMA)	612,962	3
Victoria	287,897 (CMA)	119,991	14
Kelowna	111,846 (CA)	43,636	29
Nanaimo	73,547 (CA)	23,831	38
Prince George	69,653	24,206	40
Kamloops	67,856 (CA)	25,115	42
Vernon	48,139 (CA)	18,488	56
Penticton	45,078 (CA)	18,689	60
Williams Lake	34,690 (CA)	12,230	76
Duncan	27,384 (CA)	10,269	88

Government and Politics, 1871–

A description of the division of powers between the federal and provincial governments will be found on page 4.

Lieutenant-Governor The Lieutenant-Governor is the nominal head of the British-Columbia government, and is appointed by the Governor General of Canada on the recommendation of the Prime Minister of Canada. (A description of the duties of lieutenant-governors is found on page 7.)

Lieutenant-Governors of British Columbia	*Term*
Joseph William Trutch	1871–1876
Albert Norton Richards	1876–1881
Clement Francis Cornwall	1881–1887
Hugh Nelson	1887–1892
Edgar Dewdney	1892–1897
Thomas Robert McInnes	1897–1900
Henri-Gustave Joly de Lotbinière	1900–1906
James Dunsmuir	1906–1909
Thomas Wilson Paterson	1909–1914
Francis Stillman Barnard	1914–1919
Edward Gawler Prior	1919–1920
Walter Cameron Nichol	1920–1926
Robert Randolph Bruce	1926–1931
John William Fordham Johnson	1931–1936
Eric Werge Hamber	1936–1941
William Culham Woodward	1941–1946

Charles Arthur Banks 1946–1950
Clarence Wallace 1950–1955
Frank MacKenzie Ross 1955–1960
George Randolph Pearkes 1960–1968
John Robert Nicholson 1968–1973
Walter Steward Owen 1973–1978
Henry Pybus Bell-Irving 1978–1983
Robert Gordon Rogers 1983–1988
David See-Chau Lam 1988–

Legislative Assembly The Legislative Assembly of British Columbia consists of 75 members elected by popular vote, each member representing a constituency; term of office: up to 5 years as long as the party in power maintains the confidence of the Legislative Assembly; remuneration (1992/3): $32,812 + $16,406 tax-free allowance, additional amounts for special appointments; qualifications for members: Canadian citizen, 18 years of age or older on election day, resident in British Columbia for one year prior to polling day, qualified as a voter in an electoral district in the province, not legally disqualified. (A description of the duties of provincial legislatures are found on page 7.)

Qualifications for British Columbia Voters in Provincial Elections Canadian citizen, 18 years of age or older on election day, resident in British Columbia for the six months prior to election day.

Premier Nominally appointed by the Lieutenant-Governor of British Columbia, the Premier is generally the leader of the party with the majority of seats in the Legislative Assembly. (A description of the responsibilities of provincial premiers is found on page 7.)

Premiers of British Columbia/Party/Term
John Foster McCreight
   (1871–1872)
Amor de Cosmos
   (1872–1874)
George Anthony Walkem
   (1874–1876)
Andrew Charles Elliott
   (1876–1878)

George Anthony Walkem
   (1878–1882)
Robert Beaven
   (1882–1883)
William Smithe
   (1883–1887)
Alexander Edmund Batson Davie
   (Conservative, 1887–1889)
John Robson
   (Liberal, 1889–1892)
Theodore Davie
   (1892–1895)
John Herbert Turner
   (1895–1898)
Charles Augustus Semlin
   (Conservative, 1898–1900)
Joseph Martin
   (Liberal, 1900)
James Dunsmuir
   (Conservative, 1900–1902)
Edward Gawler Prior
   (Conservative, 1902–1903)
Richard McBride
   (Conservative, 1903–1915)
William John Bowser
   (Conservative, 1915–1916)
Harlan Carey Brewster
   (Liberal, 1916–1918)
John Oliver
   (Liberal, 1918–1927)
John Duncan MacLean
   (Liberal, 1927–1928)
Simon Fraser Tolmie
   (Conservative, 1928–1933)
Thomas Dufferin Pattullo
   (Liberal, 1933–1941)
John Hart
   (Coalition Govt., 1941–1947)
Byron Ingemar Johnson
   (Coalition Govt., 1947–1952)
William Andrew Cecil Bennett
   (Social Credit, 1952–1972)
David Barrett
   (New Democratic, 1972–1975)
William Richards Bennett
   (Social Credit, 1975–1986)
Wilhelmus Nicholaas Theodore Vander Zalm
   (Social Credit, 1986–1991)
Rita Margaret Johnston
   (Social Credit, 1991)
Michael Franklin Harcourt
   (New Democratic, 1991–   )

Cabinet The Cabinet consists of ministers appointed by the Premier, usually from elected members of the majority party in the Legislative Assembly. Cabinet ministers serve at the Premier's pleasure; each member usually heads a government ministry.

Government Ministries The telephone numbers for general information are listed with the ministries. Ministries without specific information numbers can be reached through Enquiry B.C., a provincial government information referral service, (604)387-6121 (Victoria), (604)660-2421 (Vancouver), 800-661-6773 elsewhere in B.C.

Aboriginal Affairs
   (604)356-8281
Agriculture, Fisheries and Food
   (604)387-5121
Attorney General
   (604)387-4577
Education
   (604)387-4611

Employment and Investment
Energy, Mines and Petroleum Resources
Environment, Lands and Parks
   (604)387-1161 or 800-665-7027 lower mainland)
Finance and Corporate Relations
   (604)387-9278
Forests
   (604)387-5255
Government Services
Health
   (604)952-3456
Housing, Recreation and Consumer Services
Municipal Affairs
   (604)387-7912
Skills, Training and Labour
   (604)387-3165
Small Business, Tourism and Culture
Social Services
Transportation and Highways
Women's Equality

British Columbia Representation in Federal Government
House of Commons: 32 members
Senate: 6 members

Finances

A statement of British Columbia's revenue and expenditures for the years 1992/93 and 1991/92 are shown below in millions of dollars. The financial year runs from April 1 to March 31 of the year following.

	Actual 1992/93	Actual 1991/92
Revenue		
Taxation	9,818.5	9,268.3
Natural resource revenue	1,245.0	1,101.2
Contribution from government enterprises	1,017.1	700.4
Other	1,651.2	1,572.1
Government of Canada	2,435.8	2,103.0
Total revenue for the year	16,167.6	14,745.0
Expenditures		
Health	6,002.9	5,616.7
Education	4,803.8	4,519.5
Social services	2,366.5	1,993.7
Natural resources and economic development	1,151.4	1,421.0
Transportation	1,077.6	1,262.1

Protection of persons and property	878.2	786.6
Other	835.0	858.0
Interest on debt	813.5	642.8
Total expenditures for the year	17,928.9	17,100.4
Deficit for the year	1,761.3	2,355.4

Economy

Natural resources are the basis of British Columbia's economy. Its productive forest-land covers 54.6% of the province, provides both primary activities and secondary industries; its mountain ranges contain a large minerals and metals sector, while also giving it Canada's second most important potential water resources and a thriving tourist industry; and the ocean has fostered Canada's largest and most valuable fishing industry. Vancouver is the leading dry cargo port on the west coast of North America. Although only 4% of the soil is suitable for agriculture, British Columbia has an important dairy and livestock industry and is Canada's largest apple producer, its main source of apricots, and provides one-third of its blueberries.

Major Industries Forest industries are the largest component of British Columbia's manufacturing sector and accounted for 46% of all manufacturing shipments in 1992. Tourism is the second largest industry generating $5.46 billion in 1992. Other important industries include food processing, mining, and fishing.

Gross Domestic Product (1992) $76,061 million (in current dollars at factor cost); % of national G.D.P.: 12.7%; rank: 3rd.

Distribution of gross domestic product (1990)

Finance, insurance, real estate	18.3%
Manufacturing	12.1%
Construction	7.2%
Retail trade	6.1%
Government services	5.2%
Transportation, storage	5.0%
Wholesale trade	4.4%
Educational services	4.4%
Health services	4.0%
Mining	2.7%
Other utilities	2.3%
Logging	2.2%
Agriculture	1.0%
Fishing and trapping	0.4%

Value of Manufacturing Shipments $23,126 million

Farm Cash Receipts $1,247 million

Employment (seasonally adjusted) 1,500,000; participation rate: 66.4%

Unemployment (seasonally adjusted) 170,000; per capita: 10.2%

Minimum Wage (1993) $6.00, general minimum; $5.50, under 18

Exports B.C.'s exports in 1992 amounted to $16,353 million; 10.1% of total Canadian exports; rank: 4th.
Largest trading partner: United States, 50% of B.C.'s total exports
Other important markets: Japan 25%; U.K. and South Korea each 3%
Major export commodities: Forest products, mining products, energy (gas and electricity), and fish products are the major export commodities. In 1993 tourism provided 3.1% of B.C.'s GDP.

ca. 10,000 B.C.	Paleo-Indians arrive.
ca. 4,000 B.C.	Direct ancestors of west coast Indians arrive.
ca. 500 A.D.	Possibility that Hwui Shin, a Chinese Buddhist monk, explores west coast.
ca. 17th century	Bella Coola, Haida, Kwaskiutl, Nootka, Tagish, Tlingit, Tsimshian, and Wakashan peoples are on the coast; Athapaskan, Carrier, Kootenay, and Salish in the interior.
1774	*July* Juan Jose Perez Hernandez trades with Haidas off the Queen Charlotte Islands, the first recorded European contact with northwest coast Indians, and claims the area for Spain.
1778	*March 29* James Cook, the first European known to have landed in British Columbia (B.C.), arrives at Nootka Sound and claims land for Britain.
1786	*July 31* James Strange claims Vancouver Island for Britain.
1787	*July 7* Frances Barkley, wife of a ship captain, becomes the first white woman to arrive in present-day B.C.
1789	John Meares brings 30 Chinese labourers, to build a ship at Nootka, perhaps the first Chinese in North America.
	May 5 Estaban Jose Martinez arrives at Nootka Sound to enforce Spanish claims to Pacific coast.
	July Martinez seizes British ships; "Nootka Crisis" brings Spain and Britain to the brink of war.
1790	*May 31* Alferez Manuel Quimper explores the Straits of Juan de Fuca and claims area for Spain.
	October 28 Treaty of the Nootka Convention settles trading along the north Pacific coast and provides for equal rights of trade, navigation, and settlement in the unoccupied parts of the north coast of North America.
1791–1792	Robert Gray and the crew of the *Columbia* winter on the west coast of Vancouver Island, the first white men to do so.
1792	*June 4* George Vancouver claims Vancouver Island, Strait of Juan de Fuca, and the coast for Britain.
	Vancouver produces the first detailed map of Pacific coast.
1793	*July 22* Alexander Mackenzie arrives at Dean Channel, Bella Coola, the first person to cross the North American continent north of Mexico.
	Autumn William Broughton sails up the Columbia River and claims the area for Britain.
1795	*March 28* Spanish post at Nootka Sound surrenders to the British.
1805	Simon Fraser builds Rocky Mountain Portage House (present-day Hudson Hope).
1806	Fraser sends the first shipment of furs from west of the Rocky Mountains to Dunvegan, Alberta.
	Fraser builds Fort St. James on Stuart Lake as the North West Company's headquarters for New Caledonia; the oldest continuously inhabited community in B.C.
1807	David Thompson crosses Rockies and reaches Blaeberry River, the first white man to see the upper waters of the Columbia River.
	Fraser builds Fort George at New Caledonia for the North West Company.
1807–1808	*Winter* Thompson records the first systematic meteorological observations taken in B.C.

1808	*May–July* Fraser explores Fraser River reaching the Pacific on *July 2.*
1811	Thompson charts the Columbia River to the Pacific coast, raises the British flag at the juncture of the Snake and Columbia rivers, and claims country for Britain.
1812	Kamloops is founded as a North West Company post.
1825	Anglo-Russian treaty sets the Alaska boundary at 54° 41'.
1827	*July* Hudson's Bay Company begins building Fort Langley at the mouth of the Fraser River.
1835	Coal is discovered on Vancouver Island.
1846	*June 15* Oregon Treaty settles boundary dispute between the United States and Britain; it extends the 49th parallel to the west coast but gives all of Vancouver Island to Britain.
1849	*January 13* Vancouver Island is proclaimed a crown colony and Britain gives the Hudson's Bay Company a ten-year trade monopoly on the Island.
	First school on the Pacific coast is established at Fort Victoria.
1850	*March* Richard Blanchard arrives as the first governor of the colony of Vancouver Island.
	May 1 First Indian treaties on Vancouver Island arrange the purchase of all land in the vicinity of Fort Victoria.
	August Blanchard appoints a Provisional Council.
1851	Canada's first gold rush occurs on the Queen Charlotte Islands.
	June 30 Legislative Council of Vancouver Island holds its first session.
	October 30 James Douglas replaces Blanchard as governor of Vancouver Island.
1852	*July 9* British government gives Douglas a commission to assert British dominance over Queen Charlotte Islands.
	August 24 After a coal discovery, Douglas establishes Nanaimo; the Hudson's Bay Company takes possession of the coal deposits.
1853	*September 20* First jury trial is held on Vancouver Island.
	December 2 Supreme Court is established on Vancouver Island.
1854	*August 8* Sale of alcohol to Indians on Vancouver Island is made illegal.
1856	*April 16* Douglas announces the discovery of gold; all gold is declared the property of the crown.
	August 12 Legislative Assembly meets for the first time in Victoria.
1857	Gold is discovered in the sandbars of the lower Fraser River; during the following eight years gold is also discovered in other areas; gold rushes bring 25,000 prospectors to B.C. which precipitates the need for British law and rule on the mainland.
	December 28 Douglas proclaims the Crown's control of mineral rights and requires miners to take out licences.
1858	*British Colonist*, the first B.C. newspaper, is published in Victoria.
	August 2 British parliament creates the mainland colony of British Columbia.
	November 19 James Douglas is inaugurated as the first governor of the colony of British Columbia.
1859	*March* Macdonald's Bank is established at Victoria, the first bank west of the Great Lakes.
	April 25 First black settlers arrive in Victoria.
	May 4 Douglas establishes Queensborough (renamed New Westminster *July 20*) as the capital of the colony of British Columbia.
	November 3 Douglas revokes the Hudson's Bay Company's exclusive trade licence.
1860s	Haida in the Queen Charlotte Islands are stricken by epidemics.

1862–1865	Road is built from Yale to Barkerville.
1863	*July* Stickine Territory is absorbed by the colony of British Columbia.
1864	*January 22* First session of the Legislative Council of the colony of British Columbia opens at Sapperton.
1865	*August 15* First public library in B.C. opens in New Westminster.
	Esquimalt becomes a British naval station.
	Lumbermen build Hastings Mill, the beginning of Vancouver.
1866	*August* The colonies of Vancouver Island and British Columbia are united into one colony.
	August First railroad on Vancouver Island, the Esquimalt and Nanaimo Railroad, opens.
1867	*April 3* Hudson's Bay Company relinquishes all claim to Vancouver Island.
	November 19 British government rejects a request that B.C. join Canada.
	December 17 Legislature meets for the first time in Victoria.
1868	*September 16* Fire almost destroys Barkerville, the centre of the Cariboo gold rush.
1870	*March 12* Legislative Council votes to endorse union with Canada.
	July 7 B.C. agrees to terms of union with Canada that include Canada assuming British Columbia's debt and building a railroad across Canada within ten years.
1872	Public Schools Act establishes a free provincial school system.
1873	Women property holders win the right to vote in municipal elections, the first Canadian women to do so.
1876	First secondary schools in Victoria are opened.
1878	B.C. bans employment of Chinese on public works.
1884	Federal government bans the potlach, a Haida custom, for religious and political reasons.
1885	*November 7* Last spike of the Canadian Pacific Railway is driven in at Craigellachie in Eagle Pass.
1886	*April 6* Vancouver is incorporated as a city.
	June 13 Fire destroys Vancouver; 11 dead; it is immediately rebuilt.
	July 4 First passenger train from Montreal reaches Port Moody.
	Vancouver's selection as the site of the railroad terminus promotes Vancouver as B.C.'s commercial centre.
	Orientals are barred from voting.
1887	*May 3* Coal mine explodes at Nanaimo; 150 dead.
	Copper-gold deposit is discovered at Rossland and a lead-zinc deposit at Kimberley.
1888	Fire levels Gastown (Vancouver).
1890	First electric tram system in B.C. opens in Vancouver.
1891	Transpacific shipping is inaugurated making Vancouver an important port.
	Free Libraries Act is passed.
	First interurban street railway in B.C. operates between New Westminster and Vancouver.
1896	*May 26* Bridge collapses in Victoria; 55 dead.
1897	*July 14* Canadian Pacific Railway begins construction of the Crowsnest Pass to southeastern British Columbia.
1898	*February 10* Legislative buildings in Victoria are formally opened.
1902	Edison Electric Theatre, probably Canada's first permanent cinema, opens in Vancouver.
	October 31 Transpacific cable from Vancouver to Brisbane is completed.
1903	*October 20* International Joint High Commission settles the Alaska panhandle

boundary dispute; Canada is enraged by the British betrayal of Canadian interests.

1904 *March 25* Federal government disallows B.C. legislation reducing jobs available to Japanese immigrants.

September Canada's first train robbery occurs near Mission Station when Bill Miner steals $7,000.

1905 British navy leaves naval base at Esquimalt.

1906 Prince Rupert is founded by the Grand Trunk Pacific Railway.

1907–1914 Grand Trunk Pacific Railway builds a line from Edmonton through the upper Fraser, Bulkley, and Skeena valleys.

1907 *May 7* Vancouver Stock Exchange is incorporated.

1908 *March 7* University of British Columbia is chartered as a branch of McGill University; it opens in 1915 as an independent institution.

June First service station in Canada opens in Vancouver.

August 2 Fire in Kootenay Valley kills 70 and causes extensive damage.

1910 *March 5* Avalanche in Rogers Pass leaves 62 dead.

September 8 William Gibson tests first Canadian aircraft engine in a short flight at Victoria.

Most Doukhobors move from Saskatchewan to establish farming communities in the Kettle and Kootenay Valleys.

1911 Strathcona, B.C.'s first provincial park, is established.

1912 *April* Powell River Company makes the first roll of newsprint in western Canada.

May 24 Charles Saunders makes the first parachute jump in Canada at Vancouver.

Pacific Great Eastern Railway is incorporated.

1913 *July 31* Alys McKay Bryant, Vancouver, becomes the first woman in Canada to pilot an airplane.

August 6 First fatal airplane accident in Canada kills John Bryant at Victoria.

1915 *January 15* Canadian Northern Railroad between Quebec and Vancouver is completed at Basque.

Vancouver becomes a major port when the completion of the Panama Canal opens European markets.

1916 *February 13* Victoria receives its greatest one-day snowfall, 55.3 cm. (21.8 in.).

December 6 Canada's longest rail tunnel, the Connaught tunnel through Macdonald Mountain, opens.

1917 *April 4* Women are permitted to vote in provincial elections.

Helen Emma Gregory MacGill, Canada's first woman judge, is appointed to the bench of the Juvenile Court at Vancouver.

1918 *January* Mary Ellen Smith becomes the first woman elected to B.C.'s Legislative Assembly.

1919 *August 7* E.C. Hoy makes the first flight across the Rocky Mountains, from Vancouver to Lethbridge.

1920 *October 7–17* First TransCanada flight Halifax to Vancouver is made in 49 hours, 7 minutes.

October 20 B.C. votes for government control and sale of liquor rather than Prohibition.

1922 *January 1* Motorists change from left side to drive on right side of road.

12,000 coal miners in Alberta and British Columbia go on strike.

1923 *March 2* Canada and the United States sign the Halibut Treaty concerning fishing rights in the north Pacific, the first independent negotiation by the Canadian government.

1924	*December 17* B.C. legislature adopts a resolution opposing the continued immigration of oriental people to Canada.
1928	*August 25* Seven are killed in Canada's first major air disaster as an airplane flies into Puget Sound in bad weather.
1930	*February 20* Federal government transfers control of B.C.'s natural resources to the province.
1935	*January 19* In one of Vancouver's worst storms 40 cm. (15.7 in.) snow and strong winds cause 2 m. (6.6 ft.) drifts.
1937	*September 1* TransCanada Airlines (later Air Canada) makes its first commercial flight, from Vancouver to Seattle.
1938	*June 19* On "Bloody Sunday" Royal Canadian Mounted Police and Vancouver city police remove 1,500 unemployed people who have occupied public buildings since *May 20.*
1939	Lions Gate Bridge in Vancouver is opened officially.
1940	Big Bend Highway through the mountains from Golden to Revelstoke opens.
1942	*February 26* Ca. 21,000 Japanese Canadians in coastal regions are moved to inland areas and their possessions confiscated.
	June 20 Japanese submarine fires shells at a lighthouse on Estevan Point, the only time during World War II that shells fall on Canada.
	Alaska Highway is built from Dawson Creek to Fairbanks, Alaska, by the United States Army, 2,451 km. (1,523 mi.)
1946	*June 15* Frank Arthur Calder becomes the first Indian elected to a provincial legislature in Canada.
	July 29 Hailstorm in the Okanagan Valley near Penticton causes $2 million damage to crops in 15 minutes.
1948	*Spring* Melting snow in the Fraser Valley causes the worst flood in B.C. history leaving 10 dead, 9,000 homeless, and $50 million damage.
1949	*January 12* Royal Canadian Air Force North Star airplane makes the first non-stop flight across Canada from Halifax to Vancouver.
	August 21 Biggest recorded Canadian earthquake hits the west coast causing no deaths and little damage.
1950	Park Royal, the first shopping centre in western Canada, opens in West Vancouver.
	August 15 Royal Canadian Mounted Police absorb the British Columbia provincial police.
	November 21 Troop train collides with a passenger train at Canoe River; 21 dead, 53 injured.
1953	*October 15* Trans Mountain oil pipeline from Edmonton to Vancouver is completed.
1954	Aluminum Company of Canada opens a hydroelectric plant and aluminum smelter at Kitimat.
1955	Canadian Pacific Airlines flies first polar air service, Vancouver to Amsterdam.
1958	*June 17* One section of the Second Narrows Bridge in Vancouver collapses killing 18.
	July 1 Federal-provincial hospital plans takes effect in B.C.
1961	*August 3* British Columbia Electric Company is made a provincial government agency.
1962	British Columbia Hydro and Electric Power Authority is formed.
	March 6 Sons of Freedom Doukhobors detonate explosives to destroy an electric power pylon near Riondel; 9 imprisoned.
	September 3 TransCanada Highway, 7,821 km. (4,860 mi.) from St. John's, Newfoundland, to Victoria, opens in a Rogers Pass ceremony.

	October 12 Remnants of Typhoon Freda with winds up to 145 kph (90 mph) strike Victoria leaving 7 dead and $10 million damage.
1963	*July 10* B.C. and the federal government sign an agreement concerning hydroelectric power in the B.C. interior.
1964	*September 16* Canada and the United States in the Columbia River Treaty agree to develop the power of the river; three giant storage dams are to be built in B.C.
1965	*February 18* Avalanche buries a copper mining camp near Stewart; 18 dead.
1967	*April 3* Coal mine explodes near Natal; 15 dead.
	May World's largest semi-submersible oil drilling vessel (356 x 356 x 336 ft.) begins drilling for oil and gas off Vancouver Island.
1968	*June 25* Leonard Stephen Marchand, representing Kamloops-Cariboo, becomes the first Indian elected to the federal House of Commons.
1969	*February 23* First Hovercraft service in Canada begins between Vancouver and Nanaimo.
1971	*September 10* Extension of British Columbia Railway from Fort St. John to Fort Nelson is completed.
1972	Frank Arthur Calder becomes a cabinet minister in the B.C. government, the first Indian in Canada to do so.
	Rosemary Brown is elected to the B.C. Legislative Assembly becoming the first black woman elected to a Canadian legislature.
1973	Land Commission Act freezes disposition of agricultural land for non-agricultural use.
	January 25 *Irish Stardust* runs aground north of Vancouver Island spilling 378,000 l. (99,857 gal.) of fuel oil which spreads 320 km. (199 mi.) south.
1974	Pauline Jewett is appointed president of Simon Fraser University, the first woman to be head of a major coeducational university in Canada.
	March 14 B.C. government imposes rent controls.
1976	*June 30* B.C. Court of Appeal rules that B.C. owns the mineral resources on the sea bottom between Vancouver Island and the mainland.
1979	B.C. appoints Carl Friedmann as its first ombudsman.
1980	*December 4* Storm with heavy winds in southwest B.C. brings up to 30 cm. (18.6 in.) snow; 3 dead.
1983	*June 19* B.C. Place, Canada's first domed stadium, opens.
1985	Environmentalists and Indians attempt to stop logging on Meares Island.
1986	*May 2–October 13* More than 22 million visitors attend Expo 86, the world fair in Vancouver.
1991	*March 29* Rita Margaret Johnston is the first woman to become a provincial premier in Canada.
1993	*June 25* Kim Campbell, Vancouver, becomes Prime Minister of Canada, the first woman to hold this position.
	Environmentalists and Indians clash with loggers and police over the B.C. government's decision to allow logging in parts of Clayoquot Sound.
	December 10 Michael Smith, University of British Columbia, wins the Nobel Prize for Chemistry for his work in developing site-directed mutagenesis used in genetic engineering.

Culture and Education

Performing Arts In 1994 British Columbia has 77 performing companies and institutions (11 dance companies, 13 classical music organizations, 21 theatre companies, and 32 arts organizations) as well as many festivals. The major organizations are listed below. Many perform as well in other provinces and countries.

Arts Club of Vancouver Theatre, Vancouver	(604)687-5315
Belfry Theatre Society, Victoria	(604)385-6835
Ballet British Columbia, Vancouver	(604)669-5954
Folkfest, Victoria (June/July)	(604)388-5322
International Children's Festival, Vancouver (May/June)	(604)687-7697
International Comedy Festival, Vancouver (July/August)	(604)683-0883
Judith Marcuse Dance Company	(604)872-4746
Tamahnous Theatre Workshop Society, Vancouver	(604)254-4699
Vancouver Bach Choir, Vancouver	(604)921-9136
Vancouver Opera Association, Vancouver	(604)682-2871
Vancouver Symphony Orchestra, Vancouver	(604)684-9100
Vancouver Playhouse Theatre, Vancouver	(604)872-6622
Victoria International Festival, Victoria (July-August) (classical music)	(604)736-2119
Victoria Symphony Orchestra, Victoria	(604)385-9771

Provincial Museums and Galleries The following are major British Columbia institutions.

Art Gallery of Greater Victoria
Royal British Columbia Museum, Victoria
British Columbia Forest Museum, near Duncan
Science World British Columbia, Vancouver
University of British Columbia Museum of Anthropology, Vancouver
Vancouver Art Gallery, Vancouver
Vancouver Maritime Museum, Vancouver
Vancouver Museum, Vancouver

Universities and Colleges

Malaspina University College, Nanaimo
Simon Fraser University, Burnaby
Trinity Western University, Langley
University College of Fraser Valley, Abbotsford
University College of the Cariboo, Kamloops
University College of the Okanagan, Kelowna
University of British Columbia, Vancouver
University of Northern British Columbia, Prince George
University of Victoria, Victoria

Community Colleges (* indicates additional campuses in other centres)

Camosum College, Victoria
Capilano College, North Vancouver
College of New Caledonia, Prince George*
Douglas College, New Westminster
East Kootenay Community College, Cranbrook*
Kwantlen College, Surrey*
North Island College, Courtenay*
Northern Lights College, Dawson Creek*
Northwest Community College, Terrace*
Okanagan College, Kelowna*
Selkirk College, Castlegar*
Vancouver Community College, Vancouver

Miscellaneous Educational Institutions

British Columbia Institute of Technology, Burnaby
Emily Carr College of Art and Design, Vancouver
Justice Institute of British Columbia, Vancouver
Lester B. Pearson College of the Pacific, Victoria
Nicola Valley Institute of Technology, Merritt
Pacific Marine Training Institute, North Vancouver

Motor Vehicle Use

Motor Vehicles Registered for Use in British Columbia: 1,983,000

Drivers Licensed by British Columbia: (1992) ca. 2,500,000. Minimum driving age: 16

Roads Paved highways: 22,053 km. (13,704 mi.); unpaved roads: 21,584 km. (13,412 mi.); bridges maintained by the province: 2,715

Speed Limits Freeways and highways: 90–110 kph (56–68 mph); outside municipalities: 80 kph (50 mph); municipalities: 50 kph (31 mph); school and playground zones: 30 kph (19 mph)

First, Biggest, and Best

World's strongest currents: Natwakto Rapids at Slingsby Channel, up to 16 knots (18.4 mi.) per hour

World's tallest totem pole: 52.7 m. (173 ft.) in Alert Bay

World's longest and highest suspension foot bridge: Capilano Suspension Bridge, length 137 m. (450 ft.), height 70 m. (230 ft.) from the lowest point of the bridge to the river below

World's longest submarine telephone cable: ANZCAN cable Port Alberni-Hawaii-Norfolk Island-Fiji-Sydney, Australia, 15,629 km. (9,711.7 mi.)

World's largest geoscientific project currently underway: Lithoprobe, based in Vancouver, involves more than 400 scientists and students at 28 universities, 12 federal and provincial ministries, and 17 private companies

World's largest purposefully detonated non-nuclear explosion: Ripple Rock, a shipping hazard in Seymour Narrows, blown up April 5, 1958

World's tallest unsupported flagpole: 86 m. (282 ft.) originally erected at Expo 86 in Vancouver, now at a car dealership in Surrey

North America's largest man-made reservoir: Williston Lake 1,772 sq. km. (684 sq. mi.)

North America's longest railway tunnel: 14.6 km. (9.1 mi.) under Mount Macdonald

World's largest single-operator, self-powered tree crusher: LeTourneau G175 displayed at Mackenzie, length 17 m. (56 ft.), height 10.6 m. (35 ft.), width 6.4 m. (21 ft.) (it is no longer operational)

North America's greatest number of types of big game animals

Commonwealth's first female speaker in a legislature: Nancy Hodges named speaker of the British Columbia legislature December 12, 1949

British Empire's first woman cabinet minister: Mary Ellen Smith appointed minister without portfolio in the British Columbia government March 1921

North America's worst street car accident: a street car plunged into Victoria harbour when one span of the bridge collapsed; 55 dead

Sources of Information About British Columbia

Enquiry B.C.: Provincial Government Referral Service, M151 Macdonald Block, Victoria, BC V8V 1X4 (604)387-6121 (Victoria), (604)660-2421 (Vancouver), 800-663-7867 (B.C.)

Ministry of Tourism and Culture: Parliament Buildings, Victoria, BC V8V 1X4 (604)387-1642

Tourism British Columbia: 1117 Wharf Street, Victoria, BC V8W 2Z2; Telephone Discovery British Columbia (604)663-6000 (Vancouver) or 800-663-6000

British Columbia government documents are available from Crown Publications: 546 Yates Street, Victoria, BC V8W 1K8 (604)386-4636

Books About British Columbia: A Selected List

Reference Guides

Akrigg, G.P.V. and Helen B. Akrigg. *1001 British Columbia Place Names* (3rd rev. ed. 1973, rpt. 1981).

Artibise, Alan F.J. *Western Canada Since 1870: A Select Bibliography and Guide* (1978).

Barker, Mary. *The Natural Resources of British Columbia and the Yukon* (1977).

Blake, Don. *BC Trivia* (rev. ed. 1992).

Bowsfield, Hartwell (ed.). *Fort Victoria Letters, 1846–1851* (1979).

Burbridge, Joan. *Wildflowers of the Southern Interior of British Columbia and Adjacent Parts of Washington, Idaho, and Montana* (1989).

Canada. Atmospheric Environment Service. *Canadian Climate Normals, 1961–1990: British Columbia* (1993).

Canada. Energy, Mines and Resources Canada. *Gazetteer of Canada: British Columbia* (3rd ed. 1985).

Careless, Virginia. *Bibliography for the Study of British Columbia's Domestic Material History* (1976).

Chilton, Rodney R.H. *Summary of Climatic Regimes in British Columbia* (1981).

Cowan, Ian McTaggart and Charles J. Guignet. *The Mammals of British Columbia* (1956).

Cuddy, Mary Lou and James J. Scott. *British Columbia in Books: An Annotated Bibliography* (1974).

Dalzell, Kathleen E. *Queen Charlotte Islands*, 3 vols. (1981–1989).

Davis, Chuck and Shirley Mooney. *Vancouver, an Illustrated Chronology* (1986).

Edwards, Margaret H. and John C.R. Lort with Wendy J. Carmichael. *A Bibliography of British Columbia: Years of Growth, 1900–1950*, 3 vols. (1975).

Farley, A.L. *Atlas of British Columbia: People, Environment, and Resource Use* (1979).

Giles, Valerie M.E. *Annotated Bibliography of Education History in British Columbia: A Technical Report* (1992).

Hale, Linda L. (comp.). *Vancouver Centennial Bibliography*, 4 vols. (1986).

—— and Jean Barman. *British Columbia Local Histories: A Bibliography* (1991).

Hendrickson, James E. (ed.). *Journals of the Colonial Legislatures of Vancouver Island and British Columbia, 1851–1871*, 5 vols. (1980).

Holmes, Marjorie C. *Publications of the Government of British Columbia, 1871–1947* (1950).

Jackman, S.W. *The Men at Cary Castle: A Series of Portrait Sketches of the Lieutenant-Governors of British Columbia From 1871 to 1971* (1972).

——. *Portraits of Premiers: An Informal History of British Columbia* (1969).

Klinka, K. and others. *Indicator Plants of Coastal British Columbia* (1989).

Lawrence, Erma (comp.). *Haida Dictionary* (1977).

Lowther, Barbara J. and Muriel Lang (comps.). *A Bibliography of British Columbia: Laying the Foundations, 1849–1899* (1968).

Lyons, Chester P. *Trees, Shrubs and Flowers to Know in British Columbia* (1952, rpt. 1974).

Maud, Ralph. *A Guide to B.C. Indian Myth and Legend: A Short History of Myth-Collecting and a Survey of Published Texts* (1982).

Middleton, Lynn. *Place Names of the Pacific Northwest Coast: Origins, Histories and Anecdotes in Bibliographic Form About the Coast of British Columbia, Washington and Oregon* (1969).

Ouston, Rick. *Getting the Goods: Information in B.C.—How to Find It, How to Use It* (1990).

Parkin, Tom. *Wetcoast Words: A Dictionary of British Columbia Words and Phrases* (1989).

Paulson, Dennis. *Snowbirds of the Pacific Northwest* (1993).

Smith, Illoana M. (comp.). *Transportation in British Columbia: A Bibliography* (1982).

Smith, Kathleen M., Nancy J. Anderson, and Katherine I. Beamish. *Nature West Coast: A Study of Plants, Insects, Birds, Mammals and Marine Life As Seen in Lighthouse Park* (1988).

Straley, Gerald B. *Trees of Vancouver* (1992).

—— and Del Meidinger. *The Vascular Plants of British Columbia*, 4 vols. (1989).

Walbran, John T. *British Columbia Coast Names, 1592–1906, To Which Are Added a Few Names in Adjacent United States Territory: Their Origin and History . . .* (1909, rpt. 1977).

Young, George and John S. Lutz (comps. and eds.). *A Researcher's Guide to British Columbia Nineteenth Century Directories: A Bibliography and Index* (1988).

——. *A Researcher's Guide to British Columbia Directories, 1901–1940* (1992).

Young, Terry Ann. *Researching the History of Aboriginal Peoples in British Columbia: A Guide to Resources at the British Columbia Archives and Records Service and BC Lands* (1992).

Nonfiction Sources

* denotes a winner of a Governor General's Literary Award.

Affleck, Edward. *The Kootenays in Retrospect*, 3 vols. (1976).

Akrigg, G.P.V. and Helen B. Akrigg. *British Columbia Chronicle, 1778–1846: Adventures By Sea and Land (1975).

——. British Columbia Chronicle, 1847–1871: Gold & Colonists (1977).

Allison, Susan. A Pioneer Gentlewoman in British Columbia: The Recollections of Susan Allison (ed. by Margaret A. Ormsby, 1976).

Andersen, Doris. The Columbia Is Coming! (1982).

Andersen, Marnie. Women of the West Coast, Then and Now (1993).

Anderson, Kay J. Vancouver's Chinatown: Racial Discourse in Canada, 1875–1980 (1981).

Arima, E.Y. and others. Between Ports Alberni and Renfrew: Notes on West Coast Peoples (1991).

Arthur, Elizabeth. Island Sojourn (1980, rpt. 1991).

Ashwell, Reg. Coast Salish: Their Art, Culture and Legends (1978).

Baltzly, Benjamin. Benjamin Baltzly: Photographs & Journal of an Expedition Through British Columbia, 1871 (1978).

Barkley, Frances. The Remarkable World of Frances Barkley, 1769–1845 (ed. by Beth Hill, 1978).

Barman, Jean. Growing Up in British Columbia: Boys in Private Schools, 1900–1950 (1984).

——. The West Beyond the West: A History of British Columbia (1991).

—— and Robert A.J. McDonald (comps.). Readings in the History of British Columbia (1989).

Baskerville, Peter A. Beyond the Island: An Illustrated History of Victoria (1986).

Basque, Garnet (ed.). Frontier Days in British Columbia (1993).

Begg, Alexander. History of British Columbia From Its Earliest Discovery to the Present Time (1894, rpt. 1972).

Bish, Robert L. Local Government in British Columbia (1987).

Blackman, Margaret B. During My Time: Florence Edenshaw Davidson, A Haida Woman (1982).

——. Window on the Past: The Photographic Ethnohistory of the Northern and Kaigani Haida (1981).

Blake, Donald E. Two Political Worlds: Parties and Voting in British Columbia (1985).

——, R.K. Carty, and Lynda Erickson. Grassroots Politicians: Party Activists in British Columbia (1991).

Bowen, Lynne. Boss Whistle: The Coal Miners of Vancouver Island Remember (1982).

——. The Three Dollar Dreams (1987).

Brody, Hugh. Maps and Dreams: Indians and the British Columbia Frontier (1981).

Bryan, Liz. British Columbia, This Favoured Land (1982).

Cameron, Silver Donald. Seasons in the Rain: An Expatriate's Notes on British Columbia (1978).

Carey, Neil G. Puffin Cove (1982).

Carr, Emily. The Book of Small (1942, rpt. 1986). Recollections of the artist's childhood in Victoria.

——. *Klee Wyck (1941, rpt. 1986). Observations on Indian life in coastal villages.

Chadney, James G. The Sikhs of Vancouver (1984).

Cherrington, John. The Fraser Valley: A History (1992).

Clutesi, Geòrge. Potlach (1969, rpt. 1973).

Collier, Eric. Three Against the Wilderness (1959). Pioneering experiences in the 1920s.

Coulson, Barry. The Logger's Digest: From Horses to Helicopters (1992).

Cracroft, Sophia. Lady Franklin Visits the Pacific Northwest: Being Extracts From the Letters of Miss Sophia Cracroft, Sir John Franklin's Niece, February to April 1861 and April to July 1870 (ed. by Dorothy Blakey, 1974).

Dawson, George M. The Journals of George M. Dawson: British Columbia, 1875–1878, 2 vols. (ed. by Douglas Cole and Bradley Lockner, 1989).

——. Report on an Exploration in the Yukon District, N.W.T., and Adjacent Northern Portion of British Columbia, 1887 (1887, rpt. 1987).

De Volpi, Charles P. British Columbia, a Pictorial Record: Historical Prints and Illustrations of the Province of British Columbia, Canada, 1778–1891 (1973).

Downs, Art. Wagon Road North: The Story of the Caribou Gold Rush in Historical Photographs (1960, rpt. 1993).

Drushka, Ken. Working in the Woods: A History of Logging on the West Coast (1992).

Elliott, Gordon R. Barkerville, Quesnel and the Caribou Gold Rush (1978; rev. ed. of Quesnel, Commercial Centre of the Caribou Gold Rush, 1958).

Elmendorf, William W. Twana Narratives: Native Historical Accounts of a Coast Salish Culture (1993).

Emmons, George Thornton. The Tlingit Indians (ed. by Frederica de Laguna, 1991).

Farrow, Moira. Nobody Here But Us: Pioneers of the North (1975).

Fisher, Robin. Contact and Conflict: Indian-European Relations in British Columbia, 1774–1890 (2nd ed. 1992).

Fladmark, Knut R. British Columbia Prehistory (1986).

Forester, Joseph E. and Anne D. Forester. Fishing: British Columbia's Commercial Fishing History (1975).

Forward, Charles N. (ed.). British Columbia, Its Resources and People (1987).

Fraser, Simon. The Letters and Journals of Simon Fraser, 1806–1808 (ed. by W. Kaye Lamb, 1960).

Friesen, J. and H.K. Ralston (eds.). *Historical Essays on British Columbia* (1976, rpt. 1980).

Garner, Joe. *Never Chop Your Rope: A Story of British Columbia Logging and the People Who Logged* (1988).

Garr, Allen. *Tough Guy: Bill Bennett and the Taking of British Columbia* (1985).

Geddes, Gary (ed.). *Vancouver, Soul of a City* (1986).

Gibson, John Frederic. *A Small and Charming World* (1972). Life in an inland Indian village.

Gough, Barry M. *The Northwest Coast: British Navigation, Trade, and Discoveries to 1812* (1992 rev. ed. of *Distant Dominion: Britain and the Northwest Coast of North America, 1579–1809*, 1980).

Gould, Edward. *Logging: British Columbia's Logging History* (1975).

Gregson, Harry. *A History of Victoria, 1842–1970* (1970, rpt. 1977).

Griffin, Kevin. *Vancouver's Many Faces: Passport to the Cultures of a City* (1993).

Hayden, Brian (ed.). *A Complex Culture of the British Columbia Plateau: Traditional Stl'atl'imx Resource Use* (1992).

Hayman, John (ed.). *Robert Brown and the Vancouver Island Exploring Expedition* (1989).

Hill-Tout, Charles. *The Salish People*, 4 vols. (1978).

Hobson, Richmond P., Jr. *Nothing Too Good For a Cowboy* (1955, rpt. 1973).

Humuses, Paul. *Power Without Glory: The Rise and Fall of the NDP Government in British Columbia* (1976).

Hutchison, Bruce. *The Fraser* (1950, rpt. 1982).

——. *A Life in the Country* (1988).

Iglauer, Edith. *Fishing With John* (1988).

Isenor, D.E., E.G. Stephens, and D.E. Watson. *Edge of Discovery: A History of the Campbell River District* (1989).

Jensen, Doreen and Cheryl Brooks (eds.). *In Celebration of Our Survival: The First Nations of British Columbia* (1991).

Jones, Laurie. *Links to the Past: B.C.'s Birthplace Revisited: A History of Nootka and Kyuquot Sounds* (1991).

Julian, Terry. *A Capital Controversy: The Story of Why the Capital of British Columbia Was Moved From New Westminister to Victoria* (1994).

Kavic, Lorne J. and Garry Brian Nixon. *The 1200 Days, a Shattered Dream: Dave Barrett and the NDP in B.C., 1972–1975* (1979).

Keene, Roger. *Conversations With WAC Bennett* (1970).

Kew, D. and P.E. Goddard. *Indian Art and Culture of the Northwest Coast* (1974).

Kennedy, Dorothy and Randy Bouchard. *Sliammon Life and Sliammon Lands* (1983).

Kilian, Crawford. *Do Some Great Thing: The Black Pioneers of British Columbia* (1978).

Kimbley, Laurel (comp.). *Hastings and Main: Stories From an Inner City Neighbourhood* (1987).

Kloppenborg, Anne, Alice Niwinski, and Eve Johnson (eds.). *Vancouver, a City Album* (3rd ed. 1991; originally published as *Vancouver's First Century: A City Album, 1860–1960*).

Kluckner, Michael. *Vancouver, the Way It Was* (1984).

——. *Vanishing Vancouver* (1990).

——. *Victoria, the Way It Was* (1986).

Knight, Rolf. *Indians at Work: An Informal History of Native Indian Labour in British Columbia, 1858–1930* (1978).

——. *A Man of Our Times: The Life-History of a Japanese-Canadian Fisherman* (1976).

—— (ed.). *Along the No. 20 Line: Reminiscences of the Vancouver Waterfront* (1980).

Lai, David Chuenyan. *The Forbidden City With Victoria* (1991). Victoria's Chinatown.

Landale, Zoe. *Harvest of Salmon: Adventures in Fishing on the B.C. Coast* (1977).

Large, R. Geddes. *The Skeena, River of Destiny* (5th ed. 1981).

Lee, Todd. *He Saw With His Own Eyes: Stories of the Cariboo* (1992).

Leonoff, Cyril Edward. *Pioneers, Pedlars, and Prayer Shawls: The Jewish Community in British Columbia and the Yukon* (1978).

Leslie, Graham. *Breach of Promise: Sacred Ethics Under Vander Zalm* (1991).

Lewis, Claudia. *Indian Families of the Northwest Coast: The Impact of Change* (1970).

Lillard, Charles. *The Ghostland People: A Documentary History of the Queen Charlotte Islands, 1859–1906* (1989).

——. *Seven Shillings a Year: The History of Vancouver Island* (1986).

Lord, Alex. *Alex Lord's British Columbia: Recollections of a Rural School Inspector, 1915–36* (1991).

Macdonald, Bruce. *Vancouver, a Visual History* (1992).

MacDonald, George F. *Haida Monumental Art: Villages of the Queen Charlotte Islands* (1983).

MacDonald, Norbert. *Distant Neighbours: A Comparative History of Seattle & Vancouver* (1987).

Mahood, Ian and Ken Drushka. *Three Men and a Forester* (1990).

Mandy, E. Madge. *Our Trail Led Northwest: True Tale of Romance and Adventure in British Columbia* (1989).

Marchak, Patricia, Neil Guppy, and John McMullan (eds.). *Uncommon Property: The*

Fishing and Fish-Processing Industries in British Columbia (1987).

Marriott, Harry. *Cariboo Cowboy* (rev. ed. 1994).

Mason, Gary and Keith Baldry. *Fantasyland: Inside the Reign of Bill Vander Zalm* (1989).

McDonald, Robert A.J. and Jean Barman (eds.). *Vancouver's Past: Essays in Social History* (1992).

McFeat, Tom (ed.). *Indians of the North Pacific Coast* (1966, rpt. 1989).

McIlwraith, T.F. *The Bella Coola Indians,* 2 vols. (1948, rpt. with new introduction 1992).

McKervill, Hugh W. *The Salmon People: The Story of Canada's West Coast Fishing Industry* (1967).

McNaughton, Margaret. *Overland to Cariboo: An Eventful Journey of Canadian Pioneers to the Gold Fields of British Columbia in 1862* (1896, rpt. 1973).

Mitchell, David J. *Succession: The Political Reshaping of British Columbia* (1987).

———. *W.A.C. Bennett and the Rise of British Columbia* (1983).

Moran, Bridget. *Stoney Creek Woman: The Story of Mary John Tillacum* (1988).

Morice, Adrien G. *The History of the Northern Interior of British Columbia* (1978).

Morley, J. Terence and others. *The Reins of Power: Governing British Columbia* (1983).

Moroney, Catherine. *The Chief Who Danced: My Life With the Salish* (1994).

Munro, John A. (ed.). *The Alaska Boundary Dispute* (1970).

Murray, Peter. *From Amor to Zalm: A Primer on B.C. Politics and Its Wacky Premiers* (1989).

Neel, David. *Our Chiefs and Elders: Words and Photographs of Native Leaders* (1992).

Neering, Rosemary. *Down the Road: Journeys Through Small-Town British Columbia* (1991).

Nicholson, George. *Vancouver Island's West Coast, 1762–1962* (1965).

Norcross, Blanche. *Nanaimo Retrospective: The First Century* (rev. ed. 1983).

Norris, John (ed.). *Strangers Entertained: A History of the Ethnic Groups of British Columbia* (1971).

——— and Margaret Prang (eds.). *Personality and History in British Columbia: Essays in Honour of Margaret Ormsby* (1977).

Norton, Wayne and Wilf Schmidt (eds.). *Kamloops, One Hundred Years of Community, 1893–1993* (1992).

Ormsby, Margaret A. *British Columbia, a History* (1958).

Palmer, Bryan D. *Solidarity: The Rise & Fall of an Opposition in British Columbia* (1987).

Palmer, Hugh. *Circumnavigating Father* (1990). Memories of a post-World War I Vancouver family.

Paterson, T.W. *British Columbia, the Pioneer Years* (1977).

Patterson, G. James. *The Greeks of Vancouver: A Study in the Preservation of Ethnicity* (1976).

Patterson, R.M. *Trail to the Interior* (1966, rpt. 1993).

Persky, Stan. *Bennett II: The Decline & Stumbling of the Social Credit Government in British Columbia, 1979–83* (1983).

Pethick, Derek. *British Columbia Disasters* (1978, rpt. 1982).

———. *Summer of Promise: Victoria, 1864–1914* (1980).

——— and Susan Im Baumgarten. *British Columbia Recalled: A Picture History, 1741–1871* (1974).

———. *Vancouver Recalled: A Pictorial History to 1887* (1974).

———. *Vancouver, the Pioneer Years, 1774–1886* (1984).

Peterson, Jan. *The Albernis, 1860–1922* (1992).

Phillips, Daisy. *Letters From Windermere, 1912–1914* (ed. by R. Cole Harris and Elizabeth Phillips, 1984).

Poole, Francis. *Queen Charlotte Islands: A Narrative of Discovery and Adventure in the North Pacific* (1872, ed. by John W. Lyndon, 1972).

Rattray, Alexander. *Vancouver Island and British Columbia: Where They Are, What They Are, and What They May Become: A Sketch of Their History, Topography, Climate, Resources, Capabilities and Advantages, Especially as Colonies For Settlement* (1862, rpt. 1969).

Reksten, Terry. *More English Than the English: A Very Social History of Victoria* (1986).

Robin, Martin. *The Company Province,* 2 vols. (1972–1973).

Roy, Patricia E. *A White Man's Province: British Columbia Politicians and Chinese and Japanese Immigrants, 1858–1914* (1989).

Sewid, James. *Guests Never Leave Hungry: The Autobiography of James Sewid a Kwakiutl Indian* (ed. by James P. Spradley, 1969).

Shelton, W. George (ed.). *British Columbia & Confederation* (1967).

Sproat, Gilbert Malcolm. *The Nootka: Scenes and Studies of Savage Life* (1868, ed. by Charles Lillard, 1987).

Stangoe, Irene. *Cariboo-Chilcotin: Pioneer People and Places* (1994).

Stearns, Mary Lee. *Haida Culture in Custody: The Masset Band* (1981).

Steel, Stephanie Quainton. *Harvest of Light: An Artist's Journey* (1991).

Stonier-Newman, Lynne. *Policing a Province: The B.C. Provincial Police, 1858–1950* (1991).

Stores, Monica. *God's Galloping Girl: The Peace River Diaries of Monica Stores, 1929–1931* (ed. by W.L. Morton, 1979).

Sturgis, William. *The Journal of William Sturgis* (ed. by S.W. Jackman, 1978). Detailed description of Indian life.

Suttles, Wayne. *Coast Salish Essays* (1987).

Swainson, Neil A. *A Conflict Over the Columbia: The Canadian Background to an Historic Treaty* (1979).

Taylor, G.W. *Builders of British Columbia: An Industrial History* (1982).

——. *Mining: The History of Mining in British Columbia* (1977).

——. *Timber: The History of the Forest Industry in B.C.* (1975).

Tennant, Paul. *Aboriginal Peoples and Politics: The Indian Land Question in British Columbia, 1849–1989* (1990).

Thompson, David. *Columbia Journals* (ed. by Barbara Belyea, 1993).

Twigg, Alan. *Vander Zalm, From Immigrant to Premier* (1986).

Varley, Elizabeth Anderson. *Kitimat, My Valley* (1981).

Verchere, David R. *A Progression of Judges: A History of the Supreme Court of British Columbia* (1988).

Ward, W. Peter. *White Canada Forever: Popular Attitudes and Public Policy Toward Orientals in British Columbia* (2nd ed. 1990).

—— and Robert A. J. MacDonald (eds.). *British Columbia, Historical Readings* (1981).

Webb, Robert Lloyd. *On the Northwest: Commercial Whaling in Pacific Northwest, 1790–1967* (1988).

Wells, Oliver. *The Chilliwacks and Their Neighbours* (1987).

White, Howard and Jim Spilsbury. *Spilsbury's Coast: Pioneer Years in the Wet West* (1987).

Wilson, Ian and Sally Wilson. *Wilderness Seasons: Life and Adventure in Canada's North* (1987, rpt. 1993).

Woodcock, George. *British Columbia: A History of the Province* (1990).

——. *Peoples of the Coast: The Indians of the Pacific Northwest* (1977).

—— (ed.). *British Columbia, a Celebration* (1983).

Wynn, Graeme and Timothy Oke (eds.). *Vancouver and Its Region* (1992).

Yee, Paul. *Saltwater City: An Illustrated History of the Chinese in Vancouver* (1988).

British Columbia in Literature

* denotes a winner of a Governor General's Literary Award.

Baird, Irene. *Waste Heritage* (1939, rpt. 1974). Documentary novel of Vancouver and Victoria in 1938.

Bowering, George. **Burning Water* (1980). Historical fiction about Captain George Vancouver's 1792 exploration along the west coast.

——. *Caprice* (1987). French-Canadian woman in Kamloops seeks revenge in the 1890s for her brother's death.

Brandis, Marianne. *This Spring's Sowing* (1970). A dying woman chooses to spend her last days in British Columbia.

Bugnet, Georges. *The Forest* (1975). An urban couple struggle with the Peace River country wilderness.

Cameron, Anne. *Bright's Crossing: Short Stories* (1990). Stories about women who live on a west coast island.

——. *Daughters of Copper Woman* (1981). Myth and fiction combine to tell the stories of native women on Vancouver Island.

Clark, D.M. *Inside Shadows* (1973). A hunter tests his will to live when he loses his way in the British Columbia mountains.

Cohen, Matt. *Wooden Hunters* (1975). Conflicts erupt between logging concerns and the native population of a Gulf Island.

Coney, Mike. *A Tomcat Called Sabrina* (1992). Comic novel about life on a Gulf Island.

Connolly, Jay. *Dancewater Blues* (1990). Elderly white man and young Indian plan to thwart the search for a monster in Okanagan Lake.

Corcoran, David. *The West Coasters: A Sweeping Saga of the Men and Women Who Settled Canada's Pacific Coast: A Novel* (1986).

Craven, Margaret. *I Heard the Owl Call My Name* (1967, rpt. 1975). A young Anglican vicar spends his last year among the coast Indians.

Dillard, Annie. *The Living: A Novel* (1992). A story about three families in the latter half of the nineteenth century.

Emery, Maud. *A Seagull's Cry* (1975). An English couple emigrate to the British Columbia coast in the early 1900s.

Evans, Hubert. *Mist on the River* (1954, rpt. 1973). A British Columbia Indian is torn between life on the reserve and the white man's world.

Forrie, Allan, Patrick O'Rourke, and Glen Sorestad. *The Last Map is the Heart: An Anthology of Western Canadian Fiction* (1989).

Fry, Alan. *The Burden of Adrian Knowle* (1974).

Father-son conflict on a British Columbia ranch.

——. *The Revenge of Annie Charlie* (1973, rpt. 1990). Humourous tale of an Indian woman's thoughts and feelings about white laws and customs.

Gaston, Bill. *Deep Cove Stories* (1989). Linked stories about life in a village on the north shore of Burrard Inlet.

——. *Tall Lives* (1990). A story about British Columbia twins who represent the opposite ends of society.

Gerson, Carole (ed.). *Vancouver Short Stories* (1985).

Gould, Jan. *The Boathouse Question* (1978). Stories set in the Gulf Islands.

Grainger, M. Allerdale. *Woodsmen of the West* (1908, rpt. 1988). Life in turn-of-the-century British Columbia logging camps.

Gunn, Genni. *Thrice Upon a Time* (1990). British Columbia family saga that begins in the 1860s.

Haig-Brown, Roderick L. *Woods and River Tales: From the World of Roderick Haig-Brown* (1980). Nineteen stories about people in the British Columbia wilderness between 1930 and 1950.

Harlow, Robert. *Paul Nolan: A Novel* (1983). Five shattering days in the life of a Vancouver man.

——. *Royal Murdoch* (1962); *A Gift of Echoes* (1965); *Scann: A Novel* (1972, rpt. 1977). Trilogy about a fictional British Columbia town modelled on Prince George.

——. *The Saxophone Winter* (1988). A youth learns to balance his affections in a remote logging town in northern British Columbia on the eve of World War II.

Harris, Christie. *Raven's Cry* (1966, rpt. 1992). Fictional retelling of the near destruction of the Haida Indians.

Hodgins, Jack. *The Invention of the World: A Novel* (1977, rpt. 1986); **The Resurrection of Joseph Bourne; or, A Word or Two on Those Port Annie Miracles* (1979, rpt. 1990); *The Honourary Patron* (1987); *Innocent Cities* (1990). Vancouver Island, past and present, is the setting for these tales.

—— (ed.). *The West Coast Experience* (1976). Anthology.

Holdstock, Pauline. *The Burial Ground* (1991). Priest's mission to a coastal Indian village in 1860 has evil consequences.

Houston, James. *Eagle Song: An Indian Saga Based on True Events* (1983). A survivor held captive for two years relates the 1803 massacre of a ship's crew by Nootka Indians.

Hunter, Don. *Spinner's Inlet* (1989). Vignettes of a fictional small community on a Gulf Island.

Hutchison, Bruce. *The Cub Reporter Learns a Thing or Two* (1991). A tale about a 1910 by-election in Victoria.

——. *Uncle Percy's Wonderful Town* (1981). Humourous sketches about a turn-of-the-century fictional small town in the British Columbia interior.

Lawrence, Margaret. *The Fire-Dwellers* (1969, rpt. 1988). A Vancouver mother of four dreams of romance and her youth.

Lawrence, R.D. *The White Puma: A Novel* (1990). The hunted hunts the hunters in British Columbia's coast mountains.

Lee, Sky. *Disappearing Moon Cafe* (1990). Four generations of a Vancouver Chinese family from the original immigration in 1892 to the present.

Lowry, Malcolm. *October Ferry to Gabriola Island* (1970, rpt. 1988). A couple who have lost their home in Ontario travel to a British Columbia island.

Maillard, Keith. *Motet* (1989). Vancouver teacher searches for knowledge about the composer of a motet.

——. *Two Strand River* (1976). Urban Vancouver and the British Columbia coast are the settings for a quest for personal identity.

Maracle, Lee. *Ravensong* (1993). A prophetic novel about a young aboriginal woman's coming-of-age.

Marlatt, Daphne. *Ana Historic* (1988). A contemporary woman becomes obsessed with a woman who appears briefly in the 1873 Vancouver civic archives.

Mealing, F.M. *Coyote's Running Here* (1980). Legends of the Coyote-Trickster native to the Great Basin region.

O'Hagan, Howard. *Tay John* (1939, rpt. 1989). A half-breed hailed as a messiah by Shuswap Indians is outcast by both whites and natives.

Potrebenko, Helen. *Taxi!: A Novel* (2nd ed. 1989). Vancouver inhabitants are seen through the eyes of a feminist taxi-driver.

Rule, Jane. *After the Fire* (1989). Five lone women of various generations living on a Gulf Island cope with their own and each other's problems.

——. *Contract With the World* (1980). The difficult life of a Vancouver artist.

——. *The Young in One Another's Arms* (1977). People who live in a Vancouver boarding house face life's difficulties.

Schroeder, Andreas and Rudy Wiebe (eds.). *Stories From Pacific & Arctic Canada: A Selection* (1974).

Shields, Carol and Blanche Howard. *A Celibate Season* (1991). An exchange of letters reveals the problems of a non-traditional North Vancouver family when the wife accepts a temporary position in Ottawa.

Smith, Ronald and Stephen Guppy. *Rainshadow: Stories From Vancouver Island* (1982).

St. Pierre, Paul H. *Boss of the Namko Drive* (1965, rpt. 1986). A cattle drive of 200 mi. from Cariboo country to the railway.

——. *Breaking Smith's Quarter Horse* (1966, rpt. 1984); *Smith and Other Events: Tales of the Chilcotin* (1983). Stories about ranchers and Chilcotin Indians in the British Columbia interior.

Svendsen, Linda. *Marine Life* (1992). Interrelated stories about a working-class Vancouver family from the 1950s to the present.

Symons, R.D. *The Broken Snare* (1970). The positive and negative aspects of staking a claim and building a ranch.

Thomas, Audrey. *Intertidal Life: A Novel* (1984). A woman on a west coast island struggles with her husband's desertion.

——. *Munchmeyer and Prospero on the Island* (1971). The diary of a Gulf Island writer who is writing a novel about a man who keeps a diary.

Tippett, Maria. *Breaking the Cycle, and Other Stories From a Gulf Island* (1989).

Valgardson, W.D. *The Girl With the Botticelli Face* (1992). A Victoria college teacher searches his past in his struggle to cope with a nervous breakdown.

Watson, Sheila. *Deep Hollow Creek: A Novel* (1992). An urban schoolteacher tries to relate to the Indians and settlers in the Cariboo region in the 1930s.

——. *The Double Hook* (1959, rpt. 1993). A poetic and sombre novel set in Cariboo country.

Whatmough, David (ed.). *Vancouver Fiction* (1985).

White, Ellen. *Kwulasulwut: Stories From the Coast Salish* (1981).

Wilson, Ethel. *Hetty Dorval* (1947, rpt. 1990). A story about growing up in the British Columbia interior.

——. *Love and Salt Water* (1956, rpt. 1990). An unhappy childhood causes a difficult transition to adulthood.

——. *Swamp Angel* (1954, rpt. 1990). A Vancouver woman leaves her failed marriage to work in a remote British Columbia fishing camp.

Windley, Carol. *Visible Light* (1993). Stories about isolated women on the British Columbia coast.

Woodward, Caroline. *Disturbing the Peace* (1990). Short stories set in Peace River country.

MANITOBA

Manitoba, the easternmost of the three Prairie Provinces, is bordered on the west by the province of Saskatchewan; on the north by the Northwest Territories; on the east by Hudson Bay and the province of Ontario; and on the south by the states of Minnesota and North Dakota.

Name Province of Manitoba. "Manitoba" is derived from Cree Indian words "manitou" and "wapow" meaning "strait or narrows of the spirit", referring to the narrows of Lake Manitoba. *Previous names:* part of Rupert's Land (1670–1870); in 1870 most of present Manitoba was part of the North-West Territories. A small southern area called Manitoba was gradually enlarged to its present size.

Flag A red field with a Union Jack in the upper left corner and the provincial shield on the centre right. Proclaimed on May 12, 1966.

Coat of Arms The upper third of the shield is occupied by the Cross of St. George (a red cross on a white background). The lower two-thirds of the shield has a green background with a buffalo standing on rock. The shield was granted by King Edward VII on May 10, 1905. On October 23, 1992 the Governor-General signed a warrant augmenting the shield as follows. The shield is surmounted by a gold helmet with red and silver mantling and a beaver holding the province's floral emblem with a royal crown on its back. It is supported on the left by a unicorn wearing a green and sil-

ver collar with a Red River cart wheel hanging from it. The right supporter is a white horse wearing a collar of bead and bone with an Indian symbol hanging from it. The shield and supporters rest on a compartment that contains water symbols, grain, and the provincial flower and tree. A scroll with the provincial motto forms the base.

Motto *Gloriosus et Liber* (Glorious and free).

Emblems
Bird great grey owl (*Strix nebulosa*)
Flower prairie crocus or crocus anemone (*Anemone patens var. wolfgangiana*, also known as *Pulsatilla ludoviciana*)
Tree white spruce (*Picea glauca*)
Tartan maroon and green with yellow, dark green, and azure blue

Date of Entry into Confederation July 15, 1870.

Official Languages English and French have equal status in the Legislature and in the courts. In accordance with the Manitoba government's French-language services policy. French-language services are provided in designated areas of the province where the French-speaking population is concentrated. Education is provided in both languages in conformity with the requirements of the Canadian Charter of Rights and Freedoms.

Capital City Winnipeg, situated at the junction of the Red and Assiniboine rivers; population 616,790, CMA population 652,354. The first settlement, Fort Rouge, was built by Pierre Gaultier de Varennes et de Verendrye in 1738. Subsequently, Fort Gibraltar was built by the North West Company in 1804 and Fort Garry, the Hudson's Bay Company post, in 1821. Winnipeg, (from Cree Indian phrase "win-nipi" meaning "murky water") was incorporated on November 8, 1873. The Metropolitan Corporation of Greater Winnipeg, a federation of Winnipeg and surrounding urban areas, was created in 1960.

Provincial Holidays In addition to national statutory holidays (see page 2), Manitoba residents celebrate Civic Holiday (the first Monday in August).

Geography and Climate

Geography The northern three-fifths of Manitoba is covered by the Canadian Shield, among the oldest rocks in the world, rich in mineral deposits, and unsuitable for agriculture. Agricultural activity is found south and west of an imaginary line between the southeast corner of Manitoba and Flin Flon. Manitoba is relatively level with the land rising gradually to the west and south from the Hudson Bay coastal plain. One-sixth of its surface is covered by lakes and rivers. Bush-tundra and boreal forests in the north give way to mixed broadleaf forests in the centre, and open grassland and aspens in the south.

Area 649,947 sq. km. (250,946 sq. mi.), 6.5% of Canada. *Rank:* 6th among the provinces, 7th among the provinces and territories.

Inland Water 101,592 sq. km. (39,225 sq. mi.) Largest lake: Lake Winnipeg 24,387 sq. km. (9,416 sq. mi.).

Elevations Highest point: Baldy Mountain, 831 m. (2,727 ft.) Lowest point: Hudson Bay shore, sea level.

Major Rivers (*indicates a designated Canadian Heritage River) Assiniboine, *Bloodvein, Churchill, Hayes, Nelson, Red, *Seal, Winnipeg.

Climate Manitoba has a continental climate with long, cold winters and warm, short summers. It receives the most precipitation of the Prairie Provinces, 400 mm. (15.7 in.) in northern Manitoba, and 600 mm. (23.6 in.) in southeastern Manitoba. Northern Manitoba has a subarctic climate. The average daily mean temperature in January in The Pas is −22.7°C (−8.9°F); in Winnipeg −19.3°C (−2.7°F); in July in The Pas 17.7°C (63.9°F); in Winnipeg 19.6°C (67.3°F). The lowest recorded temperature in Manitoba: −52.8°C (−63.0°F) at Norway House on January 9, 1899; the highest recorded temperature 44.4°C (111.9°F) at St. Albans on July 11, 1936, and Emerson on July 12, 1936.

Average annual snowfall at The Pas, 170 cm. (66.9 in.); Winnipeg 125.5 cm. (49.4 in.). Greatest recorded snowfall over five consecutive days: 121.9 cm. (48.0 in.) at Morden on March 5, 1916. The greatest recorded Manitoba annual precipitation: 966 mm. (38.0 in.) at Peace Gardens in 1975.

Manitoba holds several Canadian records: the most rainfall received in one hour, 96 mm. (3.8 in.) on August 28, 1966, at Porcupine Mountain; the average sunniest winter (Gimli, 376 hrs.); the greatest daily range of temperatures in summer; and the greatest differences between summer and winter temperatures.

Time Zone Central.

Parks and Historic Sites

In this section * indicates the area is, or part of it is, a Unesco Biosphere Reserve.

National Park Located in Manitoba

Park	Location	Size
*Riding Mountain	Wasagaming	2,976 sq. km. (1,149 sq. mi.)

Park	Location
Atikaki	next Ontario border
Whiteshell	Falcon Lake
Grass River	east of Flin Flon
Nopiming	next Ontario border
Duck Mountain	north of Grandview
Hecla	northeast of Riverton
Clearwater Lake	north of The Pas
Grindstone	northeast of Riverton
Spruce Woods	east of Brandon
Paint Lake	southwest of Brandon

Manitoba also has 2 national wildlife areas and 2 Ramsar sites.

Major National Historic Sites and Parks in Manitoba
Cape Merry, Churchill
The Forks, Winnipeg
Fort Prince of Wales, Churchill
Lower Fort Garry, Selkirk
Riel House, Winnipeg

Provincial Parks There are 127 provincial parks covering 1,432,886 ha. (5,532 sq. mi.): 9 natural parks, 1 wilderness park, 31 recreation parks, 6 heritage parks, and 80 wayside parks. Since Manitoba's provincial parks system is under review in 1993, the following information may change. The largest parks are:

Type	Size
wilderness	406,840 ha. (1,571 sq. mi.)
natural	273,715 ha. (1,057 sq. mi.)
natural	229,133 ha. (885 sq. mi.)
natural	143,856 ha. (555 sq. mi.)
natural	127,567 ha. (493 sq. mi.)
natural	86,376 ha. (333 sq. mi.)
natural	59,616 ha. (230 sq. mi.)
recreation	25,841 ha. (100 sq. mi.)
heritage	24,883 ha. (96 sq. mi.)
recreation	22,660 ha. (88 sq. mi.)

St. Andrew's Rectory, near Winnipeg
Sloop's Cove, Churchill
York Factory, mouth of Nelson River

In addition, there are a number of historic sites in Manitoba administered by the province, municipalities, or organizations. The major sites are:

Macdonald House, Winnipeg
Norway House, Nelson River

Demography

All figures relating to Manitoba population and dwellings are 1991 data and do not include the population on 3 Indian reserves that did not cooperate in the 1991 census.

Manitoba Population: 1,091,942; 4.0% of national; *rank* 5th

Historical population data

1981	1,026,245
1971	988,250
1961	921,686
1951	776,541
1941	729,744
1921	610,118
1901	255,211
1881	62,260

Population Density: 2.0 per sq. km. (5.2 per sq. mi.)

Number of Dwellings: 407,089

Indian Reserves: 61 bands on 115 reserves

Population Characteristics:
urban: 787,175; 72.1%
rural: 304,767; 27.9%
19 and under: 319,935; 29.3%
65 and over: 146,600; 13.4%
average income for full-time employment 15 years and over (1990): $29,607; men $33,509; women $23,403

average life expectancy at birth (1987): men 73.5 years; women 79.7 years
live birth rate: 17,282; 15.8 per 1000

deaths: 8,943; 8.2 per 1000
marriages: 7,032; 6.4 per 1000
divorces: 2,790; 2.56 per 1000

Largest Cities (for definitions of CMA and CA, see page viii)

Name	Population	Dwellings	National Pop. Rank
Winnipeg	652,354 (CMA)	252,934	7
Brandon	38,567	15,461	70
Thompson	15,046 (CA)	4,992	115
Portage la Prairie	13,186	5,047	124

Government and Politics, 1870–

A description of the division of powers between the federal and provincial governments will be found on page 4.

Lieutenant-Governor The Lieutenant-Governor is the nominal head of the Manitoba government, and is appointed by the Governor General of Canada on the recommendation of the Prime Minister of Canada. (A description of the duties of lieutenant-governors is found on page 7.)

Lieutenant-Governors of Manitoba	Term
Sir Adams George Archibald	1870–1872
Francis G. Johnson	1872
Alexander Morris	1872–1877
Joseph-Edouard Cauchon	1877–1882
James Cox Aikins	1882–1888
Sir John Christian Schultz	1888–1895
James Colebrooke Patterson	1895–1900
Daniel Hunter McMillan	1900–1911
Douglas Colin Cameron	1911–1916
Sir James Albert Manning Aikins	1916–1926
Theodore Arthur Burrows	1926–1929
James Duncan McGregor	1929–1934
William Johnston Tupper	1934–1940
Roland Fairbairn McWilliams	1940–1953
John Stewart McDiarmid	1953–1960
Errick French Willis	1960–1965
Richard Spink Bowles	1965–1970
William John McKeag	1970–1976
Francis Laurence Jobin	1976–1981
Pearl Kuhlman McGonigal	1981–1986
George Johnson	1986–1993
Yvon Dumont	1993–

Legislative Assembly The Legislative Assembly of Manitoba consists of 57 members elected by popular vote, each member representing a constituency; term of office: up to 5 years as long as the party in power maintains the confidence of the Legislative Assembly; remuneration (1993): $69,098.77 + additional amounts for special appointments; qualifications for members: Canadian citizen, 18 years of age or older on election day, resident in Manitoba for six months prior to election day, not legally disqualified, e.g., a member of the Senate or House of Commons of Canada, a employee of the Crown. (A description of the duties of provincial legislatures are found on page 7.)

Qualifications for Manitoba Voters in Provincial Elections Canadian citizen, 18 years of age or older on election day, resident in Manitoba for six months prior to election day, not legally disqualified, e.g., full-time judges, those committed to an institution under The Mental Health Act.

Premier Nominally appointed by the Lieutenant-Governor of Manitoba, the Premier is generally the leader of the party with the majority of seats in the Legislative Assembly. (A description of the responsibilities of provincial premiers is found on page 7.)

Premiers of Manitoba/Party/Term
Alfred Boyd (Chief Minister)
   (1870–1871)
Marc-Amable Girard (Chief Minister)
   (1871–1872)
Henry Joseph Clarke (Chief Minister)
   (1872–1874)
Marc-Amable Girard
   (1874)
Robert Atkinson Davis
   (1874–1878)
John Norquay
   (1878–1887)
David Howard Harrison
   (1887–1888)
Thomas Greenway
   (Liberal, 1888–1900)
Sir Hugh John Macdonald
   (Conservative, 1900)
Sir Rodmond Palen Roblin
   (Conservative, 1900–1915)
Tobias Crawford Norris
   (Liberal, 1915–1922)
John Bracken
   (United Farmers of Manitoba,
   1922–1928)
John Bracken
   (Coalition, 1928–1943)
Stuart Sinclair Garson
   (Coalition, 1943–1948)
Douglas Lloyd Campbell
   (Coalition, 1948–1958)
Dufferin Roblin
   (Conservative, 1958–1967)
Walter Cox-Smith Weir
   (Conservative, 1967–1969)
Edward Richard Schreyer
   (New Democratic, 1969–1977)
Sterling Rufus Lyon
   (Conservative, 1977–1981)
Howard Russell Pawley
   (New Democratic, 1981–1988)

Gary Albert Filmon
   (Conservative, 1988–   )

Cabinet The Cabinet consists of ministers appointed by the Premier, usually from elected members of the majority party in the Legislative Assembly. Cabinet ministers serve at the Premier's pleasure; each member usually heads a government department.

Government Departments Inquiries about the work of government departments should be directed to the general Citizen's Inquiry number (204)945-4796 or 800-282-8069.

Agriculture
Consumer and Corporate Affairs
Culture, Heritage and Citizenship
Education and Training
Energy and Mines
Environment
Family Services
Finance
Government Services
Health
Highways and Transportation
Housing
Industry, Trade, and Tourism
Justice
Labour
Natural Resources
Northern Affairs
Rural Development
Urban Affairs

Manitoba Representation in Federal Government
House of Commons: 14 members
Senate: 6 members

Finances

A statement of Manitoba's revenue and expenditures for the years 1992/93 and 1991/92 is shown below in millions of dollars. The financial year runs from April 1 to March 31 of the year following.

	Actual 1992/93	*Actual 1991/92*
Revenue		
Taxation	2,668	2,751
Other	481	365
Government of Canada	1,749	1,821
Total revenue for the year	4,898	4,937
Expenditures		
Health	1,801	1,738
Education and training	1,002	956
Family services	675	606
Economic and resource development	576	600
Assistance to local governments and taxpayers	373	367
Government services	474	479
Interest on debt	563	487
Other		38
Total expenditures for the year	5,464	5,271
Deficit for the year	566	334

Economy

Manitoba has a diversified economy. While agriculture, particularly wheat and other grains, is the leading resource industry followed by livestock, plentiful hydroelectric power encourages manufacturing and the resource rich Canadian Shield provides the basis for a mining industry. Mineral production consists mainly of metals, with nickel, copper, and zinc the major products.

Major Industries Manufacturing is varied. Food processing occupies the top spot (22.1%), followed by transportation equipment (11.3%), electrical and electronic products (8.4%), and machinery (7.8%). A clothing industry (4.8%) is mainly centred on Winnipeg and there is an inland fishery out of Lake Winnipeg.

Gross Domestic Product (1992) $21,266 million (in current dollars at factor cost); % of national G.D.P.: 3.5%; *rank:* 5th

Distribution of gross domestic product (1990)

Finance, insurance, real estate	15.7%
Manufacturing	12.7%
Government services	8.7%
Construction	6.2%
Retail trade	5.9%
Educational services	5.9%
Transportation, storage	5.7%
Wholesale trade	5.7%
Health services	5.2%
Agriculture	4.5%
Mining	3.4%
Other utilities	3.1%
Logging	0.2%
Fishing and trapping	0.1%

Value of Manufacturing Shipments $6,049 million

Farm Cash Receipts $1,950 million

Employment (seasonally adjusted) 493,000; participation rate: 66.3%

Unemployment (seasonally adjusted) 44,000; per capita: 8.2%

Minimum Wage (1993) $5.00, general minimum; construction industry varies depending on job, location, and type of construction.

Exports Manitoba's exports amounted to $3,066 million; 2.2% of total Canadian exports; *rank:* 6th. Agricultural products were 38% of total domestic exports, of which cereal grains represented 66%.
Largest trading partner: United States, 60% of Manitoba's total exports; 84% of non-agricultural exports shipped to the United States.
Other important markets: Eastern Europe 7.6%; Japan 6.6%; E.E.C. 6.4%; China 6.2%. Wheat and meslin made up the major portion of export to the former USSR (95%) and to China (96%).
Major export commodities: Wheat and meslin 23%; live bovine animals 4%; aircraft and spacecraft parts 4%; motor vehicle bodies 3%; rape or canola 2%; unwrought nickel 2%.

History

ca. 11,000 B.C.	Paleo-Indians arrive.
Early centuries A.D. to arrival of Europeans	Assiniboine, Chipewyan, Ojibwa, Plains Cree, Woods Cree Indian tribes inhabit present-day Manitoba.
1612	*August* Seaman and explorer, Thomas Button, the first recorded white man to set foot in Manitoba, sails down the west coast of Hudson Bay, discovers the mouth of the Nelson River, and winters there.
1619	*September* Jens Munk, Danish sea captain, discovers the mouth of the Churchill River and winters there.
1631	Two separate expeditions, headed by Luke Foxe and Thomas James, in seeking a northwest passage explore the west coast of Hudson Bay.
1670	*May 2* Hudson's Bay Company is formed and granted trade rights over all territory draining into Hudson Bay; the territory is named Rupert's Land. *August 31* Hudson's Bay Company Governor Charles Bayley arrives at Port Nelson.
1682	Explorer Pierre-Esprit Radisson travels up the Hayes River, the first recorded European attempt to reach inland Indians.
1684	Hudson's Bay Company Governor George Geyer establishes York Factory, the first permanent settlement in Manitoba.
1690–1697	French and English struggle for control of the fur trade, capturing and recapturing forts.
1690	Explorer Henry Kelsey becomes the first white man to reach the Saskatchewan River near present-day The Pas.
1697–1713	French control the Winnipeg basin fur trade.
1700	*March* Jean-Baptiste Le Moyne de Bienville explores the Red River.
1713	*April 11* France renounces claims to Hudson Bay in the Treaty of Utrecht.
1717	James Knight builds a Hudson's Bay Company post, Churchill Factory (name changed to Prince of Wales Fort in 1719). It is destroyed by the French in 1782.
1734	Jean-Baptiste Gaultier de La Verendrye, explorer (and eventually Governor of Louisiana), builds Fort Maurepas about 10 km. (6 mi.) north of present-day Selkirk.
1738	Pierre Gaultier de Varennes et de la Verendrye and his relatives build Fort Rouge on the present site of Winnipeg. La Verendrye builds Fort La Reine on the site of present-day Portage la Prairie.

1739	La Verendrye explores Lake Winnipeg.
1740s & 1750s	La Verendrye, his relatives, and other French traders explore Manitoba.
1743	First inland Hudson's Bay Company post, Henley House, is built on the Albany River.
1750	Fort Paskoyac, the first trading post on the Saskatchewan River, is built near present-day The Pas.
	The three Frobisher brothers and their associates trade in the Red River area.
1782	*August 9* French capture Prince of Wales Fort and on *August 24* York Factory.
1783	*September* Samuel Hearne begins to build Fort Churchill.
	September 3 Places captured by the French are returned to the British in the Treaty of Paris.
1805	Drought scorches the potato crop in the Red River area bringing distress to Métis families.
1810	North West Company builds Fort Gibraltar (later called Fort Garry) on the site of present-day Winnipeg.
1811	Hudson's Bay Company grants a large tract of land, called Assiniboia, to Thomas Douglas, 5th earl of Selkirk.
1812	*August 30* The first settlers sponsored by Selkirk arrive on the banks of the Red River.
1814	Division of the Northern Department of Rupert's Land includes York Factory, Churchill Inland, West Winnipeg, and East Winnipeg.
1815	Métis attack Red River settlers whom they see as a threat to their way of life.
	First school in Manitoba opens at Selkirk.
1816	*June 19* In the Battle of Seven Oaks Métis led by Cuthbert Grant kill the governor and 20 settlers and capture Fort Douglas.
1816–1817	Selkirk restores order in the Red River Colony.
1818	*July 18* Grasshopper plague destroys crops.
	October 20 Convention of 1818 between the United States and Britain sets the southern boundary of Hudson's Bay Company territory at the 49th parallel from the Lake of the Woods to the Rocky Mountains.
1821	*March 21* Hudson's Bay Company takes over the North West Company ending strife in the fur trade industry.
	Hudson's Bay Company post, Upper Fort Garry, is built on the site of present-day Winnipeg.
1826	*May* Red River floods sweep almost every house away.
1829	First use of waterpower in Manitoba is made at Cuthbert Grant's mill in present-day Winnipeg.
1831	Building of Lower Fort Garry begins and is completed 1833.
1836	*May 4* Selkirk family sells the district of Assiniboia to the Hudson's Bay Company.
	English-speaking, white males are allowed to elect the Council.
1841	Methodist minister, James Evans, Norway House, creates the Cree syllabic alphabet.
1846	Drought causes complete crop failure in the Red River area.
1848	*June* Robert Campbell builds Fort Selkirk, a Hudson's Bay Company post.
	October 10 Public library is established at Fort Garry.
1849	People of Assiniboia throw off the Hudson's Bay Company monopoly.
1852	*Spring* Red River floods.
1855	First Prairie post office opens at Red River.
1857	Palliser Expedition sent to assess Rupert's Land's potential for agricultural settlement reports a fertile crescent extending northwest from the Red River Valley.

1859	*June Anson Northup* is the first steamboat on the Red River.
	December 28 First Manitoba newspaper, the *Nor'Wester*, is published.
1862	Henry McKenney opens a general store which will eventually become the centre of Winnipeg at Portage and Main streets.
1864–1868	Grasshopper plague around Winnipeg.
1867	Thomas Spense sets up the government of "Manitobah" in Portage la Prairie.
1868	Louis Riel becomes leader of the Métis.
1869	*October 11* Riel and 16 unarmed Métis stop Canadian surveyors.
	October 19 National Council of the Métis of Red River is formed to represent Métis in negotiations concerning the transfer of Red River lands to the government of Canada.
	October 31 Governor William McDougall is prevented from entering the area.
	November 2 Riel's troops occupy Fort Garry.
	November 19 Hudson's Bay Company transfers Rupert's Land to the British Crown.
	December 1 British Crown gives Rupert's Land to Canada, which compensates the Hudson's Bay Company in land and money. The transfer takes effect *July 15, 1870*.
	December 27 Riel becomes leader of a provisional government.
1870	*February 18* Charles Mair, John Schultz, and Thomas Scott, leaders of a force from Portage la Prairie, are arrested when they try to topple the provisional government.
	March 4 Thomas Scott is executed outside Fort Garry for insubordination.
	April Red River delegation to Ottawa wins most of the provisional government's demands for entry into the Canadian confederation except an amnesty for Riel and his followers.
	May 12 Manitoba Act (Canadian government) receives royal assent; District of Assiniboia is extended to Portage la Prairie and renamed Manitoba; Manitoba government is to consist of a lieutenant-governor, an appointed executive council, an appointed legislative council, and an elected assembly; equal status is given to English and French in the legislature and courts; dual Protestant and Catholic school systems are established; Canada retains control of natural resources.
	June 24 Provisional government approves the terms of the Manitoba Act.
	September 2 Archibald Adams, the first lieutenant-governor, arrives.
1871	*March 15* Legislature meets for first time.
	August 3 First Indian treaty is negotiated by the Canadian government in which the Cree and Objibwa Indians of southern Manitoba are compensated for land surrender.
	April First land speculators arrive heralding the beginning of land-hungry immigrants.
	May 3 St.-Boniface College receives a charter.
	October 5 American Fenians capture the unoccupied Hudson's Bay Company post at Pembina, but the United States Army returns the Fenians to the United States.
	November 28 Telegraph service opens between Winnipeg and Pembina.
	School Act provides for local administration and public funds.
	St.-Boniface Hospital is established, the first hospital in western Canada.
1872	*June* Riel returns from voluntary exile in the United States.
	Dominion Lands Act (federal government) grants 65 ha. (161 acres) of free land to settlers in Manitoba.
1873	*December* Six whiskey traders are arrested at Lake Winnipeg, the first arrests by the newly formed North-West Mounted Police.

1874	First Mennonite settlers arrive.
1875	*October 21* Two hundred thirty-five immigrants from Iceland arrive to settle on the western shore of Lake Winnipeg and conduct their affairs as the Republic of New Iceland.
	Introduction of Red Fife wheat into Manitoba increases the range of wheat production northward.
1876–1881	Forty thousand immigrants arrive, mainly Ontario British.
1876	*April 12* District of Keewatin is created, comprising northern Manitoba and northwestern Ontario.
1877	Three colleges, St.-Boniface, St. John's, and Manitoba, are united as the University of Manitoba.
	Wheat replaces fur as Manitoba's primary product.
1879	Western Canada's first grain elevator is built at Niverville.
1881–1882	"Manitoba Land Fever" causes boom.
1881	*July 26* Canadian Pacific Railway reaches Winnipeg, facilitating the export of wheat and the import of immigrants.
	August 15 Boundary is extended to present Manitoba-Saskatchewan border and to 53°N.
1882	*May 7* Manitoba Bank is chartered.
	June 1 Winnipeg has gas lighting.
1885	*November 9* Completion of the Canadian Pacific Railway begins a period of rapid growth and prosperity for Winnipeg as it becomes the wholesale distribution and financial centre of western Canada.
1887	Winnipeg Grain Exchange (renamed Western Commodity Exchange in 1972) is established, the only agricultural commodities exchange and futures market in Canada.
1889	*December 9* Ontario wins a boundary dispute with Manitoba and the federal government in Britain's highest court; the boundary is set at James Bay, Albany River, and the Lake of the Woods.
1890	*March 31* Act changes former Protestant and Catholic school systems into a single tax-supported public school system.
	Official Languages Act makes English the only official language of Manitoba (law is successfully challenged in 1892, 1909, and 1976, but the province does not act).
1895	British Privy Council upholds Manitoba's Public School Act against the federal government's order to restore separate school system.
1896	*August 11* First Ukrainian settlers arrive in southern Manitoba near Stuartburn.
1897	Amendment to the Public Schools Act allows some Catholic teachers to be hired and some religious instruction privileges.
1897–1910	Great prosperity and development, expanding settlement as immigrants arrive from eastern Canada, U.S., Britain, and Europe. Grain farming predominates.
1899	Manitoba establishes free libraries.
1902	*April 2* Prohibition is defeated.
1904	*March* Three-day blizzard with 100 kph (62 mph) winds drops 30 cm. (11.8 in.) of snow in southern Prairies; 5 trains are snowbound between Winnipeg and Calgary.
	June 16 Hydroelectric power is first generated on the Winnipeg River.
1907	Development of Marquis wheat, a fast-maturing variety well suited to the Prairies.
1908	*January 15* Manitoba Government Telephones is established, the first province to have a government telephone system.

1910	*May 4* St. Andrew's Locks, Manitoba's only canal locks, are completed allowing navigation between Winnipeg and Lake Winnipeg.
	Most of southern Manitoba, the Interlake, and Westlake areas are settled by 1910.
1912	*May 15* Boundary is extended north to the present boundary with Northwest Territories.
1913	Depression ends general prosperity.
1914	Opening of the Panama Canal ends Winnipeg's transportation supremacy.
1916	*January 27* Manitoba becomes the first province to give women the right to vote in provincial elections.
	Public Schools Act is amended to make school compulsory for all children (not previously compulsory for Catholics).
1919	*May 15–June 25* Winnipeg General Strike involves 30,000 workers and cripples the city, the only general strike in Canadian history.
	November 2 The Golden Boy, a gilded bronze statue that will become a Manitoba landmark, is raised to the top of the Manitoba legislative building.
1920	*October 20* Manitoba votes for Prohibition in a plebiscite.
1921	*December 6* James Shaver Woodsworth, Member of Parliament for Winnipeg North Centre, becomes the first socialist elected to the House of Commons.
1922	*June 22* Tornado strikes Portage la Prairie leaving 10 dead, many injured, and much damage.
1923	*June 22* Manitoba government controls the sale of liquor.
1928	*September 1* Old Age Pension Act comes into effect.
1929	Hudson Bay Railway is completed from Winnipeg to Churchill.
1930s	Long agricultural depression is caused by low world wheat prices and periods of severe drought.
1930	*July 15* Federal government announces that control of Manitoba's natural resources will be transferred to the province.
1932	*April 1* Royal Canadian Mounted Police absorbs the Manitoba provincial police force.
1934–1938	Winnipeg fur market is revived by the rehabilitation of marshes and controls on trapping.
1935	*March* 51.8 cm. (20.4 in.) of snow falls in southern Manitoba.
1936	*July* Heat wave causes over 70 heat-related deaths in Manitoba.
1938	Beginning of more prosperous times.
1940s	World War II increases productive capacity; agriculture is diversified.
1946–1954	Manitoba Power Commission pursues a program of rural electrification.
1947	Sherritt Gordon Company stakes mining claims north of Churchill resulting in a rush of prospectors to this area, a new town, Lynn Lake, and an exploitation of Manitoba's mineral resources.
1950	*May* Red River rises 10 m. (32.8 ft.) above normal forcing the evacuation of 100,000 people, the greatest flood in Canadian history.
1954	*May 31* CBWT, the first Prairie television station, goes into operation.
1955	Redistribution Act abolishes the single transferable ballot and sets up an independent committee to redraw riding boundaries.
	With the exception of Winnipeg Hydro, the Manitoba Power Commission takes over the development, production, and distribution of electric power.
1957	Thompson, a planned community, is developed to service the nickel mines in the Moak Lake area.
1958	*July 1* Federal-provincial hospital plan takes effect in Manitoba.
	Manitoba Theatre Centre is established, the first professional regional theatre in Canada.
1960s	Highway building and improvement.

1961	Worst drought year in the 20th century for Prairie wheat.
1963	*February 28* Thelma Bessie Forbes is elected the first woman speaker in the Manitoba legislature.
1966	*February 15* Manitoba and federal governments agree to the hydro development of the Nelson River.
	March 4 Blizzard with 120 kph (75 mph) winds drops 36 cm. (14 in.) of snow on Winnipeg paralyzing the city for two days.
1967	Extensive drought in the Prairies.
1968	*October 11* Red River Floodway opens, 35 km. (22 mi.) around the east side of Winnipeg.
1969	*October 10* Voting age for Manitoba elections is lowered from 21 to 18.
1970	*January 15* George Maltby is appointed Manitoba's first ombudsman.
	May 29 Hudson's Bay Company moves its head office from London, England, to Winnipeg.
	August 13 Manitoba provincial government automobile insurance is introduced with additional coverage provided by private companies.
	School instruction entirely in French is allowed.
1973	*March 30* Federal and Manitoba governments announce a guaranteed annual income experiment.
1976	*August 30* Manitoba Liquor Commission is fined for violating federal wage and price controls, the first provincial agency so fined.
1979	*April 25* Manitoba Court of Appeal disallows the 1890 laws that prohibit use of French language in the province's courts, legislature, and schools.
	December 13 Supreme Court of Canada declares Manitoba's English-language law of 1890 unconstitutional.
1982	*January 27* Manitoba Court of Appeal rules that forced retirement at age 65 contravenes Manitoba's Human Rights Act.
1983	*March 6* Ice storm with more than 28 mm. (1.1 in.) of freezing rain closes the Winnipeg airport for two days and topples several large TV towers.
	May 25 Franco-Manitobans agree to a compromise on French-language rights: French to be an official language for the courts and legislature; head offices of Manitoba government departments and agencies will offer French services.
1984	*May 24* Southwestern Manitoba receives up to 30 cm. (12 in.) of snow.
1985	*November* Supreme Court of Canada rules all Manitoba laws invalid if they were or are published in English only.
1986	*November 7* Winnipeg receives 35.8 cm. (14.1 in.) of snow with winds over 90 kph (56 mph) and snowdrifts to 2.5 m. (8. ft.); clean-up costs approach $3 million.
1987	*July 6* Two tornados strike Winnipeg bringing 40 mm. (2 in.) of rain in 2 1/2 hours causing flash floods and considerable property damage.
1988	Drought and low international wheat prices affect all sectors of the Manitoba economy.
	December 19 Premier Gary Filmon withdraws Meech Lake Accord from the legislature's agenda.
1989	*July* Twenty-three thousand northern Manitoba residents are evacuated because of forest fires.
	December First gambling house owned and operated by a Canadian province opens in Winnipeg.
1990	*June 15* Elijah Harper refuses to consent to the introduction of the Meech Lake Accord in the Manitoba Legislative Assembly, thereby causing its failure.
1992	Cold weather devastates the wheat crop.
	Supreme Court of Canada rules that Manitoba Orders-in-Council must be written in French and English.

1993   *March 4* Supreme Court of Canada rules that Manitoba's Public School Act violates language rights guaranteed to minority anglophones and francophones by the Charter of Rights and Freedoms. Francophones gain control over French language education.

Culture and Education

Performing Arts The Manitoba Arts Council funds 28 performing arts organizations. Others receive local funding. The most significant organizations based in Manitoba are listed below.

Cercle Molière, Winnipeg	(204)233-8053
Contemporary Dancers, Winnipeg	(204)452-0229
Festival du voyageur, Winnipeg (February) (western Canada's biggest winter festival)	(204)237-7692
Folklorama, Winnipeg (August) (world's largest ethno-cultural festival)	(204)982-6221 or 800-665-0234
International Children's Festival, Winnipeg (May/June)	(204)958-4730
Manitoba Chamber Orchestra, Winnipeg	(204)783-7377
Manitoba Music Festival, Winnipeg (largest music festival held in Canada)	(204)947-0184
Manitoba Opera Association, Winnipeg	(204)942-7479
Manitoba Theatre Centre, Winnipeg	(204)942-6537
Northern Manitoba Trappers' Festival, The Pas (February) (Canada's oldest winter festival)	(204)623-2912
Prairie Theatre Exchange, Winnipeg	(204)942-5483
Royal Winnipeg Ballet, Winnipeg	(204)956-0183
Winnipeg Symphony Orchestra, Winnipeg	(204)949-3999

In addition, there are many festivals that celebrate the customs and history of Manitoba's many ethnic communities.

Provincial Museums and Galleries The following are major Manitoba institutions.
Art Gallery of Southwestern Manitoba, Brandon
Living Prairie Museum, Winnipeg
Manitoba Museum of Man and Nature, Winnipeg
Mennonite Heritage Village, Steinbach
Musée de Saint-Boniface, Winnipeg
Winnipeg Art Gallery, Winnipeg

Universities and Colleges
Brandon University, Brandon
Collège universitaire de Saint-Boniface, Winnipeg
University of Manitoba, Winnipeg
University of Winnipeg, Winnipeg

Community Colleges
Assiniboine Community College, Brandon
Keewatin Community College, The Pas
Red River Community College, Winnipeg

Motor Vehicle Use

Motor Vehicles Registered for Use in Manitoba (1993): 800,710

Drivers Licensed by Manitoba (1993): 672,960. Minimum driving age: 16

Roads Highways and roads: 17,962 km. (11,161 mi.); bridges maintained by the province: ca. 3,000

Speed Limits Maximum posted speed: 100 kph (62 mph); rural roads: 90 kph (56 mph); urban: 50 kph (31 mph) unless otherwise posted

First, Biggest, and Best

North America's largest movie format: IMAX Theatre, Winnipeg, 17 m. (56 ft.) high and 22 m. (72 ft.) wide

World's first commercial motion picture: made by James Freer, a Manitoba farmer, in 1897 about life on the Prairie and used in Britain to promote immigration

World's largest ethnocultural festival: Folklorama, Winnipeg, includes more than 40 pavilions, held for 2 weeks in August

World's largest Icelandic community outside Iceland: Gimli area

World's largest collection of Inuit art: Winnipeg Art Gallery

World's first fully-integrated nickel mining and processing plant: International Nickel Company, Thompson

North America's only Tantalum mine: at Bernie Lake

World's largest known polar bear denning habitat: Cape Churchill/York Factory area

North America's largest lacustrine plain: Agassiz Lowland, 286,000 sq. km. (110,425 sq. mi.)

North America's first large city to move beyond split-level metropolitan government to a single administration: Winnipeg, 1972

North America's northernmost fort: Fort Prince of Wales, at mouth of Churchill River

North America's largest oak-log building: Musée de Saint-Boniface, Winnipeg

North America's first publicly-owned telephone system: Manitoba Government Telephones, 1908

Sources of Information About Manitoba

Government of Manitoba Citizens Inquiry Service: 511-401 York Avenue, Winnipeg, Manitoba R3C 0P8 (204)945-3744, 800-282-8060 (within Manitoba)

Travel Manitoba: 7th Floor, 155 Carlton Street, Winnipeg, Manitoba R3C 3H8 (204)945-3777, 800-665-0040 (Canada and United States)

Statutory Publications: Lower Level, 200 Vaughan Street, Winnipeg, Manitoba R3G 1T5 (204)945-3101

Books About Manitoba: A Selected List

Reference Guides

Artibise, Alan F.J. *Western Canada Since 1870: A Select Bibliography and Guide* (1978).

—— (ed.). *Gateway City: Documents on the City of Winnipeg, 1873–1913* (1979).

Budd, A.C. *Budd's Flora of the Canadian Prairie Provinces* (rev. and enlarged by J. Looman and K.F. Best, 1987).

Canada. Atmospheric Environment Service. *Canadian Climate Normals, 1961–1990: Prairie Provinces* (1993).

Canada. Energy, Mines and Resources Canada. *Gazetteer of Canada: Manitoba* (4th ed. 1994).

Dredge, L.A. and F.M. Nixon. *Glacial and Environmental Geology of Northeastern Manitoba* (1992).

Enns, Richard A. *A Bibliography of Northern Manitoba* (1991).

Friesen, Gerald and Barry Potyondi. *A Guide to the Study of Manitoba Local History* (1981).

Gilroy, Doug. *Prairie Birds in Color* (rev. and expanded ed. 1976).

Hackett, Christopher (ed.). *A Bibliography of Manitoba Local History: A Guide to Local and Regional Histories Written About Communities in Manitoba* (2nd ed. 1989).

Ham, Penny. *Place Names of Manitoba* (1980).

Historical and Scientific Society of Manitoba. Historical Committee. *Local History in Manitoba: A Key to Places, Districts, Schools and Transport Routes* (1976).

Kaye, Vladimir J. (ed.). *Dictionary of Ukrainian Canadian Biography, Pioneer Settlers of Manitoba, 1891–1900* (1975).

Kinnear, Mary and Vera Fast. *Planting the Garden: An Annotated Bibliography of the History of Women in Manitoba* (1987).

Loveridge, D.M. *A Historical Directory of Manitoba Newspapers, 1859–1978* (1981).

Manitoba Library Association. *Pioneers and Early Citizens of Manitoba: A Dictionary of Manitoba Biography From the Earliest Time to 1920* (1971).

McNicholl, Martin K. *Manitoba Bird Studies, 1744–1983: A Bibliography* (1985).

Morley, Marjorie. *A Bibliography of Manitoba From Holdings in the Legislative Library of Manitoba* (1970).

Morton, W.L. *Manitoba: The Birth of a Western Province* (1963, rpt. 1984). Documents

Peel, Bruce (comp.). *A Bibliography of the Prairie Provinces to 1953, With Bibliographical Index* (2nd ed. 1973).

Penner, Norman (ed.). *Winnipeg 1919: The Strikers' Own History of the Winnipeg General Strike* (2nd ed. 1975). Documents and chronology.

Riel, Louis. *The Collected Writing of Louis Riel*, 5 vols. (ed. George G.F. Stanley, 1985).

Rudnyts'kyi, J.B. (comp.). *Manitoba, Mosaic of Place names* (1970).

Scott, Michael M. *A Bibliography of Western Canadian Studies Relating to Manitoba* (1967).

Sloane, D. Louise, Janette M. Roseneder, and Marilyn J. Hernandez (eds.). *Winnipeg: A Centennial Bibliography* (1974).

Thomas, Lewis G. (ed.). *The Prairie West to 1905: A Canadian Sourcebook* (1975).

Vance, Fenton R., J.R. Jowsey, and J.S. McLean. *Wildflowers Across the Prairies* (rev. and expanded 1984).

Warkentin, John (ed.). *The Western Interior of Canada: A Record of Geographical Discovery, 1612–1917* (1964).

—— and Richard I. Ruggles (eds.). *Manitoba Historical Atlas: A Selection of Facsimile Maps, Plans, and Sketches From 1612 to 1969* (1970).

Weir, Thomas R. (ed.). *Atlas of Winnipeg* (1978).

—— (ed.). *Atlas of Manitoba* (1983).

Nonfiction Sources

* denotes a winner of a Governor General's Literary Award.

Allen, Sydney J. (ed.). *The Pas, Gateway to Northern Manitoba* (1983).

Angus, Terry (ed.). *The Prairie Experience* (1975).

Angel, Barbara and Michael Angel. *Charlotte Whitehead Ross* (1982). The only doctor between Winnipeg and Kenora when she began her practice in 1875.

Arnason, David and Michael Olito (eds.). *The Icelanders* (1981).

Artibise, Alan F.J. *Winnipeg: An Illustrated History* (1977).

——. *Winnipeg: A Social History of Urban Growth, 1874–1914* (1975).

—— and E.H. Dahl. *Winnipeg in Maps 1816–1972* (1975).

Begg, Alexander. *Alexander Begg's Red River Journal* (1956, rpt. 1969).

Bellan, Ruben. *Winnipeg, First Century: An Economic History* (1978).

Bercuson, David Jay. *Confrontation at Winnipeg: Labour, Industrial Relations, and the General Strike* (rev. ed. 1990).

Berton, Pierre. *The Promised Land: Settling the West, 1896–1914* (1984, rpt. 1990).

Boulanger, Tom. *An Indian Remembers: My Life as a Trapper in Northern Manitoba* (1974).

Breen, David H. *The Canadian Prairie West and the Ranching Frontier, 1874–1924* (1983).

Broadfoot, Barry. *The Pioneer Years, 1895–1914: Memories of the Settlers Who Opened the West* (1976).

Bryan, Liz. *The Buffalo People: Prehistoric Archaeology on the Canadian Plains* (1991).

Campbell, Maria. *Halfbreed* (1973, rpt. 1983).

Carbone, Stanislao. *The Streets Were Not Paved With Gold: A Social History of Italians in Winnipeg* (1993).

Chafe, J.W. *Extraordinary Tales From Manitoba* (1973).

Charette, Guillaume. *Vanishing Species: Memoirs of a Prairie Métis* (1976).

Charyk, John C. *Syrup Pails and Gopher Tails: Memories of the One-Room School* (1983).

Chiel, Arthur A. *The Jews in Manitoba: A Social History* (1961).

Coates, Kenneth and Fred McGuinness. *Manitoba, the Province and the People* (1987).

Crunican, Paul. *Priests and Politicians: Manitoba Schools and the Election of 1896* (1974).

Doern, Russell. *The Battle Over Bilingualism: The Manitoba Language Question, 1983–85* (1985).

——. *Wednesdays Are Cabinet Days: A Personal Account of the Schreyer Administration* (1981).

Donnelly, M.S. *The Government of Manitoba* (1963).

Douglas, Molly. *Going West With Annabelle* (1976).

Dumont, Gabriel. *Gabriel Dumont Speaks* (1993).

Einarsson, Helgi. *Helgi Einarsson, a Manitoba Fisherman* (1982). Pioneer life 1887–1920.

Ewanchuk, Michael (ed.). *Pioneer Profiles: Ukrainian Settlers in Manitoba* (1981).

Ffolkes, Edward. *Letters From a Young Emigrant in Manitoba* (1883, rpt. 1981).

Flanagan, Thomas. *Louis 'David' Riel: Prophet of the New World* (1979).

——. *Métis Lands in Manitoba* (1991).

Fleming, Mark. *Churchill: Polar Bear Capital of the World* (1988).

Francis, R. Douglas and Howard Palmer (eds.). *The Prairie West: Historical Readings* (2nd ed. 1992).

Friesen, Gerald. *The Canadian Prairies: A History* (1984).

Friesen, Rhinehart. *A Mennonite Odyssey* (1988).

Gerrard, Nelson S. *Icelandic River Saga* (1985).

Gray, James H. *The Boy From Winnipeg* (1970).

——. *The Roar of the Twenties* (1975).

——. *The Winter Years: The Depression on the Prairies* (1966, rpt. 1976).

Gray, John Morgan. *Lord Selkirk of Red River* (1963).

Green, Wilson F. *Red River Revelations: A Chronological Account of Early Events Leading to the Discovery, Occupation, and Development of the Red River Settlement* (1974).

Grove, Frederick Philip. *Over Prairie Trails* (1922, rpt. 1970).

Hambley, George H. *Trails of Pioneers: Records, Accounts, Historical Studies, Data, Reports, Letters of the Section of Manitoba Lying Southwest of Winnipeg in the Red River Valley . . .* (1956).

Hargrave, Letitia. *The Letters of Letitia Hargrave* (ed. Margaret Arnett McLeod, 1947, rpt. 1969). Written from the Hudson's Bay Company Post at York Factory.

Harrison, Dick. *The Struggle for a Canadian Prairie Fiction* (1977).

Healey, W.J. *Women of Red River: Being a Book Written From the Recollection of Women Surviving From the Red River Area* (1923, rpt. 1977).

Hildebrand, Jacob. *A Backward Glance* (1982). Pioneer life on a Manitoba farm.

Jackson, James A. *The Centennial History of Manitoba* (1970).

Kaplan, Harold. *Reform, Planning, and City Politics: Montreal, Winnipeg, Toronto* (1982).

Kavanagh, Martin. *The Assiniboian Basin: A Social Study of the Discovery, Exploration and Settlement of Manitoba* (1966).

Kendle, John E. *John Bracken: A Political Biography* (1979).

Kinnear, Mary (ed.). *First Days, Fighting Days: Women in Manitoba History* (1987).

Klipperstein, Lawrence and Julius G. Toews (eds.). *Mennonite Memories: Settling in Western Canada* (2nd ed. 1977).

Kristjansen, W. *The Icelandic People in Manitoba: A Manitoba Saga* (1965).

Lithman, Y. George (ed.). *People and Land in Northern Manitoba* (1992).

Livesay, Dorothy. *Beginnings: A Winnipeg Childhood* (1973). Winnipeg in the 1920s.

Lowery, Bob. *The Unbeatable Breed: People and Events in Northern Manitoba* (1981).

MacBeth, R.G. *The Making of the Canadian West: Being the Reminiscences of an Eye-Witness* (1898, rpt. 1973).

MacEwen, Grant. *Cornerstone Colony: Selkirk's Contribution to the Canadian West* (1977).

MacLeod, Margaret Arnett and W.L. Morton. *Cuthbert Grant of Grantown: Warden of the Plains of Red River* (1963, rpt. 1974).

Manitoba. Manitoba Culture, Heritage and Recreation. Historic Resources Branch. *The Old-timers: First Peoples of the Land of the North Wind* (1989).

Masters, D.C. *The Winnipeg General Strike* (1950, rpt. 1974).

McAllister, James A. *The Government of Edward Schreyer: Democratic Socialism in Manitoba* (1984).

McClung, Nellie L. *Clearing in the West: My Own Story* (1936, rpt. 1982).

McDougall, John. *In the Days of the Red River Rebellion* (1903, rpt. 1983).

McNaught, Kenneth and David J. Bercuson. *The Winnipeg General Strike, 1919* (1974).

Mitchell, Elizabeth B. *In Western Canada Before the War: Impressions of Early Twentieth Century Prairie Communities* (1915, rpt. 1981).

Morton, W.L. *Manitoba: A History* (2nd ed. with corrections 1970, rpt. 1984).

Moxham, William. *The Manitoba Journal, 1885–1889, of William Moxham* (1985).

Oppen, William A. *The Riel Rebellions: A Cartographic History* (1979).

Parr, John L. (ed.). *Speaking of Winnipeg* (1974).

Patterson, Edith. *Tales of Early Manitoba From the Winnipeg Free Press* (1970).

Payne, Michael. *The Most Respectable Place in the Territory: Everyday Life in Hudson's Bay Company Service York Factory, 1788–1870* (1989).

Pelletier, Emile. *A Social History of the Manitoba Métis* (rev. ed. 1977).

Peters, Klaas. *The Bergthaler Mennonites* (1988).

Ray, Arthur J. *Indians in the Fur Trade: Their Role as Trappers, Hunters, and Middlemen in the Lands Southwest of Hudson Bay, 1660–1870* (1974).

Rea, J.E. *The Winnipeg General Strike* (1973).

Riel, Louis. *Louis Riel: Selected Readings* (ed. Hartwell Bowsfield, 1988).

Ring, Dan. *The Urban Prairie* (1993)

Robertson, Heather. *Grass Roots* (1973).

Ross, Alexander. *The Red River Settlement: Its Rise, Progress, and Present State, With Some Account of the Native Races and Its General History, To the Present Day* (1856, rpt. 1972).

Russell, R.C. *The Carlton Trail: The Broad Highway into the Saskatchewan Country From the Red River Settlement, 1840–1880* (2nd ed. 1971).

Ryan, John. *The Agricultural Economy of Manitoba Hutterite Colonies* (1977).

Salverson, Laura Goodman. *Confessions of an Immigrant's Daughter* (1939, rpt. 1981).

Sawchuk, Joe. *The Métis of Manitoba: Reformulation of an Ethnic Identity* (1978).

Scott, Eileen M. *Porridge and Old Clothes* (1982).

Selkirk, Thomas Douglas, 5th Earl of. *The Collected Writings of Lord Selkirk, 1799–1809*, 2 vols. (ed. by J.M. Bumstead, 1984–1988).

Smith, David E. *The Regional Decline of a National Party: Liberals on the Prairies* (1981).

Stanley, George F.G. *The Birth of Western Canada: A History of the Riel Rebellions* (new ed. 1992).

——. *Louis Riel* (1963, rpt. 1985).

——. *Toil and Trouble: Military Expeditions to Red River* (1989).

Swainson, Donald (ed.). *Historical Essays on the Prairie Provinces* (1970).

Thistle, Paul C. *Indian-European Trade Relations in the Lower Saskatchewan River Region to 1840* (1986).

Thompson, William Paul. *Winnipeg Architecture* (rev. ed. 1982).

Tremaudan, A.-H. de. *Hold High Your Heads* (1982). History of the Métis nation.

Turek, Victor. *The Poles in Manitoba* (1967).

Tyman, John Langton. *By Sector, Township and Range: Studies in Prairie Settlement* (1972).

Wells, Eric. *Winnipeg, Where the New West Begins: An Illustrated History* (1982).

West, John. *The Substance of a Journal During Residence at the Red River Colony, British North America: And Frequent Excursions Among the North-West American Indians* (1824, rpt. 1966).

Wilder, Joseph E. *Read All About It: Reminiscences of an Immigrant Newsboy* (1978). Winnipeg at the beginning of the twentieth century.

Wilkins, Charles (ed.). *Winnipeg 8: The Ice-Cold Hothouse* (1982). Eight biographies.

Wilson, Keith. *Manitoba: Profile of a Province* (1975).

—— and James B. Wyndels. *The Belgians in Manitoba* (1976).

Wiseman, Nelson. *Social Democracy in Manitoba: A History of the CCF-NDP* (1983).

Yuzyk, Paul. *The Ukrainians in Manitoba: A Social History* (1953).

Manitoba in Literature

* denotes a winner of a Governor General's Literary Award; ** a winner for the title in its original French-language version.

Alexander, Katherine. *Children of Byzantium* (1993, originally published under name Katherine Vlassie, 1987). Linked stories about a Greek woman who comes to Winnipeg at the beginning of World War I.

Arnason, David. *Fifty Stories and a Piece of Advice* (1982). A collection often set in Manitoba's Icelandic communities.

Bailey, Don. *Sunflowers Never Sleep* (1990). This look at the world of petty crime and corrupt politics is set in Winnipeg.

Birdsell, Sandra. *The Chrome Suite: A Novel* (1982). As she travels from Toronto to Winnipeg, a women relives her life which started in a small Manitoba town.

——. *The Missing Child* (1989). Set in a fictitious Manitoba town.

——. *Night Travellers* (1983). Stories about a family with a Métis father and a Mennonite mother.

Blondal, Patricia. *A Candle to Light the Sun* (1960, rpt. 1976). An illegitimate boy grows up in a small Manitoba town.

Duncan, Mark (ed.). *Section Lives: A Manitoba Anthology* (1988).

Durkin, Douglas. *The Magpie* (1974). World War I veteran experiences disillusionment as a result of the failure of the Winnipeg General Strike.

Elias, David H. *Crossing the Line: Short Stories* (1992). Stories set in a southern Manitoba farming community.

Forer, Mort. *The Humback* (1969). A Métis woman in southeastern Manitoba finds joy in her many children.

Forrie, Allan, Patrick O'Rourke, and Glen Sorestad (eds.). *The Last Map Is the Heart: An Anthology of Western Canadian Fiction* (1989).

Gotlieb, Sondra. *True Confections; or, How My Family arranged My Marriage: A Novel* (1978). Humorous novel about an overweight Jewish girl in Winnipeg.

Grove, Frederick Philip. *Settlers of the Marsh* (1925, rpt. 1966). A Swedish immigrant's dreams of happiness on a northern Manitoba farm are shattered.

Haas, Maara. *The Street Where I Live: A Novel* (1976). Humorous tale of multicultural life in Winnipeg between the two world wars.

Heath, Caroline (ed.). *Double Bond: An Anthology of Prairie Women's Fiction* (1984).

Houston, James. *Running West* (1989). This story, based on fact, tells of William Stewart, a clerk at York Factory, and a Dene woman who lead an expedition to find her homeland and bring back furs and gold.

Kenyon, Michael. *Kleinberg* (1991). A young woman searches for her past in a Manitoba town.

Kleiman, Ed. *The Immortals* (1980). Short stories set in Winnipeg's north end.

Lalor, George. *The Foot of the River* (1986). Series of vignettes about the Winnipeg River region from the early people of Lake Agassiz to the twentieth century.

Laurence, Margaret. *The Stone Angel* (1961, rpt. 1988); *A Jest of God* (1966, rpt. 1988); *The Fire-Dwellers* (1969, rpt. 1988); *A Bird in the House* (1970, rpt. 1989); *The Diviners* (1974, rpt. 1988). Novels set in "Manawanka", a small Manitoba town.

Levi, Helen. *A Small Informal Dance: A Novel* (1977); *Tangle Your Web and Dosey-Do* (1978); *Honour Your Partner* (1979). The daily lives of a Manitoba town told with humour and irony.

Martyn, John. *Under the Ribs of Death* (1957, rpt. 1990). A Hungarian immigrant in the Anglo community of pre-depression Winnipeg.

McClung, Nellie L. *Sowing Seeds in Danny* (1908, rpt. 1965). The author, a well known feminist, uses humour to highlight the foibles of a small Manitoba community.

McRae, Garfield. *A Room on the River* (1977). Eleven stories with a Manitoba setting.

Mitchell, Ken (ed.). *Horizon: Writings of the Canadian Prairies* (1977).

Ostenso, Martha. *Wild Geese* (1925, rpt. 1989); also published as *The Passionate Flight*. A Manitoba farm family experiences domestic tyranny.

Parr, Joan (ed.). *Manitoba Stories* (1981).

——, Carol Kleiman, and David Williamson (eds.). *Winnipeg Stories* (1974).

Reimer, Douglas. *Older Than Ravens* (1989). Short stories about Mennonites in southern Manitoba.

Rosenstock, Janet and Dennis Adair. *Riel* (1979). Historical fiction about the Métis leader.

Roy, Gabrielle. *Where Nests the Water Hen* (1951, rpt. 1989); *Street of Riches* (1957, rpt. 1991); *The Road Past Altamont* (1966, rpt. 1989); **Children of My Heart* (1979). Stories about Franco-Manitobans.

Salverson, Laura Goodman. *The Viking Heart* (rev. ed. 1947, rpt. 1975). Fictionalized story of Icelandic immigration to Gimli, 1876–1919.

Schulman, Audrey. *The Cage* (1994). A suspense-filled novel about four people who are in Chuchill to photograph polar bears.

Shields, Carol. *Republic of Love* (1992). A thirty-five-year-old Winnipeg woman meets a thrice-divorced night-talk radio host.

Shipley, Nan. *Return to the River* (1976). A sympathetic portrayal of an Indian woman in the Manitoba of the 1950s.

Silver, Alfred. *Red River Story* (1990); *Where the Ghost Horse Runs* (1991). Novels about Cuthbert Grant, an early Métis leader.

Stead, Robert J.C. *The Homesteaders* (1916, rpt. 1973); *Grain* (1926, rpt. 1969); *Dry Water: A Novel of Western Canada* (1983). Three novels set in Manitoba farm communities during the last decades of the nineteenth century to the 1920s.

Stewart, Molly. *The Tartan Unicorn: A Collection of Short Stories* (1987).

Sweatman, Margaret. *Fox* (1991). Historical and fictional characters are woven into a novel about the Winnipeg General Strike.

Tefs, Wayne. *The Canasta Players* (1990). A Winnipeg professor suffers middle-age angst.

—— (comp.). *Made in Manitoba: An Anthology of Short Fiction* (1990).

Thiessen, Jack. *The Eleventh Commandment: Mennonite Low German Short Stories* (1990). Many stories are set in Manitoba.

Tracy, Ann. *Winter Hunger: A Novel* (1990). A man moves with his family to northern Manitoba to study three aboriginal communities.

Valgardson, W.D. *Bloodflowers: Ten Stories* (1973); *God Is not a Fish Inspector* (1975); *Red Dust: Stories* (1978); *The Gentle Sinners* (1980). The Icelandic community around Gimli is the setting for these three collections of short stories and a novel.

Wiebe, Armin. *The Salvation of Yasch Siemens* (1984). A youth grows to manhood in a fictional Manitoba village.

Wiseman, Adele. *Crackpot: A Novel* (1974). A humorous tale set in the Jewish community in north Winnipeg.

NEW BRUNSWICK

New Brunswick, located in Atlantic Canada, is the westernmost and the largest of the Maritime Provinces. It is bordered on the north by the province of Quebec and the Bay of Chaleur; on the east by the Gulf of St. Lawrence and Northumberland Strait; on the south by the Bay of Fundy and the province of Nova Scotia, joined at the Isthmus of Chignecto; on the west by the state of Maine.

Name Province of New Brunswick. "New Brunswick" was named by King George III in honour of his German dominions, the Duchy of Brunswick-Lunenberg. *Previous names:* from 1534–1713 it was a part of Acadia, from 1713–1784 a part of Nova Scotia.

Flag The top third displays a golden lion on a red background; the bottom two-thirds, an ancient oared galley riding on waves. Proclaimed on February 24, 1963.

Coat of Arms The content of the central shield is similar to the provincial flag and is supported on either side by a white-tailed deer with antlers and a collar of Maliseet wampum from which hang smaller shields, bearing on the left the Union Jack and on the right three golden fleur-de-lys on a blue background. The central shield rests on a grassy mound from which purple violets and fiddleheads grow (the compartment). Beneath this is the provincial motto on a scroll. Above the central shield is a helm with wreath, supporting a coronet with four maple leaves and on top an Atlantic salmon holding on its back a royal crown. Arms granted by

Queen Victoria on May 27, 1868, the motto, supporters, compartment, and supporters by Queen Elizabeth II on September 24, 1984.

Motto *Spem Reduxit* (Hope was restored).

Emblems
Bird black-capped chickadee (*Parus atricapillus*)
Flower purple violet (*Viola cucullata*)
Tree balsam fir (*Abies balsamea*)
Tartan blue, forest green, meadow green, interwoven with gold on red

Date of Entry into Confederation July 1, 1867; one of the four original provinces in Confederation.

Official Languages English and French.

Capital City Fredericton, situated on the Saint John River 135 km. (84 mi.) upstream from the Bay of Fundy; population 46,466, CA population 71,869. Previous settlements on this site: Fort Nashwaak was established as the capital of Acadia in 1691 and abandoned in 1698; Sainte-Anne, an Acadian settlement, flourished from 1732 to 1759; in 1784 the site was surveyed as a planned settlement for Loyalists and named Osnaburg. This name was changed on February 22, 1785, to Frederick's Town in honour of Prince Frederick, Bishop of Osnaburg; in August 1785 it was referred to as Fredericton for the first time. Fredericton was chosen by Governor Thomas Carleton as the capital of New Brunswick on April 25, 1785 (Saint John had briefly been the previous capital). It was incorporated as a city on May 30, 1848.

Provincial Holidays In addition to national statutory holidays (see page 2), New Brunswick residents celebrate New Brunswick Day (the first Monday in August).

Geography and Climate

Geography New Brunswick is nearly rectangular in shape with uplands in the north, gently rolling hills on a central plateau, and a lowland plain in the southeast. Almost 90% of New Brunswick is covered with forests. Much of the soil is rocky and unfit for agriculture except in the fertile river valleys and Bay of Fundy lowlands. There are many rivers and streams and several natural harbours.

Area Total 73,437 sq. km. (28,354 sq. mi.); 0.7% of Canada. *Rank:* 8th among the provinces, 10th among the provinces and territories.

Inland Water 1,344 sq. km. (519 sq. mi.), includes ca. 2,000 lakes; 1,000 are natural lakes, 1,000 are man-made, the result of mining, gravel pits, etc. Largest lake: Grand Lake 30 km. (19 mi. long).

Elevations Highest point: Mount Carleton, 820 m. (2,690 ft.). Lowest point: coastline, sea level.

Major Rivers (* indicates a designated Canadian Heritage River): Miramichi, Nepisiguit, Peticodiac, Restigouche, Salmon, *St. Croix, Saint John, Tobique.

Climate Northern and central New Brunswick have a continental climate while the coastal areas are moderated by the surrounding waters. The average daily mean temperature in January in Grand Falls is −12.2°C (10°F); in Saint John −6.7°C (19.9°F); in July in Grand Falls 18.2°C (64.8°F); in Saint John 16.9°C (62.4°F). The lowest recorded temperature in New Brunswick: −47.2°C (−53°F) at Sisson Dam on February 2, 1955; the highest recorded temperature 39.4°C (102.9°F) at Nepisiguit Falls and Woodstock on August 18, 1935, and Rexton on August 19, 1935.

Average annual snowfall in Edmundston is 364 cm. (143.3 in.); in Fredericton 290.4 cm. (114.3 in.). Greatest recorded snowfall over five consecutive days: 124.8 cm. (49.1 in.) at Turtle Creek on December 24, 1970. Greatest recorded annual snowfall: 704 cm. (277.2 in.) at Tide Head, winter of 1954/55. New Brunswick is the snowiest Maritime Province.

The average annual precipitation in Edmundston is 1121 mm. (44.1 in.); in Fredericton 1109.3 mm. (43.7 in.). The greatest recorded New Brunswick annual precipitation: 2,150 mm. (84.6 in.) at Alma in 1979.

Time Zone Atlantic.

Parks and Historic Sites

National Parks Located In New Brunswick

Park	Location	Size
Fundy	Alma	206 sq. km. (80 sq. mi.)
Kouchibouguac	near Richibucto	239 sq. km. (92 sq. mi.)

Provincial Parks There are 42 provincial parks covering 21,561 ha. (53,278 acres): 23 recreation parks, 3 campground parks, 4 beach parks, 11 picnic parks, and 1 resource park. The largest parks are:

Park	Location	Type	Size
Mount Carleton	near Saint-Quentin	resource	17,427 ha. (43,064 acres)
Sugar Loaf	Campbellton	recreation	1,149 ha. (2,840 acres)
Mactaquac	near Fredericton	recreation	526 ha. (1,299 acres)
Herring Cove	Campobello Island	beach	424 ha. (1,047 acres)
Parlee Beach	Shediac	beach	96 ha. (237 acres)
The Rocks	Hopewell Cape	recreation	72 ha. (178 acres)
Les Jardins de la Republique	Saint-Jacques	recreation	44 ha. (108 acres)

New Brunswick has 2 national bird sanctuaries, 4 national wildlife areas, and 3 Ramsar sites. In addition, it has Canada's largest park wholly contained within a city, Rockwell Park in Saint John, 870 ha. (2,200 acres).

International Parks in New Brunswick
Roosevelt Campobello International Park, Campobello Island (joint Canada/U.S.)

Major National Historic Sites and Parks in New Brunswick
Acadian Odyssey, Saint-Joseph
Beaubears Island, Nelson-Miramichi
Carleton Martello Tower, Saint John
Fort Beausejour, near Sackville

Partridge Island, Saint John Harbour
St. Andrews Blockhouse, St. Andrews

In addition, there are a number of historic sites in New Brunswick administered by the province, municipalities, or organizations. The major sites are:

Bonar Law Historic Park, Rexton
Doak Historic Site, Doaktown
Guard House and Soldiers Barracks, Fredericton
King's Landing Historical Settlement, Prince William
MacDonald Farm Historic Park, Bartibog Bridge
Ministers Island, St. Andrews
Sheriff Andrews House, St. Andrews
Village historique acadien, Caraquet

Demography

All figures relating to New Brunswick population and dwellings are 1991 data and do not include the population on 8 Indian reserves that did not cooperate in the 1991 census. Staff at Statistics Canada estimate that there are 2,066 people on these reserves.

New Brunswick Population: 723,900; 2.7% of national; *rank* 8th

Historical population data

1981	696,405
1971	634,560
1961	597,936
1951	515,697
1941	457,401
1921	387,876
1901	331,120
1881	321,233
1861	252,047

Population Density: 10.1 persons per sq. km. (26.2 per sq. mi.)

Number of Dwellings: 255,042

Indian Reserves: 19

Population Characteristics:
urban: 345,214; 47.7%
rural: 378,686; 52.3%
19 and under: 208,810; 28.8%
65 and over: 88,145; 12.2%
average income for full-time employment 15 years and over (1990): $30,274; men $34,921; women $22,799

average life expectancy at birth (1987):
   men 72.47 years; women 80.01 years
live birth rate: 9,497; 13.7 per 1000

deaths: 5,469; 7.5 per 1000
marriages: 4,521; 6.2 per 1000
divorces: 1,652; 2.28 per 1000

Largest Cities (for definitions of CMA and CA, see page viii)

Name	Population	Dwellings	National Pop. Rank
Saint John	124,981 (CMA)	45,359	24
Moncton	106,503 (CA)	38,971	30
Fredericton	71,869 (CA)	26,635	39
Bathurst	36,167 (CA)	12,545	73
Edmundston	22,478 (CA)	8,169	98
Campbellton	17,183 (CA)	6,012	106

Government and Politics, 1867-

A description of the division of powers between the federal and provincial governments will be found on page 4.

Lieutenant-Governor The Lieutenant-Governor is the nominal head of the New Brunswick government, and is appointed by the Governor General of Canada on the recommendation of the Prime Minister of Canada. (A description of the duties of lieutenant-governors is found on page 7.)

Lieutenant-Governors of New Brunswick	Term
Charles Hastings Doyle	1867
Francis Pym Harding	1867–1868
Lemuel Allan Wilmot	1868–1873
Samuel Leonard Tilley	1873–1878
Edward Barron Chandler	1878–1880
Robert Duncan Wilmot	1880–1885
Samuel Leonard Tilley	1885–1893
John Boyd	1893
John James Fraser	1893–1896
Abner Reid McClelan	1896–1902
Jabez Bunting Snowball	1902–1907
Lemuel John Tweedie	1907–1912
Josiah Wood	1912–1917
Gilbert Whiting Ganong	1917
William Pugsley	1917–1923
William Freeman Todd	1923–1928
Hugh Havelock McLean	1928–1935
Murray MacLaren	1935–1940
William George Clark	1940–1945
David Lawrence MacLaren	1945–1958
Joseph Leonard O'Brien	1958–1965
John Babbitt McNair	1965–1968
Wallace Samuel Bird	1968–1971
Hedard-Joseph Robichaud	1971–1982
George Francis Gillman Stanley	1982–1987
Gilbert Finn	1987–1994
Margaret Norrie McCain	1994–

Legislative Assembly The Legislative Assembly of New Brunswick consists of 55 members elected by popular vote, each member representing a constituency; term of office: up to 5 years as long as the party in power maintains the confidence of the Legislative Assembly; remuneration (1993): $35,807 + $14,323 expense allowance, additional amounts for special appointments; qualifications for members: Canadian citizen or British subject resident in the province prior to January 1, 1979, 18 years of age or older on polling day, ordinarily resident in New Brunswick six months immediately preceding the issue of the writ of election, ordinarily resident in the electoral district for six months immediately preceding the issue of the writ, not legally disqualified, e.g., a member of the Senate or House of Commons of Canada, a mayor or councillor of a municipality. (A description of the duties of provincial legislatures are found on page 7.)

Qualifications for New Brunswick Voters in Provincial Elections Canadian citizen or British subject resident in the province prior to January 1, 1979, 18 years of age or older on polling day, ordinarily resident in New Brunswick six months immediately preceding the issue of the writ of election, ordinarily resident in the electoral district for six months immediately preceding the issue of the writ, not legally disqualified, e.g., a prisoner in a penal institution, Chief Electoral Officer.

Premier Nominally appointed by the Lieutenant-Governor of New Brunswick, the Premier is generally the leader of the party with the majority of seats in the Legislative Assembly. (A description of the duties of provincial premiers is found on page 7.)

Premiers of New Brunswick/Party/Term
Peter Mitchell
  (1866–1867)
Andrew Rainsford Wetmore
  (1867–1870)
George Luther Hatheway
  (1871–1872)
George Edwin King
  (1872–1878)
John James Fraser
  (1878–1882)
Daniel Lionel Hanington
  (1882–1883)
Andrew George Blair
  (Liberal, 1883–1896)
James Mitchell
  (Liberal, 1896–1897)
Henry Robert Emmerson
  (Liberal, 1897–1900)
Lemuel John Tweedie
  (Liberal, 1900–1907)
William Pugsley
  (Liberal, 1907)
Clifford William Robinson
  (Liberal, 1907–1908)
John Douglas Hazen
  (Conservative, 1908–1911)

James Kidd Fleming
  (Conservative, 1911–1914)
George Johnson Clarke
  (Conservative, 1914–1917)
John Alexander Murray
  (Conservative, 1917)
Walter Edward Foster
  (Liberal, 1917–1923)
Peter John Veniot
  (Liberal, 1923–1925)
John Babington Macaulay Baxter
  (Conservative, 1925–1931)
Charles Dow Richards
  (Conservative, 1931–1933)
Leonard Percy de Wolfe Tilley
  (Conservative, 1933–1935)
Albert Allison Dysart
  (Liberal, 1935–1940)
John Babbitt McNair
  (Liberal, 1940–1952)
Hugh John Flemming
  (Conservative, 1952–1960)
Louis Joseph Robichaud
  (Liberal, 1960–1970)
Richard Bennett Hatfield
  (Conservative, 1970–1987)
Frank Joseph McKenna
  (Liberal, 1987–)

Cabinet The Cabinet consists of ministers appointed by the Premier, usually from elected members of the majority party in the Legislative Assembly. Cabinet ministers serve at the Premier's pleasure; each member usually heads a government department.

Government Departments The telephone numbers of the ministers are listed with the departments.

Advanced Education and Labour
  (506)453-2342
Agriculture
  (506)453-2448
Economic Development and Tourism
  (506)453-3009
Education
  (506)453-2523
Environment
  (506)453-2558

Finance
(506)453-2451
Fisheries and Aquaculture
(506)453-2662
Health and Community Services
(506)453-2581
Municipalities, Culture and Housing
(506)585-7041
Natural Resources and Energy
(506)453-2510
Soliciter General
(506)453-7414

Supply and Services
(506)453-2591
Transportation
(506)453-2559

New Brunswick Representation in Federal Government
House of Commons: 10 members
Senate: 10 members

Finances

A statement of New Brunswick's ordinary revenue and expenditures for the years 1992/93 and 1991/92 is shown below in millions of dollars. The financial year runs from April 1 to March 31 of the year following.

	Actual 1992/93	Actual 1991/92
Revenue		
Taxation	1,910.0	2,052.3
Other provincial sources	337.5	288.9
Government of Canada	1,721.0	1,421.1
Total revenue for the year	3,968.5	3,762.3
Expenditures		
Health	1,174.6	1,142.9
Education	897.2	884.0
Income assistance	336.7	325.5
Other social services	90.1	91.4
Municipal affairs	443.8	433.4
Economic development	246.5	249.7
Central government	231.0	219.3
Transportation	128.1	125.6
Interest on debt	538.0	475.8
Total expenditures for the year	4,086.0	3,947.6
Deficit for the year	117.5	185.3

Economy

The economy of New Brunswick is based on the land and the surrounding waters. The forests that cover 90% of its land area, a higher percent than any other Canadian province, are its greatest natural resource and mineral deposits have encouraged mining production. The province has 40% of Canada's proven reserves of lead, silver, and zinc. Although the fishery is the third largest in Atlantic Canada, it is an impor-

tant part of the economy. Potato farming averages about 79% of New Brunswick's farm cash income and the province is the largest potato-producing area in Canada. Manufacturing is mostly based on the processing of primary products. Tourism is becoming a major industry.

Major Industries New Brunswick's manufacturing industries are involved in the processing of forest products, such as pulp and paper, and food from farms and the sea. It has Canada's only tuna processing plant. Mining production includes base metals, potash, and coal.

Gross Domestic Product (1992) $11,992 million (in current dollars at factor cost); % of national G.D.P.: 2.0%; *rank:* 8th

Distribution of gross domestic product

Commercial, business, personal services	19.8%
Finance, insurance, real estate	14.3%
Manufacturing	12.5%
Trade, wholesale and retail	11.9%
Public administration	11.0%
Construction	8.2%
Utilities	5.5%
Transportation and communication	5.4%
Other (not elsewhere classified)	5.2%
Other primary	4.7%
Agriculture	1.5%

Value of Manufacturing Shipments $5,405 million

Farm Cash Receipts $254 millions

Employment (seasonally adjusted) 287,000; participation rate: 58.9%

Unemployment (seasonally adjusted) 43,000; per capita: 13.0%

Minimum wage $5.00

Exports New Brunswick's exports in 1992 amounted to $3,013 million; 2.0% of total Canadian exports; *rank:* 7th
Largest trading partner: United States; 64.2% of New Brunswick's total exports, 84% of non-agricultural exports shipped to the United States
Other important markets: E.E.C. 19.8%; Japan 5.8%
Major export commodities: Paper and paper board were 22.5% of total domestic exports, petroleum products (other than crude) 20.3%, wood pulp and similar pulp 15.3%, and fish and fish preparation 10.2%

History

ca. 10,000 B.C.	Paleo-Indians arrive.
ca. 7000 B.C.	Maritime Archaic Culture.
ca. 1000 B.C.	Evidence of pottery and widespread trading.
	By 1600 A.D. Micmacs live in south and east, Malecites along upper Saint John River Valley.
1534	Jacques Cartier explores the coast.
1604	*June 24* Samuel de Champlain and Pierre de Gua, Sieur de Monts sail into Saint John Harbour and claim land for France. They winter at Sainte Croix, but move in 1605 to Port-Royal.
1621	*September 10* King James I grants William Alexander, Earl of Stirling, the region from the Gaspé to the Saint Croix River to which Alexander gives the name Nova Scotia.
1630–1650	Struggle among the French for trade and territory in southern New Brunswick.
1630	Charles de Saint-Etienne de La Tour establishes a trading post, Fort La Tour, on the site of present-day Saint John.
1645	Charles Menou d'Aulnay, La Tour's rival for governor, captures Fort La Tour.
1654	*July 17* English expedition led by Robert Sedgewick captures Fort Sainte-Marie at the mouth of the Saint John River.
1655	*November 3* Acadia is restored to France in the Treaty of Westminster.
1659	British establish a fort at Jemseg.
1667	*November 3* Treaty of Breda returns Acadia to the French.

1692	Joseph Robinau de Villebon builds Fort Saint-Joseph on the Saint John River.
1696	New Englanders successfully attack Beaubassin and Fort Saint Jean.
1701	Governor Jacques-Francois de Brouillan destroys Fort La Tour and moves forces to Port-Royal.
1713	*April 11* France surrenders present-day New Brunswick to England in the Treaty of Utrecht.
1715	*June 25* Acadians refuse to take oath of allegiance to England.
1726	*September 25* Acadians ask exemption from bearing arms.
1727	*September 6* Acadians ask exemption from oath of allegiance to Britain.
1730	Acadians in Chignecto region swear allegiance to Britain.
1749	French occupy trading post at present-day Saint John.
	October French forces attempt to limit British settlement in the Saint John River and Chignecto Isthmus areas.
1750	*October* French build Fort Beausejour, near present-day Sackville.
1755	*June 16* British capture Fort Beausejour and rename it Fort Cumberland.
	June 17 French abandon Fort Gaspereau.
	July 23 British demand Acadians swear an oath of allegiance; Acadians from Fort Beausejour to the Ana River who refuse (ca. 6,000) are deported; many are scattered around the American colonies.
1758	British capture trading post at present-day Saint John. Fort La Tour rebuilt and named Fort Frederick.
1760	*September 13* Maliseet and Micmac swear allegiance to King George.
1762	*May 16* New England settlers arrive at Maugerville, the first British settlers in New Brunswick.
1763	*February 10* Treaty of Paris: France formally cedes its North American possessions to Britain.
1764	British enact legislation allowing Acadians to return if they swear allegiance.
1767	Acadians establish settlements along the northeast shore of the Bay of Chaleur.
1775	Fort Frederick is destroyed by American troops.
1778	British build Fort Howe at the mouth of the Saint John River.
	September 24 Micmac and Malecite take oath of allegiance to Britain at Fort Howe.
1783	*May 18* Seven thousand loyalists land at Parrtown (Saint John); in all 11,000 loyalists settle in the Saint John Valley.
	September 3 Treaty of Paris: formal end of British-United States conflict sets boundaries between Canada and the United States from mouth of the St. Croix River to the watershed between the St. Lawrence and the Atlantic.
	December 12 First newspaper in New Brunswick, the *Royal Saint John Gazette and Nova-Scotia Intelligencer,* is published at Parrtown.
1784	*June 18* Formal order for the separation of New Brunswick from Nova Scotia; provision is made for a governor, appointed council, and elected assembly.
	July 28 Thomas Carleton is appointed first governor.
1785	Carleton and Parrtown are incorporated as the city of Saint John, the first incorporated city in British North America.
	University of New Brunswick begins as an Anglican-affiliated academy.
	The oldest continuing farmer's market in Canada opens in Saint John.
	Fredericton High School, the oldest English-language high school in Canada, opens.
	November First elections are held in New Brunswick.
1786	*January 9* First legislative assembly opens in Saint John.
	October 23 Government of New Brunswick is moved from Saint John to Saint Anne's Point (Fredericton).

1788	Legislative Assembly first meets in Fredericton.
1789	First theatrical performances in New Brunswick, *The Busy Body* and *Who's the Dupe*, take place in a private room in the Mallard Tavern in Saint John.
1791	First lighthouse in New Brunswick is built on Partridge Island in Saint John harbour.
1800	*February 12* College of New Brunswick is founded in Fredericton.
	New Brunswick court denies slave owners the right to regain possession of escaped slaves.
	Early 1800s New Brunswick's lumber industry gets a boost from Britain's preferential tarriffs for its colonies.
1809	Napoleon's continental blockade brings prosperity to New Brunswick's saw-mills and ports.
1810	Acadians gain the right to vote in New Brunswick.
1813	Julia Catherine Beckwith, Fredericton, is the first Canadian-born author to publish a work of fiction in Canada (published in 1824).
1814	*December 24* Treaty of Ghent ends conflict between Britain and U.S.
1816	*May 21* First steamboat in the Maritimes, the *General Smythe*, begins operation on the Saint John River.
1817	*November 24* A commission established by the Treaty of Ghent awards the islands in Passamaquoddy Bay to Britain.
1820	*March 25* Canada's first chartered bank, the Bank of New Brunswick, is incorporated at Saint John.
1822	New Brunswick's first steam-powered sawmill opens in Saint John.
1825	*October 5* Forest fire in Miramichi region destroys several towns, kills 160, and burns 15,000 sq. km. (5,792 sq. mi.) of forest, crippling lumber trade for many years.
1826	First paid police force in Canada is established at Saint John.
1829	*February 10* King's College in Fredericton receives a royal charter.
1837	*January 14* Fire devastates Saint John.
1839	*February 8* Clash of Maine and New Brunswick lumbermen leads to American and Canadian troops in Aroostock Valley in response to a dispute over the Maine/New Brunswick border.
1840s	Arrival of 30,000 immigrants fleeing the potato famine in Ireland.
1840	*August 10* Louis Anselm Lauriat ascends in his balloon, the *Star of the East*, from Barrack Square in Saint John, the first known balloon flight in Canada.
1842	*April 5* Abraham Gesner founds first natural history museum in Canada at the Mechanics Institute in Saint John (now New Brunswick Museum).
	August 9 Ashburton-Webster Treaty settles the Maine/New Brunswick border dispute.
	Charles Fenerty of Sackville discovers a practical way to make paper from wood pulp.
	Benjamin Tibbits invents the compound marine engine which is installed in the *Reindeer* for service on the Saint John River.
1847	New Brunswick achieves responsible government.
1849	*January 1* New Brunswick Electric Telegraph opens.
	George and Joseph Salter establish a shipyard at The Bend (Moncton), bringing the area prosperity.
	Martha Hamm Lewis becomes the first woman to attend Normal School in New Brunswick; an Order-in-Council dictates that she must wear a veil and not mix with, or speak to, classmates.
1851	*April 12* British government transfers operation of the post office to the New Brunswick legislature.
	April 30 Telegraph line from Saint John to St. Andrews is established.

Thomas Turnbull drives Canada's first automobile, a three-wheeled horseless carriage, through Saint John.

William Brydone Jack Observatory on the University of New Brunswick campus, the oldest observatory in Canada, opens.

Canada's first industrial exhibition opens in Saint John.

1853   *January 1* Law prohibits the importation of alcoholic beverages.

September 14 Construction begins on New Brunswick's first railroad, the European and North American Railway, crossing New Brunswick from Nova Scotia to Maine.

1854   *June 6* Reciprocity Treaty with the United States brings prosperity to New Brunswick.

University of New Brunswick offers first English course in Canada.

1855   The Bend (Moncton) is incorporated as a town. The incorporation is lost in 1862.

1856   *January 1* Law prohibiting alcoholic beverages in New Brunswick comes into effect.

1858   Canada's first steam locomotive is built in Saint John.

1859   *April 19* King's College is chartered as the non-denominational University of New Brunswick.

1860s   Shipbuilding industry declines as steel, steam-powered ships replace wooden sailing vessels.

1864   *Spring* New Brunswick legislature passes a resolution to have a conference to discuss Maritime Union with the two other Maritime provinces.

September 7 Conference to discuss Maritime Union concludes that a union is hopeless, but a British North America union highly desirable.

1865   *March 4* Anti-Confederation forces win the New Brunswick election.

Canada's first board of fire underwriters is established in Saint John.

1866   *March 16* United States abrogates the Reciprocity Treaty resulting in a swing of New Brunswick opinion to a Canadian Confederation.

April First American Fenian raid on the New Brunswick frontier helps to sway public opinion toward Confederation.

April 17 Pro-Confederation forces form the government.

1867   *July 1* New Brunswick joins three other British North American colonies in Confederation.

July 8 First French language newspaper in New Brunswick, *Le Moniteur Acadien*, is published.

1869   British garrison leaves Fredericton.

1871   *May 17* Common Schools Act establishes free public schools, abandoning an informal system of separate schools.

Canada's first YWCA is orgainized in Saint John.

1875   *January* Riots in Caraquet leave two dead and lead to amendments to the Common School Act that improve the Catholic position.

1877   *June 20* Fire destroys two-thirds of Saint John, leaving 18 dead and 15,000 homeless.

1879   *August 6* Tornado demolishes Buctouche; 7 dead.

1880s   Railway expansion linking New Brunswick with the rest of Canada stimulates commerce.

1880   *February 25* Fire destroys the legislative building in Fredericton.

1882   New provincial legislative assembly building opens.

1883   *December 21* First Royal Canadian Regiment is raised in Fredericton.

Canada's first tax-supported free public library is established in Saint John.

1888   New Brunswick Telephone Company is incorporated.

1889	Canadian Pacific Railway reaches Saint John.
1890	Moncton is incorporated as a city.
1891	*April 16* Act abolishes the Legislative Council.
1908	*April 30* New Brunswick votes to retain Prohibition.
1910	*July 11* Fire on Campobello Island leaves only four houses standing.
1918	New Brunswick government establishes the first ministry of health in Canada.
1919	*April 17* Women are allowed to vote in provincial elections, but not to hold office.
1920s	Climax of Maritime Rights Movement, a regional protest against the Maritimes declining influence since Confederation. Rise of a vigorous pulp and paper industry.
1920	*July 10* New Brunswick votes for Prohibition.
1921	*October 10* New Brunswick votes against the importation of liquor for personal use.
1923	Shipbuilding industry is revived with the establishment of the Saint John Drydock and Shipbuilding Company.
1924	Kenneth Colin Irving founds the Irving Oil Company.
1927	*April 19* Prohibition ends when New Brunswick votes to have the sale of liquor placed under provincial government control. Federal government passes the Maritime Freight Rates Act providing for statutory reductions in freight rates and establishes the Maritime Freight Rates Commission (later Atlantic Provinces Transportation Commission) with headquarters in Moncton.
1929	New Brunswick passes the Free Libraries Act.
1930s	Depression following several decades of economic stagnation lowers New Brunswick's standard of living below the national average.
1932	Royal Canadian Mounted Police absorb the New Brunswick provincial police.
1934	*March 9* Women gain right to run for office in New Brunswick.
1936	*March 19* Ice jam sweeps away a railway bridge across the Saint John River.
1950s	Canadian Forces Base Gagetown becomes the largest land-manoeuvres training ground in the Commonwealth.
1959	*July 1* Federal-provincial hospital plan goes into effect in New Brunswick.
1960s	Federal-provincial efforts to improve New Brunswick's economy lead to rural development and government investment in small industry.
1960	*June 27* Louis Joseph Robichaud becomes the first Acadian to be Premier of New Brunswick.
1963	*June 19* Université de Moncton is founded from the amalgamation of three colleges.
1966	*June 10* Municipalities Act gives the provincial government responsibility for education, medical, judicial, and social services and municipalities responsibility for services to property. *July 17* Schools Act requires all schools to provide identical services.
1967	*October* New Brunswick appoints William Thomas Ross Flemington its first ombudsman.
1968	*April 12* Official Language Act is passed giving French and English equal status.
1969	Federal government repeals the Maritime Freight Rates Act in favour of one creating a regional committee to administer transportation subsidies. *October 16* New Brunswick announces the construction of a container shipping terminal in Saint John.
1972	*April 24* Fishing off New Brunswick is banned temporarily as a measure to conserve stocks.

1973   Council of Maritime Premiers is formed to deal with cooperation in internal development and external influence.
        April 29/30 Saint John River floods the Fredericton area.
1974   *May 23* New Brunswick becomes first province to draft statutes in English and French.
1976   *February 2* One of the fiercest storms in the twentieth century in the Bay of Fundy hits southern New Brunswick with 188 kph (117 mph) winds and 12 m. (39 ft.) waves.
1977   Federal government declares 200 mi. (322 km.) sovereignty off Canada's coasts.
        February 1 Federal-provincial agreement gives New Brunswick 100% of the royalties from offshore mineral discoveries within 5 km. (3 mi.) of the coast and 75% from resources beyond.
1981   Provincial act guarantees equal status to English and French communities with right to their own institutions in certain fields.
1982   *January 9* Two earthquakes measuring 5.5 and 4.9 on Richter scale hit New Brunswick but cause no damage.
1986   *January 4* 67 cm. (26 in.) of snow, accompanied by 110 kph (68 mph) winds, falls on Moncton.
1990   *January 15* New Brunswick legislature approves Meech Lake Accord.
1993   *February 1* Federal government passes amendment to the Constitution entrenching English and French language rights in New Brunswick.

Culture and Education

Performing Arts New Brunswick has a number of performing arts companies and institutions. The most significant organizations are listed below.

DanceEast, Moncton	(506)854-2863
Symphony New Brunswick, Saint John	(506)634-8379
Theatre New Brunswick, Fredericton	(506)458-8344
	800-442-9779
Théâtre populaire d'Acadie, Caraquet (autumn)	(506)727-0920
Théâtre l'Escaouette, Moncton	(506)855-0001

Among the many festivals in New Brunswick are:

Atlantic Waterfowl Celebration, Sackville (August)	(506)364-8080
Festival By the Sea, Saint John (August)	(506)632-0086
Foire Brayonne, Edmundston (July) (largest francophone festival in Canada outside Quebec)	(506)739-6608
Irish Festival, Chatham/Newcastle (July) (largest Irish festival in Canada)	(506)778-8810
Loyalist Days, Saint John (July)	(506)634-8123

Provincial Museums and Galleries The following are major New Brunswick institutions.
Acadian Museum and Art Gallery, Université de Moncton
Beaverbrook Art Gallery, Fredericton
Miramichi Atlantic Salmon Museum, Doaktown
New Brunswick Museum, Saint John

Universities
Mount Allison University, Sackville
St. Thomas University, Fredericton
Université de Moncton, Moncton
University of New Brunswick, Fredericton

Community Colleges
New Brunswick Community College has campuses in 10 centres:

Bathurst
Campbellton
Dieppe
Edmundston
Grand-Sault
Miramichi
Moncton
St. Andrews

Saint John
Woodstock

Miscellaneous Educational Institutions
Atlantic School of the Performing Arts,
Sackville
New Brunswick College of Craft and Design, Fredericton

Motor Vehicle Use

Motor Vehicles Registered for Use in New Brunswick (1993): 498,524

Drivers Licensed by New Brunswick (1993): 475,526. Minimum driving age: 16

Roads Hard surface: 7,120.5 km. (4,424.6 mi.); gravel: 2,540.3 km. (1,578.5 mi.);

bridges maintained by the province: 2,698

Speed Limits Controlled access highways: 90–100 kph (56–62 mph); Trans-Canada routes: 90 kph (56 mph); rural roads: 80 kph (50 mph); urban and populated areas: 50–70 kph (31–43 mph)

First, Biggest, and Best

World's longest covered bridge: spans Saint John River at Hartland, 390.8 m. (1,282 ft.)
North America's only museum devoted to Papal history: Popes Museum and Art Gallery, Grande-Anse
North America's largest Danish community: New Denmark
British Empire's first entirely new cathedral foundation since the Norman Conquest: 1845 for Christ Church Cathedral, Fredericton
British Empire's first Public Health Centre: Saint John, 1919
World's first variable-pitch propeller: tested in flight 1927 by inventor Wallace Turnbull of Rothesay
North America's first undersea telegraph cable: laid November 22, 1852 between Cape Tormentine and Carleton Head, Prince Edward Island, by Frederick Newton Gisbourne
North America's first deep-water terminal for super tankers: Mispec Point, September 9, 1970
World's fastest individual bottle-filling operation: Moosehead Brewery, Saint John, turns out 1,642 units per minute
World's first steam-operated foghorn: installed on Partridge Island 1859; plan first presented by Robert Foulis in 1853
World's first compound marine engine: developed by Benjamin Tibbets, Saint John, in 1842
British Empire's first penny newspaper: *Saint John Morning News*, first published 1838
World's largest ax: 18.3 m. (60 ft.) long by 7 m. (23 ft.) wide in Nackawic
North America's first paid police force: March 20, 1826, Saint John
World's first police union: Saint John, 1919
British Empire's first degree awarded to a woman: Bachelor of Science and English Literature from Mount Allison University on May 25, 1875, to Grace Annie Lockhart
North America's first orchestra to accompany silent movies: Saint John 1907
World's first Boy Scout Apple Day: organized by Eli Boyaner, Saint John in 1932
World's first five-cent chocolate nut bar: invented by Arthur D. Ganong and George F. Fisher of Ganong Brothers Ltd. in 1910

Sources of Information About New Brunswick

New Brunswick Inquiries: P.O. Box 6000, Fredericton, N.B. E3B 5H1 (506) 543–2525, 800-442-4400

New Brunswick Tourism: P.O. Box 12345, Fredericton, N.B. E3B 5C3 (506) 453–2377, 800-561-0123

New Brunswick government publications are available from New Brunswick Inquiries.

Books About New Brunswick: A Selected List

Reference Guides

Abbott, D. (ed.). *Bibliography of New Brunswick Geology* (1965).

Atlantic Provinces Economic Council. *Atlantic Canada Today* (1987).

Baker, Lori. *"Benedict Arnold Slept Here?": Saint John Dictionary* (5th ed. 1992).

Bird, Richard W. *Coins of New Brunswick* (1993).

Bishop, Olga B. *Publications of the Governments of Nova Scotia, Prince Edward Island, New Brunswick, 1758–1952* (1957).

Blouin, Glen. *Weeds of the Woods: Some Small Trees and Shrubs of New Brunswick* (1984).

Burrows, Roger. *A Birdwatchers Guide to Atlantic Canada. Vol. 3, New Brunswick, Prince Edward Island, Maritime Quebec* (1982).

Canada. Atmospheric Environment Service. *Canadian Climate Normals, 1961–1990: Atlantic Provinces* (1993).

Canada. Energy, Mines and Resources Canada. *Gazetteer of Canada: New Brunswick* (2nd ed. 1972 and supplement 1977).

Craig, Helen (comp.). *New Brunswick Newspaper Directory, 1783–1988* (1989).

Curtis, Herb. *Look What the Cat Drug In: Miramichi Dictionary* (2nd ed. 1990).

—— with Iris Young and Colleen Thompson. *Slow Men Working in Trees: Fredericton Dictionary* (1991).

Dilworth, Tim (ed.). *Land Mammals of New Brunswick* (1984).

Elections in New Brunswick, 1784–1984 (1984).

Erskine, Anthony J. *Atlas of Breeding Birds of the Maritime Provinces* (1992).

Fellows, Robert F. *Researching Your Ancestors in New Brunswick, Canada* (1979).

Fleming, Patricia Lockhart. *Atlantic Canadian Imprints, 1801–1820: A Bibliography* (1991).

Folster, David. *The Great Trees of New Brunswick* (1987).

Frank, David (comp.). *The New Brunswick Worker in the 20th Century, a Reader's Guide: A Selective Annotated Bibliography* (1986).

Hamilton, W.D. and W.S. Spray (eds.). *Source Materials Relating to the New Brunswick Indian* (1976).

Hickey, Daniel, Louise Charlebois, and Bruce Oliver (comps.). *A Guide to Archival Sources on the New Brunswick Forest Industry* (1990).

Hinds, Harold R. *The Flora of New Brunswick: A Manual for the Identification of All Vascular Plants, Including Ferns and Fern Allies and Flowering Plants Growing Without Cultivation in New Brunswick, Canada* (1986).

Johnson, D.F. *The Saint John County Alms and Work House Records: The Irish in New Brunswick & Their Origins* (1985).

Laugher, Charles T. *Atlantic Province Authors of the Twentieth Century: A Bio-bibliographical Checklist* (1982).

Lawrence, Joseph Wilson. *The Judges of New Brunswick and Their Times* (1905–1907, rpt. 1983).

McCalla, Robert J. *The Maritime Provinces Atlas* (new ed. 1991).

Moore, Diana and Andrea Schwenke (comps.). *New Brunswick Schools: A Guide to Archival Sources* (1992).

Morley, William F.E. *The Atlantic Provinces: Newfoundland, Nova Scotia, New Brunswick, Prince Edward Island* (1967). A bibliography.

Murphy, Peter. *Together in Exile* (1990). Genealogy of immigrants from Louth, Ireland, to Saint John.

Myles, Diane. *Speakers of the Legislative Assembly, Province of New Brunswick, 1786–1985* (1985).

Norton, Judith Ann (comp.). *New England Planters of the Maritime Provinces of Canada, 1759–1800: Bibliography of Sources* (1993).

Rayburn, Alan. *Geographical Names of New Brunswick* (1975).

Scott, W.B. and M.G. Scott. *Atlantic Fishes of Canada* (1988).

Squires, W. Austin. *The Birds of New Brunswick* (2nd ed. 1976).

——. *The Mammals of New Brunswick* (1968).

Swanick, Eric L. (comp.). *New Brunswick History: A Checklist of Secondary Sources* (1974).

Nonfiction Sources

Acheson, T.W. *Saint John: The Making of a Colonial Urban Community* (1985).

Alexander, David G. *Atlantic Canada and Confederation: Essays in Canadian Political Economy* (1983).

Allen, Sadie Harper. *A Full House and Fine Singing: Diaries and Letters of Sadie Harper Allen* (ed. by Mary Biggar Peck, 1992). A 1890s teenager in Shediac and at Mount Allison University.

Ashe, Robert. *Just Enough Fog To Keep It Cool: The People of Saint John, N.B.* (1985).

Aunger, Edmund A. *In Search of Political Stability: A Comparative Study of New Brunswick and Northern Ireland* (1981).

Bell, D.G. *Early Loyalist Saint John: The Origin of New Brunswick Politics, 1783–1786* (1983).

Belliveau, John Edward. *The Monctonians: Citizens, Saints and Scoundrels*, 2 vols. (1981).

Bogaard, Paul A. *Profiles of Science and Society in the Maritimes Prior to 1914* (1990).

Bruce, Harry. *Down Home: Notes of a Maritime Son* (1988).

Brym, Robert J. and R. James Sacouman (eds.). *Underdevelopment and Social Movements in Atlantic Canada* (1979).

Buckner, Phillip A. and David Frank (eds.). *Atlantic Canada Before Confederation* (2nd ed. 1990).

Buckner, Phillip A. and John G. Reid (eds.). *The Atlantic Region to Confederation: A History* (1994).

Burrill, Gary and Ian McKay (eds.). *People, Resources, and Power [Critical Perspectives on Underdevelopment and Primary Industries in the Atlantic Region]* (1987).

Calder, Doris. *All Our Born Days: A Lively History of New Brunswick's Kingston Peninsula* (1984).

Carleton University. History Collaborative. *Urban and Community Development in Atlantic Canada, 1867–1991* (1993).

Clarke, George Frederick. *Someone Before Us: Our Maritime Indians* (3rd ed. 1974).

Condon, Ann Gorman. *The Envy of the American States: The Loyalist Dream for New Brunswick* (1984).

Conrad, Mary (ed.). *They Planted Well: New England Planters in Maritime Canada* (1988).

Cormier, Michel and Achille Michaud. *Richard Hatfield: Power and Disobedience* (1992).

Curtis, Wayne. *Currents in the Stream: Miramichi People and Places* (1988).

Daigle, Jean (ed.). *Acadians of the Maritimes: Thematic Studies* (1982).

Davies, Gwendolyn. *Studies in Maritime Literary History, 1760–1930* (1991).

—— (ed.). *Myth and Milieu: Atlantic Literature and Culture 1918–1939* (1993).

DeMont, John. *Citizens Irving: K.C. Irving and His Legacy: The Story of Canada's Wealthiest Family* (1991).

Dodge, Helen Carmichael. *My Childhood in the Canadian Wilderness* (1961).

Doyle, Arthur T. *Heroes of New Brunswick* (1984).

——. *Premiers of New Brunswick* (1983).

Ewing, Juliana Horatia. *Canada Home: Juliana Horatia Ewing's Fredericton Letters, 1867–1869* (ed. by Mary Howard Blom and Thomas E. Blom, 1983).

Fisher, Peter. *The First History of New Brunswick* (1980).

Fleming, Berkeley (ed.). *Beyond Anger and Longing: Community Development in Atlantic Canada* (1988).

Foote, Annie. *Voices of the Bay: Reflections on Changing Times Along Fundy Shores* (1992).

Forbes, Ernest R. *The Maritime Rights Movement, 1919–1927: A Study in Canadian Regionalism* (1979).

——. *Challenging the Regional Stereotype: Essays on the 20th Century Maritimes* (1989).

—— and D.A. Mulse (eds.). *The Atlantic Provinces in Confederation* (1993).

Gair, Reavley (ed.). *A Literary and Linguistic History of New Brunswick* (1985).

Grant, B.J. *When Rum Was King* (1984).

Griffiths, Naomi E.S. *The Contexts of Acadian History, 1686–1874* (1992).

Hale, C. Anne. *The Rebuilding of Saint John, New Brunswick, 1877–1881* (1990).

Hill, Isabel. *Some Loyalists and Others* (rev. ed. 1977).

House, J.D. *Fish Versus Oil: Resources and Rural Development in North Atlantic Societies* (1986).

Howell, Colin and Richard Twomey (eds.). *Jack Tar in History: Essays in the History of Maritime Life and Labour* (1991).

Hughes, Gary K. *Music of the Eye: Architectural Drawings of Canada's First City, 1822–1914* (1992).

Hynes, Leo J. *Irish Catholics in New Brunswick* (1992).

Inwood, Kris (ed.). *Farm, Factory and Fortune: New Studies in the Economic History of the Maritime Provinces* (1993).

Koven, Marcia. *Weaving the Past Into the Present: A Glimpse Into the 130 Year History of the Saint John Jewish Community* (1989).

Lawrence, Joseph Wilson. *The Judges of New Brunswick and Their Times* (1983).

MacBeath, George and Donald F. Taylor. *Steamboat Days: An Illustrated History of the Steam-*

boat Era on the Saint John River, 1816–1946 (1982).

MacDonald, M.A. *Fortune & La Tour: The Civil War in Acadia* (1983).

——. *Rebels and Royalists: The Lives and Material Culture of New Brunswick Early English-Speaking Settlers, 1758–1783* (1990).

MacFarlane, W.G. *Fredericton History: Two Centuries of Romance, War, Privation, and Struggle* (1893, rpt. 1981).

MacKenzie, Michael. *Glimpses of the Past: True Stories Old and New* (1984).

MacNutt, W.S. *The Atlantic Provinces: The Emergence of a Colonial Society, 1712–1857* (1965).

——. *New Brunswick, A History 1784–1867* (1963, rpt. 1984).

The Maritimes: Tradition, Challenge and Change (1987).

Martin, Lois. *Historical Sketches of the Miramichi* (1985).

Maxwell, Lilian M. Beckwith. *An Outline of the History of Central New Brunswick to the Time of Confederation* (1937, rpt. 1984).

McCann, Larry (ed.). *People and Place: Studies of Small Town Life in the Maritimes* (1987).

—— and Carrie MacMillan (eds.). *The Sea and Culture of Atlantic Canada: A Multidisciplinary Sampler* (1992).

McGee, Harold Franklin (ed.). *The Native Peoples of Atlantic Canada: A History of Indian-European Relations* (1972, rpt. 1983).

McGahan, Elizabeth W. *The Port of Saint John*, 2 vols. (1982).

Medjuck, Sheva. *The Jews of Atlantic Canada* (1986).

Mitcham, Allison. *Offshore Islands of Nova Scotia and New Brunswick* (1984).

——. *Paradise or Purgatory: Island Life in Nova Scotia & New Brunswick* (1986).

Monro, Alexander. *New Brunswick: With a Brief Outline of Nova Scotia and Prince Edward Island* (1855, rpt. 1972).

Nowlan, Michael O. *The Last Bell: Memories of New Brunswick Christmas* (1992).

—— (ed.). *The Maritime Experience* (1975).

Paratte, Henri-Dominique. *Acadians* (1991).

Paul, Daniel N. *We Are Not the Savages: A Micmac Perspective on the Collision of European and Aboriginal Civilizations* (1993).

Peck, Mary. *The Bitter With the Sweet: New Brunswick 1604–1984* (1983).

——. *A New Brunswick Album: Glimpses of the Way We Were* (1987).

Power, Thomas P. (ed.). *The Irish in Atlantic Canada, 1780–1900* (1991).

Rawlyk, George A. (ed.). *Historical Essays on the Atlantic Provinces* (1967).

Robb, James. *The Letters of James and Ellen Robb: Portrait of a Fredericton Family in Early Victorian Times* (ed. by Alfred Goldsworth Bailey, 1983).

Robinson, Charlotte Gourlay. *Pioneer Profiles of New Brunswick Settlers* (1980). Twenty profiles of loyalist women.

Sager, Eric W. with Gerald E. Panting. *Maritime Capital: The Shipping Industry in Atlantic Canada, 1820–1914* (1990).

Samson, Daniel (ed.). *Contested Countryside: Rural Workers and Modern Society in Atlantic Canada, 1800-1950* (1994).

Sandberg, L. Anders (ed.). *Trouble in the Woods: Forest Policy and Social Conflict in Nova Scotia and New Brunswick* (1992).

Saunders, S.A. *The Economic History of the Maritime Provinces* (1939, rpt. 1984).

Savoie, Donald J. *Federal-Provincial Collaboration: The Canada-New Brunswick General Development Agreement* (1981).

Schuyler, George W. *Saint John: Two Hundred Years Proud* (1984).

See, Scott W. *Riots in New Brunswick: Orange Nativism and Social Violence in the 1840s* (1993).

Southham, Nancy (ed.). *Remembering Richard: An Informal Portrait of Richard Hatfield By His Friends, Family and Colleagues* (1993).

Spicer, Stanley T. *Maritimers Ashore and Afloat: Interesting People, Places, and Events Related to the Bay of Fundy and Its Rivers*. Vol. 1 (1993).

Spray, W.A. *The Blacks in New Brunswick* (1972).

—— and Carole L. Spray. *New Brunswick: Its History and Its People* (1984).

Squires, W. Austin. *History of Fredericton: The Last Two Hundred Years* (1980).

Stanley, Della M.M. *Louis Robichaud: A Decade of Power* (1984).

Starr, Richard. *Richard Hatfield: The Seventeen Year Saga* (1987).

Stewart, George. *The Story of the Great Fire in St. John, N.B., June 20th, 1877* (1980).

Swanick, Eric L. (ed.). *Hardiness, Perseverance and Faith: New Brunswick Library History* (1991).

Thomas, Peter. *Strangers From a Secret Land: The Voyages of the Brig Albion and the Founding of the First Welsh Settlements in Canada* (1986).

Thorburn, H.G. *Politics of New Brunswick* (1961).

Thurston, Harry. *Tidal Life: A Natural History of the Bay of Fundy* (1990).

Toner, P.M. (ed.). *New Ireland Remembered: Historical Essays on the Irish in New Brunswick* (corrected ed. 1989).

Trueman, Stuart. *The Fascinating World of New Brunswick* (1979).

——. *An Intimate History of New Brunswick* (1970, rpt. 1982).

——. *Tall Tales and True Tales From Down East: Eerie Experiences, Heroic Exploits, Extraordinary Personalities, Ancient Legends and Folklore From New Brunswick and Elsewhere in the Maritimes* (1979).

Tuck, James A. *Maritime Provinces Prehistory* (1984).

Tweedie, R.A. *On With the Dance: A New Brunswick Memoir, 1935–1960* (1986).

Upton, Leslie F.S. *Micmacs and Colonists: Indian-White Relations in the Maritimes, 1713–1867* (1979).

Van den Hoonaard, Will. C. *Silent Ethnicity: The Dutch of New Brunswick* (1991).

Wade, Mason. *Mason Wade, Acadia and Quebec: The Perception of an Outsider* (ed. by N.E.S. Griffiths and G.A. Rawlyk, 1991).

Wallis, Wilson D. and Ruth Sawtell Wallis. *The Malecite Indians of New Brunswick* (1957).

Whitehead, Ruth Holmes. *The Old Man Told Us: Excerpts From Micmac History 1500–1950* (1991).

Wilbur, Richard. *The Rise of French New Brunswick* (1989).

Winslow, William Odber (ed.). *Winslow Papers*, A.D. *1776–1826* (1901, rpt. 1972).

Wright, Esther Clark. *The Loyalists of New Brunswick* (1955, rpt. 1985).

Wright, Harold E. and Byron E. O'Leary. *Fortress Saint John: An Illustrated Military History, 1640–1985* (1985).

Wynn, Graeme. *Timber Colony: A Historical Geography of Early Nineteenth Century New Brunswick* (1981).

New Brunswick in Literature

* denotes a winner of a Governor General's Literary Award.

Bauer, Nancy. *Flora, Write This Down* (1982). A portrayal of a New Brunswick family.

Bonnie, Fred. *Squatter's Rights* (1979). Seven stories about people in the New Brunswick/Maine border region.

Brewster, Elizabeth. *The Sisters: A Novel* (1974). Three New Brunswick sisters grow apart in the depression years.

Burningham, Bradd. *The Sad Eye* (1991). Stories narrated by a variety of characters.

Choyce, Lesley (ed.). *Chezzetcook: An Anthology of Contemporary Poetry and Fiction From Atlantic Canada* (1977).

Corey, Deborah Joy. *Losing Eddie* (1993). Connected short stories about Eddie, returned from reform school to home in a rural New

Brunswick town, seen through the eyes of his younger sister.

Creighton, Helen. *A Folktale Journey Through the Maritimes* (1993).

Curtis, Herb. *Currents in the Stream* (1988); *The Americans Are Coming: A Novel* (1989); *The Last Tasmanian* (1991); *The Lone Angler* (1993). Novels set in the Miramichi region.

——. *Hoofprints on the Sheet: New Brunswick Short Stories* (1993).

——. *One Indian Summer* (1993). A novel about the dying days of a New Brunswick farm in the 1950s.

Donaldson, Allan. *Paradise Siding* (1984). Seven stories depict growing up in Woodstock in the 1930s.

Fraser, Raymond. *The Bannonbridge Musicians* (1978). A tale of rural New Brunswick youth in the 1960s.

——, Clyde Rose, and Jim Stewart (eds.). *East of Canada: An Atlantic Anthology* (1976).

Gibbs, Robert. *I've Always Felt Sorry For Decimals: Stories* (1978). Six stories about two brothers in the 1930s growing up in a New Brunswick town.

Livesay, Dorothy. *The Husband: A Novella* (1990). A Fredericton woman's estranged marriage is reconciled through a love affair with a younger man.

Maillet, Antonine. *Mariaagelas: Maria, Daughter of Gelas* (1986). A young Acadian living in a coastal village in the 1930s becomes involved in smuggling.

McGahan, Elizabeth W. (ed.). *Whispers From the Past: Selections From the Writings of New Brunswick Women* (1986).

Nowlan, Alden. *Miracle at Indian River and Other Stories* (1968, rpt. 1982). Eighteen portraits of rural New Brunswick people.

——. *Will Ye Let the Mummies In?: Stories* (1984). Twenty-two stories about life in the Maritimes.

Nowlan, Michael O. (ed.). *Stubborn Strength: A New Brunswick Anthology* (1983).

Richards, David Adams. *The Coming of Winter* (1974, rpt. 1992); *Blood Ties* (1976, rpt. 1992); *Dancers at Night: Stories* (1978); *Lives of Short Duration* (1981, rpt. 1992); *Road to Stilt House* (1985); **Nights Below Station Street* (1988); *Evening Snow Will Bring Such Peace* (1990); *For Those Who Hunt the Wounded Down* (1993). Miramichi Valley is the setting for these novels and stories.

Thomas, Peter. *The Welsher* (1987). A sad comedy about a man who seeks refuge in a New Brunswick forest cabin.

Thompson, Kent. *A Local Hanging and Other Sto-*

ries (1984). Short stories about ordinary folk in New Brunswick.

———. *Married Love: A Vulgar Entertainment: A Novella* (1988). A comedy about a visit from Ontario relatives to a Fredericton household.

———. *Playing in the Dark: A Novel* (1990). This story alternates between a bank teller in Fredericton and her lover in a Kingston, Ontario, penitentiary.

———. *Stories From Atlantic Canada: A Selection* (1973).

Walker, David. *Ash* (1976). A pilot convalescing in a New Brunswick cabin finds some purpose and meaning in his botched-up life.

———. *Mallabec* (1965). A Boston man returns with his wife to fish salmon in the River Mallabec, and finds that he cannot forget the tragic events from a previous visit in 1939.

NEWFOUNDLAND AND LABRADOR

Newfoundland and Labrador (commonly called Newfoundland), Canada's most easterly province, is divided into two parts separated by the Strait of Belle Isle: to the southeast the island of Newfoundland lying off the east coast of Canada and to the northwest Labrador, a much larger mainland area. The province of Newfoundland and Labrador is bordered on the west by the province of Quebec and the Gulf of St. Lawrence; on the south and east by the Atlantic Ocean; on the north by the Hudson Strait. Cape Spear is the most eastern point in North America.

Name   Province of Newfoundland and Labrador. Early fishermen and explorers named the island "New Founde Lande", "Terra Nova", "Terre-Neuve", or "Terra de Bacalao". "Newfoundland", Canada's oldest place-name of European origin, was first mentioned in 1503 in The English Daybooks of King's Payments. Gaspar Corte-Real named the mainland "Terra del Lavrador" (Land of the Farmer); later anglicized as "Labrador".

Flag   White background with four blue right-angle triangles forming a horizontal rectangle on left; on right two white right-angled triangles bordered in red separated by a golden arrow. It was adopted on June 6, 1980.

Coat of Arms   The shield has a red background with a white cross dividing it in quarters, each part bearing a lion or unicorn, and is supported on either side by an Indian carrying a bow. Above the shield is an elk standing on a double argent of red and gold. The shield and sup-

porters rest on a grassy mound emblazoned with the provincial motto on a scroll. The arms were granted by King Charles I on January 1, 1637, and officially adopted by the Newfoundland government on January 1, 1928.

Motto   *Quaerite Prime Regnum Dei* (Seek ye first the kingdom of God).

Emblems
Bird   Atlantic puffin (*Fratercula arctica*)
Flower   pitcher plant (*Sarracenia purpurea*)
Gemstone   labradorite
Tartan   (unofficial) dark green, gold, white, brown, and red on a medium green background
Tree   black spruce (*Picea mariana*)

Date of Entry into Confederation
March 31, 1949, the last province to join Canada.

Official Language   English.

Capital City St. John's, situated on the east coast of the Avalon Peninsula, Canada's most easterly city; population 154,269, CMA population 171,859. Myth says that John Cabot named the region St. John's Isle because he arrived June 24, 1497. First established in 1504 as a base for the English fisheries, the town, founded in 1583, became the seat of government in 1832 when Newfoundland was granted a colonial legislature. It was incorporated in 1888 and received a city charter in 1921.

Provincial Holidays In addition to national statutory holidays (see page 2), Newfoundland and Labrador residents celebrate the closest prior Mondays to St. Patrick's Day (March 17), St. George's Day (April 23), Discovery Day (June 24), and Orangemen's Day (July 12).

Geography and Climate

Geography The island of Newfoundland is roughly triangular in shape with many bays and harbours and a deeply indented east coast. The interior plateau is half forested and half barren and boggy. A mountain range, a narrow coastal plain, and commercial forests are found in the west. Labrador's northern region contains rugged mountains, deep fiords, and subarctic vegetation. Its interior is well forested and its southern coastal plain barren and rugged.

Area 405,720 sq. km. (156,649 sq. mi.); 4.1% of Canada. *Rank:* 7th among the provinces, 9th among the provinces and territories.

Inland Water 34,032 sq. km. (13,140 sq. mi.), includes more than 800 lakes. Largest lake: Michikamau Lake 7,666 sq. km. (2,960 sq. mi.).

Elevations Highest point: Mount Caubvick, 1,652 m. (5,420 ft.). Lowest point: coastline, sea level.

Major Rivers (* indicates a designated Canadian Heritage River): *Bay du Nord, Churchill, Exploits, Fraser, Gander, Humber, Kanairiktok, Kogaluk, Little Mecatina, *Main, Naskaupi, Terra Nova.

Climate Labrador has a rigorous climate with cold winters and cool summers ranging from subarctic in the north to continental in the interior. The coastal areas of the island of Newfoundland have a maritime climate characterized by changeable weather and moderate temperatures. Waters over the Grand Banks are among the foggiest in the world. The average daily mean temperature in January in Goose Bay is −16.4°C (2.5°F); in St. John's −3.9°C (25°F); in July in Goose Bay 15.8°C (60.4°F); in St. John's 15.5°C (59.9°F). The lowest recorded temperature in the province: −51.1°C (−60°F) at Esker Station, Labrador, on February 17, 1973; the highest recorded temperature 41.7°C (107.1°F) at Northwest River, Labrador, on August 11, 1914.

The average snowfall in Goose Bay is 445.2 cm. (175.3 in.) per year; in St. John's 359.4 cm. (141.5 in.) per year. The average precipitation in Goose Bay is 946.1 mm. (37.2 in.) per year; in St. John's 1,513.6 mm. (59.6 in.) per year. The province's greatest recorded annual precipitation: 2,253 mm. (88.7 in.) at Pools Cove in 1983.

The Province of Newfoundland and Labrador holds several Canadian records: St. John's is the foggiest, windiest, cloudiest, wettest, major city in Canada; the highest average number of hours of fog per year, 1,890 hours at Argentia; greatest recorded snowfall over five consecutive days, 182 cm. (71.7 in.) at Cartwright on January 1, 1965; the lowest sea-level pressure 94.02 kPa at St. Anthony on January 2, 1977.

Time Zones Newfoundland time zone (one half hour ahead of Atlantic time) on the island and the south coast of Labrador; Atlantic time zone in the rest of Labrador.

Parks and Historic Sites

In this section, the following designations are used: * indicates the area is, or part of it is, a Unesco World Heritage Site; ** indicates the area is, or part of it is, a National Bird Sanctuary.

National Parks Located in Newfoundland and Labrador

Park	Location	Size
Gros Morne	Rocky Harbour	1,943 sq. km. (750 sq. mi.)
**Terra Nova	Glovertown	399 sq. km. (154 sq. mi.)

Provincial Parks There are 95 provincial parks covering 449,428 ha. (1,735 sq. mi.), 1.1% of Newfoundland and Labrador's area: 20 natural and scenic reserve parks, 15 wilderness and ecological reserves, 34 natural environment parks, 1 waterway park, 20 outdoor recreation parks, and 5 park reserves. The largest parks are:

Park	Region	Type	Size
Bay du Nord	Eastern	wilderness	289,500 ha. (1,118 sq. mi.)
Avalon	Avalon	wilderness	107,000 ha. (413 sq. mi.)
Sepoy Hill	Avalon	reserve	4,500 ha. (17 sq. mi.)
Barachois Pond	western	natural environment	3,497 ha. (14 sq. mi.)
Watt's Point	western	ecological	3,090 ha. (12 sq. mi.)
Butter Pot	Avalon	natural environment	2,833 ha. (11 sq. mi.)
Chance Cove	Avalon	natural environment	2,068 ha. (8 sq. mi.)
Sir Richard Squires Memorial	central	natural environment	1,574 ha. (6 sq. mi.)
Grand Lake	Labrador	reserve	1,505 ha. (6 sq. mi.)
Winter Tickle Lake	central	reserve	1,500 ha. (6 sq. mi.)

Newfoundland and Labrador has 1 national bird sanctuary and 1 Ramsar site.

Major National Historic Sites and Parks in Newfoundland and Labrador

*L'Anse aux Meadows, north of St. Anthony

Basque Whaling Archaeological Site, Red Bay

Cape Spear, near St. John's

Castle Hill, Placentia

Port au Choix, Port au Choix

Signal Hill, St. John's

In addition, there are a number of historic sites in Newfoundland and Labrador administered by the province, municipalities, or organizations. The major sites are:

Beothuk Village, Grand Falls-Windsor

Cape Bonavista Lighthouse, Bonavista

Commissariat House, St. John's

Grenfell House, St. Anthony

Heart's Content Cable Station, Heart's Content

Lester-Garland Premises, Trinity

Point Amour Lighthouse, Point Amour

Quidi Vidi Battery, St. John's

Trinity Interpretation Centre, Trinity

Demography

Newfoundland and Labrador Population:
568,474; 2.1% of national; *rank* 9th

Historical population data
1981   567,685
1971   522,104
1961   457,853
1951   361,416

Population Density: 1.5 persons per sq. km. (4.0 per sq. mi.) (lowest of the provinces)

Number of Dwellings: 175,665

Indian reserves: 1

Population Characteristics:
urban: 304,451; 53.6%
rural: 264,023; 46.4%
19 and under: 182,030; 32.0%
65 and over: 55,160; 9.7%
average income for full-time employment 15 years and over (1990); $30,993; men $36,211; women $23,346
average life expectancy at birth (1987); men 72.72 years; women 79.36 years
live birth rate: 7,166; 12.6 per 1000 (lowest in Canada)
deaths: 3,798; 6.6 per 1000
marriages: 3,480; 6.1 per 1000
divorces: 912; 1.6 per 1000

Largest Cities and Towns *(for definitions of CMA and CA, see page viii)*

Name	Population	Dwellings	National Pop. Rank
St. John's	171,859 (CMA)	55,750	19
Corner Brook	33,790 (CA)	10,804	78
Grand Falls-Windsor	25,285 (CA)	7,918	91
Labrador City	11,392 (CA)	3,403	131
Gander	11,063 (CA)	3,547	135

Government and Politics, 1949–

A description of the division of powers between the federal and provincial governments will be found on page 4.

Lieutenant-Governor The Lieutenant-Governor is the nominal head of the Newfoundland and Labrador government, and is appointed by the Governor General of Canada on the recommendation of the Prime Minister of Canada. (A description of the duties of lieutenant-governors is found on page 7.)

Lieutenant-Governors of Newfoundland and Labrador	Term
Albert Joseph Walsh	1949
Leonard Cecil Outerbridge	1949–1957
Campbell Leonard Macpherson	1957–1963
Fabian O'Dea	1963–1969
Ewart John Arlington Harnum	1969–1974
Gordon Arnaud Winner	1974–1981
William Anthony Paddon	1981–1986
James Aloysius McGrath	1986–1991
Frederick William Russell	1991–

Legislative Assembly The Legislative Assembly of Newfoundland and Labrador consists of 52 members elected by popular vote, each member representing a constituency; term of office: up to 5 years as long as the party in power maintains the confidence of the Legislative Assembly; remuneration (1993/4): $36,807 + $18,158.37 tax-free allowance + constituency allowance to a maximum of $7,500, additional amounts for special appointments; qualifications for members: Canadian citizen, 18 years of age or older on nomination day, ordinarily resident in the province immediately preceding the election (a person who goes to a place outside the province for a continuous period of more than six months ceases to be ordinarily resident), not legally disqualified. (A description of the duties of provincial legislatures are found on page 7.)

Qualifications for Newfoundland and Labrador Voters in Provincial Elections Canadian citizen, 18 years of age or older on polling day, ordinarily resident in the province immediately preceding the election, ordinarily resident in the electoral district on polling day (a person who goes to a place outside the province for a continuous period of more than six months ceases to be ordinarily resident, exceptions for certain people, e.g., students).

Premier Nominally appointed by the Lieutenant-Governor of Newfoundland and Labrador, the Premier is generally the leader of the party with the majority of seats in the Legislative Assembly. (A description of the responsibilities of provincial premiers is found on page 7.)

Premiers of Newfoundland and
Labrador/Party/Term
Joseph Roberts Smallwood
(Liberal, 1949–1972)
Frank Duff Moores
(Conservative, 1972–1979)
Alfred Brian Peckford
(Conservative, 1979–1989)
Thomas Gerard Rideout
(Conservative, 1989)
Clyde Kirby Wells
(Liberal, 1989–   )

Cabinet The Cabinet consists of ministers appointed by the Premier, usually from elected members of the majority party in the Legislative Assembly. Cabinet ministers serve at the Premier's pleasure; each member usually heads a government department.

Government Departments The telephone numbers of public relations directors/specialists are listed with the departments.

Education
(709)729-5909
Employment and Labour Relations
(709)729-1072
Environment and Lands
(709)729-3394
Finance
(709)729-0110
Fisheries
(709)729-3733
Forestry and Agriculture
(709)729-3760
Health
(709)729-0110
Industry, Trade and Technology
(709)729-0050
Justice
(709)729-0110
Mines and Energy
(709)729-2622
Municipal and Provincial Affairs
(709)729-3142
Social Services
(709)729-0110
Tourism and Culture
(709)729-0928
Works, Services and Transportation
(709)729-0110

Newfoundland and Labrador Representation in Federal Government
House of Commons: 7 members
Senate: 6 members

Finances

A statement of Newfoundland and Labrador's current revenues and expenditures for the years 1992/93 and 1991/92 is shown below in thousands of dollars. The financial year runs from April 1 to March 31 of the year following.

	Actual 1992/93	Actual 1991/92
Revenue		
Taxation	1,311,103	1,324,300
Other	365,442	321,506
Government of Canada	1,373,315	1,328,496
Total revenue for the year	3,049,860	2,974,302
Expenditures		
Education	739,240	707,907
Health	763,252	741,565
Debt charges and other financial expenses	486,678	493,900
Social welfare	432,285	402,061
General government	168,450	163,705
Transportation and communication	105,649	103,341
Other	435,877	421,365
Total expenditures for the year	3,131,431	3,033,844
Deficit for the year	81,571	59,542

Economy

The economy of Newfoundland and Labrador is based on its natural resources and their processing. While its land-based resources, such as mining and hydroelectric power, continue to contribute to the economy, its large fishing and fish processing industry, a former staple of the economy, is in decline due to the paucity of fish off its shores. Poor soils and an adverse climate have restricted agriculture to a limited supply of local markets.

Major Industries Newfoundland and Labrador's manufacturing industries include pulp and paper and, until recently, food processing from the fisheries. It is Canada's largest producer of iron ore and has significant mining of lead, zinc, and other minerals. Hydroelectric power developments in Labrador and offshore oil and gas deposits are a significant part of the economy.

Gross Domestic Product (1992) $8,113 millions (in current dollars at factor cost); % of national G.D.P.: 1.4%; rank: 9th

Distribution of gross domestic product (1992)

Finance, insurance, real estate	15.3%
Government services	12.3%
Construction	9.2%
Educational services	8.9%
Retail trade	8.2%
Manufacturing	7.7%
Health services	6.7%
Other utilities	4.9%
Wholesale trade	3.6%
Mining	3.5%
Transportation, storage	2.6%
Fishing and trapping	0.9%
Agriculture	0.4%

Value of Manufacturing Shipments $1,647 million

Farm Cash Receipts $62 million

Employment (seasonally adjusted) 197,000; participation rate: 54.3%

Unemployment (seasonally adjusted) 41,000; per capita: 17.2%

Minimum wage $5.00

Exports Newfoundland's exports in 1992 amounted to $1,224.0 million; 0.8% of total Canadian exports; *rank:* 9th
Largest trading partner: United States, 50% of Newfoundland's exports
Other important markets: U.K., ca. 10%; Netherlands, 6%; Italy, 5%; Germany and Japan, ca. 4%
Major export commodities: fish and fish products, newsprint, mining products

History

ca. 7000 b.c.	Maritime archaic culture is found in Labrador; it spreads to Newfoundland by 3000 b.c.
ca. 700 b.c.	Dorset culture reaches Labrador; it spreads to Newfoundland by 500 b.c.
ca. 550 a.d.	Legend that St. Brendan arrives in Newfoundland.
ca. 900	Algonkian people are in Labrador.
ca. 1000	Ancestors of Beothuk Indians are in Newfoundland.
1000	Vikings visit Labrador and build a settlement at present-day L'Anse aux Meadows.
1400s	French, Spanish, Basque, and Portuguese fish on the Grand Banks and Labrador Sea.
1497	*June 24* John Cabot sails along the Newfoundland coast and probably lands on the east coast.
1500s	Whale oil industry is on the Labrador coast at Red Bay.
1500–1501	Gaspar Corte-Real explores Newfoundland and Labrador coasts, establishing Portuguese claim to fisheries.
1506	Jean Denys makes the first known Norman fishing voyage to Newfoundland, landing at present-day Renews.
1509	*Winter* Colony is established at St. John's to secure the area for the British. None survive.
1523–1524	Giovanni de Verrazano explores the North American coast and names present-day Newfoundland and Nova Scotia Arcadia.
1527	*Summer* John Rut explores the Labrador coast.
1528	Merchant named Bute builds the first permanent residence at St. John's.
1534	*May 10* Jacques Cartier reaches Newfoundland, explores and maps the coast.
1558	First settlers arrive at Trinity.
1583	*August 5* Humphrey Gilbert in St. John's claims land for British.
1585	*October 10* Bernard Drake destroys the Spanish fishery in Newfoundland waters.
1586–1587	John Davis charts the Labrador coast.
1610	*May 2* King James I grants a charter to the Company of Adventurers and Planters to colonize Newfoundland. *August* Governor John Guy brings settlers to Cupids. Pirate Peter Easton builds a fort on the headland of Harbour Grace as a base to attack shipping.
1612	*October* Guy explores Trinity Bay.
1614	English colony at Conception Bay is established.
1616	*June 17* William Vaughan buys Avalon Peninsula and makes several attempts to establish a colony of Welsh settlers at Trepassey and Renews.
1621	George Calvert, first Baron Baltimore, buys the Avalon Peninsula from Vaughan and establishes a colony at Ferryland.
1623	*April 7* Calvert obtains a royal charter for the Province of Avalon.
1633	In the Western Charter King Charles I forbids settlement on Newfoundland and designates as governor of the "Fishing Admirals" the first ship captain to reach the island each year.
1637	*November 13* King Charles I grants all Newfoundland to a group of nobles headed by David Kirke, but gives no authority over fishermen.
1638	Kirke becomes first governor of Newfoundland and subsequently builds forts at Ferryland, St. John's, and Bay de Verde; he brings 100 colonists.
1662	French establish a fishing settlement at Placentia.

1665	*December 13* Dutch plunder St John's.
1673	Ship Captain Christopher Martin beats off attack by three Dutch ships at the entrance to St. John's harbour.
1675	*January 27* King Charles II issues new charter designed to protect the rights of the Fishing Admirals and merchants which includes no settlement within six miles of the shoreline.
1689–1690s	Forts William, George, and Castle are built to protect St. John's harbour.
1694	*August 31* William and Mary defeats seven French ships at Ferryland.
1696	*November* Pierre Le Moyne, Sieur d'Iberville, destroys English settlements and captures St. John's.
1697	*October 30* Treaty of Ryswick returns all territory captured in North America during King William's War.
	King William III grants Labrador to Joseph de La Penja, a Rotterdam merchant.
1702	*October 17* Augustin Le Gardeur de Courtemanche is granted a ten-year trading and fishing concession for Labrador, heralding French settlement of Labrador.
1704	*August* French and Indians destroy Bonavista.
	British build Fort Amherst on the south side of St. John's harbour narrows.
1705	French capture or destroy many settlements on Conception and Trinity Bays.
1709	*January 1* French capture St. John's; they abandon it in *April.*
1713	*April 11* France surrenders Newfoundland to England in the Treaty of Utrecht; French retain some fishing rights.
1720	First Church of England in North America is established in St. John's.
1726	First school in Newfoundland opens in Bonavista, organized by the Society for the Propagation of the Gospel in Foreign Parts.
1728	Earthquake and tidal wave cause great destruction along Burin Peninsula; 27 dead.
1729	*April* Henry Osborn, first of the naval governors, is appointed to bring order to the fishing industry.
1762	*June 27* French capture St. John's; British retake it on *September 16* in the Battle of Signal Hill, the last encounter between British and French soldiers in North America.
1763	*February 10* Treaty of Paris: France formally cedes its North American possessions to Britain.
	October 7 Labrador is given to Newfoundland.
1769	Moravian Brothers from Germany are granted 40,470 ha. (100,000 acres) on the Labrador coast to establish Christian settlements among the Inuit.
1771	Jens Haven opens the first Moravian mission post.
1774	*June 22* Quebec Act enlarges the boundaries of Quebec to include Labrador (in effect *May 1, 1775*).
1775	*September 9* Hurricane strikes eastern Newfoundland drowning ca. 4,000 seamen.
1778	*May* American privateer raids Placentia Bay.
1783	*September 20* Treaty of Paris allows United States fishermen to dry catch on unsettled Labrador shores.
1787	Rigolet is built as a Hudson's Bay Company post in Labrador.
1791	*July* First civil court in Newfoundland, the Court of Civil Jurisdiction, is established.
1792	Supreme Court of Criminal Jurisdiction is established.
	August André Michaux becomes the first naturalist to explore interior of the Quebec-Labrador peninsula.
1800–1840	Apex of the sealing industry.

1807	*Royal Gazette*, Newfoundland's first newspaper, is published in St. John's.
1809	*March 30* Labrador Act transfers coasts of Labrador from the Saint-Jean River to Hudson Strait and Anticosti Island from Quebec to Newfoundland.
1813	*June* Governor Richard Keats allows the first land grants for farming, each not to exceed four acres.
1815–1818	Islanders experience famine.
1816	*February 12* St. John's is almost destroyed by fire.
1822	*November 4* William Epps Cormack with a Micmac guide completes the first recorded walk across Newfoundland's interior from Smith Sound to St. George's Bay.
1823	*December 26* Chamber of Commerce is established in St. John's.
1825	First official coach road opens from St. John's to Portugal Cove.
	British Parliament restores Anticosti Island and part of the southwest coast of Labrador to Quebec.
	April 16 Thomas Cochrane is appointed the first resident governor of Newfoundland.
1826	Supreme Court of Newfoundland is established.
1827	First Mechanics Institute in Canada opens in St. John's.
1829	*June 6* Shananditti, the last of the Beothuk people, dies at St. John's.
1832	*March 2* British government gives control of almost all Crown revenue to the colony, requiring it to pay for office holders.
	August 22 Colony is granted representative government; while the appointed governor and legislative council hold the most power, the House of Assembly is elected by popular ballot with 15 representatives from 9 electoral districts.
1836	Education Act distributes funds among societies promoting education; non-denominational boards of education are established.
1838	*January 1* Newfoundland's first representative assembly meets in St. John's.
1839	John McLean becomes the first white man to see Churchill Falls.
1842	*August 31* In the Newfoundland Act Britain imposes a single legislature with appointed and elected members.
1846	*June 9* St. John's is leveled by fire.
1847	Britain revives the Council and makes it into an upper house.
	September 11 Hurricane kills 300 in Newfoundland.
1850	*January 28* Colonial Building, the Newfoundland legislative building to 1959, is opened officially by Governor Sir John LeMarchant.
1855	Newfoundland achieves responsible government when the Legislative Council is made responsible to the House of Assembly; membership in the Assembly is increased to 30.
1856	Frederick Newton Gisbourne and Cyrus Field complete a telegraph line from Cape Ray to Cape Breton Island, Nova Scotia.
	Newfoundland issues its first postage stamp.
1863	*Anglo-Saxon* is wrecked off Cape Race; 237 dead.
1864	Lumber industry is encouraged when Gay Silver builds a sawmill on Corner Brook stream.
1866	*March* House of Assembly passes resolution postponing indefinitely the issue of confederation with Canada.
1869	*December 7* Newfoundland voters reject Confederation.
1870	British troops withdraw from St. John's.
1881	*August 10* Construction of a railroad from St. John's to Hall Bay begins; it is finished *October 19, 1897*.
1885	*October 12* Storm on Labrador coast leaves 300 dead.
1890	Newfoundland tries to sell Labrador to Canada for $9 million.

1891	*December* Britain vetoes Newfoundland's free trade agreement with the United States.
1892	*July 8–9* Most of St. John's is destroyed by fire.
1893	Wilfred Thomason Grenfell builds a hospital at Battle Harbour for Labrador fishermen.
1894	Iron ore mines open on Bell Island.
	December 10 Newfoundland's two principal banks fail; the economy is in crisis.
1895	*February–May* Talks about Confederation fail because Canada refuses to give Newfoundland money to pay for debts and local services.
1897	Ferry service between Placentia (later Port-aux-Basques) to North Sydney, Nova Scotia, begins.
1898	Narrow gauge railway from St. John's to Port-aux-Basques, the "Newfie Bullet", is completed.
1902	*October 18* Britain permits Newfoundland's free trade agreement with the United States.
1904	*July 9* French government relinquishes rights over part of the Newfoundland coast.
1905	*March* United States Congress cancels free trade with Newfoundland.
	June 15 Newfoundland prohibits sale of bait and fishing licences to foreign fishing vessels.
1908	*November 3* Fishermen's Protective Union is formed at Herring Cove.
1910	*September 7* Hague Tribunal rules Newfoundland may regulate fisheries in its territorial waters including three nautical miles outside a straight line drawn across the mouths of its bays.
	Pulp and paper manufacturing is started at Grand Falls.
1917	*January 1* Prohibition is in effect.
1919	Avalon Telephone Company is incorporated (later the Newfoundland Telephone Company).
1923	Newfoundland offers to sell Labrador to Canada for $30 million, later lowered to $15 million.
	Newfoundland government takes over the trans-island railway, essential steamship and telegraph services.
1925	Newfoundland ends Prohibition in favour of government control and sale of liquor.
	April 25 Women over 25 gain right to vote in Newfoundland.
	Memorial University College is founded and opens its doors *September 15*.
1926	British government grants Newfoundland dominion status.
1927	*March 1* Judicial Committee of the British Privy Council settles a long-standing dispute between Quebec and Newfoundland by giving Labrador to Newfoundland; it establishes the boundary between Canada and Labrador.
1928	Mining of base metals is started at Buchans.
1929	*November 18* Earthquake and tidal wave in Burin Peninsula sweeps away houses and boats; 27 dead.
1930	First Canadian talking movie, *The Vikings*, is made about Newfoundland's sealing industry.
1932	*March 5* House of Assembly is attacked by ca. 10,000 demanding investigation into government corruption.
	Newfoundland offers to sell Labrador to Canada for $110 million.
1933	Newfoundland government is bankrupt.
	December 2 Newfoundland loses its dominion status; the constitution is suspended and it reverts to a crown colony.

1934	*February 16* Newfoundland is governed by a Commission of Government appointed by Britain, composed of a governor, three Newfoundlanders, and three others.
1935	Gander is selected by British and Canadian governments to accommodate regular transatlantic flights.
	Public Libraries Act is passed.
1939–1945	World War II brings prosperity because of construction and maintenance of large defence bases at Argentia, Gander, Goose Bay, St. John's, and Stephenville.
1940	*September* Britain-United States agreement allows three United States military bases to be established in Newfoundland; an economic boom ensues.
1941	*August 14* Atlantic Charter is signed by Winston Churchill and Franklin Roosevelt at Placentia Bay.
1942	*February 18* Residents of Chamber's Cove and nearby communities save 180 from three storm-tossed, grounded United States warships; two ships sink, 300 dead.
	September 4 German submarines sink two ships loading iron ore at Bell Island.
	October 14 Newfoundland-Nova Scotia ferry, *Caribou*, is sunk by German submarines; 136 dead.
	December 12 Arson fire at the Knights of Columbus hostel in St. John's kills 99, the most deadly structural fire in Canada.
1943	Secret German naval mission establishes a battery-operated automatic weather station at Martin Bay.
1945	*December* British government announces an elected National Convention of Newfoundlanders to make suggestions about future government.
1946	*October* Joseph Smallwood's motion to the National Convention to send a delegation to Ottawa is defeated.
	Commission of Government declares union with the United States is outside the National Convention's terms of reference.
	British state an independent Newfoundland can expect no assistance.
1948	*March 11* British announce referendum choices: Commission of Government to continue for five years, confederation with Canada, or responsible government.
	June 3 No clear choice emerges in the referendum.
	July 14 Six Royal Air Force Vampires land at Goose Bay, completing the first Atlantic crossing by jet-propelled aircraft.
	July 22 Second referendum brings vote for confederation with Canada.
	December 11 Terms of union with Canada are signed to take effect *March 31, 1949.*
1949	*July 13* First legislature of the province of Newfoundland and Labrador opens in St. John's.
1950s	Exploration of natural resources leads to a mining industry.
1950	*August 1* Royal Canadian Mounted Police absorbs the Newfoundland Rangers and assumes policing of the province.
1953	Resettlement program begins involving the relocation of communities that lack health, education, and other facilities.
1954	Sir Richard Squires Memorial Park is established as the first Newfoundland and Labrador provincial park.
1955	Province's first television station, CJON, starts.
1956	Humbermouth, Townsite, Corner Brook West, and Curling are incorporated as the city of Corner Brook.
1957	*June* Conne River Indian Reserve, the only Indian reserve in the province, is

established when the province transfers 26.9 sq. km. (2.1 sq. mi.) to the Conne River Band.

1958 *July 1* Federal-provincial hospital plan goes into effect in Newfoundland and Labrador.

1959 *February 16* Province's worst blizzard leaves six dead and 70,000 without power; roads are blocked with 5 m. (16.4 ft.) drifts.

1960 *April 20* Newfoundland and Labrador legislature holds its first session in the new Confederation Building.

1961 *June 23* Forest fires in Bonavista Bay leave 3,000 homeless.
October 9 Memorial University College becomes Memorial University.

1962 *September 3* TransCanada Highway from St. John's to Victoria, British Columbia, opens, 7,821 km. (4,860 mi.).

1965 *March 8* Provincial government announces free tuition for all Newfoundland and Labrador students enrolled at Memorial University, the first province to take this step.
Paved highway across Newfoundland is completed.

1966 *October 6* Agreement is reached between Hydro-Quebec and British Newfoundland Corporation that Quebec will subsidize the development of Churchill Falls and buy all surplus power at a fixed rate for 40 years (negotiations between Newfoundland and Quebec are not completed until 1969).

1967 *September 5* Czech airliner crashes near Gander killing 35 people.

1968 *June* Grenfell Mission's services to northern Newfoundland and Labrador end.

1969 *April 15* "Newfie Bullet" train operations are replaced by buses.
May 4 Federal government bans fishing in Placentia Bay because of pollution.

1971 *February 10* Federal government establishes quotas for seal hunt that affect Newfoundland and Labrador.

1972 *April 24* Fishing off Port-aux-Basques is banned temporarily as a measure to conserve stocks.
June 16 Churchill Falls power project is inaugurated.

1973 Oil refinery at Come By Chance begins production (declared bankrupt *March 12, 1976*).

1975 Province appoints Ambrose Peddle as its first and only ombudsman.

1977 Federal government declares 200 mi. (322 km.) sovereignty off Canada's coasts which includes 95% of Grand Banks.

1978 *September 5* Hurricane Ella with winds exceeding 220 kph (136.7 mph) hits Newfoundland.
October 25 Discovery of Spanish galleon sunk off Labrador in 1525 is announced.

1979 *July 13* Ca. 133 pothead whales beach themselves at Point au Gaul; efforts to tow them out to sea are unsuccessful.
First commercial discovery of hydrocarbons beneath continental shelf leads to the Hibernia oil development.

1980 *July 21* Fishing industry is shut down completely by strikes, lockouts, and layoffs leaving 35,000 without work.

1982 *February 15 Ocean Ranger,* the world's largest submersible drill rig, sinks during a storm on the Grand Banks; 84 dead.

1983 *February 17* Newfoundland Supreme Court rules against Newfoundland in its dispute with the federal government over offshore mineral rights.
Stephenville is designated as Canada's first international trade zone.

1984 *March 8* Supreme Court of Canada rules that the federal government controls offshore mineral rights.

April 11–14 Ice storm in Avalon Peninsula leaves 200,000 people without electricity.

December 11 Federal and Newfoundland governments agree on control and sharing of offshore oil and gas reserves.

1985 *February 10* Canada-Newfoundland Development Fund is established to finance major offshore projects.

December 12 Airplane carrying United States military personnel crashes at Gander Airport killing 258, the worst air disaster on Canadian soil.

1986 Canada closes its ports to European Community fishing vessels to discourage overfishing.

1987 *January 29* Federal government apologizes to Newfoundland for not consulting it when discussing disputed maritime boundaries with France.

1988 *July 18* Federal and Newfoundland governments and a five-oil-company consortia sign an agreement to develop the Hibernia oil field. (Further deal signed *September 14, 1990* involves only four oil companies.)

Innu in Labrador stage sit-ins at local air force base to protest NATO low-level training flights.

1989–1990 Several fish processing plants close because of reduced fishing quotas eliminating many jobs.

1990 *March* Office of Ombudsman is abolished for budgetary reasons.

June 22 Meech Lake agreement fails when Premier Clyde Wells declines to put it to a legislative vote.

1992 *February 24* Domestic cod quotas cut by 35%.

March 6 Commercial salmon fishing is banned for five years.

March 27 Fishermen protest for four days against foreign vessels continuing to fish on Grand Banks outside Canadian territory.

June 30 School tax and school tax authorities are abolished.

July 2 Federal government shuts down northern cod fisheries for two years; 20,000 lose jobs.

September 15 European Economic Community members close fishery outside Canada's territorial waters.

1993 *January* Federal government and some new partners revive the Hibernia project.

Further closures of fisheries and fish plants are announced.

1994 *September 27* American forces leave Argentia, the last major American military base in Canada.

Culture and Education

Performing Arts Newfoundland and Labrador has 12 professional performing arts companies, 10 amateur theatre companies, and many festivals. The major organizations and events are:

Newfoundland and Labrador Folk Festival, St. John's (August)	(709)576-8508
Newfoundland Symphony Orchestra, St. John's	(709)753-6492
Rising Tide Theatre Company, St. John's	(709)753-6905 or (709)576-3867
South Shore Folk Festival, Ferryland (July) (Irish heritage)	(709)432-2820
Stephenville Festival, Stephenville (summer theatre)	(709)643-4445
Theatre Newfoundland and Labrador, Corner Brook	(709)939-7238

Provincial Museums and Galleries The following are major institutions.

Labrador Heritage Museum, Happy Valley-Goose Bay

Memorial University Art Gallery, St. John's

Newfoundland and Labrador Museum of Transportation, St. John's

Newfoundland Museum, St. John's, and its branches in other centres

Piulimatsivik-Nain Museum, Nain

University

Memorial University of Newfoundland, St. John's

Colleges of Applied Arts, Technology and Continuing Education (* indicates additional campuses in other centres)

Cabot College, St. John's*

Central Newfoundland Regional College, Grand Falls-Windsor*

Eastern Regional College, Clarenville*

Labrador College, Happy Valley*

Westviking College, Stephenville*

Miscellaneous Educational Institutions

Fisher Institute of Applied Arts and Technology, Corner Brook

Sir Wilfred Grenfell College, Corner Brook

Motor Vehicle Use

Motor Vehicles Registered for Use in Newfoundland and Labrador (1993): 397,210

Drivers Licensed by Newfoundland and Labrador (1993): 336,958. Minimum driving age: 17

Roads Paved highways: 6,500 km. (4,039 mi.); unpaved roads: 2,400 km. (1,491 mi.); bridges maintained by the province: 850

Speed Limits TransCanada highway: 100 kph (62 mph) with paved shoulder, 90 kph (56 mph) without paved shoulder; trunk roads: 80–90 kph (50–56 mph); secondary roads: 70–80 kph (43–50 mph); local roads: 50–60 kph (31–37 mph); gravel roads: 60 kph (37 mph) or less

First, Biggest, and Best

North America's largest island: Newfoundland 108,857.2 sq. km. (42,030 sq. mi.)

American continent's first English-speaking colony: 1583 founded by Humphrey Gilbert

North America's oldest settlement continuously inhabited by Europeans: St. John's established as a shore base for English fishermen in 1504

North America's closest city to Europe: St. John's

World's longest sea-fogs: Grand Banks average visibility less than 915 m. (3,000 ft.) more than 120 days per year

World's only fully preserved sixteenth-century Basque fishing vessel: Basque Whaling Archaeological Site, Red Bay

Western world's largest single-site hydroelectric power station: Churchill Falls

North America's first court of admiralty: established at Trinity by Richard Whitbourne in 1615

North America's oldest regiment: Royal Newfoundland Regiment, 1708

World's first nonstop transatlantic flight: June 15, 1919, John Williams Alcock and Arthur Whitton Brown from St. John's to Clinton, Ireland

World's first transatlantic wireless message: received by Guglielmo Marconi at St. John's, December 12, 1901

World's first successful laying of a transatlantic submarine cable for telegraphic purposes: Heart's Cove from Valencia, Ireland, 1858; first message sent on August 16
World's first aerial survey: timber survey of Labrador, August 1919
North America's first smallpox vaccination: administered by John Clinch in Trinity, 1800
North America's first child born of European parents: Snorri, child of Thorfin and Gudrid born near L'Anse aux Meadows ca. 1000
First letter sent from North America: letter from John Rut in St. John's to King Henry VIII on August 31, 1527
North America's oldest continuous sporting event: St. John's Regatta, first formal race September 22, 1818, but can be traced continuously from 1828
World's largest caribou herd: northern Labrador
North America's first book of verse: *Quodlibets* by Robert Hayman written while governor of Harbour Grace, 1618–1628, published in London 1628

Sources of Information About Newfoundland and Labrador

Newfoundland Information Service: P.O. Box 8700, St. John's, NF A1B 4J6 (709)729-3610
Department of Tourism and Culture: P.O. Box 8730, St. John's, NF A1B 4K2 (709)729-2830, 800-563-6353
Newfoundland and Labrador government publications can be obtained from the Queen's Printer: P.O. Box 8700, Confederation Building, St. John's, NF A1B 4J6 (709)729-3649

Books About Newfoundland and Labrador: A Selected List

Reference Guides

Anderson, T.C. *The Rivers of Labrador* (1985).
Atlantic Provinces Economic Council. *Atlantic Canada Today* (1987).
Burrows, Roger. *A Birdwatchers Guide to Atlantic Canada. Vol. 1, Offshore Islands, Pelagic Ferries, Newfoundland & Labrador* (1981).
Canada. Atmospheric Environment Service. *Canadian Climate Normals, 1961–1990: Atlantic Provinces* (1993).
Canada. Energy, Mines and Resources Canada. *Gazetteer of Canada: Newfoundland* (2nd ed. 1983).
Carignan, Paul. *Beothuck Archaeology in Bonavista Bay* (1977).
Cell, Gillian T. (ed.). *Newfoundland Discovered: English Attempts at Colonization, 1610–1630* (1982). Documents.
Chan, Margaret (comp.). *A Guide to the Government Records of Newfoundland* (1983).
Clarke, Sandra. *North-West River (Sheshatshit) Montagnais: A Grammatical Sketch* (1982).
Collins, Michael. *Life on the Newfoundland Seashore: Seaweeds, Invertebrates and Fish* (1993).

Cooke, Alan and Fabien Caron (comps.). *Bibliography of the Quebec-Labrador Peninsula*, 2 vols. (1968).
Cuff, Robert H. (ed.). *Dictionary of Newfoundland and Labrador Biography* (1990).
De Leon, Lisa. *Writers of Newfoundland and Labrador: Twentieth Century* (1985).
Ellison, Suzanne. *Historical Directory of Newfoundland and Labrador Newspapers, 1807–1987* (1989).
Encyclopedia of Newfoundland and Labrador, 5 vols. (1981–1994).
Fleming, Patricia Lockhart. *Atlantic Canadian Imprints, 1801–1820: A Bibliography* (1991).
Harrington, Michael. *Prime Ministers of Newfoundland* (rev. ed. 1991).
Laugher, Charles T. *Atlantic Province Authors of the Twentieth Century: A Bio-bibliographical Checklist* (1982).
Markham, W.E. *Ice Atlas: Eastern Canadian Seaboard* (1981).
Matthews, K.A. *"Who Was Who" of Families Engaged in Fishery and Settlement of Newfoundland, 1660–1840* (1971).
McManus, Gary E. and Clifford H. Wood. *Atlas of Newfoundland and Labrador* (1991).

Morley, William F.E. *The Atlantic Provinces: Newfoundland, Nova Scotia, New Brunswick, Prince Edward Island* (1967). A bibliography.

O'Dea, Agnes C. (comp.). *Bibliography of Newfoundland*, 2 vols. (1986).

Peters, Harold S. and Thomas D. Burleigh. *The Birds of Newfoundland* (1951).

Prowse, D.W. *A History of Newfoundland From the English, Colonial and Foreign Records* (1895, rpt. 1972).

Reeves, John. *History of the Government of the Island of Newfoundland, With an Appendix Containing the Acts of Parliament Made Respecting the Trade and Fishery* (1793, rpt. 1967).

Robertson, A., Stuart Porter, and George Brodie (eds.). *Climate and Weather of Newfoundland and Labrador* (1993).

Samuelson, Karl. *Fourteen Men Who Figured Prominently in the Story of Newfoundland and Labrador* (1984).

Scott, W.B. and M.G. Scott. *Atlantic Fishes of Canada* (1988).

Seary, E.R. *Place Names of the Avalon Peninsula of the Island of Newfoundland* (1971).

—— with Sheila M.P. Lynch. *Family Names of the Island of Newfoundland* (1977).

Sterns, Maurice A. with Philip Hiscock and Bruce Daley. *Newfoundland and Labrador Social Science Research: A Select Annotated Bibliography* (1975).

Story, G.M., W.J. Kirwin, and J.D.A. Widdowson (eds.). *Dictionary of Newfoundland English* (2nd ed. 1990).

Summers, William F. and Mary E. Summers. *Geography of Newfoundland* (1972).

Taft, Michael. *A Regional Discography of Newfoundland and Labrador, 1904–1972* (1975).

Todd, W.E. Clyde. *Birds of the Labrador Peninsula and Adjacent Areas: A Distributional List* (1963).

Wheeler, E.P. *List of Labrador Eskimo Place Names* (1953).

White, Jack A. *The Streets of St. John's*, 2 vols. (1989–1990).

Nonfiction Sources

Alexander, David. *The Decay of Trade: An Economic History of the Newfoundland Saltfish Trade, 1935–1965* (1977).

Alexander, David G. *Atlantic Canada and Confederation: Essays in Canadian Political Economy* (1983).

Andrews, Ralph L. *Integration and Other Developments in Newfoundland Education, 1915–1949* (1985).

——. *Post-Confederation Developments in Newfoundland Education, 1949–1975* (1985).

Andrieux, J.P. *Newfoundland's Cod War: Canada or France?* (1987).

Baker, Melvin. *Aspects of Nineteenth Century St. John's Municipal History* (1982).

Banfill, B.J. *Labrador Nurse* (1952).

Barbour, Florence Grant. *Memories of Life on the Labrador and in the North* (1973).

Ben-Dor, Shmuel. *Makkovik: Eskimos and Settlers in a Labrador Community: A Contrastive Study in Adaptation* (1966).

Bennett, Margaret. *The Last Stronghold: Scottish Gaelic Traditions in Newfoundland* (1987).

Brice-Bennett, Carol. *Our Footsteps Are Everywhere: Inuit Land Use and Occupancy in Labrador* (1977).

Brown, Cassie. *Death on the Ice: The Great Newfoundland Sealing Disaster of 1914* (1972, rpt. 1988).

——. *Standing Into Danger: A Dramatic Story of Shipwreck and Rescue* (1979).

Brox, Ottar. *Newfoundland Fishermen in the Age of Industry: A Sociology of Economic Dualism* (1972).

Brym, Robert J. and R. James Sacouman (eds.). *Underdevelopment and Social Movements in Atlantic Canada* (1979).

Buckner, Phillip A. and David Frank (eds.). *Atlantic Canada Before Confederation* (2nd ed. 1990).

Buckner, Phillip A. and John G. Reid (eds.). *The Atlantic Region to Confederation: History* (1994).

Butler, Gary R. *Saying Isn't Believing: Conversational Narrative and the Discourse of Tradition in a French-Newfoundland Community* (1990).

Butler, Victor. *The Little Nord Easter: Reminiscences of a Placentia Bayman* (1975, rpt. 1980).

Candow, James E. *Of Men and Seals: A History of the Newfoundland Seal Hunt* (1989).

Cardoulis, John N. *A Friendly Invasion: The American Military in Newfoundland, 1940–1990* (1990).

Carleton University. History Collaborative. *Urban and Community Development in Atlantic Canada, 1968–1991* (1993).

Cell, Gillian T. *English Enterprise in Newfoundland, 1577–1660* (1969).

Channing, J.G. *The Effects of Transition to Confederation on Public Administration in Newfoundland* (1982).

Clark, Rex (ed.). *Contrary Winds: Essays on Newfoundland Society in Crisis* (1986).

Cochrane, Candace. *Outport: Reflections From the Newfoundland Coast* (1981).

Codignola, Luca. *The Coldest Harbour in the Land: Simon Stock and Lord Baltimore's Colony in Newfoundland, 1621–1649* (1988).

Coish, E. Calvin. *Distant Shores: Pages From Newfoundland's Past* (1994).

——. *Season of the Seal: The International Storm Over Canada's Seal Hunt* (1979).

Davies, Gwendolyn (ed.). *Myth and Milieu: Atlantic Literature and Culture 1918–1939* (1993).

Davies, K.G. with A.M. Johnson (eds.). *Northern Quebec and Labrador Journals and Correspondence, 1819–35* (1963).

De Boileau, Lambert. *Recollections of Labrador Life* (1861, ed. by Thomas F. Bredin, 1969).

De Volpi, Charles P. *Newfoundland, a Pictorial Record: Historical Prints and Illustrations of the Province of Newfoundland, Canada, 1497–1887* (1972).

Diack, Lesley. *Labrador Nurse* (1963).

Doel, Priscilla. *Port O'Call: Memories of the Portuguese White Fleet in St. John's, Newfoundland* (1992).

Fardy, B.D. *Demsduit: Native Newfoundlander* (1988).

——. *Under Two Flags: The French-English Struggle for Newfoundland, 1696–1796* (1987).

Faris, James C. *Cat Harbour: A Newfoundland Fishing Settlement* (1972).

Feltham, John. *Bonavista Bay Revisited* (1992).

Fitzgerald, Jack. *Strange But True Newfoundland Stories* (1989).

Fleming, Berkeley, (ed.). *Beyond Anger and Longing: Community Development in Atlantic Canada* (1988).

Forbes, Ernest R. and D.A. Mulse (eds.). *The Atlantic Provinces in Confederation* (1993).

Galgay, Frank and Michael McCarthy. *Shipwrecks of Newfoundland and Labrador*, 2 vols. (1987–1990).

Gobineau, Joseph Arthur de. *A Gentleman in the Outports: Gobineau and Newfoundland* (ed. by Michael Wiltshire, 1993).

Goudie, Elizabeth. *Women of Labrador* (1973, rpt. 1983).

Goulding, Jay. *The Last Outport: Newfoundland in Crisis* (1982).

Graham, Frank W. *"We Love Thee Newfoundland": Biography of Sir Cavendish Boyle, K.C.M.G., Governor of Newfoundland, 1901–1904* (1991).

Greene, John P. *Trial and Triumph: The History of Newfoundland and Labrador* (1982).

Grenfell, Sir Wilfred Thomason. *The Best of Wilfred Grenfell* (selected by William Pope, 1990).

——. *A Labrador Doctor: The Autobiography of Sir Wilfred Thomason Grenfell* (1919, rpt. 1961).

Guihan, Bill. *Sketches of the Old City: An Introduction to the History and Architecture of St. John's* (1988).

Gunn, Gertrude E. *The Political History of Newfoundland, 1832–1864* (1966, rpt. 1977).

Gwyn, Richard. *Smallwood, the Unlikely Revolutionary* (rev. ed. 1972).

Halpert, Herbert and G.M. Story (eds.). *Christmas Mummery in Newfoundland: Essays in Anthropology, Folklore and History* (1969, rpt. 1990).

Handcock, W. Gordon. *Soe Longe As There Comes Noe Women: Origins of English Settlement in Newfoundland* (1989).

Harris, Michael. *Rare Ambition: The Crosbies of Newfoundland* (1992).

Head, C. Grant. *Eighteenth Century Newfoundland: A Geographer's Perspective* (1976).

Henriksen, Georg. *Hunter in the Barrens: The Naskapi on the Edge of the White Man's World* (1973).

Hiller, James and Peter Neary (eds.). *Newfoundland in the Nineteenth and Twentieth Centuries* (1980).

——. *Twentieth Century Newfoundland: Explorations* (1994).

Hodgson, Douglas. *Fishing Communities in Labrador and the Great Northern Peninsula of Newfoundland North of 50* (1991).

Hornung, Rick. *The Edge of Time: A Journey in Search of Labrador* (1993).

Horwood, Harold. *Corner Brook: A Social History of a Paper Town* (1986).

——. *The Foxes of Beachy Cove* (1967, rpt. 1975).

——. *Historic Newfoundland* (1986).

——. *Joey: The Life and Political Times of Joey Smallwood* (1989).

Hornung, Rick. *The Edge of Time: A Journey in Search of Labrador* (1993).

Houlihan, Eileen. *The Uprooted: The Argentia Story* (1992).

House, J.D. *The Challenge of Oil: Newfoundland's Quest for Controlled Development* (1985).

——. *Fish Versus Oil: Resources and Rural Development in North Atlantic Societies* (1986).

Hoy, Claire. *Clyde Wells: A Political Biography* (1992).

Hubbard, Mina. *A Woman's Way Through Unknown Labrador* (1981).

Ingstad, Anne Stine. *The Norse Discovery of America*, 2 vols. (1985).

Iverson, Noel and D.R. Matthews. *Communities in Decline: An Examination of Household Resettlement in Newfoundland* (1968).

Jackson, Douglas. *On the Country: The Micmacs of Newfoundland* (1993).

Jackson, F.L. *Surviving Confederation* (rev. ed. 1986; original title *Newfoundland in Canada*).

Jukes, J.B. *Excursions In and About Newfoundland*

During the Years 1839 and 1840, 2 vols. (1969).

Kahn, Alison. *Listen While I Tell You: A Story of the Jews of St. John's, Newfoundland* (1987).

Kealey, Linda (ed.). *Pursuing Equality: Historical Perspectives on Women in Newfoundland and Labrador* (1993).

Kennedy, John C. *Holding the Line: Ethnic Boundaries in a Northern Labrador Community* (1982).

Le Messurier, Sally Lou. *The Fishery of Newfoundland and Labrador* (1980).

Loder, Millicent Blake. *Daughter of Labrador* (1989).

Lounsbury, Ralph Greenlee. *The British Fishery in Newfoundland, 1634–1763* (1934, rpt. 1969).

Lysaght, A.M. *Joseph Banks in Newfoundland, 1766: His Diary, Manuscripts and Collections* (1971).

Macfarlane, David. *The Danger Tree: Memory, War, and the Search for a Family's Past* (1991; published in the United States as *Come From Away*).

MacKenzie, David. *Inside the Atlantic Triangle: Canada and the Entrance of Newfoundland into Confederation, 1939–1949* (1986).

MacKenzie Michael. *Glimpses of the Past: True Stories Old and New* (1984).

———. *Reflections of Yesteryear: True Stories Old and New* (1978).

MacLeod, Malcolm. *Peace of the Continent: The Impact of the Second World War and American Bases in Newfoundland* (1986).

MacNutt, W.S. *The Atlantic Provinces: The Emergence of a Colonial Society, 1712–1857* (1965).

Mannion, John J. (ed.). *The Peopling of Newfoundland: Essays in Historical Geography* (1977).

Marshall, Ingeborg C.L. *Reports and Letters by George Christopher Pulling Relating to the Beothuk Indians of Newfoundland* (1989).

Martin, Cabot. *No Fish in Our Lives: Some Survival Notes For Newfoundland* (1992).

Matthews, Keith. *Lectures on the History of Newfoundland, 1500–1830* (1973, rpt. 1988).

Matthews, Ralph. *"There's No Better Place Than Here": Social Change in Three Newfoundland Communities* (1976).

McCann, Larry and Carrie MacMillan (eds.). *The Sea and Culture of Atlantic Canada: A Multidisciplinary Sampler* (1992).

McCann, Phillip. *Blackboards and Briefcases: Personal Stories of Newfoundland Teachers, Educators and Administrators* (1982).

McDonald, Ian D.H. *"To Each His Own": William Coaker and the Fishermen's Protective Union in Newfoundland Politics, 1908–1925* (1987).

McGee, Harold Franklin (ed.). *The Native Peoples of Atlantic Canada: A History of Indian-European Relations* (1972).

Merrick, Elliott. *Northern Nurse* (1942, rpt. 1994).

———. *True North* (1933, rpt. 1989).

Momatiuk, Yva and John Eastcott. *This Marvellous Terrible Place: Images of Newfoundland and Labrador* (1988).

Mowat, Claire. *The Outport People* (1983).

Mowat, Farley. *New Founde Land* (1968, rpt. 1989).

———. *This Rock Within the Sea: A Heritage Lost* (1968, rpt. 1976).

———. *The Wake of the Great Sealers* (1973).

———. *A Whale for the Killing* (1972, rpt. 1981).

Moyles, R.G. *"Complaints Is Many and Various, But the Odd Divil Likes It": Nineteenth Century Views of Newfoundland* (1975).

Murphy, Tony. *War at Our Doorstep: St. John's During World War II: An Album* (1989).

——— and Paul Kenny. *The Trail of the Caribou* (1991). Newfoundland in World War I.

Murray, Hilda Chaulk. *More the Fifty Percent: Woman's Life in a Newfoundland Outport, 1900–1950* (1979).

Nadel-Klein, Jane and Donna Lee Davis. *To Work and to Weep: Women in the Fishing Economies* (1988).

Neary, Peter. *Newfoundland in the North Atlantic World, 1929–1949* (1988).

———. (ed.). *The Political Economy of Newfoundland, 1929–1972* (1973).

——— and Patrick O'Flaherty. *Part of the Main: An Illustrated History of Newfoundland and Labrador* (1983).

Noel, S.J.R. *Politics in Newfoundland* (1971).

O'Brien, Patricia (ed.). *The Grenfell Obsession: An Anthology* (1992).

O'Flaherty, Patrick. *The Rock Observed: Studies in the Literature of Newfoundland* (1979).

O'Neill, Paul. *The Story of St. John's, Newfoundland*, 2 vols. (1975–1976).

Paddon, Harold G. *Green Woods and Blue Waters: Memories of Labrador* (1989).

Paddon, W.A. *Labrador Doctor: My Life With the Grenfell Mission* (1989).

Paine, Robert (ed.). *Patrons and Brokers in the East Arctic* (1971).

Pastore, Ralph T. *Shananditti's People: The Archaeology of the Beothuks* (1992).

Peckford, A. Brian. *The Past in the Present: A Personal Perspective on Newfoundland's Future* (1983).

Perkins, Robert F. *Against Straight Lines: Alone in Labrador* (1983).

Philbrook, Tom. *Fisherman, Logger, Merchant, Miner: Social Change and Industrialism in Three Newfoundland Communities* (1966).

Plaice, Evelyn. *The Native Game: Settler Percep-*

tions of Indian/Settler Relations in Central Labrador (1990).

Pocius, Gerald L. *A Place to Belong: Community, Order, and Everyday Space in Calvert, Newfoundland* (1991).

Poole, George. *A Lifetime Listening to the Waves: Memories of a Labrador Fisherman* (1987).

Pottle, Herbert L. *Fun on the Rock: Toward a Theory of Newfoundland Humour* (1983).

Powell, Ben. *Labrador By Choice* (1984).

——. *Trapline: The Story of Danny* (1990).

Power, Thomas P. (ed.). *The Irish in Atlantic Canada, 1780–1900* (1991).

Proulx, Jean-Pierre. *Basque Whaling in Labrador in the 16th Century* (1992).

Rawlyk, George A. (ed.). *Historical Essays on the Atlantic Provinces* (1967).

Richards, J.T. *Snapshots of Grenfell* (1989).

Rolfe, Hedley. *Water Down My Neck: Memoirs of an Outport Doctor* (1992).

Rompkey, Ronald. *Grenfell of Labrador: A Biography* (1991).

Rowe, Frederick W. *Education and Culture in Newfoundland* (1976).

——. *Extinction: The Beothuks of Newfoundland* (1977).

——. *A History of Newfoundland and Labrador* (1980).

——. *Into the Breach: Memoirs of a Newfoundland Senator* (1988).

——. *The Smallwood Era* (1985).

Russell, Franklin. *The Secret Islands* (1965).

Ryan, Shannon. *Fish Out of the Water: The Newfoundland Saltfish Trade, 1814–1914* (1986).

Sager, Eric W. with Gerald E. Panting. *Maritime Capital: The Shipping Industry in Atlantic Canada, 1820–1914* (1990).

Samson, Daniel (ed.). *Contested Countryside: Rural Workers and Modern Society in Atlantic Canada, 1800–1950* (1994).

Saunders, Gary L. *Rattles and Steadies: Memoirs of a Gander River Man* (1986).

Sider, Gerald M. *Culture and Class in Anthropology and History: A Newfoundland Illustration* (1986).

Sinclair, Peter R. *From Traps to Draggers: Domestic Commodity Production in Northwest Newfoundland, 1850–1982* (1985).

—— (ed.). *A Question of Survival: The Fisheries and Newfoundland Society* (1988).

Smallwood, Joseph R. *I Chose Canada: The Memoirs of the Honourable Joseph R. "Joey" Smallwood* (1973).

——. *The Time Has Come to Tell* (1967, rpt. 1979).

Smith, Ed. *Some Fine Times!* (1991). Memoir of growing up in Newfoundland.

Such, Peter. *Vanished Peoples: The Archaic Dorset & Beothuk People of Newfoundland* (1978).

Taylor, Stephen and Harold Horwood. *Beyond the Road: Portraits & Visions of Newfoundlanders* (1976).

Thomas, Gerald and J.D.A. Widdowson (eds.). *Studies in Newfoundland Folklore: Community and Process* (1991).

Thomas, Gordon W. *From Sled to Satellite: My Years With the Grenfell Mission* (1987).

Thompson, Robert. *"Persistence and Change": The Social and Economic Development of Rural Newfoundland and Labrador, 1971–1981* (1983).

Tuck, James A. *Ancient People of Port au Choix: The Excavation of an Archaic Indian Cemetery in Newfoundland* (1976, rpt. 1993).

——. *Newfoundland and Labrador Prehistory* (1977).

Wadden, Marie. *Nitassinan: The Innu Struggle to Reclaim Their Homeland* (1991).

Wadel, Cato. *Marginal Adaptations and Modernization in Newfoundland: A Study of Strategies and Implications of Resettlement and Redevelopment of Outport Fishing Communities* (1969).

Walker, Mary. *The Lady and the Trapper* (1991).

Wallace, Dillon. *The Lure of the Labrador Wild* (1905, rpt. 1990).

Whiffen, Bruce. *Prime Berth: An Account of Bonavista's Early Years* (1993).

Whiteley, George. *Northern Seas, Hardy Sailors* (1982).

Williamson, Eileen M. *Outport: A Newfoundland Journal* (1980).

Winter, Keith. *Shananditti: The Last of the Beothuks* (1975).

Woodford, Paul. *"We Love the Place, Oh Lord": A History of the Written Musical Tradition of Newfoundland and Labrador to 1949* (1988).

Wright, Guy David. *Sons and Seals: A Voyage on the Ice* (1986).

Zimmerly, David. *Cain's Land Revisited: Culture Change in Central Labrador, 1775–1972* (1975).

Newfoundland and Labrador in Literature

Baksh, Ishmael. *Black Light* (1988). An East Indian immigrant from Trinidad adjusts to a new culture in St. John's.

Batstone, Bert. *The Mysterious Mummer and Other Newfoundland Stories* (1984).

Beahan, G. *Hard Target* (1990). A comic novel about oil exploration in Newfoundland.

Bird, Will R. *Angel Cove* (1972). Nineteen short stories set in an outport.

—— (ed.). *Atlantic Anthology* (1959).

Bice, Clare. *The Great Island: A Story of Mystery in Newfoundland* (1954).

Choyce, Lesley (ed.). *Chezzetcook: An Anthology of Contemporary Poetry and Fiction From Atlantic Canada* (1977).

Clark, Joan. *Eiriksdottir: A Tale of Dreams and Luck: A Novel* (1994). Historical fiction about Eric the Red's daughter who led an expedition to Newfoundland.

Davidson, James West and John Rugge. *Great Heart: The History of a Labrador Adventure* (1988). Based on expeditions made in 1903 and 1905.

Dodds, Donald G. *A Long Night in Codroy* (1992). A collection of yarns from the Codroy Valley.

Dohaney, M.T. *The Corrigan Women* (1988). Three generations of women in a rugged coastal village.

——. *To Scatter Stones* (1992). A Newfoundland woman eventually returns to win an election as a Liberal candidate in a traditionally Conservative constituency.

Duley, Margaret. *Cold Pastoral* (1939, rpt. 1977); *The Eyes of the Gull* (1939, rpt. 1976); *Highway to Valour* (1941, rpt. 1977). Newfoundland setting portrayed vividly.

Duncan, Norman. *The Way of the Sea* (1903, rpt. 1982). Short stories explore outport life.

Finn, Tom. *Prince* (1991). Stories about the fictional Prince family of pre-Confederation Bonavista Bay.

Fisk, Alan. *The Strange Things of the World: A Historical Novel* (1988). Based on Thomas Buts voyage to Newfoundland in 1536.

Fletcher, Peggy. *When the Moon is Full* (1977). Fifteen stories in rural Newfoundland settings.

Fraser, Raymond, Clyde Rose, and Jim Stewart (eds.). *East of Canada: An Atlantic Anthology* (1976).

Garrett, Helen. *The Brothers From North Bay* (1966).

Gough, Helen. *Maud's House* (1984). A woman who defies convention is ostracized by an outport community.

Gough, William. *Chips and Gravey: A Ghostly Love Story* (1991). A story about an outport youth's love for the ghost of a country singer.

Grenfell, Sir Wilfred Thomason. *Labrador Days: Tales of the Sea Toilers* (1919, rpt. 1971).

Guy, Ray. *Beneficial Vapours* (1981). Boyhood experiences of a merchant's son in Placentia Bay.

—— (comp.). *That Far Greater Bay* (rev. ed. 1985). Writings about Newfoundland.

Hambling, Jack. *Stage Heads and Warm Dandelions* (1985). Stories set in Newfoundland.

Hill, Douglas. *The Second Trap* (1982). A student doing field research in a small village learns that violence lurks beneath the quiet surface of the community.

Horwood, Harold. *Tomorrow Will Be Sunday* (1966, rpt. 1992); *Remembering Summer* (1987). Scandal in an outport leads to a trial; followed by a novel about the protagonist as a young man.

——. *White Eskimo: A Novel of Labrador* (1972). Based on a legendary blond hunter.

Janes, Percy. *Eastmall* (1982). A municipal dump in St. John's causes local concern.

——. *House of Hate* (1970, rpt. 1990). A domineering father in Corner Brook has a corrosive effect on his children.

——. *Newfoundlanders: Short Stories* (1981).

——. *No Cage for Conquerors: A Novel* (1984). Newfoundland setting.

——. *Requiem for a Faith: A Novel* (1984). Two generations of a Conception Bay farm family.

—— and Harry Cuff (eds.). *Twelve Newfoundland Short Stories* (1982).

Johnston, Wayne. *The Divine Ryans* (1990). A comic novel about an eccentric St. John's family.

——. *The Story of Bobby O'Malley* (1985, rpt. 1991). A fictional memoir of a Catholic boyhood in a Newfoundland town.

——. *The Time of Their Lives* (1987, rpt. 1991). A bitter patriarch destructively dominates his family in a small Newfoundland town.

Lannon, Alice and Mike McCarthy. *Fables, Fairies & Folklore of Newfoundland* (1991).

Moore, Tom. *Good-bye Momma* (1976, rpt. 1993). A boy in an outport copes with his father's remarriage after his mother's death.

Morgan, Bernice. *Random Passage* (1992); *Waiting For Time* (1993). The past and present is interwoven into this story of English immigrants in the Bonavista Peninsula in the 1800s.

——, Helen Porter, and Geraldine Rubia. *From This Place; A Selection of Writings by Women of Newfoundland and Labrador* (1977).

Murphy, Mike. *Ned 'n Me* (1986). A dockside observer chronicles the life in St. John's.

Neary, Peter and Patrick O'Flaherty. *By Great Waters: A Newfoundland and Labrador Anthology* (1974).

Norman, Eric, Stanley Sparkes, and June Warr. *Landings: A Newfoundland & Labrador Literature Anthology* (1984).

O'Flaherty, Patrick. *Priest of God* (1989). A doubting priest and an accidental death in a divided Newfoundland community.

——. *A Small Place in the Sun* (1989). Short stories mostly set in Newfoundland.

O'Neill, Paul. *Breakers: Stories From Newfoundland and Labrador* (1982).

——. *Legends of a Lost Tribe: Folk Tales of the Beothuk Indians of Newfoundland* (1976).

Peacock, F.W. *Labrador Inuit Lore and Legend* (1981).

Pinsent, Gordon. *John & the Missus: A Novel* (1974). Humour and pathos in a Newfoundland mining community.

——. *The Rowdyman: A Novel* (1973). A man makes his unpredictable, but charming way in Grand Falls and St. John's.

Pitman, Al. *The Boughwolfen and Other Stories* (1984). Fourteen short stories about the childhood world of working-class Newfoundland.

Pitt, David G. *Tales From the Outer Fringe: Five Stories and a Novella* (1990). Newfoundland outport life.

Porter, Helen Fogwell. *Hard Target* (1990). A comic novel about Newfoundland's oil patch.

——. *A Long and Lonely Ride* (1991). Short stories with a Newfoundland setting.

Roberts, T.G. *The Red Feathers* (1907, rpt. 1983). A romantic tale of Beothuk life.

Rose, Clyde (ed.). *Baffles of Wind and Tides: A Selection of Newfoundland Writings* (1974).

——. *The Blasty Bough* (1976). An anthology.

Rowe, William M. *Clapp's Rock* (1983). An ambitious man is involved in corrupt politics.

Roy, Gabrielle. *Windflower* (1970, rpt. 1991). The white and traditional worlds are explored as an Inuit woman in northern Labrador struggles to bring up her half-breed son.

Russell, Ted. *The Chronicles of Uncle Mose* (1975);

Tales From Pigeon Inlet (1977). Tales of outport life.

Ryan, D.W.S. (ed.). *Legends of Newfoundland & Labrador* (1990).

—— and T.P. Rossiter (eds.). *The Newfoundland Character: An Anthology of Newfoundland and Labrador Writings* (1987).

Salter, Robina. *Hannah: A Novel* (1986). A story about a midwife in the outports at the time of Newfoundland's confederation with Canada.

Scammell, Arthur Reginald. *My Newfoundland: Stories, Poems, Songs* (1966).

Schull, Joseph. *The Jinker* (1968). Newfoundland captains of two ships on a seal-hunting expedition in 1891.

Sellars, Walter. *Hard Aground* (1992). Three men in Labrador search for a submarine twenty years overdue.

Steffler, John. *The Afterlife of George Cartwright* (1992). Fiction based on an eighteenth-century English gentleman who spent almost sixteen years on the coast of Labrador.

Such, Peter. *Riverrun* (1973). Historical fiction about the last winter of the Beothuk Indians.

Thompson, Kent. *Stories From Atlantic Canada: A Selection* (1973).

Tucker, Otto. *A Collection of Stories* (1977).

A Way With Words: An Anthology for the Twentieth Anniversary of the Newfoundland Writers' Guild (1987).

White, Marian Frances (ed.). *"The Finest Kind": Voices of Newfoundland and Labrador Women* (1992).

NOVA SCOTIA

Nova Scotia, located in Atlantic Canada, includes the most easterly part of mainland North America, Cape Breton Island, and many smaller islands. With the exception of the Isthmus of Chignecto which joins it to New Brunswick, Nova Scotia is surrounded by water: on the north by the Gulf of St. Lawrence and Northumberland Strait; on the east and south by the Atlantic Ocean; on the west by the Bay of Fundy.

Name Province of Nova Scotia. "Nova Scotia" was named by William Alexander after Scotland, his homeland. *Previous name:* Acadia (to 1713).

Flag The blue cross of St. Andrew on a white background with a shield bearing the lion of Scottish kings in the middle. Granted by King Charles I in 1625.

Coat of Arms The content of the central shield is similar to the provincial flag and is supported on the left side by a royal unicorn and on the right by a North American Indian holding an arrow. The shield and supporters rest on a base of entwined Scottish thistles and mayflowers. Above the shield is a helm and two joined hands, one armoured, supporting a spray of laurel and thistle. A scroll with the provincial motto completes the top. First granted by King Charles I in 1625 and reinstated by King George V on January 19, 1929.

Motto *Munit Haec et Altera Vincit* (One defends and the other conquers).

Emblems
Flower mayflower or trailing arbutus (*Epigaea repens*)
Gemstone agate
Mineral stilbite

Tartan blue, white, green, red, and gold; the first provincial tartan in Canada (1956)
Tree red spruce (*Picea rubens*)

Date of Entry into Confederation July 1, 1867; one of the four original provinces in Confederation.

Official Language English.

Capital City Halifax, situated on a large east coast harbour, the largest city and principal port in Atlantic Canada; population 114,456, CMA population 332,501. The site, originally named Chebucto (Micmac for "great, long harbour"), was occupied by Micmac Indians and later the French. Halifax, the first permanent English-speaking settlement in Nova Scotia, was founded by Edward Cornwallis on June 21, 1749, and named for George Montagu Dunk, second Earl of Halifax, Chief Lord of Trade and Plantations. It was incorporated as a city April 10, 1841. On January 1, 1969, Halifax was enlarged by the annexation of five western suburbs.

Provincial Holidays There are no provincial holidays in addition to the national statutory holidays (see page 2).

Geography and Climate

Geography The Nova Scotia mainland with a deeply indented coastline and a series of ridges running through the centre of the province is an area of low relief. Fertile plains and river valleys are found on the slopes facing the Gulf of St. Lawrence and the Bay of Fundy. Cape Breton Island rising from lowlands in the south to a high plateau in the north is mostly a rugged area.

Area 55,490 sq. km. (21,425 sq. mi.); 0.6% of Canada. *Rank:* 9th among the provinces, 11th among the provinces and territories.

Inland Water 2,650 sq. km. (1,023 sq. mi.), includes more than 3,000 lakes. Largest lake: Bras d'Or Lake, a tidal saltwater lake, 1,150 sq. km. (444 sq. mi.).

Elevations Highest point: North Barren Mountain, 532 m. (1,745 ft.). Lowest point: coastline, sea level.

Major Rivers (* indicates a designated Canadian Heritage River): Annapolis, *Margaree, Medway, Mersey, *Shelburne, Shubenacadie, St. Mary's.

Climate Nova Scotia has a maritime climate modified by the surrounding waters: warmer in areas affected by the Gulf Stream, cooler where washed by the Atlantic Ocean or the Bay of Fundy. Winters are stormy on the Atlantic coast and there is extensive fog. Inland, summers are warmer and winters colder than coastal areas. The average daily mean temperature in January in Halifax is −3.1°C (26.4°F), in July 18.2°C (64.8°F). The lowest recorded temperature in Nova Scotia: −41.1°C (−42.0°F) at Upper Stewiacke on January 31, 1920; the highest recorded temperature 38.3°C (100.9°F) at Collegeville on August 19, 1935.

The average annual snowfall in Halifax is 271 cm. (107 in.); greatest recorded snowfall over five consecutive days, 122 cm. (48 in.) at Whitehead on March 3, 1916; greatest recorded annual snowfall, 653 cm. (257 in.) at Cheticamp, winter of 1964/65; greatest one-day snowfall, 69 cm. (27 in.) at Yarmouth on March 19, 1885.

The average annual precipitation in Halifax is 1,490.6 mm. (58.7 in.); greatest recorded Nova Scotia annual precipitation: 2,360 mm. (92.9 in.) at Wreck Cove Brook in 1983.

Time Zone Atlantic.

Parks and Historic Sites

National Parks Located in Nova Scotia

Park	Location	Size
Cape Breton Highlands	Ingonish Beach	951 sq. km. (367 sq. mi.)
Kejimkujik	Maitland Bridge	384 sq. km. (148 sq. mi.)

Provincial Parks There are 122 provincial parks covering almost 30,000 acres (121 sq. km.) including campsites, picnic, beach, roadside, wildlife, and historic parks, some combining two or three of these aspects. The largest parks are:

Park	County	Size
Dollar Lake	Halifax	2,949 acres
Taylor Head	Halifax	2,036 acres
Blomidon	Kings	1,875 acres
North River	Victoria	1,472 acres
Five Islands	Cumberland	1,020 acres
Amherst Shore	Cumberland	810 acres

Upper Clements	Annapolis	712 acres
Lawrencetown	Halifax	609 acres
Whycocomagh	Inverness	507 acres
Two Rivers	Cape Breton	470 acres

Nova Scotia has 8 national bird sanctuaries, 6 national wildlife areas, and 3 Ramsar sites.

Major National Historic Sites and Parks in Nova Scotia

Alexander Graham Bell, Baddeck
Fort Anne, Annapolis Royal
Fort Edward, Windsor
Fort McNab, Halifax
Fortress of Louisbourg, Louisbourg
Grassy Island, Canso
Grand-Pré, Grand-Pré

Halifax Citadel, Halifax
Marconi, Glace Bay
Port Royal, Granville Ferry
Prince of Wales Tower, Halifax
St. Peters Canal, St. Peters
York Redoubt, Halifax

In addition, there are a number of historic sites in Nova Scotia administered by the province, municipalities, or organizations. The major sites are:

Hector Heritage Quai, Pictou
Nova Scotia Highland Village, Iona

Demography

Nova Scotia Population: 899,942; 3.3% of national; *rank* 7th

Historical population data

1981	847,440
1971	788,960
1961	737,007
1951	642,584
1941	577,962
1921	523,837
1901	459,574
1881	440,572
1861	330,857

Population Density: 17.0 persons per sq. km. (44.1 per sq. mi.)

Number of Dwellings: 326,484

Indian Reserves: 13

Population Characteristics:
urban: 481,508; 53.5%
rural: 418,434; 46.5%
19 and under: 251,350; 27.9%
65 and over: 113,400; 12.6%
average income for full-time employment 15 years and over (1990): $30,841; men $35,841; women $23,828
average life expectancy at birth (1987): men 72.25 years; women, 79.20 years (lowest of the provinces)
live birth rate: 12,016; 13.4 per 1000
deaths: 7,255; 8.1 per 1000
marriages: 5,845; 6.5 per 1000
divorces: 2,280; 2.53 per 1000

Largest Cities and Towns *(for definitions of CMA and CA, see page viii)*

Name	Population	Dwellings	National Pop. Rank
Halifax	320,501 (CMA)	119,450	13
Sydney	116,100 (CA)	39,764	27
Truro	44,003 (CA)	16,285	62
New Glasgow	38,676 (CA)	13,826	69
Kentville	24,060 (CA)	8,901	93

Government and Politics, 1867–

A description of the division of powers between the federal and provincial governments will be found on page 4.

Lieutenant-Governor The Lieutenant-Governor is the nominal head of the Nova Scotia government, and is appointed by the Governor General of Canada on the recommendation of the Prime Minister of Canada. (A description of the duties of lieutenant-governors is found on page 7.)

Lieutenant-Governors of Nova Scotia	Term
Charles Hastings Doyle	1867–1873
Joseph Howe	1873
Adams George Archibald	1873–1883
Matthew Henry Richey	1883–1888
Archibald Woodbury McLelan	1888–1890
Malachy Bowes Daly	1890–1900
Alfred Gilpin Jones	1900–1906
Duncan Cameron Fraser	1906–1910
James Drummond McGregor	1910–1915
David McKeen	1915–1916
MacCallum Grant	1916–1925
James Robson Douglas	1925
James Cranswick Tory	1925–1930
Frank Stanfield	1930–1931
Walter Harold Covert	1931–1937
Robert Irwin	1937–1940
Frederick Francis Mathers	1940–1942
Henry Ernest Kendall	1942–1947
John Alexander Douglas McCurdy	1947–1952
Alistair Fraser	1952–1958
Edward Chester Plow	1958–1963
Henry Poole MacKeen	1963–1968
Victor deBedia Oland	1968–1973
Clarence Lloyd Gosse	1973–1978
John Elvin Schaffner	1978–1984
Alan Rockwell Abraham	1984–1989
Lloyd Roseville Crouse	1989–

House of Assembly The House of Assembly of Nova Scotia consists of 52 members elected by popular vote, each member representing a constituency; term of office: up to 5 years as long as the party in power maintains the confidence of the House of Assembly; remuneration (1993/4): $30,130 + $15,065 expense allowance, additional amounts for special appointments; qualifications for members: British subject, 19 years of age or older. (A description of the duties of provincial legislatures are found on page 7.)

Qualifications for Nova Scotia Voters in Provincial Elections Canadian citizen or British subject on polling day, 18 years of age or older on polling day, ordinarily resident in Nova Scotia for the six months immediately preceding the date of writ of election, in the polling division on the day of the writ, not legally disqualified, e.g., a returning officer, a prisoner in a penal institution.

Premier Nominally appointed by the Lieutenant-Governor of Nova Scotia, the Premier is generally the leader of the party with the majority of seats in the House of Assembly. (A description of the responsibilities of provincial premiers is found on page 7.)

Premiers of Nova Scotia/Party/Term
Hiram Blanchard
  (Liberal, 1867)
William Annand
  (Anti-Confederation, 1867–1875)
Philip Carteret Hill
  (Liberal, 1875–1878)
Simon Hugh Holmes
  (Conservative, 1878–1882)
John Sparrow David Thompson
  (Conservative, 1882)
William Thomas Pipes
  (Liberal, 1882–1884)
William Stevens Fielding
  (Liberal, 1884–1896)
George Henry Murray
  (Liberal, 1896–1923)
Ernest Howard Armstrong
  (Liberal, 1923–1925)
Edgar Nelson Rhodes
  (Conservative, 1925–1930)

Gordon Sydney Harrington
(Conservative, 1930–1933)
Angus Lewis Macdonald
(Liberal, 1933–1940)
Alexander Stirling MacMillan
(Liberal, 1940–1945)
Angus Lewis Macdonald
(Liberal, 1945–1954)
Harold Joseph Connolly
(Liberal, 1954)
Henry Davies Hicks
(Liberal, 1954–1956)
Robert Lorne Stanfield
(Conservative, 1956–1967)
George Isaac Smith
(Conservative, 1967–1970)
Gerald Augustine Regan
(Liberal, 1970–1978)
John MacLennan Buchanan
(Conservative, 1978–1990)
Roger Stuart Bacon
(Conservative, 1990–1991)
Donald William Cameron
(Conservative, 1991–1993)
John Patrick Savage
(Liberal, 1993–   )

Cabinet The Cabinet consists of ministers appointed by the Premier, usually from elected members of the majority party in the House of Assembly. Cabinet ministers serve at the Premier's pleasure; each member usually heads a government department.

Government Departments The toll-free number for enquiries about the Nova Scotia government made from within Nova Scotia is 800-424-5200. The general government operator is 800-424-0000. The telephone numbers of information/communications/public relations officers are listed with the departments. Where a department does not have an information officer, the number of the minister is given, indicated with *.

Agriculture and Marketing
*(902)424-4388
Community Services
(902)424-3265
Economic Development
(902)424-6810
Education
(902)424-2615
Environment
(902)424-2575
Finance
*(902)424-5720
Fisheries
(902)424-0308
Health
(902)424-5925
Housing and Consumer Affairs
(902)424-8998
Intergovernmental Affairs
*(902)424-6600
Justice
(902)424-6811
Labour
(902)424-4680
Municipal Affairs
*(902)424-5550
Natural Resources
*(902)424-2900
Tourism and Culture
(902)424-8687

Nova Scotia Representation in Federal Government
House of Commons: 11 members
Senate: 10 members

Finances

A statement of Nova Scotia's revenues and expenditures for the years 1992/93 and 1991/92 is shown below in thousands of dollars. The financial year runs from April 1 to March 31 of the year following.

	Actual 1992/93	Actual 1991/92
Revenue		
Taxation	1,836,051	1,858,218
Other	409,881	367,079
Government of Canada	1,264,648	1,305,197
Total revenue for the year	3,510,580	3,530,494
Expenditures		
Health	1,326,791	1,248,205
Education	1,017,447	1,017,288
Social services	242,620	303,074
Resource development	216,183	207,043
Transportation and communication	291,543	245,428
Other	373,325	363,596
Interest on debt	912,740	803,065
Total expenditures for the year	4,380,649	4,187,699
Deficit for the year	870,114	657,205

Economy

The economy of Nova Scotia is based largely on its natural resources. The most important mineral commodity is coal, more than 3.3 million tonnes having been mined in 1989. It is Canada's largest producer of gypsum and has Canada's biggest barite deposits. Nova Scotia mines also produce lead, zinc, and industrial minerals like salt, limestone, anhydrite, and dolomite. There are substantial oil and gas reserves being developed around Sable Island. The large forest resources form the basis for its pulp and paper and lumber industry, its access to the sea the basis for what has been the largest fisheries in Atlantic Canada. Only 10% of the land is suitable for agriculture; however, the rich soil in these areas, mainly around the Annapolis Valley, produces Canada's highest yield per unit area for many crops. Port facilities at Halifax, Sydney, and Point Tupper are the closest to Europe in mainland North America and provide an important entry and exit point for North American trade.

Major Industries Most manufacturing plants in Nova Scotia are small scale and process primary products, such as pulp and paper and food processing. Mining production includes salt, gypsum, coal, and construction materials. Until the recent fish stock crisis, cod, haddock, lob-

sters, and scallops formed the largest part of the fishing industry. The main agricultural products are dairy, poultry, and fruit. Nova Scotia supplies one half Canada's blueberries. North American plants for Volvo automobiles and Michelin tires are located in Nova Scotia. The very many historic sites contribute to Nova Scotia's large tourist industry with the Cabot Trail, a 296 km. (184 mi.) long loop around the Highlands of Cape Breton Island, being a major attraction.

Gross Domestic Product (1992) $15,560 million (in current dollars at factor cost); % of national G.D.P.: 2.6%; *rank:* 7th

Distribution of gross domestic product (1992)

Community, business, and personal services	24.3%
Finance, insurance, real estate	15.4%
Public administration and defence	13.6%
Manufacturing	13.6%
Wholesale and retail trade	12.3%
Transportation, storage	8.8%
Construction	5.3%
Utilities	2.8%
Fishing	2.2%
Agriculture	1.4%
Mining	1.1%
Forestry	0.6%

Value of Manufacturing Shipments $5,245 million

Farm Cash Receipts 311 million

Employment (seasonally adjusted) 370,000; participation rate: 60.8%

Unemployment (seasonally adjusted) 51,000; per capita: 12.1%

Minimum Wage $5.15, experienced workers; $4.70, inexperienced workers

Exports Nova Scotia's exports in 1992 amounted to $2,284 million; 1.5% of Canadian exports; rank: 8th. Nova Scotia is the world's largest exporter of lobster, Christmas trees, gypsum, and wild blueberries.
Largest trading partner: United States, 69% of Nova Scotia's exports
Major export commodities (1992): Fish and fish preparartion 32.7%; non-metallic minerals and mineral fuels 10.5%; paper and paper board 10.3%; wood and similar pulp 9.9%

History

ca. 10,000 B.C.	Paleo-Indians arrive.
ca. 7000 B.C.	Maritime Archaic Culture.
ca. 875 A.D.	Irish monks are believed to have settled on Cape Breton Island and been absorbed by Micmac Indians.
ca. 1000	Norsemen visit.
by 1600	Micmac Indians inhabit present-day Nova Scotia.
1358	*June 30* Henry Sinclair is believed to have landed in Guysborough Harbour and travelled inland.
1497	*June 24* John Cabot plants a flag on Sugarloaf Mountain claiming land for England.
1523–1524	Giovanni de Verrazano explores the North American coast and names present-day Nova Scotia and Newfoundland Arcadia.
ca. 1525	Portuguese attempt a settlement near Ingonish.
1583	*August 29 Delight* is wrecked on Sable Island with 85 deaths, Canada's first marine disaster.
1598	*March* Troilus de Mesgouez, Marquis de la Roche, settles convicts in a semi-military colony on Sable Island.
1605	Samuel de Champlain and Pierre de Gua, Sieur de Monts, move the settlement originally established at Sainte Croix to Port-Royal.
1606	Francois Gravé du Pont launches two small boats at Port-Royal, the first sailing ships built in Canada.
1610	First horses from France arrive in Acadia.
1613	English expedition led by Samuel Argall destroys French settlements in Acadia.
1621	*September 10* King James I grants Acadia to William Alexander, Earl of Stirling; Alexander names it Nova Scotia.
1629	*July 1* James Stuart, Lord Ochiltree, arrives with 60 colonists at Baleine. Alexander and Charles de Saint-Etienne de la Tour build Charles Fort at Port Royal.
1630	*April 30* La Tour transfers allegiance to Britain and receives a huge grant of land in Nova Scotia.
1632	*March 29* Treaty of Saint-Germain-en-Laye returns Acadia to France. *September 8* Isaac de Launoy de Razilly brings settlers and moves the capital of Acadia from Port-Royal to La Hàve (present-day Riverport).

1647	Acadia is granted to Charles Menou d'Aulnay as a hereditary fief.
1651	*February 25* La Tour is appointed governor of Acadia.
1653	*December 3* Nicholas Denys is granted lands between Cape Canso and Cape Rosier.
1654	*August 16* English expedition captures Port-Royal.
1667	*November 3* Treaty of Breda returns Acadia to the French.
1670	*July 17* French government returns to Acadia when the new governor, Hector Andigne de Grandfontaine, arrives.
1680	First Acadian settlers arrive at Grand-Pré.
1690	*May 11* William Phips captures Port-Royal and renames it Annapolis Royal.
1691	*November 27* Joseph Robinau de Villebon reclaims Acadia from the British.
1697	*October 30* Treaty of Ryswick returns all territory captured in North America during King William's War.
1701–1713	Acadia passes from French to English several times during Europe's War of the Spanish Succession.
1713	*April 11* France surrenders Nova Scotia to England in the Treaty of Utrecht. French begin construction of Louisbourg fortress on Île Royale (Cape Breton Island).
1715	*June 25* Acadians refuse to take an oath of allegiance to England.
1721	Governor Richard Philipps begins a settlement at Canso.
1725	New Englanders begin to settle in Nova Scotia and soon surpass Acadians in number.
1726	*September 25* Acadians ask exemption from bearing arms.
1727	*September 6* Acadians ask exemption from an oath of allegiance to Britain.
1728	Richard Watts, first English teacher in Canada, opens a school at Annapolis Royal.
1730	*April–May* Acadians at Annapolis, Chignecto, and Minas sign an oath of allegiance to Britain.
1734	*April 1* First lighthouse in Canada is built at Louisbourg.
1744	*May 24* British settlers at Canso surrender to the French.
1745	*June 17* British troops and New England militia capture Louisbourg.
1746	Many Micmacs in western Nova Scotia die of typhus.
1747	*February 11* French attack on Grand-Pré leaving 100 dead convinces the British that Acadians should be deported.
1748	*October 18* Louisbourg and Île Royale are returned to France in the Treaty of Aix-La-Chapelle.
1749	Capital of Nova Scotia is moved from Annapolis Royal to Halifax.
1749	*September 6* Representatives declare Acadians will not take oath.
1750–1753	Ca. 2,500 mostly German Protestants settle in the Lunenburg area; Lunenburg is founded *June 7, 1753*.
1750–1760	Ca. 7,000 British colonists arrive in Nova Scotia.
1750	*May 15* First divorce in Canada occurs at Halifax between Lieutenant Williams and his wife.
	September 2 St. Paul's Church, the oldest Protestant church in Canada, opens in Halifax.
	Governor Charles Lawrence builds Fort Lawrence near present-day Amherst.
1752	*March 23* Canada's earliest newspaper, the *Halifax Gazette,* is published.
1754	*October 21* Jonathan Belcher is appointed the first Chief Justice of Nova Scotia.
1755	*July 23* British demand that Acadians swear an oath of allegiance; Acadians who refuse are deported; the order of expulsion is made on *September 5;* many are scattered around the American colonies.
	December 9 First post office in Canada opens in Halifax.
1758	*July 26* British capture Louisbourg and repatriate inhabitants to France.

	October 2 Nova Scotia Assembly is founded, the oldest elected representative assembly in British North America.
1759	*September 13* First settlers arrive at Truro.
1760s	Immigration from New England and Northern Ireland.
1760	*September 13* Micmacs swear allegiance to King George III.
1761	*June 25* In Halifax Micmacs and British formally conclude a treaty signed in 1760.
1763	*February 10* Treaty of Paris: France formally cedes its North American possessions to Britain.
	October 7 Cape Breton Island (formerly Île Royale) is annexed to Nova Scotia.
1772–1774	One thousand people from Yorkshire settle in the Isthmus of Chignecto.
1773	First Scottish settlers arrive in Pictou.
1775	*June 24* Nova Scotia Assembly swears loyalty to the British crown in reaction to the American rebellion.
	September 25 Vaccine is administered at Lunenburg, the first recorded use in Nova Scotia.
1776	*April 1* Over 1,000 New England refugees arrive in Halifax.
	November 6 Americans unsuccessfully attack Fort Cumberland.
	Halifax booms as the supply centre for British troops.
1781	*August 28* American privateers raid Annapolis Royal.
1782–1784	Large influx of loyalists swamps the existing population in Nova Scotia.
1782	*July 1* American privateers attack Lunenburg.
1783	*September 3* Treaty of Paris: formal end of British-United States conflict.
1784	*May 2* Britain declares Cape Breton Island a separate colony.
	June 18 Formal order is made for the separation of New Brunswick from Nova Scotia.
1785	*September 1* Sydney becomes the capital of Cape Breton Island.
1787	Halifax Chess, Pencil, and Brush Club becomes the first artists' organization in British North America.
1788	Regular sailing packet service is established between Halifax and Britain.
	King's Edgehill, the oldest existing private school in Canada, is founded in Windsor.
1789	University of King's College, the oldest English-language university in Canada, opens in Windsor.
1792	One thousand black loyalists leave Nova Scotia for Sierra Leone.
1798	Coal is discovered in Pictou County.
1800–1830	Fifty thousand Highland Scots settle in Pictou and Antigonish counties and on Cape Breton Island.
1800	Nova Scotia courts deny the rights of slave owners.
	September 11 Corner stone for Government House is laid in Halifax.
1809	First fire insurance company in Canada, the Fire Assurance Association of Halifax, is founded.
1813	First Sunday school in Canada for black people opens in Halifax.
1814	Seventeen hundred released slaves from the southern United States settle around Halifax.
1815–1851	Fifty-five thousand immigrants arrive from the British Isles.
1818	George Ramsay, 9th Earl of Dalhousie, founds Dalhousie College.
1819	*February 11* Nova Scotia legislature opens for first time in Province House, Halifax, Canada's oldest parliament building.
	April 6 Supreme Court of Nova Scotia first sits in Province House.
1820	*October* Cape Breton Island is re-annexed to Nova Scotia.

1823	*January 1* Nova Scotia becomes the first part of Canada to issue its own currency.
	April 3 Lawrence Kavanagh becomes the first Catholic to sit in the Nova Scotia legislature.
	October 10 Public subscription library opens in Halifax.
1825	*September* Halifax Banking Company incorporates Nova Scotia's first bank.
1827	*April 23* Shubenacadie Canal connecting Halifax with the Bay of Fundy is begun.
	First railway in Canada, powered by horses, opens in Pictou to haul coal.
1832	*March 30* Bank of Nova Scotia is incorporated.
1835	*March 3* Freedom of the press in Nova Scotia is guaranteed when Joseph Howe is acquitted of libel for publishing an article critical of Halifax magistrates.
1836	First public garden in Canada opens in Halifax.
	The Clockmaker by Thomas Chandler Haliburton is published, the first Canadian fiction writer to achieve an international reputation.
1837	*January 31* Simon D'Entremont becomes the first Acadian to sit in the House of Assembly.
	August 2 First yacht club in Canada, the Halifax Yacht Club, is founded.
1839	*September 19* First steam railway in the Maritimes, the Albion Mines Railway, opens between Stellarton and Pictou Harbour.
1840	*July 16 Britannia*, the first ship of the Cunard Line founded by Samuel Cunard of Halifax, arrives at Halifax with transatlantic mail, establishing a regular, fast, steam packet service.
1842	*January 11* Gas lighting is first used in Halifax.
	March Indian Act brings government assistance to the Micmac Indians.
1847	*August 15* Simultaneous polling occurs for the first time in a Nova Scotia election.
	Reform Party wins a majority in the House of Assembly leading to responsible government.
	Andrew Downs opens Canada's first zoo in Halifax.
1848	Chloroform is used for the first time in Canada at Pictou.
	Responsible government is formed under James Boyle Uniacke.
1849	*November 1* Gas lighting is first used on Halifax streets.
1851	*April 12* British government transfers operation of post office to the Nova Scotia legislature.
	September 1 Postage stamps are first sold in Nova Scotia.
1853	*September 14* Construction begins on the European and North American Railway, crossing New Brunswick from Nova Scotia to Maine.
1856	Frederick Newton Gisbourne and Cyrus Field complete a telegraph line from Cape Ray, Newfoundland, to Cape Breton Island.
1857	First Canadian school for the deaf and speech-impaired opens in Halifax.
1858	*June 8* Nova Scotia flag is used for the first time in Halifax.
1859	*September 9* Fire destroys midtown Halifax.
1860	*January 1* Decimal system of accounting becomes law.
1861	First cooperative society store in British North America opens in Stellarton.
1863	*January 3* First covered skating rink in Canada opens in Halifax.
	April 26 Dalhousie College opens as Dalhousie University.
1864	*Spring* Nova Scotia legislature passes a resolution to have a conference to discuss Maritime Union with the two other Maritime Provinces.
	September 7 Conference to discuss Maritime Union concludes that a union is hopeless, but a British North America union highly desirable.
1865	Act provides for compulsory assessment and a free, common school system

of education; Nova Scotia becomes the first province to provide free secondary education.

1866 *March 16* United States abrogates the Reciprocity Treaty resulting in a swing of Nova Scotia opinion to a Canadian confederation.

April 17 Nova Scotia House of Assembly votes to support Confederation.

1867 *July 1* Nova Scotia joins three other British North American colonies in Confederation.

September Anti-Confederation forces win the Nova Scotia election; a delegation to London seeks Nova Scotia's release.

1868 *June 14* British government informs the Canadian government that it will not allow Nova Scotia to withdraw from Confederation.

1869 *January 15* Joseph Howe enters the federal cabinet signalling the collapse of the anti-Confederation movement.

August 19 Windsor and Annapolis Railway opens between Annapolis and Grand-Pré.

St. Peters Canal is completed.

1873 *May 13* Fire and explosion in a Pictou County mine kills 60, Canada's first mine disaster.

August 25 Cyclone on Cape Breton Island kills 500 and destroys 900 buildings and 1,200 vessels.

1875 *May 6* Truro is incorporated as a town.

1878 *March 8* First long distance call in Nova Scotia is made from Halifax to Truro.

1879 *December 6* Telephone service is first offered to the Nova Scotia public.

1880 *February 15* First quintuplets in Canada are born in Little Egypt; all die.

November 12 Explosion in Foord Pit, Stellarton, kills 49 coal miners.

1882 *April 12* Nova Scotia Steel Company is formed and produces the first steel ingots in Canada.

1885 *November 17* Gold is discovered in Hants County.

1886 *May* Legislature passes resolutions about the release of Nova Scotia from Confederation.

1887 *February* Pro-Confederation forces win 14 of 21 seats in the federal election leading to the collapse of the repeal movement.

First art college in Canada, the Nova Scotia College of Art and Design, opens in Halifax.

1888 Nova Scotia Telephone Company is formed.

1890 *November 24* Cape Breton Railway opens.

1891 *February 21* Gas explosion in the Springhill mine kills 125.

Minimum age for boy labourers in mines is raised to 12.

1892 *July 22* United States and Britain sign a boundary convention concerning Passamaquoddy Bay.

1893 *April 19* House of Assembly refuses to debate a woman's suffrage bill.

1894 *March 15* Nova Scotia votes for Prohibition.

November 11 First recorded game of basketball in Canada is played in Halifax.

1895 *December 18* First home and school association in Canada is formed in Baddeck.

1896 *February 12* First electric trams in Halifax begin operation.

1897 Ferry service between Placentia (later Port-aux-Basques), Newfoundland, and North Sydney begins.

1899 *March* Dominion Iron and Steel Corporation is incorporated in Nova Scotia.

1904 *April 11* Sydney is incorporated as a city.

1906 *January 16* Control of the garrison at Halifax is transferred to the Canadian government when the last British soldiers leave Canada.

1907	*November 26* Dial telephones are used at Sydney Mines, believed to be the first in Canada.
1914	*Evangeline*, the first feature film produced in Canada, is photographed in Annapolis Valley.
1917	*July 25* Coal mine disaster in Cape Breton Island leaves 65 dead.
1918	*January 23* Coal mine explosion in Pictou County kills 88.
	April 26 Women are allowed to vote in provincial elections.
1919	Nova Scotia Power Commission is formed.
1920s	Climax of Maritime Rights Movement, a regional protest against the Maritimes declining influence since Confederation.
1920	*October 7–17* First transcanada flight, Halifax to Vancouver, is made in 49 hours, 7 minutes.
	October 25 Nova Scotia votes for Prohibition.
	Universal suffrage for men and women over 21 comes into effect.
1921	*February 19* First permanent dial exchange in Nova Scotia is installed in Halifax.
1923	*April 15* Change from left- to right-hand drive on Nova Scotia highways is effected.
	Boys under 16 are prohibited from working in mines.
1927	Federal government passes the Maritime Freight Rates Act providing for statutory reductions in freight rates and establishes the Maritime Freight Rates Commission (later Atlantic Provinces Transportation Commission).
1928	*May 31* Legislative Council is abolished.
	Antigonish Movement has its beginnings in the Extension Department of St. Francis Xavier University.
1929	*October 30* Nova Scotia ends Prohibition in favour of provincial government control of liquor.
1930	*April 10* Legislation creating a Nova Scotia police force comes into effect.
1931	*January 14* Public Archives of Nova Scotia are opened on the Dalhousie University campus.
1932	*April 1* Royal Canadian Mounted Police absorbs the Nova Scotia provincial police.
1936	*September 5* Beryl Markham, the first woman to fly solo over Atlantic Ocean from east to west, lands at Baleine Cove.
	October 13 Mary Teresa Sullivan, the first woman alderman in Canada, is sworn in as a member of the Halifax City Council.
1937	Free Library Act is passed.
1938	*December 6* Broken cable causes 16 deaths at Sydney Mines.
1939	*September* First convoy of supplies to Britain sails out of Halifax.
1940s	Halifax's role as a major port for supplies to western allies sparks Nova Scotia prosperity.
1942	*October 14* Newfoundland-Nova Scotia ferry, *Caribou*, is sunk by German submarines; 136 dead.
1945	*May 7* VE Day celebrations in Halifax turn into riots; 2 dead.
1946	Act provides for an equal level of education across Nova Scotia financed by the provincial government and municipal taxes.
1949	*January 15* Royal Canadian Air Force North Star airplane makes the first non-stop flight across Canada from Halifax to Vancouver.
1952	*January 14* Coal mine explosion at Stellarton leaves 19 dead.
1955	*August 13* Canso Causeway to Cape Breton Island is officially opened.
1956	*November 1* Springhill mine accident kills 39; 88 are rescued.
1957	*May 8* First Atlantic Premiers Conference is held in Halifax.

1958	*October 22* Blanche Margaret Meagher of Halifax becomes Canada's first woman ambassador when she is appointed ambassador to Israel.
	October 23 Springhill mine disaster kills 74; some survivors are trapped for 8 days.
1959	*January 1* Federal-provincial hospital plan goes into effect in Nova Scotia.
1960	*February 2–3* Snowstorm brings up to 96 cm. (37.8 in.) to the Halifax area.
1961	*February 8* Gladys Porter becomes the first woman to sit in the Nova Scotia legislature.
	March 13 Dartmouth is incorporated as a city.
	November 4 Interprovincial School for the Deaf opens in Amherst.
1962	*October 25* First oceanographic institution in Canada, Bedford Institute of Oceanography, is founded in Dartmouth.
1963	*June* Circus ship *Fleurus* catches fire at Yarmouth.
	November 18 Last segregated black school in Nova Scotia is closed.
1967	Edgar Spinney Archibald of Yarmouth is awarded the first Order of Canada.
	November 22 Nova Scotia government buys Dominion Steel and Coal Company, Sydney, and operates it as the Sydney Steel Corporation.
1969	*August 15–24* First Canada Summer Games are held in Halifax-Dartmouth.
	September 13 Union of Nova Scotia Indians is formed at Sydney.
	Federal government repeals the Maritime Freight Rates Act in favour of one creating a regional committee to administer transportation subsidies.
	November CSS *Hudson* leaves Halifax to begin the first circumnavigation of the Americas and arrives back in Halifax in *November 1970.*
1970	*February 3 Arrow* goes aground in Chedabucto Bay spilling oil on the water and beaches.
	Voting age reduced to 19 for provincial elections.
1971	*March 22* Television cameras are allowed into the Nova Scotia legislature, the first province to permit this on a regular basis.
	April 15 Harry Douglas Smith is appointed Nova Scotia's first ombudsman.
	August 15–16 Hurricane Beth drops 296 mm. (11.7 in.) rain on the Halifax area sweeping away bridges and damaging buildings and farmland.
	Oil and gas discoveries on Sable Island are announced.
	Atlantic School of Theology opens, Canada's first ecumenical college.
1973	Council of Maritime Premiers is formed to deal with cooperation in internal development and external influence.
	Nova Scotia Power Commission and Nova Scotia Light and Power Company are amalgamated to form Nova Scotia Power Corporation, a crown corporation.
	Voting age is reduced to 18 for provincial elections.
1975	Art Gallery of Nova Scotia is established.
1976	*February 4* Supreme Court of Nova Scotia rules that the province does not have the right to censor motion pictures.
1977	Federal government declares 200 mi. (322 km.) sovereignty off Canada's coasts.
	November 1 Freedom of Information Act is proclaimed in Nova Scotia.
1978	*January 3* Ellen Richardson becomes Deputy Minister of Consumer Affairs, the first woman deputy minister in Nova Scotia.
1979	*February 24* Mine disaster in Glace Bay leaves 12 dead.
	March 15 Kurdistan breaks up off Cape Breton Island; oil spreads from Bras d'Or to Halifax.
1980	*November* Alexa McDonough is elected leader of the provincial New Democratic Party, the first woman leader of a political party in Canada, with the exception of the territories.

1981	*October 6* First election in Nova Scotia in which all members of the House of Assembly are chosen by single-member constituencies.
	Legislation is passed providing education in French for Acadian children where practical.
1982	*March 2* Federal-provincial agreement on offshore resources gives the federal government final say on the development of oil and gas and Nova Scotia most of the revenue.
	July 30 Federal government issues permits for a three-year drilling project off Nova Scotia's north coast.
1984	Test project to harness Bay of Fundy's tidal power begins generating power.
	World Court resolves dispute with the United States over the ownership of Georges Bank by giving Canada one-sixth, the most valuable portion.
	Drought in southwest Nova Scotia dries up many streams and wells.
	December 22 Doreen Lewis becomes the mayor of Annapolis Royal, the first black mayor in Canada.
1987	*July 13* One hundred seventy-four illegal southeast Asian immigrants land on Nova Scotia's coast.
1988	*April 18* Federal government calls a 12-year halt to oil and gas drilling in the Canadian portion of Georges Bank.
1990	*December* Due to reduced cod quotas, several fish plants close.
1991	Eighty-thousand-year-old mastodon bones are found in a gypsum quarry near Halifax, the first time such a complete find is made in Nova Scotia.
1992	*May 9* Disaster at Westray Mines in Pictou County leaves 26 dead.
1993	*May 25* Wayne Adams becomes the first black member of the Nova Scotia legislature and on *June 11* the first black cabinet minister.
	December 31 United States and Canada agree to a five-month shutdown of the Georges Bank fishery.

Culture and Education

Performing Arts Nova Scotia has a number of performing companies and institutions. The major organizations are:

Festival Antigonish, Antigonish (summer)	(902)867-2100
Jest in Time Theatre, Halifax (mime and physical theatre)	(902)423-4647
Mermaid Theatre of Nova Scotia, Windsor (professional puppet theatre)	(902)798-5841
Mulgrave Road Co-op Theatre, Guysborough	(902)533-2092
Neptune Theatre, Halifax	(902)429-7300
Ship's Company Theatre, Parrsboro (Canadian plays)	(902)254-2003
Symphony Nova Scotia, Halifax	(902)421-7311

Among the 350 community festivals and events in Nova Scotia are:

Atlantic Jazz Festival, Halifax (July)	(902)422-8221
Antigonish Highland Games, Antigonish (August)	(902)863-4275
Festival acadien d'Halifax/Dartmouth (May)	(902)421-1772
Halifax Busker Festival (August)	(902)425-4329
Nova Scotia International Tattoo, Halifax (June/July)	(902)420-1114
Scotia Festival of Music, Halifax (May/June)	(902)429-9467

Provincial Museums and Galleries The following are major Nova Scotia institutions.

Acadian Museum, Cheticamp

Art Gallery of Nova Scotia, Halifax
Maritime Museum of the Atlantic, Halifax
Nova Scotia Museum, Halifax with divisions in other centres

Nova Scotia Museum of Industry, Stellarton

Universities Nova Scotia has Canada's highest per capita network of institutions of higher education and the highest level of university enrollment largely due to out-of-province students

Acadia University, Wolfville
Atlantic School of Theology, Halifax
Dalhousie University, Halifax
Mount St. Vincent University, Halifax
Nova Scotia Agricultural College, Truro
Nova Scotia College of Art and Design, Halifax
Nova Scotia Teachers College, Halifax
St. Francis Xavier University, Antigonish
St. Mary's University, Halifax
Technical University of Nova Scotia, Halifax
Université Sainte-Anne, Pointe-de-l'Eglise

University College of Cape Breton, Sydney
University of King's College, Halifax

Community Colleges
Cobatec Community College, Truro
Kingstec Community College, Kentville
Nova Scotia Community College, Halifax, has branches in:
Bridgewater
Dartmouth
Lawrencetown
Middleton
Port Hawksbury
Springhill
Shelburne
Stellarton
Sydney
Windsor
Yarmouth

Miscellaneous Educational Institutions
Canadian Coast Guard College, Sydney
Nova Scotia Fisheries Training Centre

Motor Vehicle Use

Motor Vehicles Registered for Use in Nova Scotia: 580,667

Drivers Licensed by Nova Scotia: over 579,225. Minimum driving age: 16

Roads Paved: 13,205 km. (8,205 mi.); unpaved: 12,770 km. (7,935 mi.); bridges maintained by the province: ca. 3,500

Speed Limits TransCanada and 100 series highways: 100 kph (62 mph); other highways: 80 kph (50 mph); urban and school zones on school days, 8 A.M. to 5 P.M.: 50 kph (31 mph)

First, Biggest, and Best

World's largest tides: Burncoat Head in Minas Basin range from 14.5–16 m. (47.5–52.5 ft.)
North America's first tidal power station: Annapolis Tidal Generating Station built 1984, and also North America's only saltwater hydroelectric power station
World's second largest natural harbour: Halifax (after Sydney, Australia)
North America's largest collection of fossils: unearthed January 29, 1986, on the Minas Basin shore
World's deepest causeway: across Strait of Canso, 65 m. (213.3 ft.)
North America's oldest operating salt-water ferry service: Halifax-Dartmouth, established 1752
North America's oldest naval dockyard: HMC Dockyards, Halifax, established 1758
North America's first lighthouse: built at Louisbourg 1720
North America's largest fortress: Louisbourg
North America's first round church: St. George's of England, Halifax, built 1800

World's only church designed by a member of the British Royal Family: St. George's Church by the Duke of Kent.

North America's oldest continuously occupied executive mansion: Province House, Halifax, built 1819

North America's oldest permanent agricultural fair: now site of Hants Exhibition in Windsor, begun 1765 and held without interruption since 1815

North America's first zoo and botanical garden north of Mexico: Halifax, 1847

World's biggest man-made explosion before Hiroshima: Halifax Explosion, December 6, 1917, when a Belgian relief ship collided with a French munitions ship in the Halifax harbour; more than 1,600 dead, 4,000 injured, 6,000 homeless, and 5.2 sq. km. (2 sq. mi.) of Halifax destroyed

North America's first European drama performed north of Mexico: "Théâtre de Neptune en la Nouvelle France" by Marc Lescarbot at Port Royal November 14, 1606

Western hemisphere's first public library: established by Marc Lescarbot, 1606

British Empire's first cathedral: St. Paul's, Halifax, 1750

British Empire's first colony to win responsible government: 1848

British Empire's first use of a secret ballot: House of Assembly adopts a resolution to apply secret balloting to the election of its members, February 13, 1759

North America's first telegraph system by flags: Duke of Kent, Halifax, 1793

North America's first yacht squadron: Royal Nova Scotia, 1836

North America's first chamber of commerce: 1750 in Halifax

North America's first discovery of iron ore: St. Mary's Bay, 1604

North America's first coal mining on a commercial basis: Port Morien, 1720

North America's first fireproof concrete building: Louisbourg lighthouse, 1733

World's first paper made from wood fiber: Charles Fenerty, Halifax, started experimenting in 1839 and produced paper from wood pulp in 1841

World's first vessel to cross the Atlantic Ocean wholly under steam power: *Royal William* left Pictou on August 18, 1833, and arrived in Gravesend, England, September 11

British Empire's first recorded flight of a heavier-than-air machine: Alexander Graham Bell's tetrahedral cell kite lifts Neil MacDiarmid at Baddeck, December 23, 1905

British Empire's first powered flight by a heavier-than-air machine: John Alexander Douglas McCurdy flies Silver Dart at Baddeck, February 23, 1909

World's discovery of kerosene: in 1846 Abraham Gesner, Cornwallis, developed a process for distilling kerosene, the start of the modern petroleum refining industry

North America's first self-contained breathing apparatus for mine rescue: used by Glace Bay collieries in 1906

British Empire's first flag: granted by King Charles I, 1625

North America's highest ratio of educational facilities to population

British Empire's first institution to teach British common law: Dalhousie University Law School, Halifax, 1883–1884

World's first solo circumnavigation: Joshua Slocum, a native of Westport, left Boston April 24, 1897, and arrived in Newport, R.I., on June 27, 1898 after travelling ca. 74,000 km. (ca. 46,000 mi.) alone in a rebuilt oyster sloop

World's first black person to win the Victoria Cross: William Hall of Hantsport, 1854, while serving with the British Navy in India; also the first Canadian to win

North America's first female police officer: Rose Fortune, Annapolis Royal, ca. 1830

British Empire's first Anglican bishop: Charles Inglis was consecrated Bishop of Nova Scotia, August 12, 1787

British Empire's longest continuous leadership of a political entity: 27 years, George Henry Murray, Premier of Nova Scotia, 1896–1923

World's largest known bluefin tuna: 678.6 kg. (1,496 lb.) caught by Ken Fraser, Auld Cove, October 26, 1979

Sources of Information About Nova Scotia

Nova Scotia Department of Supply and Service, Information and Communication Service: One Government Place, P.O. Box 608, Halifax, N.S. B3J 2R7 (902)424-5200, 800-424-5200 (Nova Scotia)

Nova Scotia Department of Tourism and Culture: P.O. Box 456, Halifax, N.S. B3J 2R5 (902)424-4709, 800-565-0000 (Canada), 800-341-6096 (United States)

Nova Scotia Government Bookstore: Box 637, Halifax, N.S. B3J 2T3 (902)424-7580

Books About Nova Scotia: A Selected List

Reference Guides

Antoft, Kell (ed.). *A Guide to Local Government in Nova Scotia* (3rd ed. 1992).

Atlantic Provinces Economic Council. *Atlantic Canada Today* (1987).

Bishop, Olga B. *Publications of the Governments of Nova Scotia, Prince Edward Island, New Brunswick, 1758–1952* (1957).

Burrows, Roger. *A Birdwatchers Guide to Atlantic Canada. Vol. 2, Nova Scotia* (1982).

Canada. Atmospheric Environment Service. *Canadian Climate Normals, 1961–1990: Atlantic Provinces* (1993).

Canada. Energy, Mines and Resources Canada. *Gazetteer of Canada: Nova Scotia* (3rd ed. 1993).

Claridge, Edward and Betty Ann Milligan. *Animal Signatures* (4th ed. 1992). Field guide to the animals most commonly encountered in Nova Scotia and their signs.

Dawson, Joan. *The Mapmaker's Eye: Nova Scotia Through Early Maps* (1988).

Doull, John. *Sketches of the Attorney-Generals of Nova Scotia, 1750–1925* (1964).

Elliott, Shirley B. (ed.). *The Legislative Assembly of Nova Scotia, 1758–1983: A Biographical Directory* (1984).

Elliott, Shirley. *Nova Scotia Book of Days: A Calendar of the Province's History* (1979).

Erskine, Anthony J. *Atlas of Breeding Birds of the Maritime Provinces* (1992).

Fleming, Patricia Lockhart. *Atlantic Canadian Imprints, 1801–1820: A Bibliography* (1991).

Gilhen, John. *Amphibians and Reptiles of Nova Scotia* (1984).

Haliburton, Gordon. *Clansmen of Nova Scotia* (1979).

Halifax Library Association. *Nova Scotia in Books, from the First Printing in 1752 to the Present Time, Commemorating the Centennial of Confederation* (1967).

Laugher, Charles T. *Atlantic Province Authors of the Twentieth Century: A Bio-bibliographical Checklist* (1982).

Marble, Allan Everett. *Nova Scotians at Home and Abroad: Biographical Sketches of Over Six Hundred Native Born Nova Scotians* (rev. ed. 1989).

McCalla, Robert J. *The Maritime Provinces Atlas* (new ed. 1991).

Milner, Philip (ed.). *Nova Scotia Writes* (1979).

Morley, William F.E. *The Atlantic Provinces: Newfoundland, Nova Scotia, New Brunswick, Prince Edward Island* (1967). A bibliography.

Morrison, James H. *Common Heritage: An Annotated Bibliography of Ethnic Groups in Nova Scotia* (1984).

Multicultural Association of Nova Scotia. *People of Nova Scotia*, 2 vols. (1980).

Natural History of Nova Scotia, 2 vols. (1984)

Newton, Pamela. *The Cape Breton Book of Days: A Daily Journal of the Life and Times of an Island* (1984).

Norton, Judith Ann (comp.). *New England Planters of the Maritime Provinces of Canada, 1759–1800: Bibliography of Sources* (1993).

Nova Scotia. Department of Development. *Resource Atlas* (1986).

Nova Scotia. Department of Natural Resources. *A Map of the Province of Nova Scotia* (1992).

Nova Scotia. Women's Directorate. *Women in Nova Scotia: A Statistical Handbook* (1990).

Penney, Allen. *Houses of Nova Scotia: An Illustrated Guide to Architectural Style Recognition* (1989).

Peterson, Jean (comp.). *The Loyalist Guide: Nova Scotian Loyalists and Their Documents* (1983).

Public Archives of Nova Scotia. *Place-Names and Places of Nova Scotia* (2nd ed. 1976, rpt. 1982).

Punch, Terrence M. *Genealogical Research in Nova Scotia* (3rd rev. ed. 1983).

——. *Some Sons of Erin in Nova Scotia* (1980).

Roland, Albert E. *Geological Background and Physiology of Nova Scotia* (1982).

—— and E.C. Smith. *Flora of Nova Scotia* (1969).

—— and A. Randall Olson. *Spring Wildflowers* (1993).

Saunders, Gary and Donald R. Pentz. *Trees of Nova Scotia: A Guide to Native and Exotic Species* (rev. ed. 1989).

Scott, W.B. and M.G. Scott. *Atlantic Fishes of Canada* (1988).

Sellick, Lester B. *Notable Nova Scotians* (1981).

Smith, Leonard H. *Nova Scotia Genealogy and Local History: A Trial Bibliography* (2nd ed. 1984).

Stewart, Gordon T. (ed.). *Documents Relating to the Great Awakening in Nova Scotia, 1760–1791* (1982).

Tennyson, Brian (comp.). *Cape Breton: A Bibliography* (1978).

Tratt, Gertrude E.N. *A Survey and the Listing of Nova Scotia Newspapers, 1752–1957: With Particular Reference to the Period Before 1867* (1979).

Tufts, Robie W. *Birds of Nova Scotia* (3rd ed. rev. by Ian A. McLean, 1986).

Vaison, Robert (comp.). *Studying Nova Scotia, Its History and Present State, Its Politics and Economy: A Bibliography and Guide* (1974).

——. *Nova Scotia Past and Present: A Bibliography and Guide* (1976).

Villebon, Joseph Robineau de. *Acadia at the End of the Seventeenth Century: Letters, Journals and Memoirs of Joseph Robineau de Villebon, Commandant in Acadia, 1690–1700 and Other Contemporary Documents* (ed. by John Clarence Webster, 1934, rpt. 1979).

Wetmore, Don and Lester B. Sellick. *Loyalists in Nova Scotia* (1983).

Wright, Esther Clark. *Planters and Pioneers* (rev. ed. 1982).

Nonfiction Sources

* denotes a winner of a Governor General's Literary Award.

Alexander, David G. *Atlantic Canada and Confederation: Essays in Canadian Political Economy* (1983).

Arsenault, Bona. *History of the Acadians* (1966).

Barnard, Murray. *Sea, Salt, & Sweat: A Story of Nova Scotia and the Vast Atlantic Fisheries* (2nd ed. rev. by Jim Brett, 1986).

Barthomeuf, Jacques. *Governing Nova Scotia* (1985).

Beck, J. Murray. *Joseph Howe*, 2 vols. (1982–1983).

——. *Politics of Nova Scotia* (1985).

Bell, Winthrop Pickard. *The "Foreign Protestants" and the Settlement of Nova Scotia: The History of a Piece of Arrested British Colonial Policy in the Eighteenth Century* (2nd ed. 1990).

Bickerton, James P. *Nova Scotia, Ottawa, and the Politics of Regional Development* (1990).

Binkley, Marian. *Voices From Off Shore: Narratives of Risk and Danger in the Nova Scotian Deep Sea Fishery* (1994).

Bird, Michael J. *The Town That Died: The True Story of the Greatest Man-Made Explosion Before Hiroshima* (1962).

Black Cultural Centre for Nova Scotia. *Traditional Lifetime Stories: A Collection of Black Memories*, 2 vols. (1987–1990).

Bogaard, Paul A. (ed.). *Profiles of Science and Society in the Maritimes Prior to 1914* (1990).

Bourneuf, François Lambert. *Diary of a Frenchman: François Lambert Bourneuf's Adventures From France to Acadia, 1787–1871* (ed. by J. Alphonse Deveau, 1990).

Brown, Roger David. *Blood on the Coal: The Story of the Springhill Mining Disasters* (1976).

Bruce, Harry. *A Basket of Apples: Recollections of Historic Nova Scotia* (1982).

——. *Down Home: Notes of a Maritime Son* (1988).

Brym, Robert J. and R. James Sacouman (eds.). *Underdevelopment and Social Movements in Atlantic Canada* (1979).

Buckner, Phillip A. and David Frank (eds.). *Atlantic Canada Before Confederation* (2nd ed. 1990).

Buckner, Phillip A. and John G. Reid (eds.). *The Atlantic Region to Confederation: A History* (1994).

Burrill, Gary and Ian McKay (eds.). *People, Resources, and Power [Critical Perspectives on Underdevelopment and Primary Industries in the Atlantic Region]* (1987).

Cameron, Silver Donald. *Wind, Whales and Whisky: A Cape Breton Voyage* (1991).

Campbell, D. and R.A. MacLean. *Beyond the Atlantic Roar: A Study of Nova Scotia Scots* (1974).

Carleton University. History Collaborative. *Urban and Community Development in Atlantic Canada, 1867–1991* (1993).

Choyce, Lesley. *An Avalanche of Ocean: The Life and Times of a Nova Scotia Immigrant* (1987).

Clark, Andrew Hill. *Acadia: The Geography of Early Nova Scotia to 1760* (1968).

Clarke, George Frederick. *Expulsion of the Acadians: The True Story, Documented* (8th ed. 1988).

——. *Someone Before Us: Our Maritime Indians* (3rd ed. 1974).

Cuthbertson, Brian. *The Loyalist Governor: Biography of Sir John Wentworth* (1983).

Daigle, Jean (ed.). *Acadians of the Maritimes: Thematic Studies* (1982).

Dalhousie, George Ramsay, Earl of. *The Dalhousie Journals* (ed. by Marjorie Whitelaw, 1978–1982).

Davies, Gwendolyn. *Studies in Maritime Literary History, 1760–1930* (1991).

—— (ed.). *Myth and Milieu: Atlantic Literature and Culture 1918–1939* (1993).

Davis, Anthony. *Dire Straits, the Dilemmas of a Fishery: The Case of Digby Neck and the Islands* (1991).

Denys, Nicolas. *The Native People of Acadia* (1993). Part of a seventeenth century work.

DeRoche, Constance P. *The Village, the Vertex: Adaptation to Regionalism and Development in a Complex Society* (1985).

—— and John deRoche (eds.). *"Rock in a Stream": Living With the Political Economy of Underdevelopment in Cape Breton* (1987).

DeVolpi, Charles P. *Nova Scotia, a Pictorial Record: Historical Prints and Illustrations of the Province of Nova Scotia, Canada, 1605–1878* (1974).

Donovan, Kenneth. *The Island: New Perspectives on Cape Breton's History, 1713–1990* (1990).

—— (ed.). *Cape Breton at 200: Historical Essays in Honour of the Island's Bicentennial, 1785–1985* (1985).

Dunn, Charles W. *Highland Settler: A Portrait of the Scottish Gael in Nova Scotia* (1953, rpt. 1968).

Earle, Michael (ed.). *Workers and the State in 20th Century Nova Scotia* (1989).

Erickson, Paul A. *Halifax's North End: An Anthropologist Looks at the City* (1986).

Fergusson, Bruce. *Honourable W.S. Fielding*, 2 vols. (1970–1971).

——. *Joseph Howe of Nova Scotia* (1973).

Fingard, Judith. *The Dark Side of Life in Victorian Halifax* (1989).

Fleming, Berkeley (ed.). *Beyond Anger and Longing: Community Development in Atlantic Canada* (1988).

Forbes, Ernest R. *The Maritime Rights Movement, 1919–1927: A Study in Canadian Regionalism* (1979).

——. *Challenging the Regional Stereotype: Essays on the 20th Century Maritimes* (1989).

—— and D.A. Mulse (eds.). *The Atlantic Provinces in Confederation* (1993).

Fraser, Sarah. *Pasture Spruce* (1971). Rural life in Nova Scotia at the turn of the century.

Fry, Bruce W. *"An Appearance of Strength": The Fortifications of Louisbourg*, 2 vols. (1984).

Gilman, Dorothy. *A New Kind of Country* (1978, rpt. 1989).

Girard, Philip and Jim Phillips (eds.). *Essays in the History of Canadian Law. Vol. 3, Nova Scotia* (1990).

Griffiths, Naomi E.S. *The Contexts of Acadian History, 1686–1874* (1992).

Haliburton, E.D. *My Years With Stanfield* (1972).

Hawkins, John. *The Life and Times of Angus L.* [Macdonald] (1969).

——. *Recollections of the Regan Years: A Political Memoir* (1990).

Hill, Kay. *Joe Howe, the Man Who Was Nova Scotia* (1980).

Horwood, Harold. *Dancing on the Shore: A Celebration of Life in the Annapolis Valley* (1987).

House, J.D. *Fish Versus Oil: Resources and Rural Development in North Altlantic Societies* (1986).

Howell, Colin and Richard Twomey (eds.). *Jack Tar in History: Essays in the History of Maritime Life and Labour* (1991).

Inwood, Kris (ed.). *Farm, Factory and Fortune: New Studies in the Economic History of the Maritime Provinces* (1993).

Jobb, Dean. *Crime Wave: Con Men, Rogues, and Scoundrels From Nova Scotia's Past* (1991).

Johnson, Ralph S. *Forests of Nova Scotia: A History* (1986).

Johnston, A.J.B. *The Summer of 1744: A Portrait of Life in 18th Century Louisbourg* (rev. ed. 1991).

—— and others. *Louisbourg: An Eighteenth Century Town* (1991).

Jones, Sonia. *It All Began With Daisy* (1987). A New York family moves to a farm near Halifax and starts a yogurt business.

Kavanagh, Peter. *John Buchanan: The Art of Political Survival* (1988).

Kimball, R.E. *The Bench: The History of Nova Scotia's Provincial Courts* (1989).

Kitz, Janet F. *Shattered City: The Halifax Explosion and the Road to Recovery* (1989).

Kroll, Robert E. (ed.). *Intimate Fragments: An Irreverent Chronicle of Early Halifax* (1985).

Leefe, Peter L. and John G. McCreath. *History of Early Nova Scotia* (3rd ed. 1990).

MacDonald, Andy. *Bread & Molasses* (1976, rpt. 1986) *Don't Slip on the Soap* (1978, rpt. 1985). Recollections of a coal miner's family of eleven children in the Depression.

MacDonald, M.A. *Fortune & La Tour: The Civil War in Acadia* (1983).

MacEwen, Paul. *Miners and Steelworkers: Labour in Cape Breton* (1976).

Macgillivray, Don and Brian Tennyson (eds.). *Cape Breton Historical Essays* (2nd ed. 1981).

MacKay, Don. *Scotland Farewell: The People of the Hector* (1980).

MacKenzie, A.A. *The Irish in Cape Breton* (1979).

MacKenzie, Michael. *Glimpses of the Past: True Stories Old and New* (1978).

———. *Reflections of Yesteryear: True Stories Old and New* (1984).

MacKinnon, Neil. *This Unfriendly Soil: The Loyalist Experience in Nova Scotia, 1783–1791* (1986).

MacMillan, C. Lamont. *Memoirs of a Cape Breton Doctor* (1975, rpt. 1993).

MacNutt, W.S. *The Atlantic Provinces: The Emergence of a Colonial Society, 1712–1857* (1965).

The Maritimes: Tradition, Challenge and Change (1987).

McCann, Larry (ed.). *People and Place: Studies of Small Town Life in the Maritimes* (1987).

——— and Carrie MacMillan (eds.). *The Sea and Culture of Atlantic Canada: A Multidisciplinary Sampler* (1992).

McCulloch, Thomas. *The Mephibosheth Stepsure Letters* (ed. by Gwendolyn Davies, 1990). Satire on the manners and mores of nineteenth-century Nova Scotia written between 1821 and 1823.

McGee, Harold Franklin (ed.). *The Native Peoples of Atlantic Canada: A History of Indian-European Relations* (1972, rpt. 1983).

McLennan, J.S. *Louisbourg From Its Foundation to Its Fall, 1713–1758* (4th ed. 1979).

McLeod, Mary K. and James O. St. Clair. *No Place Like Home: The Life and Times of Cape Breton Heritage Houses* (1992).

McNeil, Neil. *The Highland Heart in Nova Scotia* (1948, rpt. 1980).

McPherson, Flora. *Watchman Against the World: The Remarkable Story of Norman McLeod & His People From Scotland to Cape Breton Island to New Zealand* (1962, rpt. 1993).

Medjuck, Sheva. *The Jews of Atlantic Canada* (1986).

Metson, Graham. *The Halifax Explosion: Dec. 6, 1917* (1978).

——— with Cheryl Lean (eds.). *East Coast Port—Halifax at War, 1939–1945* (1981).

Mitcham, Allison. *Offshore Islands of Nova Scotia and New Brunswick* (1984).

———. *Paradise or Purgatory: Island Life in Nova Scotia & New Brunswick* (1986).

Moody, Barry. *The Acadians* (1981).

Moore, Christopher. *Louisbourg Portraits: Life in an Eighteenth-Century Garrison Town* (1982).

Moorsom, W.S. *Letters from W.S. Moorsom Comprising Sketches of a Young Country* (1830, ed. by Marjorie Whitelaw 1986).

Morrison, James. *"We Have Held Our Own": The Western Interior of Nova Scotia, 1800–1940* (1981).

Nova Scotia. Department of Natural Resources. *One of the Great Treasures: Geology and History of Coal in Nova Scotia* (rev. ed. 1993).

Nowlan, Michael O. (ed.). *The Maritime Experience* (1975).

Pacey, Elizabeth. *Historic Halifax* (1988).

Paratte, Henri-Dominique. *Acadians* (1991).

Paul, Daniel N. *We are Not the Savages: A Micmac Perspective on the Collision of European and Aboriginal Civilizations* (1993).

Payzant, Joan M. *Halifax: Cornerstone of Canada* (1985).

Peach, Earle. *Memories of a Cape Breton Childhood* (1990).

Peck, Mary Biggar. *A Nova Scotia Album: Glimpses of the Way We Were* (1989).

Perkins, Simeon. *The Diary of Simeon Perkins, 1804–1812* (ed. by Charles Bruce Fergusson, 1969, rpt. 1978).

Powell, Thomas P. (ed.). *The Irish in Atlantic Canada, 1780–1900* (1991).

Raddall, Thomas H. *Halifax, Warden of the North* (1948, rpt. 1993).

Rawlyk, George A. *Nova Scotia's Massachusetts: A Study of Massachusetts-Nova Scotia Relations 1630–1784* (1973).

——— (ed.). *Historical Essays on the Atlantic Provinces* (1967).

Redman, Stanley R. *Open Gangway: The Real Story of the Halifax Navy Riot* (1981).

Richardson, Evelyn M. *B . . . Was for Butter and Enemy Craft* (1976).

———. *My Other Islands* (1960).

———. *We Keep a Light* (1945, rpt. 1985).

Ripley, Donald. *Bagman: A Life in Nova Scotia Politics* (1993).

Ross, Sally. *The Acadians of Nova Scotia Past and Present* (1992).

Sager, Eric W. with Gerald E. Panting. *Maritime Capital: The Shipping Industry in Atlantic Canada, 1820–1914* (1990).

Salusbury, John. *Expeditions of Honour: The Journal of John Salusbury in Halifax, Nova Scotia, 1749–53* (1982).

Samson, Daniel (ed.). *Contested Countryside: Rural Workers and Modern Society in Atlantic Canada, 1800–1950* (1994).

Sandberg, L. Anders (ed.). *Trouble in the Woods: Forest Policy and Social Conflict in Nova Scotia and New Brunswick* (1992).

Saunders, S.A. *The Economic History of the Maritime Provinces* (1939, rpt. 1984).

Sinclair, Gladys Jessie. *Growing Up on a Farm in Nova Scotia, 1915–1923: Personal Memoirs of the Period in Mill Valley, N.S.* (1992).

Spicer, Stanley T. *Maritimers Ashore and Afloat: Interesting People, Places, and Events Related to the Bay of Fundy and Its Rivers.* Vol. 1 (1993).

Stewart, Gordon and George Rawlyk. *A People Highly Favoured of God: The Nova Scotia Yankees and the American Revolution* (1972).

Tennyson, Bruce Douglas (ed.). *Impressions of Cape Breton* (1986).

Thurston, Harry. *Tidal Life: A Natural History of the Bay of Fundy* (1990).

Trueman, Stuart. *Tall Tales and True Tales From Down East: Eerie Experiences, Heroic Exploits, Extraordinary Personalities, Ancient Legends and Folklore From New Brunswick and Elsewhere in the Maritimes* (1979).

Tuck James A. *Maritime Provinces Prehistory* (1984).

Upton, Leslie F.S. *Micmacs and Colonists: Indian-White Relations in the Maritimes, 1713–1867* (1979).

Wade, Mason. *Mason Wade, Acadia and Quebec: The Perceptions of an Outsider* (ed. by N.E.S. Griffiths and G.A. Rawlyk, 1991)

Walker, James W. St. G. *The Black Loyalists: The Search for a Promised Land in Nova Scotia and Sierra Leone, 1783–1870* (1976, rpt. 1992).

Whitehead, Ruth Holmes. *The Old Man Told Us: Excerpts From Micmac History 1500–1950* (1991).

Nova Scotia in Literature

Akerman, Jeremy. *Black Around the Eyes: A Novel* (1981). A picture of Cape Breton coal miners during the depression.

Baker, Kent. *A Man Wanders Sometimes* (1989). A story about a man, his girlfriend, and a dog living in a house by the ocean in Nova Scotia.

Bell, John (ed.). *Halifax: A Literary Portrait* (1990).

Bird, Will R. *An Earl Must Have a Wife* (1969). Historical fiction about Joseph Des Barres, Lieutenant-Governor of Cape Breton Island 1784–1787.

——. *Here Stays Good Yorkshire* (1945); *Tristam's Salvation* (1957); *Despite the Distance* (1961). Novels about Yorkshire settlers in the Chignecto region during the time of the American Revolution.

——. *The Passionate Pilgrim* (1949). Set in Chignecto region during the Acadian expulsion.

——. *To Love and Cherish* (1953). Historical fiction about the founding of Shelburne by the Loyalists.

Bruce, Charles. *The Channel Shore* (1954, rpt. 1988). Three generations living on the Nova Scotia coast between 1919 and 1950.

——. *The Township of Time: A Chronicle* (1959, rpt. 1986). The Channel Shore is the background for these interrelated stories set in 1786 to 1950.

Buckler, Ernest. *The Mountain and the Valley* (1952, rpt. 1989). A young man grows up on an Annapolis Valley farm.

——. *Ox Bells and Fireflies* (1968, rpt. 1974). A novel based on the author's boyhood on a Nova Scotia farm.

——. *Rebellion of Young David and Other Stories* (1975). Vignettes of personal relationships in a Nova Scotia setting.

Choyce, Lesley. *Eastern Sure: Short Fiction* (1980). Consumerism conflicts with the life of the rural poor.

——. *The Republic of Nothing* (1994). In the 1950s a man decides to declare the independence of an island off the coast of Nova Scotia.

—— (ed.). *Cape Breton Collection* (1984).

—— (ed.). *Chezzetcook: An Anthology of Contemporary Poetry and Fiction From Atlantic Canada* (1977).

Clark, Joan. *Swimming Toward the Light: Short Stories* (1990). Thirteen stories dealing with the same characters stretch from the wartime Nova Scotia coast to present-day Halifax.

Creighton, Helen. *A Folktale Journey Through the Maritimes* (1993).

Currie, Sheldon. *The Company Store* (1988). A novel about a family in a coal-mining town on Cape Breton Island.

Davidson, Heather. *Hot Tongue, Cold Shoulder: A Diary: A Novel* (1981); *The Cow's Tail: A Diary: A Novel* (1982). A Connecticut family moves to Nova Scotia in the eighteenth century.

Day, Frank Parker. *Rockbound: A Novel* (1928, rpt. 1989). Two Nova Scotia fishermen's families feud on an island off the coast of Nova Scotia.

Donovan, Rita. *Dark Jewels: A Novel* (1990). Memories of the past surface in a miner's life.

Doucet, Clive. *My Grandfather's Cape Breton* (1980). A boy spends the summer with his grandfather.

——. *The Priest's Boy* (1992). Seventeen interrelated short stories about life on Cape Breton Island during the depression.

Dow, David Stuart. *The Cliff Hanger House* (1978). In the eighteenth century Scottish immigrants prosper on Cape Breton Island through crime and piracy.

Foster, Malcolm Cecil. *Annapolis Valley Saga* (1976). Fictionalized account of the life of the author's father, 1856–1951.

Fraser, Raymond, Clyde Rose, and Jim Stewart

(eds.). *East of Canada: An Atlantic Anthology* (1976).

Fraser, William Douglas. *Nor'east for Louisbourg* (1978). A Massachusetts man's involvement in the siege of Louisbourg.

Gillis, Tessie. *The Promised Land: Stories of Cape Breton* (1992).

Gordon, Mark. *Head of the Harbour: A Novel* (1982). A man returning from Israel explores Halifax, his home town, and himself.

Hale, Alice and Sheila Brooks (eds.). *Nearly an Island: A Nova Scotia Anthology* (1979).

Haliburton, Thomas Chandler. *The Clockmaker; or, The Sayings and Doings of Sam Slick of Slickville* (1836, rpt. 1993). A satiric picture of nineteenth-century Nova Scotia.

——. *The Old Judge; or, Life in a Colony* (1849, rpt. 1968). Humourous sketches and stories.

Hall, Chipman. *Lightly* (1977). A boy and his grandfather find empathy for each other in an isolated fishing village.

Lewis, David E. *A Lover Needs a Guitar and Other Stories* (1983). Amusing stories set in Bridgetown.

Lotz, Jim. *The Sixth of December* (1981). A novel about the Halifax explosion.

MacDonald, D.R. *Eyestone: Stories* (1988). Most of these nine stories are set in Scottish communities on Cape Breton Island.

MacLennan, Hugh. *Barometer Rising* (1941, rpt. 1989). A novel about the Halifax explosion.

——. *Each Man's Son* (1951, rpt. 1993). Puritan heritage is explored in Cape Breton mining country.

MacLeod, Alistair. *As Birds Bring Forth the Sun and Other Stories* (1986, rpt. 1992); *Lost Salt Gift of Blood* (1976, rpt. 1989). Short stories set on Cape Breton Island.

MacNeil, Robert. *Burden of Desire* (1992). A novel about the Halifax explosion.

Mosher, Edith. *Farm Tales* (1976). Stories about a small family farm.

Nowlan, Alden. *Various Persons Named Kevin O'Brien: A Fictional Memoir* (1973, rpt. 1981). The writer relives his childhood and adolescence in the Nova Scotia village of his youth.

——. *The Wanton Troopers: A Novel* (1988). A story about a boy living in an isolated village in Nova Scotia.

——. *Will Ye Let the Mummers In?: Stories* (1984). Twenty-two stories about life in the Maritimes.

Powell, Robert B. *Gaskell's Cove: A Novel of Early Nova Scotia* (1975).

Raddall, Thomas H. *The Governor's Lady* (1960, rpt. 1992). Historical novel about Frances Wentworth, wife of the governor of Nova Scotia.

——. *Hangman's Beach* (1966, rpt. 1992). The grim realities of war are felt in Halifax during the Napoleonic Wars.

——. *His Majesty's Yankees* (1942, rpt. 1977). Nova Scotians experience conflicting emotions during the American revolution.

——. *The Nymph and the Lamp: A Novel* (1950, rpt. 1994). Marriage problems trouble a Sable Island couple.

——. *Roger Sudden* (1944, rpt. 1977). A historical novel set in Nova Scotia during the Seven Years' War involves the capture of Louisbourg.

——. *The Wings of the Night* (1956). The decline of a once prosperous Nova Scotia lumber town.

Ritchie, Cicero T. *The Willing Maid* (1958). Nova Scotia in the eighteenth century is the background for this novel.

Robertson, Ellison. *Cranberry Head: Stories and Paintings* (1985). Cape Breton Island in fiction and art.

Sauer, Julia L. *Fog Magic* (1943, rpt. 1986).

Taylor, James D. (ed.). *An Underlying Reverence: Stories of Cape Breton* (1994).

Thompson, Kent. *Stories From Atlantic Canada: A Selection* (1973).

Tudor, Kathleen and Renee Davis (eds.). *Islands in the Harbour: A Collection of Stories By Writers From Nova Scotia's South Shore* (1990).

Ward, Frederick. *A Room Full of Balloons* (1981). Based on a true story about a black boy's rebellion.

Weekes, Mary. *Acadian Betrayal* (1955). Historical fiction.

Wilson, Helen Dacey. *Tales From Barrett's Landing: A Childhood in Nova Scotia* (1964); *More Tales From Barrett's Landing: A Childhood in Nova Scotia* (1967).

Wynne-Jones, Tim. *Odd's End* (1980). An unknown person menaces a couple in an isolated house in Nova Scotia.

ONTARIO

Ontario, located in central Canada, is Canada's most populous province. It is bordered on the west by the province of Manitoba; on the north by Hudson Bay and James Bay; on the east by the province of Quebec; and on the south by the states of New York, Pennsylvania, Ohio, Michigan, Wisconsin, and Minnesota. Middle Island, Ontario, (N41° 41') in Lake Erie is the southernmost point in Canada.

Name Province of Ontario. "Ontario" is adapted from an Iroquois Indian word meaning "beautiful water" or "beautiful lake". *Previous names:* Upper Canada (1791–1841), Canada West (1841–1867); before 1791 it was regarded as the upper part of the Province of Quebec.

Flag A red field with a Union Jack in the upper left corner and the provincial shield on the centre right. Proclaimed on May 21, 1965.

Coat of Arms Shield is supported by a moose at left, a bear resting on a bar of gold and green above, a Canadian deer at right, the provincial motto below. The lower two-thirds of the shield has three golden maple leaves on a green background; the upper third, the Cross of St. George (a red cross on a white background). The shield was granted by Queen Victoria in 1868, the motto and supporters by King Edward VII on February 27, 1909.

Motto *Ut Incepit Fidelis Sic Permanet* (Loyal it began, loyal it remains).

Emblems
Bird common loon (*Gavia immer*) (unofficial)

Flower white trillium (*Trillium grandiflorum*)
Mineral amethyst
Tree white pine (*Pinus strobus L.*)

Date of Entry into Confederation July 1, 1867; one of the four original provinces in Confederation.

Official Language English.

Capital City Toronto, situated in southern Ontario on the north shore near the western end of Lake Ontario; population 635,395. The site was selected by Governor John Graves Simcoe as the capital of Upper Canada and named York on August 27,1793; the capital was transferred from Newark (Niagara-on-the-Lake) February 1, 1796. York was incorporated on March 6, 1834. In 1835 its name was changed to Toronto (adapted from Indian word meaning "place of meeting"). The Municipality of Metropolitan Toronto, a federation of Toronto and suburbs, was created January 1, 1953; population 2,275,771, CMA population 3,893,046, the largest metropolitan area in Canada.

Provincial Holidays In addition to national statutory holidays (see page 2), Ontario residents celebrate Civic Holiday (the first Monday in August).

Geography and Climate

Geography Most of northern Ontario and two-thirds of the total land mass of the province is covered by the Canadian Shield, among the oldest rocks in the world, rich in mineral deposits, and unsuitable for agriculture. Except where a few northern clay belts exist, most agricultural activity takes place in southern Ontario where fertile soil is found. The forest cover ranges from the stunted black spruce and willows of the extreme north changing gradually to aspen, jack pine, and spruce as one moves south and finally to the mixed forests of the southern part of Ontario.

Area 1,068,582 sq. km. (412,473 sq. mi.); 10.8% of Canada. *Rank:* 2nd among the provinces, 3rd among the provinces and territories.

Inland Water 177,388 sq. km. (68,472 sq. mi.), includes more than 250,000 lakes. Largest lake wholly in Ontario: Lake Nipigon 4,848 sq. km. (1,871 sq. mi.).

Elevations Highest point: Ishpatina Ridge, Timiskaming District (N47° 20' W80° 44'), 693 m. (2,274 ft.). Lowest point: Hudson Bay shore, sea level.

Major Rivers (* indicates a designated Canadian Heritage River; ** indicates a Ramsar site): Abitibi, Albany, Attawapiskat, *Bloodvein, Detroit, */**French, */**Grand, Mattagami, *Mattawa, *Missinaibi, Moose, Niagara, Ottawa, Rainy, Rouge, St. Clair, St. Lawrence, Severn, the Trent-Severn Canal and the Rideau Canal systems, *the boundary waters/Voyageur Waterway in La Verendrye, Quetico, and Middle Falls Provincial Parks.

Climate Because Ontario stretches more than 15° latitude, there can be a large range in temperature from north to south. Northern Ontario has a subarctic climate while southern Ontario is in the temperate zone. (The dividing line between north and south for climate data is Sault Ste. Marie, Sudbury, and Ottawa.) The average daily mean temperature in January in northern Ontario is −20°C (−4°F); in southern Ontario −7.5°C (18.5°F); in July in northern Ontario 16°C (60.8°F); in southern Ontario 20°C (68°F). The lowest recorded temperature in Ontario: −58.3°C (−72.9°F) at Iroquois Falls on January 23, 1935; the highest recorded temperature 42.2°C (107°F) at Atikokan on July 11–12, 1936, and Fort Francis on July 13, 1936.

Average annual snowfall in northern Ontario: 200 cm. (78.7 in.); in southern Ontario 150–200 cm. (59–78.7 in.); in the lee of the Great Lakes 300 cm. (118.1 in.). Greatest recorded snowfall in one day: 101.6 cm. (40 in.) at Nolalu on March 24, 1975. Greatest recorded annual snowfall: 766 cm. (301.6 in.) at Steep Hills Falls winter of 1938–39. The greatest recorded Ontario annual precipitation: 1,620 mm. (63.8 in.) at Stratford in 1884.

Southwestern Ontario has the highest frequency of hot humid weather in Canada; 32°C (89.6°F) is the mean humidex in Windsor during the last week of July; London has the highest Canadian average number of thunderstorm days, 34.

Time Zones Most of the province is in the eastern time zone; the area west of the 90th meridian near the Manitoba border is in the central time zone.

Parks and Historic Sites

In this section, * indicates that the area is, or part of it is, a Ramsar site.

National Parks Located In Ontario

Park	Location	Size
Bruce Peninsula	Bruce Peninsula	266 sq. km. (103 sq. mi.)
Georgian Bay Islands	near Honey Harbour	24 sq. km. (9 sq. mi.)

*Point Pelee	near Leamington	16 sq. km. (6 sq. mi.)
Pukaska	near Marathon	1,878 sq. km. (725 sq. mi.)
St. Lawrence Islands	near Mallorytown	6 sq. km. (2 sq. mi.)

Unesco Biosphere Reserves Located in Ontario

Reserve	Location	Size
Long Point	north shore Lake Erie	26,250 ha. (101 sq. mi.)
Niagara Escarpment	Bruce Peninsula south to Niagara River	207,000 ha. in 725 km. (799 sq. mi. in 450 mi.)

Provincial Parks   There are 260 provincial parks covering 6% of Ontario's area: 82 nature reserve parks, 8 wilderness parks, 64 natural environment parks, 29 waterways parks, 73 recreation parks, and 4 historical parks. The largest parks are:

Park	District	Type	Size
*Polar Bear	Moosonee	wilderness	2,408,700 ha. (9,300 sq. mi.)
Algonquin	Algonquin	natural environment	765,345 ha. (2,995 sq. mi.)
Quetico	Atikokan	wilderness	475,819 ha. (1,837 sq. mi.)
Opasquia	Red Lake	wilderness	473,000 ha. (1,826 sq. mi.)
Woodland Caribou	Red Lake	wilderness	450,000 ha. (1,737 sq. mi.)
Lake Superior	Wawa	natural environment	155,659 ha. (601 sq. mi.)
Wabakimi	Nipigon	wilderness	155,000 ha. (598 sq. mi.)
Winisk River	Geraldton	waterway	152,500 ha. (589 sq. mi.)
Missinaibi	Chapleau	waterway	99,152 ha. (383 sq. mi.)
Pipestone River	Sioux Lookout	waterway	97,375 ha. (376 sq. mi.)

Ontario also has 360 conservation areas including 12 national bird sanctuaries (plus one shared with the Northwest Territories) and 9 national wildlife areas. There are 5 Ramsar sites.

Major National Historic Sites and Parks in Ontario

Bellevue House, Kingston
Bethune Memorial House, Gravenhurst
Butler's Barracks, Niagara-on-the-Lake
Fort George, Niagara-on-the-Lake
Fort Malden, Amherstburg
Fort Mississauga, Niagara-on-the-Lake
Fort St. Joseph, St. Joseph Island
Fort Wellington, Prescott
Fort York, Toronto
Queenston Heights and Brock Monument, Queenston
Woodside, Kitchener

In addition, there are a large number of historic sites in Ontario administered by the province, municipalities, or organizations. The major sites are:

Black Creek Pioneer Village, Metropolitan Toronto
Fort Henry, Kingston
Old Fort William, Thunder Bay
Ste. Marie Among the Hurons, Midland
Upper Canada Village, near Morrisburg

Demography

All figures relating to Ontario population and dwellings are 1991 data and do not include the population on 34 Indian reserves that did not cooperate in the 1991 census. Staff at Statistics Canada estimate that there are between 5,000 and 6,000 residents on these reserves.

Ontario Population: 10,084,885; 36.9% of national; *rank* 1st

Historical population data
1981	8,625,107
1971	7,703,106
1961	6,236,092

1951	4,597,542
1941	3,787,655
1921	2,933,662
1901	2,182,947
1881	1,926,922
1861	1,396,091

Population Density: 11 persons per sq. km. (28.5 per sq. mi.)

Number of Dwellings: 3,661,671

Indian Reserves: 126 bands on 128 reserves and 9 Indian settlements

Population Characteristics:
urban: 8,253,842; 81.8%
rural: 1,831,043; 18.2%
19 and under: 2,734,300; 27.1%
65 and over: 1,183,475; 11.7%
average income for full-time employment 15 years and over (1990): $36,031; men $41,509; women $27,862
average life expectancy at birth (1987): men 73.5 years; women 79.7 years
live birth rate: 151,478; 15.0 per 1000
deaths: 72,917; 7.4 per 1000
marriages: 72,938; 7.2 per 1000
divorces: 27,699; 2.75 per 1000

Largest Cities (all CMAs) (for a definition of CMA, see page viii)

Name	Population	Dwellings	National Pop. Rank
Toronto	3,893,046	1,373,056	1
National Capital District (Ottawa part)	920,857 (693,900)	352,411 (267,796)	4
Hamilton	599,760	221,777	9
London	381,522	147,990	10
St. Catherines-Niagara	364,552	138,433	11
Kitchener	356,421	138,433	12
Windsor	262,075	97,759	15
Oshawa	240,140	83,076	16
Sudbury	157,613	57,805	21
Thunder Bay	124,427	47,104	25

Government and Politics, 1867–

A description of the division of powers between the federal and provincial governments will be found on page 4.

Lieutenant-Governor The Lieutenant-Governor is the nominal head of the Ontario government, and is appointed by the Governor General of Canada on the recommendation of the Prime Minister of Canada. (A description of the duties of lieutenant-governors is found on page 7.)

Lieutenant-Governors of Ontario

	Term
Henry William Sisted	1867–1868
William Pearcy Howland	1868–1873
John Willoughby Crawford	1873–1875
Donald Alexander Macdonald	1875–1880
John Beverly Robinson	1880–1887
Alexander Campbell	1887–1892
George Airey Kirkpatrick	1892–1897
Oliver Mowat	1897–1903
William Mortimer Clark	1903–1908
John Morison Gibson	1908–1914
John Strathearn Hendrie	1914–1919
Lionel Herbert Clarke	1919–1921
Henry Cockshutt	1921–1927
William Donald Ross	1927–1932
Herbert Alexander Bruce	1932–1937
Albert Matthews	1937–1946
Ray Lawson	1946–1952
Louis Orville Breithaupt	1952–1957
John Keiller MacKay	1957–1963
William Earl Rowe	1963–1968
William Ross Macdonald	1968–1974
Pauline Emily McGibbon	1974–1980

John Black Aird	1980–1985
Lincoln MacCauley Alexander	1985–1991
Henry Newton Rowell Jackman	1991-

Legislative Assembly The Legislative Assembly of Ontario consists of 130 members elected by popular vote, each member representing a constituency; term of office: up to 5 years as long as the party in power maintains the confidence of the Legislative Assembly; remuneration (1993/4): $44,675 + $14,984 expense allowance, additional amounts for special appointments; qualifications for members: Canadian citizen, 18 years or older on polling day, ordinarily resident in Ontario six months prior to polling day, not legally disqualified. (A description of the duties of provincial legislatures are found on page 7.)

Qualifications for Ontario Voters in Provincial Elections Canadian citizen, 18 years or older on polling day, ordinarily resident in Ontario six months prior to polling day, ordinarily resident in electoral district six months prior to polling day, not legally disqualified.

Premier Nominally appointed by the Lieutenant-Governor of Ontario, the Premier is generally the leader of the party with the majority of seats in the Legislative Assembly. (A description of the responsibilities of provincial premiers is found on page 7.)

Premiers of Ontario/Party/Term
John Sandfield Macdonald
   (Liberal-Conservative, 1867–1871)
Edward Blake
   (Liberal, 1871–1872)
Oliver Mowat
   (Liberal, 1872–1896)
Arthur Sturgis Hardy
   (Liberal, 1896–1899)
George William Ross
   (Liberal, 1899–1905)
James Pliny Whitney
   (Conservative, 1905–1914)
William Howard Hearst
   (Conservative, 1914–1919)

Ernest Charles Drury
   (United Farmers of Ontario, 1919–1923)
George Howard Ferguson
   (Conservative, 1923–1930)
George Stewart Henry
   (Conservative, 1930–1934)
Mitchell Frederick Hepburn
   (Liberal, 1934–1942)
Gordon Daniel Conant
   (Liberal, 1942–1943)
Harry Corwin Nixon
   (Liberal, 1943)
George Alexander Drew
   (Conservative, 1943–1948)
Thomas Laird Kennedy
   (Conservative, 1948–1949)
Leslie Miscampbell Frost
   (Conservative, 1949–1961)
John Parmenter Robarts
   (Conservative, 1961–1971)
William Grenville Davis
   (Conservative, 1971–1985)
Frank Miller
   (Conservative, 1985)
David Robert Peterson
   (Liberal, 1985–1990)
Robert Keith Rae
   (New Democratic, 1990–   )

Cabinet The Cabinet consists of ministers appointed by the Premier, usually from elected members of the majority party in the Legislative Assembly. Cabinet ministers serve at the Premier's pleasure; each member usually heads a government ministry.

Government Ministries The telephone numbers for general information are listed with the ministries.

Agriculture and Food
   (416)326-3400
Attorney General
   (416)326-2220
Citizenship
   (416)314-7226
Community and Social Services
   (416)325-5666
Consumer and Commercial Relations
   (416)326-8555
Culture, Tourism and Recreation
   (416)314-7400

Economic Development and Trade
(416)325-6666
Education and Training
(416)325-2929
Environment and Energy
(416)323-4321 800-565-4923
Finance
(416)325-0400 800-263-7965
Health
(416)327-4327 800-263-1153
Housing
(416)585-7041
Intergovernmental Affairs
(416)325-4760
Labour
(416)326-7565 800-267-9517

Municipal Affairs
(416)585-7041
Natural Resources
(416)314-2000
Northern Development and Mines
(416)965-1683
Soliciter General and Correctional Services
(416)326-5000
Transportation
(416)235-4686 800-268-0637

Ontario Representation in Federal Government
House of Commons: 99 members
Senate: 24 members

Finances

A statement of Ontario's revenue and expenditures for the years 1992/93 and 1991/92 are shown below in millions of dollars. The financial year runs from April 1 to March 31 of the year following.

	Actual 1992/93	*Actual 1991/92*
Revenue		
Taxation	30,041	30,738
Other	4,212	3,691
Government of Canada	7,554	6,324
Total revenue for the year	41,807	40,753
Expenditures		
Health	16,973	16,834
Education	6,197	6,414
Colleges and universities	3,396	3,296
Social services	9,413	8,314
Other	12,535	12,629
Interest on debt	5,193	4,196
Total expenditures for the year	53,707	51,683
Deficit for the year	11,900	10,930

Economy

Ontario is the most industrialized and urbanized province and produces the most wealth. The largest Canadian stock exchange, the head offices of many of the major chartered banks, insurance companies, and large corporations are located here, principally in Toronto. More than 50% of Canada's manufactured goods are made in Ontario. It has Canada's largest and most diverse agricultural activity in-cluding more commercial livestock farms than other provinces and the most fruit production mainly from the Niagara Peninsula.

Major Industries Ontario is Canada's largest producer of motor vehicles and parts, steel, computers, and minerals. Principal industries include all types of manufacturing, finance, construction, service industries including tourism, agriculture, and forestry.

Gross Domestic Product (1992) $236,811 million (in current dollars at factor cost); % of national G.D.P.: 39.4%; *rank:* 1st

Distribution of gross domestic product (1990):

Commercial, business, personal services	23.9%
Manufacturing	23.8%
Finance, insurance, real estate	16.7%
Trade, wholesale and retail	11.5%
Transportation and communication	7.0%
Public administration	6.0%
Construction	5.9%
Utilities	2.6%
Other primary	1.4%
Agriculture	1.2%

Value of Manufacturing Shipments $146,018 million

Farm Cash Receipts 5,414 million

Employment (seasonally adjusted) 4,734,000; participation rate: 67.5%

Unemployment (seasonally adjusted) 517,000; per capita: 9.8%

Minimum Wage (1994) $6.70, general minimum; $5.90, liquor servers and students under 18.

Exports Ontario's total exports in goods and services in 1992 amounted to $82,226 million, 48% of total Canadian merchandising exports; *rank:* 1st. Ontario exports more per capita than any G-7 nation. Largest trading partner: United States; more than 88% of Ontario's export is shipped to the United States. Major export commodities: vehicles (other than railways/trams rolling stock) 42%; industrial equipment (nuclear reactors, boilers, machinery and mechanical appliances) 12%.

History

ca. 10,000 B.C.	Paleo-Indians arrive.
ca. 1000 B.C.	Evidence of pottery and wide-spread trading.
Early centuries A.D.	Algonquin, Cree, Huron, Neutral (or Attiwandron), Nipissing, Ojibwa (or Chippewa), Ottawa, Petun (or Tobacco) Indian tribes inhabit present-day Ontario.
ca. 1600	Huron, Neutral, Ojibwa, Ottawa, Petun are the dominant tribes.
ca. 1610	Huron confederacy is formed making it the strongest political unit at the time Europeans arrive.
1610	Henry Hudson explores Hudson Bay. Etienne Brulé, the first European to see Lakes Ontario, Huron, and Superior, lives with the Hurons.
1611	*June 23* Henry Hudson, cast adrift by his crew, lands on northern shores of present-day Ontario.
1613	Samuel de Champlain explores the Ottawa River.
1615	Champlain winters with the Hurons.
1620–1650	Hurons act as middlemen in fur trade.
1626	*July* Jean de Brebeuf, Jesuit missionary, arrives in Huron country.
1638	An epidemic kills more than half the Hurons.
1639	Jerome Lalemant begins construction of Sainte Marie, a Jesuit mission near present-day Midland, the first European-built community in present-day Ontario.
1649	*May 15* Jesuits burn and abandon Sainte Marie. Iroquois from present-day United States conquer southern Ontario Indians to gain control of the fur trade; southern Ontario is depopulated by death and dispersal.

1650	Ottawa tribe assumes position as middlemen in the link between New France and the fur trade.
1670	*May 2* Hudson's Bay Company is formed and granted trade rights over all territory draining into Hudson Bay.
1672	Charles Bayley establishes the second Hudson's Bay Company post at Moose Fort, the first English settlement in Ontario.
1673	*June 13* French establish Fort Cataraqui (later Fort Frontenac) at present-day Kingston, the first permanent (with brief interruptions) European settlement in the Great Lakes region.
1686	French capture English posts on James Bay: Moose Fort (*June 20*) and Fort Albany (*July 26*).
1692	Hudson's Bay Company recaptures Fort Albany.
1713	*April 11* France returns Hudson Bay drainage basin to Britain in the Treaty of Utrecht.
1720	French establish Fort Toronto, a small post; it is abandoned in 1730.
1749	Land grants on the site of present-day Windsor are given to French Canadian farmers, the first permanent agricultural settlement in Ontario.
1750	French build Fort Rouillé on the site of present-day Toronto.
1754	Beginning of French and Indian War; most fighting takes place outside Ontario's borders.
1758	*August 27* Fort Frontenac is captured and destroyed by American colonial troops.
1759	French burn Fort Rouillé to keep it from the British.
1760	French capitulate; Canada becomes a British colony.
1763	*February 10* Treaty of Paris: France formally cedes its North American possessions to Britain including all of Canada east of the Rocky Mountains.
1774	*June 22* Quebec Act, passed by the British Parliament, extends the borders of Quebec to include all of present-day southern Ontario, establishes English criminal law, restores French civil law, and grants religious freedom for Catholic Canadians. In effect, *May 1, 1775*.
1776	Ontario is used as a base of operation for British and loyalist troops during the American Revolution.
1783	*September 3* Treaty of Paris: formal end of British-United States conflict sets a line running through the middle of the Great Lakes and their connecting rivers as the southern boundary of Ontario.
1784	Mass migration of United Empire Loyalists from the United States to Ontario starts with about 6,000 Americans and 1,000 Iroquois led by Joseph Brant. The largest settlements are established in southeastern Ontario. The total immigration reaches 10,000 by the end of the decade.
1785	John Stuart opens first school in Ontario at Kingston.
1787	*September 23* Land is purchased from the Indians at present-day Toronto.
1789	*December 27* First stage coach service in Ontario, Fort Erie-Queenston, begins.
1790	*May 19* Land south of Lake St. Clair and Thames River to the northwest shore of Lake Erie is purchased from Indians.
1791	*June 10* Constitutional Act or Canada Act (British Parliament) divides Quebec into Upper and Lower Canada, establishes English law and land tenure in Upper Canada, a system of government which includes an elected legislative assembly and an appointed lieutenant-governor, legislative council, and executive council, and sets aside one-seventh of the land each for the support of the lieutenant-governor and the Protestant clergy.
1792	John Graves Simcoe, Upper Canada's first lieutenant-governor, arrives. *September 17* First legislature is convened at Newark (present-day Niagara-on-

the Lake), Upper Canada's first capital. First statute introduces English law for property and civil rights.

1793 *April 18* First Ontario newspaper, the *Upper Canada Gazette*, is published in Newark.

August 24 Simcoe founds York (present-day Toronto).

1794 Simcoe transfers capital of Upper Canada to York.

1800 *June 8* First circulating library in Upper Canada is established at Niagara.

1802 Fort William becomes the chief Ontario fur headquarters for the North West Company.

1803 Thomas Talbot begins his promotion of settlement in the London district; by 1836 he has settled portions of 29 townships in southwestern Upper Canada.

1807 *February 2* District Grammar School Act signals the beginning of the Ontario education system.

1812 *June 18* United States declares war on Britain.

July 11 Americans invade Canada from Detroit.

September 29 Americans raid Gananoque.

October 13 Canadian victory at Battle of Queenston Heights.

1813 *February 7* Americans raid Brockville.

April 27 Americans burn York.

May 27 Americans capture Fort George.

June 5 Canadian victory at Battle of Stoney Creek.

June 24 Canadian victory at Battle of Beaver Dam.

September 10 American victory at Battle of Put-in-Bay, Lake Erie.

October 5 American victory at Battle of Moraviantown.

November 11 Canadian victory at Battle of Crysler's Farm.

December 10 Americans burn Newark and part of Queenston.

1814 *July 5* American victory at Battle of Chippewa.

July 25 Canadian victory at Battle of Lundy's Lane.

December 24 Treaty of Ghent ends conflict and both sides return what has been captured.

1817 *April 27* Rush-Bagot Treaty limits the number of battleships on the Great Lakes leading to naval disarmament in that area.

Road between Toronto and Montreal is completed.

1820–1850 Mass immigration from British Isles results in southern Ontario being substantially settled by the mid-1850s.

1821 *April 21* Bank of Upper Canada is incorporated.

1824 First novel by a Canadian-born author to be published in British North America, *St. Ursala' Convent: The Nun of Canada* by Julia Catherine Hart is published in Kingston.

1825 Peter Robinson settles ca. 2,000 Irish immigrants around present-day Peterborough.

1826 *May 26* Naturalized Upper Canada residents have the right to vote for, and be elected to, the Assembly.

1827 *March 31* King's College (later University of Toronto) is founded.

1829 *November 29* Welland Canal opens linking Lake Erie and Lake Ontario around Niagara Falls.

1831 First museum in Canada is established in Niagara Falls.

Canada's oldest weekly newspaper, the *Coburg Star,* is published.

1832 *May 29* Rideau Canal is completed linking Kingston to Bytown (later Ottawa).

1834 William Lyon Mackenzie becomes the first mayor of York (Toronto).

Printers in York form Ontario's first trade union.

	March 6 First railway in Upper Canada, the London and Gore Railroad, is incorporated.
	December 30 Fire destroys Upper Canada's Parliament building in York (Toronto).
1835–1836	North America's first plank road is laid leading east from Toronto.
1835	*March 11* First formal police force in Canada is established in Toronto.
1837	*November 25* Mackenzie proclaims the Provisional Government of the State of Upper Canada.
	December 5–7 Rebellion led by Mackenzie is defeated at Toronto.
	December 29 Upper Canada militia burns the United States ship *Caroline* with one American death and one injury.
1838	British government sends Lord Durham to investigate Canadian problems; he briefly visits Upper Canada.
	February 26 Five hundred American Fenians occupy Pelee Island; they are defeated by British troops and local militia on *March 3.*
	November 12–16 Americans capture a windmill near Prescott and eventually are defeated.
	December 4 American raid at Windsor is routed.
1839	*February 4* Lord Durham recommends the union of Upper and Lower Canada and the establishment of responsible government for local and regional affairs.
1840	*September 6* First official weather observation in Canada is taken by Charles Riddell at Toronto.
1841	*February 10* Act of Union (British Parliament) creates the Province of Canada; Upper Canada becomes Canada West.
1841–1843	Kingston is the capital of the Province of Canada.
1841	*June 14* First Union Parliament meets.
1842	*August 9* Ashburton-Webster Treaty defines the southern boundary of Ontario west to Lake of the Woods.
1844	*September 17* First suspension bridge in Canada opens across the Ottawa River at the Chaudière Falls.
1846	*December 19* First telegram in Canada is sent from Toronto to Hamilton.
1848	*March 11* Reformers Robert Baldwin (Canada West) and Robert Lafontaine (Canada East) are elected and achieve responsible government.
	March 29–31 Ice jam on Lake Erie near Buffalo causes Niagara Falls to run dry.
1849	*February 1* Amnesty Act grants immunity to those involved in the Rebellion of 1837.
	April 7 Fire destroys much of Toronto.
	Municipal Corporations Act sets a framework for local self-government which forms the basis of the present system in Ontario.
1849–1865	Capital of the Province of Canada alternates every four years between Toronto and Quebec City.
1850	Common School Act is the beginning of modern Ontario's system of public-supported schools and provides for a public library system.
1852	*October 24* Toronto Stock Exchange opens.
1853	Catholics are exempted from school taxes if they wish to pay taxes for Catholic schools.
	April 16 James Goode, Toronto Locomotive Works, produces the first Canadian-made locomotive for the Ontario, Simcoe and Huron Railway.
1854	*June 6* Reciprocity Treaty with the United States, together with railroad building and other factors, brings an economic boom to Ontario.
	Clergy reserves are abolished.

	Printers undertake first Canadian labour strike.
	First railway tunnel in Canada opens at Brockville.
1856	*June* First Ontario French-language newspaper, *Le Progress*, is published in Ottawa.
1857	*December 31* Queen Victoria selects Ottawa as the capital of the Province of Canada.
1850–1869	A primarily agricultural society gives way to urban and industrial growth with manufacturing in farm implements, machinery, metalworking, and textiles.
1862	Oil is discovered near Sarnia.
1863	Scott Act establishes separate schools in rural areas and is the basis of the modern school system.
1864	*June 1* Harvey Farrington opens the first cheese factory in Canada in Oxford County.
1866	*March 16* United States abrogates the Reciprocity Treaty.
	May 31–June 3 American Fenians raid across Niagara frontier, defeat the Canadian militia at Ridgeway, and retreat to the United States.
1867	*July 1* Canada West, renamed Ontario, joins three other British North American colonies in Confederation; Ottawa becomes the capital of the Dominion of Canada.
	September First Ontario election is held.
	December 27 First Legislative Assembly of Ontario meets.
	Emily Howard Stowe, the first woman doctor in Canada, practices medicine in Toronto.
1868	*April 7* American Fenian assassinates Thomas D'Arcy McGee, a Father of Confederation, in Ottawa.
	Vote is given to male British subjects 21 years old, who own, rent, or occupy property of specified values.
1869	*November 19* Canada purchases Rupert's Land from the Hudson's Bay Company; the transfer in effect *July 15, 1870* increases Ontario's size.
1870	A matron and deputy matron are hired at the Kingston Penitentiary, the first female federal civil servants.
1872	Dual representation by one person in the federal and Ontario legislatures is abolished.
1873	*June* Canada's oldest winery still operating, Barnes Wines Ltd., opens in St. Catherines.
1874	Vote is extended to male British subjects 21 years old with an annual income of $400 and to "enfranchised Indians".
1876	Local school systems are made accountable to a new Department of Education.
	April 12 Present-day northwestern Ontario becomes part of the District of Keetwatin.
	June 1 Royal Military College, Canada's first military college, is established at Kingston.
1879	First long distance line in Canada is erected from Hamilton to Dundas.
	Toronto has first telephone directory in Canada.
1881	First public telephone in Canada operates in Lancefield's stationery store, Hamilton.
	May 24 Paddle-steamer *Victoria* capsizes on Thames River; 182 dead.
1882	Ontario's largest wheat crop represents the apex of wheat farming in Ontario which, thereafter, declined in favour of other crops.
	Free Libraries Act is passed.

1883	*March 23* Manhood suffrage is instituted.
	May 7 Toronto takes over the Mechanic's Institute to develop a library that will become the largest public library system in Canada.
	July 10–11 77 mm. (3 in.) of rain causes a flash flood in the Thames River at London that kills 18 and sweeps away buildings.
	First woman to graduate in medicine, Ann Augusta Stowe-Gullen, receives a degree from Victoria College.
1884	Legislation is passed to protect women and youth in factories; 14 minimum age for females, 12 for males, 10 hours maximum work day.
	Spinsters and widows are permitted to vote in municipal elections.
	July 4 Imperial Privy Council defines Ontario's borders.
	October 8 Pembroke becomes the first town in Ontario to use electricity for street lighting.
1885	*July* Well is sunk at Port Colborne from which a gas utility is established the following August.
1886	First electric tram system in Canada opens in Windsor.
	March 25 First Workman's Compensation Act in Canada.
1888	First nickel smelter is built at Copper Cliff.
	Vote is extended to all adult male British subjects except unenfranchised Indians living on reserves.
	Hydroelectric power is generated for the first time in Canada at John Barber's paper mill in Georgetown.
1889	*December 9* Ontario wins boundary dispute with Manitoba and the federal government in Britain's highest court; Ontario's boundary is extended to James Bay, Albany River, and Lake of the Woods.
1891	Ontario Hockey Association is founded, the first organized league promoting hockey as a spectator sport.
	Toronto establishes the first children's aid society in Canada.
	October 2 Grand Trunk Railway opens the St. Clair Tunnel between Sarnia and Port Huron, Michigan, the first underwater train tunnel in Canada.
1893	*April 4* Ontario legislative buildings are officially opened.
	May First provincial forest reserve, Algonquin Park, is established.
1894	Ontario votes for Prohibition.
1896	*May 10* Imperial Privy Council upholds Ontario's right to enforce Prohibition, but denies the right to stop its manufacture or importation.
1897	Iron is discovered north of Sault Ste. Marie; gold is discovered at Wawa.
	Lady Ishbel Aberdeen receives an honourary degree from Queen's University, Kingston, the first Canadian university to award an honourary degree to a woman.
1899	Ontario militia regiments go to the South African War.
1900	Great Fire destroys one-fifth of Ottawa.
1902	*May 12* Work begins on the Temiskaming and Northern Ontario Railway, the first railway owned by a Canadian province.
1903	Seven miles per hour speed limit is established for automobiles.
1904	Albert Evanturel, Prescott, becomes Ontario's first French Canadian cabinet minister.
	Canadian automotive industry begins when Ford Motor Company of Canada is formed in Windsor.
1906	Allan Studholme, Hamilton East, becomes the first elected Labour member of the Legislative Assembly.
1909	*April 13* Supreme Court of Ontario is established.
	May 1 Prohibition comes into effect.

	July 13 Gold is discovered in the Cochrane area.
1910	Association canadienne-française d'education d'Ontario is established to promote French language education for Ontario French children.
1912	Ontario achieves its present boundaries.
	Ontario children are to be educated in English; Regulation 17 limits French to the first two years as a language of instruction and after that as a regular subject.
	July 6 Fred Eells flies the first seaplane in Canada at Toronto Harbour.
1913	*October 8* W. Robinson makes the first commercial inter-city flight, Montreal to Ottawa.
1914–1918	Almost 10% of Ontario's population is in uniform; 68,000 are killed, wounded, or missing in World War I.
1914	Algoma Central Railway, Sault Ste. Marie to Hearst, is completed.
1915	*July 14* First Canadian-produced aircraft, the Curtiss JN-3, is test flown near Toronto.
1916	*March 2* Temperance Act is passed making it illegal to possess alcohol outside a private dwelling or to sell it as a beverage.
	July 29 Forest fire engulfs Cochrane and Matheson; ca. 230 dead.
1917	*April 12* Vote in provincial and municipal elections is extended to women.
1918	*June 24* First Canadian airmail flight, Montreal to Toronto.
1920	*May* First exhibition of the Group of Seven painters is held at the Art Gallery of Ontario, Toronto.
1921	*December 6* Agnes Macphail from Grey County becomes the first woman elected to the federal parliament.
	April 18 Ontario votes for Prohibition.
1922	*October 4* Forest fire almost destroys Haileybury and spreads over 18 townships, killing 43 and dispossessing 2,900 people.
1923	Frederick Grant Banting and John Rickard Macleod, University of Toronto, are given the Nobel Prize in physiology/medicine for their discovery of insulin.
1924	*September* First Canadian regular airmail service begins between Haileybury, Ontario, and Rouyn, Quebec.
1926	Red Lake gold rush starts in northern Ontario leading to a boom peak in the 1930s and 1940s.
	December 1 Ontario government control of liquor sales rather than Prohibition is preferred by voters.
1927	*June 12* British Privy Council rules against an appeal for separate Catholic schools in Ontario.
1930	*February 20* Cairine Reay Wilson becomes the first woman appointed to the Senate.
1931	Ontario Farm Marketing Board is established.
1934	Standard Stock and Mining Exchange is amalgamated with the Toronto Stock Exchange.
1936	*July* One of the most intense heat waves in Canadian history hits Ontario leaving 600 dead, crops devastated, and causing forest fires.
	November 2 Federal government establishes the Canadian Broadcasting Corporation as a crown corporation with English-language services based in Toronto.
1937	Ontario's first minimum wage for men is instituted.
	Thames River at London floods leaving 4,000 homeless.
1938	*January 27* Ice on the Niagara River causes the Honeymoon Bridge to collapse.
1941	*September 25* Hurricane with 130 kph (81 mph) winds hits southwestern Ontario.

1943	Joseph Salsberg and Albert MacLeod are the first and only Communists elected to the Ontario Legislative Assembly.
1944	*December 11* 57 cm. (22.4 in.) of snow, strong winds, and huge drifts paralyze Toronto for several days.
1945	*September 5* Canada's first nuclear reactor begins operation at Chalk River.
1946–1969	Large postwar baby boom and immigration increase Ontario's population.
1946	*June 17* Tornado moving from Windsor to Tecumseh leaves 17 dead, hundreds injured, and much property damage.
	July 10 First drive-in theatre in Canada opens in Stoney Creek.
1949	Ontario's first four-lane restricted-access highway, the Queen Elizabeth Way from Toronto to the American border at Buffalo, is completed.
	September 17 Excursion ship *Noronic* burns at a pier in the Toronto Harbour, leaving 118 dead.
1952	*September 8* CBLT, Canada's first English-language television station, begins broadcasting in Toronto.
1953	*April–May* Franc Joubin and Joseph Herman Hirshhorn stake the biggest uranium find in history near Blind River.
	May 21 Tornado hits Sarnia leaving five dead and much damage.
	July 3 Stratford Festival opens.
	First indoor shopping mall in Canada, Lawrence Plaza, opens in Toronto.
1954	*March 30* Canada's first subway opens in Toronto.
	October 15 Hurricane Hazel drops up to 214 mm. (8.4 in.) of rain on Toronto in 72 hours, causing Canada's severest flood; 83 people dead, millions in property damage.
	Last restrictions on Ontario Indians' voting rights are removed.
1957	*June* Ellen Louks Fairclough, Hamilton, becomes the first woman federal cabinet minister.
1959	*January 1* Federal-provincial hospital plan is in effect in Ontario.
	April 20 St. Lawrence Seaway opens to commercial traffic.
1962	*June 4* First Canadian nuclear power generating station opens at Rolphston.
	July 30 TransCanada Highway officially opens at the half-way mark, 61 km. (38 mi.) north of Sault Ste. Marie.
	August 1 Ontario Construction Act makes employers responsible for the safety of their staff.
	December 11 Canada's last execution, a double hanging, takes place at the Don Jail, Toronto.
1964	*August 17* Important copper-silver-zinc discovery near Timmins causes big stock-gambling activity.
1965	*January 16* Automotive Products Trade Agreement between Canada and the United States causes major restructuring in Ontario's automotive industry.
1967	*August 24* Plans to establish French-language secondary schools are announced.
	Grade 13 matriculation examinations are abolished.
1968	Hall-Dennis report is published and influences the destructuring of the educational system.
	April 12 Lincoln MacCauley Alexander, Hamilton West, becomes the first black person to sit in the federal parliament.
	August 19 Severe hailstorm in Lambeth leaves 17.5 cm. (6.9 in.) of ice on streets and extensive damage to crops and property.
1969	*October 16* Herbert Eser Gray, Windsor, becomes the first Jew to be appointed to the federal cabinet.
1970	TV Ontario, a provincially-owned, noncommercial television network, begins broadcasting in English on Monday to Saturday and French on Sunday.

July 5 Air Canada flight crashes at Toronto airport killing all 109 aboard.

August 20 Tornado at Sudbury leaves 6 dead, 200 injured, and much property damage.

1971 *July* Legal age of majority in Ontario is 18.

September 13 Ontario government establishes free hospital and medical care for citizens 65 years and over effective *January 1, 1972*, and for low income earners effective *April 1, 1972*.

December Gerhard Herzberg, National Research Council, Ottawa, is awarded the Nobel Prize in chemistry for his studies of chemical reactions that help produce smog.

1974 *April 3* Tornado at Windsor leaves 9 dead, 30 injured, and much property damage.

1975 *April 1* CN Tower is completed.

May 22 Arthur Maloney is appointed Ontario's first ombudsman.

1977 First commercial CANDU reactor begins operation in Pickering.

December 7–9 Storm drops 101 cm. (39.8 in.) of snow on London; drifts block all roads; army emergency unit is brought to the city.

1978 *January 6* Sun Life Assurance Company announces head office move from Montreal to Toronto because of Quebec language laws and political instability; many other firms make similar moves.

1979 *November 10* Two hundred twenty thousand people are evacuated from Mississauga because of a derailed tanker car containing dangerous chemicals.

1981 Massive gold deposits are found at Hemlo.

1982 *March 4* Bertha Wilson of the Ontario Court of Appeal becomes the first woman to sit on the Supreme Court of Canada.

1983 Drought in southern Ontario is the worst in the twentieth century.

1984 *June 12* Ontario government announces full public funding for Catholic separate schools to the end of the secondary school level.

1985 Alvin Curling, Scarborough North, becomes Ontario's first black cabinet minister and Lincoln Alexander the first black lieutenant-governor.

May 30 Golf-ball size hailstones flatten crops and smash greenhouses in Windsor and Leamington.

May 31 Eight tornadoes move through Barrie and central Ontario; 8 dead, thousands homeless, millions in property damage.

1986 *December 10* John Charles Polanyi, University of Toronto, shares the Nobel Prize in chemistry for his work on infrared chemiluminescence.

1987 *June* Pay Equity Act mandates equal pay for work of equal value, the first pay equity legislation for the private sector in North America.

1988 *September 23* Ontario Court of Appeal rules Christian religious exercises in public schools unconstitutional.

1989 *July* Thunderstorm brings 264 mm. (10.4 in.) of rain to Harrow, the Canadian record for a 24-hour rainfall east of Vancouver Island.

French Languages Services Act requires the province to offer services in the French language in areas where 10% or more of the population is French speaking.

1990 *January 29* Despite the fact that the French Language Services Act does not apply to municipalities, Sault Ste. Marie's city council declares English to be the city's only official language.

February More than 40 other Ontario cities and towns declare English to be the only official language.

1991 *July 18* Fierce 15-minute storm in northwestern Ontario destroys between 20 and 50 million trees in a 1,500 sq. km. (579 sq. mi.) area.

October Employee Wage Protection Program helps workers recover wages of up to $5,000, lost as a result of bankruptcy, etc.

1992   *May 18* Explosion caused by anti-abortionists destoys Dr. Henry Morganthaler's abortion clinic in Toronto.

1993   Provincial government forces a social contract on public service unions causing labour unrest.

October 26 Jean Augustine, the first black woman to sit in the House of Commons, is elected in the Toronto riding of Etobicoke/Lakeshore.

December 9 Ontario passes Bill 79, the employment equity law.

1994   *December 10* Announcement is made that Bertram Neville Brockhouse, a retired McMaster University professor, will share the Nobel Prize in physics for his work in providing evidence about the strength and nature of forces that hold solids and liquids together.

Culture and Education

Performing Arts In 1993 Ontario had 447 performing arts facilities, 95 professional theatre companies, 87 major festivals involving the arts, 57 symphonies, and 16 professional dance troupes. Toronto with the world's third largest English-language theatre industry is the centre for this activity with 140 theatre and dance companies. Only the most significant organizations based in Ontario are listed below. Many perform as well in other provinces and countries.

Blyth Festival, Goderich (mid-June to mid-September) (Canadian plays)	(519)523-9300
Canadian Opera Company, Toronto	(416)363-6671
Canadian Stage Company, Toronto	(416)368-3110
Caribana, Toronto (July/August) (largest Caribbean festival in North America)	(416)925-5435
Elmer Iseler Singers, Toronto	(416)971-4840
Le Franco, Ottawa (June) (largest artistic and cultural festival for francophones in North America)	(613)230-0056
Guelph Spring Festival, Guelph	(519)821-7570
Hamilton Philharmonic Orchestra, Hamilton	(905)526-6555
International Festival of Authors, Toronto (October)	(416)973-4000
Kitchener-Waterloo Symphony Orchestra, Kitchener-Waterloo	(519)578-1570 800-265-8977
National Ballet of Canada, Toronto	(416)362-0201
Oktoberfest, Kitchener (largest Bavarian festival in North America)	(519)570-4267
Opera Atelier, Toronto	(416)925-3767
Second City, Toronto (Comedy skits)	(416)863-1111
Shaw Festival, Niagara-on-the-Lake (May to October) (works of George Bernard Shaw and plays and musicals written during his lifetime, 1856–1950)	(905)468-2172 800-267-4759
Stratford Festival, Stratford (May to mid-November) (Shakespeare and his contemporaries, other classical works, musicals, and Canadian plays; productions based on classical theatre standards)	(519)273-1600 or 800-567-1600; Toronto line 363–4471; Kitchener-Waterloo line 662–2215; London line 227–1352

Tafelmusik, Toronto (baroque music)	(416)964-6337
Tarragon Theatre, Toronto	(416)531-1827
Théâtre français de Toronto, Toronto	(416)534-6604
Theatre Passe Muraille, Toronto	(416)363-2416
Toronto Dance Theatre, Toronto	(416)967-1365
Toronto International Film Festival, Toronto (September)	(416)968-FILM
Toronto Mendelssohn Choir, Toronto	(416)598-0422
Toronto Symphony Orchestra, Toronto	(416)872-4255
Winterlude, Ottawa (February) (festival of winter)	(613)239-5000

Provincial Museums and Galleries There are 300 museums and galleries in Ontario. The following are major Ontario institutions.

Art Gallery of Ontario, Toronto
Canadian Museum of Nature, Ottawa
Canadian War Museum, Ottawa
McMichael Canadian Collection, Kleinberg
Museum of Currency, Ottawa
National Aviation Museum, Ottawa
National Gallery of Canada, Ottawa
National Museum of Science and Technology, Ottawa
Ontario Agricultural Museum, Milton
Ontario Science Centre, Toronto
Royal Ontario Museum, Toronto
Science North, Sudbury

Universities and Colleges
Brock University, St. Catherines
Carleton University, Ottawa
University of Guelph, Guelph
Lakehead University, Thunder Bay
Laurentian University, Sudbury
McMaster University, Hamilton
Nipissing University, North Bay
Ontario College of Art, Toronto
Ontario Institute for Studies in Education
University of Ottawa, Ottawa
Queen's University, Kingston
Royal Military College of Canada, Kingston
Ryerson Polytechnic University, Toronto
University of Toronto, Toronto (Canada's largest university)
Trent University, Peterborough
University of Waterloo, Waterloo
University of Western Ontario, London
Wilfrid Laurier University, Waterloo
University of Windsor, Windsor
York University, Metropolitan Toronto

Colleges of Applied Arts and Technology
(* indicates additional campuses in other centres)

Algonquin College, Ottawa suburb
Cambrian College, Sudbury
Canadore College, North Bay
Centennial College, Metropolitan Toronto
Conestoga College, Kitchener
Confederation College, Thunder Bay
Durham College, Oshawa
Fanshawe College, London
George Brown College, Toronto
Georgian College, Barrie*
Humber College, Metropolitan Toronto
La Cité collegiale, Ottawa
Lambton College, Sarnia
Loyalist College, Belleville
Mohawk College, Hamilton*
Niagara College, Welland*
Northern College, South Porcupine*
St. Clair College, Windsor*
St. Lawrence College, Brockville*
Sault College, Sault Ste. Marie*
Seneca College, Metropolitan Toronto*
Sheridan College, Oakville*
Sir Sandford Fleming College, Peterborough*

Colleges of Agricultural Technology
Centralia College, Huron Park
Collège de technologie agricole et alimentation d'Alfred, Alfred
Kemptville College, Kemptville
Ridgetown College, Ridgetown

Miscellaneous Educational Institutions
Canadian Memorial Chiropractic College, Toronto
Michener Institute for Applied Health Sciences, Toronto
Niagara Parks Commission School of Horticulture, Niagara Falls

Motor Vehicle Use

Motor Vehicles Registered for Use in Ontario (1994): 8,127,573

Drivers Licenced by Ontario (1994): 6,688,760. Minimum driving age: 16

Roads Highways: 27,200 km. (16,902 mi.); municipal roads: 134,400 km. (83,516 mi.); bridges maintained by the province: 2,882

Speed Limits Controlled access highways: 100 kph (62 mph); TransCanada routes: 90 kph (56 mph); rural roads: 80–90 kph (50–56 mph); urban and populated areas: 40–60 kph (25–37 mph)

First, Biggest, and Best

World's largest annual exhibition: Canadian National Exhibition, Toronto (August–early September)
World's tallest free-standing structure: CN Tower, Toronto, 553 m. (1814.4 ft.)
World's tallest chimney: at International Nickel Company's Copper Cliff smelter, 381.3 m. (1,251 ft.)
Commonwealth's tallest office building: First Canadian Place, Toronto, 240 m. (787.4 ft.)
North America's only hydraulic-lift locks: Trent Canal at Peterborough and Kirkfield
World's first fully retractable roof: Skydome, Toronto, opened June 3, 1989
World's greatest waterfall by volume: Niagara Falls, 169,000,00 litres (37,180,000 gal.) per min.; 91.7% of this flows over the Canadian side of the Falls
World's longest street: Yonge Street, from Lake Ontario shore in Toronto to the Manitoba border at Rainy River, 1900.5 km. (1171.3 mi.)
World's largest island within a lake: Manitoulin Island in Canadian section of Lake Huron, 2,766 sq. km. (1,068 sq. mi.)
World's largest lake within a lake: Manitou Lake on Manitoulin Island, an island in Lake Huron, 106.4 sq. km. (41.1 sq. mi.)
World's largest known crater: 250 km. (155 mi.) in diameter buried in a depression near Sudbury
World's largest known reserves of uranium: Elliott Lake area
World's richest silver vein: discovered September 1, 1903, at Long Lake
World's largest single source of nickel: discovered 1883 near Sudbury
World's largest amount of shatter-coned rock: Sudbury Basin
North America's first successful commercial oil well: Oil Springs in Enniskillen Township, southeast of Sarnia, 1858
North America's first oil company: International Petroleum and Mining Company, Hamilton, established 1854
World's first nationalized electric utility: Hydro-Electric Power Commission of Ontario, incorporated May 14, 1906
World's invention of the telephone described by Alexander Graham Bell as "conceived in Brantford in 1874 and born in Boston in 1875"
World's first long distance telephone call: Brantford to Paris, Ontario, August 10, 1876
British Empire's first telephone exchange: Hamilton, July 15, 1878, opened by Hamilton District Telegraph
World's first newspaper to produce a full text commercial database containing every story from each issue: *Globe & Mail*, Toronto, 1979; it is also the first to publish electronically and in print the same day

World's largest and most sensitive neutrino observatory and the world's largest man-made cavity: Sudbury Neutrino Observatory, Sudbury, 2 km. (1.2 mi.) below the earth's surface, 10 storeys high, and over 20 m. (65.6 ft.) in diameter

World's first pressurized aviation suit: invented by Dr. Wilbur Rounding Franks, University of Toronto, 1940

North America's first flight of a jet transport: August 10, 1949, Jetliner C-102 built by A.V. Roe Company, Toronto

World's first airmail carried by a jet-powered aircraft: Jetliner, April 18, 1950

World's first straight-winged aircraft to break the sound barrier without rocket power: Avro CF-100, December 18, 1952

World's first plant to run on hydroelectric power: John R. Barber's paper mill, Georgetown, 1888

World's first electric street car system: St. Catherines, 1887

World's largest collection of grain elevators: 23 at Thunder Bay

World's greatest blackout: failure of an Ontario Hydro relay device at Queenston causes a power blackout in Ontario and seven northeastern U.S. states, November 9, 1965

World's first patient treated with cobalt-60 therapy: Ontario Cancer Foundation, London, October 27, 1951

World's first published suggestion about standard time: Sandford Fleming, Toronto, February 8, 1879

World's first alternating-current radio tube: invented by Edward Rogers, Toronto, April, 1925

North America's first electron microscope: built by Eli Franklin Burton and others, University of Toronto, 1935–1939

World's largest motion pictures: IMAX motion pictures produced by IMAX Systems Corporation, Toronto

World's first panoramic camera: patented by John Connon, Elora, 1887

World's first electronic organ: patented by Frank Morse Robb, Belleville, 1928

World's first railway sleeping car: built by Thomas Burnley, Brantford, 1860

World's most comprehensive collection of Canadian art: National Gallery of Canada, Ottawa

World's largest public collection of Henry Moore's art: Art Gallery of Ontario, Toronto

North America's largest (Stratford Festival) and second largest (Shaw Festival) theatre companies

World's largest computer science and mathematics faculty: University of Waterloo

North America's only theatre devoted to a bilingual, multidisciplinary program: National Arts Centre, Ottawa

North America's first metropolitan federation: Municipality of Metropolitan Toronto on January 1, 1953

British Empire's first anti-slavery act: Upper Canada's Abolition Act, July 9, 1793, designed to prevent further introduction of slaves and to limit the term of present servitude

British Empire's first woman admitted to the profession of law: Clara Brett Martin, 1897

Commonwealth's first female lieutenant-governor: Pauline McGibbon, January 17, 1974

World's first baseball game played with a nine-player per team format: Beachville, 1838

World's first wild west show: Niagara Falls, August 28, 1872

World's largest brook trout caught: 6.57 km. (14 lbs., 8 oz.), Nipigon River by Dr. W.J. Cook, July 1916

World's first recorded game of ice hockey: December 25, 1855, Kingston

World's invention of five-pin bowling: by Thomas F. Ryan, Toronto, 1908–1909

North America's oldest continuously-run turf stakes: Queen's Plate started by Queen Victoria in 1859 for a race in Toronto or some other Ontario locality

World's longest skating rink: Rideau Canal at Ottawa, 17.8 km. (11.1 mi.)

North America's largest number of international commercial flights: Pearson International Airport, Toronto

North America's first saints: eight Jesuit martyrs killed by the Hurons near present-day Midland, canonized June 29, 1930

World's first surviving quintuplets: Dionne quintuplets (5 girls) born May 28, 1934, at Callander

World's first electrically cooked meal: Windsor Hotel, Ottawa, August 29, 1892

Sources of Information About Ontario

Government of Ontario Citizens Inquiry Bureau: M151 Macdonald Block, 900 Bay Street, Toronto, Ontario M7A 1N3 (416)326-1234 (will accept collect calls from Ontario)

Ontario Travel: Queen's Park, Toronto, Ontario M7A 2E5 (416)314-0944 (English), (416)314-0956 (French), 800-668-2746 (English), 800-268-3736 (French)

Publications Ontario: 50 Grosvenor Street, Toronto, Ontario M7A 1N8 (416)326-5300, 800-668-9938

Books About Ontario: A Selected List

Reference Guides

Aitken, Barbara B. *Local Histories of Ontario Municipalities, 1951–1977: A Bibliography With Representative Trans-Canada Locations of Copies* (1978).

———. *Local Histories of Ontario Municipalities, 1977–1987: A Bibliography With Representative Cross-Canada Locations of Copies* (1989).

Armstrong, Frederick H. *Handbook of Upper Canada Chronology* (rev. ed. 1985).

Bennet, Doug and Tim Tiner. *Up North: A Guide to Ontario's Wilderness From Blackflies to Northern Lights* (1993).

Bishop, Olga B. *Bibliography of Ontario History, 1867–1976: Cultural, Economic, Political, Social*, 2 vols. (1980).

———. *Publications of Ontario, 1867–1900* (1976).

———. *Publications of the Province of Upper Canada and of Great Britain Relating to Upper Canada, 1791–1840* (1984).

Brown, D.M., G.A. McKay, and L.J. Chapman. *The Climate of Southern Ontario* (1980).

Cadman, Michael D., Paul F.J. Eagles, and Frederick M. Helleiner (comps.). *Atlas of the Breeding Birds of Ontario* (1987).

Canada. Atmospheric Environment Service. *Canadian Climate Normals, 1961–1990: Ontario* (1993).

Canada. Energy, Mines and Resources Canada. *Gazetteer of Canada: Ontario* (4th ed. 1988).

Carter, Floreen Ellen. *Place Names of Ontario*, 2 vols. (1984).

Crowder, Norman. *Early Ontario Settlers: A Sourcebook* (1993).

Crowe, R.B. *The Climate of Ottawa-Hull* (1984).

Dagg, Anne Innis. *Mammals of Ontario* (1974).

Dean, William G. (ed.). *Economic Atlas of Ontario* (1969).

Defoe, Deborah (comp.). *Kingston: A Selected Bibliography* (2nd ed. 1982).

Elliott, Noel Montgomery (ed.). *People of Ontario, 1600–1900: Alphabetized Directory of the People, Places and Vital Dates*, 3 vols. (1984).

Elliott, Robbins. *Ontario Book of Days* (1988).

Fitzgerald, E. Keith. *Ontario People, 1796–1803* (1993).

Firth, Edith G. (ed.). *The Town of York, 2 vols. (1962–1966)*. Primary documents, 1793–1834.

Fleming, Patricia Lockhart. *Upper Canada Imprints, 1801–1841: A Bibliography* (1988).

Forman, Debra. *Legislators and Legislatures of Ontario*, 4 vols. (1984–1992).

Garry, Lorraine and Susan Holland (comps.). *Northern Ontario: A Bibliography* (1968).

Gervais, Gaetan, Gwenda Hallsworth, and Ashley Thomson. *The Bibliography of Ontario History, 1976–1986* (1989).

Goodwin, Clive E. *A Bird-Finding Guide to Ontario* (1982).

James, Ross D. *Annotated Checklist of the Birds of Ontario* (2nd ed. 1991).

Judd, W.W. and J. Murrary Speirs (eds.). *Naturalist's Guide to Ontario* (1964).

Mandrak, Nicholas E. and E.J. Crossman. *A Checklist of Ontario Freshwater Fishes: Annotated With Distribution Maps* (1992).

Mika, Nick and Helma Mika. *Historic Sites of Ontario* (1974).

———. *Places in Ontario, Their Name Origins and History*, 3 vols. (1977–1983).

———. *United Empire Loyalists: Pioneers of Upper Canada* (1976).

Morley, William F.E. *Ontario and the Canadian North* (1978). The first part of this bibliography is devoted to local histories of Ontario.

Murray, Florence B. *Muskoka and Haliburton, 1615–1875: A Collection of Documents* (1963).

National Capital Commission. *A Bibliography of the History and Heritage of the National Capital Region* (1976).

Ontario Historical Society. *Directory of Heritage Organizations and Institutions in Ontario* (1989).

Ontario. Ministry of Colleges and Universities. *Ontario Since 1967: A Bibliography* (1973).

Reid, William D. *The Loyalists in Ontario: The Sons and Daughters of the American Loyalists of Upper Canada* (1973).

Saulesleja, Andrej. *Great Lakes Climatological Atlas* (1986).

Scott, David. *Ontario Place Names: The Historical, Offbeat or Humourous Origins of Close to 1,000 Communities* (1993).

Soper, James H. and Margaret L. Heimburger. *Shrubs of Ontario* (1982).

Speirs, Murray. *Birds of Ontario*, 2 vols. (1985).

Thurston, P.C. and others (eds.). *The Geology of Ontario* (1991).

Walshe, Shan. *Plants of Quetico and the Ontario Shield* (1980).

Wilson, William. *Canadiana Guidebook: Antique Collecting in Ontario* (1974). Includes sources to collecting antiques.

Zichmanis, Zile and James Hodgins. *Flowers of the Wild: Ontario and the Great Lakes Region* (1982).

Nonfiction Sources

*denotes a winner of a Governor General's Literary Award.

Acton, Janice, Penny Goldsmith, and Bonnie Sheppard. *Women at Work, Ontario, 1850–1930* (1974).

Addison, Ottelyn. *Early Days in Algonquin Park* (1974).

Akenson, Donald Harman. *The Irish in Ontario: A Study of Rural History* (1984).

Allen, Robert Thomas. *My Childhood and Yours: Happy Memories of Growing Up* (1977). Toronto's east end in the 1920s.

Armstrong, Christopher. *The Politics of Federalism: Ontario's Relations With the Federal Government, 1867–1942* (1981).

Armstrong, F.H., H.A. Stevenson, and J.D. Wilson (eds.). *Aspects of Nineteenth-Century Ontario: Essays Presented to James J. Talman* (1974).

Armstrong, Frederick H. *A City in the Making: Progress, People & Perils in Victorian Toronto* (1988).

Arnopoulos, Sheila McLeod. *Voices from French Ontario* (1982).

Arthur, Eric. *Toronto, No Mean City* (3rd ed. rev. by Stephen A. Otto, 1986).

Beardon, Jim and Linda Jean Butler. *Shadd: The Life and Times of Mary Shadd Cary.* (1977). A black woman in 19th-century Canada West who assisted fugitive slaves from the U.S. and fought for women's rights.

Bell, George G. and Andrew D. Pascoe. *The Ontario Government: Structure and Functions* (1988).

Blake, Verschoyle Benson and Ralph Greenhill. *Rural Ontario* (1969). Photographs and histories of nineteenth-century buildings.

Boyle, Harry J. *Mostly in Clover* (1961) *Homebrew and Patches* (1963). Memories of boyhood on an Ontario farm.

Bothwell, Robert. *A Short History of Ontario* (1986).

Brand, Dionne (ed.). *No Burden to Carry: Narratives of Black Working Women in Ontario 1920s to 1950s* (1992).

Bray, Matt and Ernie Epp (eds.). *A Vast and Magnificent Land: An Illustrated History of Northern Ontario* (1984).

Breckenridge, Muriel. *The Old Ontario Cookbook* (1976). Notes about everyday life in early Ontario introduces groups of recipes.

Brode, Patrick. *Sir John Beverley Robinson: Bone and Sinew of the Compact* (1984).

Burkholder, Mabel. *History of Central Ontario* (1952).

Burnford, Sheila. *Without Reserve* (1969, rpt. 1974). Cree and Ojibwa communities in northwestern Ontario.

Caplan, Gerald L. *The Dilemma of Canadian Socialism: The C.C.F. in Ontario* (1973).

Careless, J.M.S. *Brown of the Globe*, 2 vols. (1959–1963, rpt. 1989).

———. *Ontario, A Celebration of Our Heritage* (Vol. 1, 1991).

—— (ed.). *Pre-Confederation Premiers: Ontario Government Leaders, 1841–1867* (1980).

——. *Toronto to 1918: An Illustrated History* (1984).

Chapman, L.J. and D.F. Putnam. *The Physiography of Southern Ontario* (1984).

Coombs, A.E. *History of the Niagara Peninsula* (1950).

Craig, Gerald. *Upper Canada: The Formative Years, 1784–1841* (1963).

Dale, Clare A. *"Whose Servant I Am": Speakers of the Assemblies of the Province of Upper Canada, Canada and Ontario, 1792–1992* (1992).

Dear, M.J., J.J. Drake, and L.G. Reeds (eds.). *Steel City: Hamilton and Region* (1987).

De Visser, John. *Southwestern Ontario* (1982).

Drummond, Ian M. *Progress Without Planning: The Economic History of Ontario From Confederation to the Second World War* (1987).

Dunham, Aileen. *Political Unrest in Upper Canada* (1927, rpt. 1963).

Dunham, Mabel. *Trail of the Conestoga* (1942, rpt. 1973).

Elliott, George and John Reeves. *God's Big Acre: Life in 401 Country* (1986).

Evans, A. Margaret. *Sir Oliver Mowat* (1992).

Filey, Mike. *Toronto Sketches: "The Way We Were"* (1992).

Finnigan, Joan. *Some of the Stories I Told You Were True* (1981). Ottawa Valley in the past two centuries.

Firth, Edith. *Toronto in Art: 150 Years Through Artist's Eyes* (1983).

Fowler, Peter. *Niagara* (1981).

Fyrer, Mary Beacock. *Elizabeth Postuma Simcoe, 1792–1850 : A Biography* (1989).

Gabori, Susan. *In Search of Paradise* (1993). Italian immigration to Ontario.

Gagan, David. *Hopeful Travellers: Families, Land, and Social Change in Mid-Victorian Peel County, Canada West* (1981).

Galbraith, John Kenneth. *The Scotch* (1964).

Gentilcore, R. Louis and C. Grant Head. *Ontario's History in Maps* (1984).

Glazebrook, G.P. de T. *Life in Ontario: A Social History* (1975).

——. *The Story of Toronto* (1971).

Godfrey, Charles M. *The Cholera Epidemics in Upper Canada, 1832–1866* (1968).

Graham, Roger. *Old Man Ontario: Leslie M. Frost* (1990).

Graham, W.H. *The Tiger of Canada West* (1962). Biography of William Dunlop, 1792–1848, pioneer and politician.

Guillet, Edwin C. *Early Life in Upper Canada* (1933, rpt. 1963).

Gwyn, Sandra. *The Private Capital: Ambition and Love in the Age of Macdonald and Laurier* (1984).

Hall, Roger and Gordon Dodds. *Ontario, 200 Years in Pictures* (1991).

Harney, Robert F. and Harold Troper. *Immigrants: A Portrait of the Urban Experience, 1890–1930* (1975). European immigrants in Toronto.

Heidenreich, Conrad. *Huronia: A History of the Huron Indians, 1600–1650* (1971).

Humber, Charles J. (ed.). *Allegiance: The Ontario Story* (1991).

Iacovetta, Franca. *Such Hardworking People: Italian Immigrants in Postwar Ontario* (1992).

Johnson, James K. and Bruce G. Wilson (eds.). *Historical Essays on Upper Canada: New Perspectives* (1989).

Jones, Donald. *Fifty Tales of Toronto* (1992).

Kaplan, Harold. *Reform, Planning, and City Politics, Montreal, Winnipeg, Toronto* (1982).

Keane, David and Colin Read (eds.). *Old Ontario: Essays in Honour of J.M.S. Careless* (1990).

Keith, W.J. *Literary Images of Ontario* (1992).

Kenyon, W.A. *The History of James Bay 1610–1686: A Study in Historical Archaeology* (1986).

Kilbourn, William. *The Firebrand: William Lyon Mackenzie and the Rebellion in Upper Canada* (1956).

——. *The Toronto Book: An Anthology of Writing Past and Present* (1976).

Killan, Gerald. *Protected Places: A History of Ontario's Provincial Parks System* (1993)

Ladell, John and Monica Ladell. *A Farm in the Family: The Many Faces of Ontario Agriculture Over the Centuries* (1985).

Langton, Anne. *A Gentlewoman in Upper Canada: The Journals of Anne Langton* (1950).

Lemon, James. *Toronto Since 1918: An Illustrated History* (1985).

Magee, Joan. *The Belgians in Ontario: A History* (1987).

——. *The Swiss in Ontario* (1991).

Mandelthorpe, Jonathan. *Power and the Tories: Ontario Politics 1943 to the Present* (1974).

Mays, John Bentley. *Emerald City: Toronto Revisited* (1994).

McBurney, Margaret and Mary Byers. *Homesteads: Early Buildings and Families From Kingston to Toronto* (1979).

McCalla, Douglas. *Planting the Province: The Economic History of Upper Canada, 1784–1870* (1993).

McCallum, John. *Unequal Beginnings: Agriculture and Economic Development in Quebec and Ontario Until 1870* (1980).

McDougall, A.K. *John P. Robarts, His Life and Government* (1986).

McInnis, Marvin. *Perspectives on Ontario Agriculture, 1815–1930* (1992).

McKenty, Neil. *Mitch Hepburn* (1967).

McKillop, A.B. *Matter of the Mind: The University in Ontario 1791–1951* (1994).

McRae, Marion. *The Ancestral Roof: Domestic Architecture of Upper Canada* (1963).

Merritt, Richard, Nancy Butler, and Michael Power (eds.). *The Capital Years: Niagara-on-the-Lake, 1792–1796* (1991).

Middleton, Jesse Edgar and Fred Landon. *The Province of Ontario: A History, 1615–1927*, 4 vols. (1927–1928).

Minhinnick, Jeanne. *At Home in Upper Canada* (1970).

Moodie, Susanna. *Roughing It in the Bush; or, Forest Life in Canada* (1852, rpt. 1988).

Noel, S.J.R. *Patrons, Clients, Brokers: Ontario Society and Politics, 1791–1896* (1990).

Oliver, Peter G. *Howard Ferguson, Ontario Tory* (1977).

Piva, Michael J. (ed.). *A History of Ontario: Selected Readings* (1988).

Potter-MacKinnon, Janice. *While the Women Only Wept: Loyalist Refugee Women in Eastern Ontario* (1993).

Radforth, Ian. *Bushworkers and Bosses: Logging in Northern Ontario, 1900–1980* (1980).

Rea, K.J. *The Prosperous Years: The Economic History of Ontario, 1939–1975* (1985).

Read, Colin and Ronald J. Stagg (eds.). *The Rebellion of 1837 in Upper Canada* (1985).

Reaman, George Elmore. *The Trail of the Black Walnut* (1974). The settlement of Pennsylvania German families in Upper Canada during the American Revolution.

Reid, Richard M. *The Upper Ottawa Valley to 1855* (1990).

Robinson, Percy J. *Toronto During the French Regime: A History of the Toronto Region From Brulé to Simcoe, 1615–1793* (2nd ed. 1965).

Rogers, Edward S. and Donald B. Smith (eds.). *Aboriginal Ontario: Historical Perspectives on the First Nations* (1994).

Ross, Eric. *Full of Hope and Promise: The Canadas in 1841* (1991).

Russell, Victor L. (ed.). *Forging a Consensus: Historical Essays on Toronto* (1984).

Saywell, John T. *Just Call Me Mitch: The Life of Mitchell F. Hepburn* (1991).

Scadding, Henry. *Toronto of Old* (1873, ed. by Fred Armstrong, 1966, rpt. 1987).

Schmalz, Peter S. *The Ojibway of Southern Ontario* (1991).

Schull, Joseph. *Ontario Since 1867* (1978).

Shackleton, Philip. *The Furniture of Old Ontario* (1973).

Sheppard, George. *Plunder, Profit and Paroles: A Social History of the War of 1912 in Upper Canada* (1994).

Spelsman, Stephen A. *The Jews of Toronto: A History* (1979).

Spelt, Jacob. *Toronto* (1973).

——. *Urban Development in South Central Ontario* (1983).

Stamp, Robert M. *The Schools of Ontario, 1876–1976* (1982).

St.-Denis, Guy. *Simcoe's Choice: Celebrating London's Bicentennial, 1793–1993* (1992).

Stouffer, Allen P. *The Light of Nature and the Law of God: Antislavery in Ontario, 1833–1877* (1992).

Taylor, John H. *Ottawa: An Illustrated History* (1986).

Thomson, Gary. *Village Life in Upper Canada* (1988).

Tivy, Louis. *Your Loving Anna* (1972). A southern Ontario pioneer's letters home to England.

Traill, Catherine Parr. *The Backwoods of Canada: Being Letters From the Wife of an Emigrant Officer, Illustrative of the Domestic Economy of British North America* (1836, rpt. 1966).

Trigger, Bruce G. *The Children of Aataentic: A History of the Huron People to 1660* (1987).

Tulchinsky, Gerald (ed.). *To Preserve & Defend: Essays on Kingston in the Nineteenth Century* (1976).

Van Steen, Marcus. *Governor Simcoe and His Lady* (1968).

Walker, Franklin A. *Catholic Education and Politics in Upper Canada: A Study of Documentation Relating to the Origin of Catholic Elementary Schools in the Ontario School System* (1985).

——. *Catholic Education and Politics in Ontario: A Documentary Study* (1985).

Webster, Michael. *Home Farm: One Family's Life on the Land* (1989).

Westfall, William. *Two Worlds: The Protestant Culture of Nineteenth-Century Ontario* (1989).

White, Graham (ed.). *The Government and Politics of Ontario* (4th ed. 1990).

White, Randall. *Ontario 1610–1985: A Political and Economic History* (1985).

——. *Too Good to be True: Toronto in the 1920s* (1993).

Wilson, Barbara M. (ed.). *Ontario and the First World War, 1914–1918* (1977).

Wright, J.V. *Ontario Prehistory: An Eleven-Thousand-Year Archaeological Outline* (1972).

Zucchi, John E. *Italians in Toronto: Development of a National Identity, 1875–1935* (1988).

Ontario in Literature
*denotes a winner of a Governor General's Literary Award.

Beresford-Howe, Constance. *Night Studies* (1985). Humour and irony highlight the differences between staff and students of an urban community college.

Bodsworth, Fred. *The Sparrow's Fall* (1966). In the northern Ontario wilderness a young Indian and a pregnant woman strive to keep alive.

Boissoneau, Alice. *Eileen McCullough* (1976, rpt. 1984). The pregnant, adopted daughter of an immigrant copes with life in wartime Toronto alone.

Braithwaite, Max. *A Privilege and a Pleasure* (1975). A story about hypocrisy in an upper-middle-class family in an affluent Toronto suburb.

Brodeur, Helene. *A Saga of Northern Ontario* (1983). The land and people of early 20th-century northern Ontario are depicted in this romantic adventure novel.

Callaghan, Morley. *Strange Fugitive* (1928, rpt. 1973). Toronto in the 1920s.

Clark, Joan. *The Victory of Geraldine Gull* (1988. rpt. 1994). The difficult lives of the inhabitants of a community on the Ontario shores of Hudson Bay.

Clarke, Austin. *The Meeting Point* (1972); *Storm of Fortune* (1973); *The Bigger Light* (1975). A trilogy depicting the lives of West Indian domestics and their circle living in Toronto.

Cobb, Jocelyn. *Belmullet* (1982). A young girl lives with relatives on a northern Ontario farm.

Cohen, Matt. *The Disinherited* (1974); *The Colours of War* (1977); *The Sweet Second Summer of Kitty Malone* (1979); *Flowers of Darkness* (1981). Novels about the lives of inhabitants in a fictional town north of Kingston.

Connor, Ralph. *The Man From Glengarry* (1901, rpt. 1993); *Glengarry Schooldays: A Story of Early Days in Glengarry* (1902, rpt. 1993). Rural Ontario and a one-room schoolhouse in the nineteenth century.

Davies, Robertson. *Deptford Trilogy* (1983; contains *Fifth Business: A Novel* 1970); **Manticore: A Novel* (1972); *World of Wonders* (1975). A snowball thrown by a child in the imaginary village of Deptford in 1908 has consequences that reveal the mysteries of the human character.

—— *Tempest-tost* (1951, rpt. 1987). A comedy of manners based in a small fictional Ontario city.

De La Roche, Mazo. *Jalna* (1927, rpt. 1961). This novel and its fifteen sequels tell a saga about a well-off family in rural Ontario beginning in pioneer times.

Dewdney, Selwyn. *Wind Without Rain* (1974). Three teachers in a small town in pre–World War II Ontario.

Doucet, Clive. *Coe's War* (1983). World War II and the world of jazz face a young man in Toronto.

Downie, Mary Alice and Mary Alice Thompson (eds.). *Written in Stone: A Kingston Reader* (1993).

Duncan, Helen. *Across the Bridge: A Prelude to W.W. I* (1988). Tragedy is the centre of this novel set in a small town near London in the summer before World War I.

Duncan, Sara Jeannette. *The Imperialist* (1904, rpt. 1971). A picture of Brantford at the turn of the century.

Engel, Marion. *Lunatic Villas* (1981). A humourous picture of contemporary life in Toronto.

Evans, Hubert. *O Time in Your Flight: A Novel* (1979). Small-town Ontario at the time of the Boer War seen through the eyes of a child.

Faessler, Shirley. *Everything in the Window* (1979); *A Basket of Apples and Other Stories* (1988). Portraits of Toronto's Jewish community in the pre–World War II years.

Fagan, Cary and Robert MacDonald (eds.). *Streets of Attitude: Toronto Stories* (1990).

Gane, Margaret Drury. *Parade on an Empty Street* (1978). A boy's childhood in the Toronto of 1939–1940 remembered.

Garner, Hugh. *Cabbagetown: A Novel* (1960, rpt. 1978); *Silence on the Shore* (1962, rpt. 1983). Novels about Toronto's poor and working poor.

Gear, Kathleen O'Neal. *This Widowed Land* (1993). Historical fiction about Jesuit missionaries and Huron Indians.

Glover, Douglas. The Life and Times of Captain N: A Novel (1993). Historical fiction set in the Niagara frontier in the final days of the American Revolution.

Govier, Katherine. *Fables of Brunswick Avenue* (1985). Short stories about people who have once lived on Brunswick Avenue in Toronto.

——. *Going Through the Motions* (1982). Trained for the ballet, a woman becomes a striptease dancer in Toronto.

——. *Hearts of Flame* (1991). A portrait of Toronto emerges in this story of four members of an Alberta folk group who move to Toronto.

Gutteridge, Don. *How the World Began: A Parable of 1812* (1991).

——. *St. Vitus Dance: A Novel* (1987); *Shaman's Ground* (1988). A woman's life in a small village on Lake Huron in the nineteenth and early twentieth century.

Helwig, David. *The Glass Knight* (1976); *Jennifer* (1979) *It Is Always Summer* (1982); *A Sound Like Laughter: A Novel* (1983). Novels set in Kingston and vicinity.

Hood, Hugh. *A New Athens* (1981). Life in southeastern Ontario towns.

——. *The Swing in the Garden* (1980). A boy's life in the Toronto of the 1930s.

Huggan, Isabel. *The Elizabeth Stories* (1984). Small-town life in southwestern Ontario seen through a girl's eyes.

Kilodney, Crad. *Girl on the Subway and Other Stories* (1990). Most of these eleven stories are situated in and around Toronto.

Knister, Raymond. *White Narcissus* (1929, rpt. 1962). A young woman's sense of duty keeps her in a rural Ontario town.

Leacock, Stephen. *Sunshine Sketches of a Little Town* (1912, rpt. 1990). A classic of Canadian humour.

MacGregor, Roy. *Shoreline: A Novel* (1980). The Algonquin region figures in this combination of fact and fiction which tells about an American woman who believes she is the illegitimate daughter of the painter Tom Thomson's fiancé.

Mestern, Pat Mattaini. *Clara: An Historical Novel of an Ontario Town, 1879–1930* (1977). Based on fact this novel relates episodes in Fergus.

Moore, Brian. *Black Robe* (1985). A seventeenth-century French priest struggles with his faith and his missionary zeal in the Ontario wilderness.

Munro, Alice. **Dance of the Happy Shades: Stories* (1968); *Lives of Girls & Women* (1971); **Who Do You Think You Are?: Stories* (1978); *Moons of Jupiter: Stories* (1982, rpt. 1994); **Progress of Love* (1986). Short stories about girls and women mostly set in Huron County.

Murphy, Phil. *Summer Island* (1984). Seven stories set on Ward's Island, Toronto, in the 1930s summers.

Paci, F.G. *The Italians: A Novel* (1978). The cultural adjustments of an immigrant Italian family in a small Ontario town.

——. *Black Madonna: A Novel* (1982); *The Father* (1984). Two novels about an Italian immigrant family in Sault Ste. Marie.

Purdy, Al. *A Splinter in the Heart: A Novel* (1990). A young man's journey into adulthood takes place in Trenton in the 1930s.

Quarrington, Paul. *The Life of Hope* (1985). A humourous novel about the life of a writer in the fictional town of Hope, Ontario.

——. *Logan in Overtime* (1990). Amusing story about an ex-hockey player in Falconbridge.

Richardson, John. *Wacousta; or, The Prophecy: A Tale of the Canadas*, 3 vols. (1832, abr. ed. rpt. 1982). Melodrama set in the 1760s during Pontiac's uprising.

Richardson, R.L. *Colin of the Ninth Concession: A Tale of Scottish Pioneer Life in Eastern Ontario* (1903, rpt. 1973).

Ross, Paul. *Four Corners on Main Street* (1990). An Ontario village is seen through the eyes of a social worker.

Sears, Dennis T. Patrick. *The Lark in the Clear Air* (1974). Humourous novel about a young man's experiences in rural Ontario during the 1930s.

Shadd-Evelyn, Karen. *I'd Rather Live in Buxton* (1993). Poetry and fiction about black people in North Buxton.

Sheard, Sarah. *The Swing Era* (1993). A woman returns from a Nepali Buddhist monastery to her Georgian Bay home town.

Stein, David Lewis. *Taking Power* (1992). Fact and fiction are mixed in this novel about Toronto city politics from 1969 to 1979.

Torgov, Morley. *A Good Pace to Come From* (1974). A lighthearted novel with a Sault Ste. Marie setting.

——. *Outside Chances of Maximilian Glick: A Novel* (1982). Humourous tale about growing up in a small Jewish community in a northern Ontario city.

Tourbin, Dennis. *The Port Dalhousie Stories* (1987). Short stories about teenage boys in Port Dalhousie.

Vassanji, M.G. *No New Land: A Novel* (1991). Immigrants from Dar es Salaam living in a Toronto apartment building struggle to "make it" in a new land.

Wallace, Garth. *Fly Yellow Side Up* (1990). Humourous story about a young man's first summer as a bush pilot near Georgian Bay.

Weinzweig, Helen. *Basic Black With Pearls* (1980). Tired of a conventional life a middle-aged woman in Toronto imagines a life of intrigue.

Wolfe, Morris and Douglas Daymond (eds.). *Toronto Short Stories* (1977).

Woods, Grahame. *Bloody Harvest* (1977). A former teenage hockey star and war hero, now middle aged, struggles for a living as a farm labourer in Ontario.

Young, Phyllis Brett. *The Torontonians: A Novel* (1960).

PRINCE EDWARD ISLAND

Prince Edward Island, an island located east of the provinces of New Brunswick and Nova Scotia, is Canada's smallest province. It is surrounded by the waters of the Northumberland Strait on the south and west and the Gulf of St. Lawrence on the north and east.

Name   Province of Prince Edward Island. "Prince Edward Island" is named for Prince Edward, Duke of Kent, a son of George III, then commander of the British troups in North America. *Previous names:* Abegweit (Micmac Indian name meaning "land cradled on the water"); Île Saint-Jean (1534–1758), Island of Saint John (1758–1799).

Flag   The provincial shield in a rectangular format with an alternating red and white border. Adopted March 24, 1964.

Coat of Arms   The top third of the shield contains a golden lion on a red background; the lower two-thirds contains three small oak trees under the protection of a larger oak tree. The provincial motto surrounds the bottom of the shield. Granted by King Edward VII on May 30, 1905.

Motto   *Parva Sub Ingenti* (The small under the protection of the great).

Emblems
Bird   blue jay (*Cyanocitta cristata*)

Flower   lady's slipper (*Cypripedium acaule*)
Tree   northern red oak (*Quercus ruba*)
Tartan   reddish-brown, green, white, and yellow

Date of Entry into Confederation   July 1, 1873.

Official Language   English.

Capital City   Charlottetown, situated at the confluence of three rivers on a broad harbour leading into the Northumberland Strait; population 15,396, CA population 57,472. The French established Port La Joie in 1730 as the administrative centre of Île Saint-Jean. The name was changed by the British in 1758 to Fort Amherst. On October 25, 1768, a new townsite across the harbour was named Charlotte Town in honour of Queen Charlotte, consort of George III. Charlottetown was incorporated on April 17, 1855.

Provincial Holidays   There are no holidays in addition to the national statutory holidays (see page 2).

155

Geography and Climate

Geography Prince Edward Island, crescent-shaped with a deeply indented coastline and many small harbours, has distinctive red soil. The western part is nearly flat rising to hilly sections in the central region and rolling hills in the east. The north shore has extensive sand dunes and beaches. The original forest cover is gone, now replaced with mixed forests of spruce, red maple, and balsam fir.

Area 5,660 sq. km. (2,185 sq. mi.); 0.1% of Canada. *Rank:* 10th among the provinces, 12th among the provinces and territories.

Inland Water Many streams, but only small lakes and rivers.

Elevations Highest point: Springton, Queen's County, 152 m. (499 ft.). Lowest point: shore, sea level.

Major Rivers Clyde, Kidore, Hillsborough, Mill, Southwest, West.

Climate Prince Edward Island (P.E.I.) has a moderate climate throughout the year with long, fairly mild winters, late, cool springs, and mild, breezy summers. It experiences more variable weather than other parts of Canada. The average daily mean temperature in January is −7°C (19.4°F); in July 18.5°C (65.3°F). The lowest recorded temperature in P.E.I.: −37.2°C (−35°F) at Kilmahumaig on January 26, 1884; the highest recorded temperature 36.7°C (98.1°F) at Charlottetown on August 19, 1935.

Average snowfall: 330.6 cm. (130.2 in.) per year. Greatest recorded snowfall over five consecutive days: 92.7 cm. (36.5 in.) at Charlottetown on December 30, 1921. Average annual precipitation: 1,169.4 mm. (46.1 in.).

Time Zone Atlantic.

Parks and Historic Sites

National Parks Located on Prince Edward Island

Park	Location	Size
Prince Edward Island	north shore	18 sq. km. (7 sq. mi.)

Provincial Parks There are 30 provincial parks. All parks are recreational and have evolved around beaches and two golf courses. The largest parks are:

Park	Location	Size
Brudenell	east shore	476 ha. (1,177 acres)
Brookvale Provincial Ski Park	highway 13	175 ha. (433 acres)
Mill River	northwest	153 ha. (378 acres)
Cabot Beach	north shore	131 ha. (324 acres)
Green Park	north shore	89 ha. (219 acres)
Buffaloland	Milltown Cross	62 ha. (154 acres)
Lord Selkirk	south shore	62 ha. (153 acres)
Strathgartney	Strathgartney	54 ha. (133 acres)
Panmure Island	east shore	40 ha. (99 acres)
Cedar Dunes	southwest shore	37 ha. (42 acres)

Prince Edward Island has 1 national bird sanctuary and 1 Ramsar site.

Major National Historic Sites and Parks on Prince Edward Island

Fort Amhert/Port-La-Joie, near Charlottetown

Province House, Charlottetown

In addition, there are a number of historic sites on Prince Edward Island adminis-tered by the province, municipalities, or organizations. The major sites are:

Beaconsfield Historic House, Charlottetown

Orwell Corner Historic Village, Orwell

Village pionnier acadien, Mont-Carmel

Demography

Prince Edward Island Population: 129,765; 0.5% of national; *rank* 10th

Historical population data

1981	122,505
1971	111,640
1961	104,629
1951	98,429
1941	95,047
1921	88,615
1901	103,259
1881	108,891
1861	80,857

Population Density: 22.9 persons per sq. km. (59.4 per sq. mi.) (highest in Canada)

Number of Dwellings: 44,751

Indian Reserves: 4

Population Characteristics:

urban: 51,813; 39.9%

rural: 77,952; 60.1%

19 and under: 39,385; 30.4%

65 and over: 17,075; 13.1%

average income for full-time employment 15 years and over (1990): $28,617; men $32,538; women $22,857

average life expectancy at birth (1987): men 73.5 years; women 79.7 years

live birth rate: 1,885; 14.5 per 1000

deaths: 1,188; 9.1 per 1000 (highest in Canada)

marriages: 876; 6.8 per 1000

divorces: 269; 2.07 per 1000

Largest Cities and Towns (for a definition of CA, see page viii)

Name	Population	Dwellings	National Pop. Rank
Charlottetown	57,472 (CA)	20,346	50
Summerside	15,237 (CA)	5,433	112

Government and Politics, 1873–

A description of the division of powers between the federal and provincial governments will be found on page 4.

Lieutenant-Governor The Lieutenant-Governor is the nominal head of the Prince Edward Island government, and is appointed by the Governor General of Canada on the recommendation of the Prime Minister of Canada. (A description of the duties of lieutenant-governors is found on page 7.)

Lieutenant-Governors of Prince Edward Island	*Term*
William C.F. Robinson	1873–1878
Robert Hodgson	1878–1879
Thomas Heath Haviland	1879–1884
Andrew Archibald Macdonald	1884–1889
Jedediah Slason Carvell	1889–1894
George William Howlan	1894–1899
Peter Adolphus McIntyre	1899–1904
Donald Alexander MacKinnon	1904–1910

Benjamin Rogers	1910–1915
Augustine Colin Macdonald	1915–1919
Murdock MacKinnon	1919–1924
Frank Richard Heartz	1924–1930
Charles Dalton	1930–1933
George Des Brisay DeBlois	1933–1939
Bradford W. Lepage	1939–1945
Joseph Alphonse Bernard	1945–1950
Thomas William Lemuel Prowse	1950–1958
Frederick Walter Hyndman	1958–1963
Willibald Joseph MacDonald	1963–1969
John George MacKay	1969–1974
Gordon Lockhart Bennett	1974–1980
Joseph Aubin Doiron	1980–1985
Lloyd George McPhail	1985–1990
Marion Loretta Reid	1990–

Legislative Assembly The Legislative Assembly of Prince Edward Island consists of 32 members elected by popular vote, with one councillor and one assemblyman from each of the 16 electoral districts; term of office: up to 5 years as long as the party in power maintains the confidence of the Legislative Assembly; remuneration (1994): $32,000 + $9,700 expense allowance, additional amounts for special appointments; qualifications for members: Canadian citizen, 18 years of age or older, qualified as an elector in one of the electoral districts within the province, not legally disqualified. (A description of the duties of provincial legislatures are found on page 7.)

Qualifications for Prince Edward Island Voters in Provincial Elections Canadian citizen, 18 years of age or older on polling day, ordinarily a Prince Edward Island resident for six months immediately preceding the date of the writ of election, in the polling division on the date of the writ.

Premier Nominally appointed by the Lieutenant-Governor of Prince Edward Island; the Premier is generally the leader of the party with the majority of seats in the Legislative Assembly. (A description of the responsibilities of provincial premiers is found on page 7.)

Premiers of Prince Edward Island/Party/Term
James Colledge Pope
  (Conservative, 1873)
Lemuel Cambridge Owen
  (Conservative, 1873–1876)
Louis Henry Davies
  (Liberal, 1876–1879)
William Wilfred Sullivan
  (Conservative, 1879–1889)
Neil McLeod
  (Conservative, 1889–1891)
Frederick Peters
  (Liberal, 1891–1897)
Alexander Bannerman Warburton
  (Liberal, 1897–1898)
Donald Farquharson
  (Liberal, 1898–1901)
Arthur Peters
  (Liberal, 1901–1908)
Francis Longworth Haszard
  (Liberal, 1908–1911)
Herbert James Palmer
  (Liberal, 1911)
John Alexander Mathieson
  (Conservative, 1911–1917)
Aubin-Edmond Arsenault
  (Conservative, 1917–1919)
John Howatt Bell
  (Liberal, 1919–1923)
James David Stewart
  (Conservative, 1923–1927)
Albert Charles Saunders
  (Liberal, 1927–1930)
Walter Maxfield Lea
  (Liberal, 1930–1931)
James Davis Stewart
  (Conservative, 1931–1933)
William Joseph Parnell MacMillan
  (Conservative, 1933–1935)
Walter Maxfield Lea
  (Liberal, 1935–1936)
Thane Alexander Campbell
  (Liberal, 1936–1943)
John Walter Jones
  (Liberal, 1943–1953)
Alexander Wallace Matheson
  (Liberal, 1953–1959)
Walter Russell Shaw
  (Conservative, 1959–1966)
Alexander Bradshaw Campbell
  (Liberal, 1966–1978)
William Bennett Campbell
  (Liberal, 1978–1979)

John Angus McLean
(Conservative, 1979–1981)
James Matthew Lee
(Conservative, 1981–1986)
Joseph Atallah Ghiz
(Liberal, 1896–1993)
Catherine Sophia Callbeck
(Liberal, 1993–   )

Cabinet The Cabinet consists of ministers appointed by the Premier, usually from elected members of the majority party in the Legislative Assembly. Cabinet ministers serve at the Premier's pleasure; each member usually heads a government department.

Government Departments The telephone numbers for general information are listed with the departments.

Agriculture, Fisheries and Forestry
(902)368-4880
Economic Development and Tourism
(902)368-4240
Education and Human Resources
(902)368-4600
Environment
(902)368-5000
Health and Social Services
(902)368-4900
Provincial Affairs and Attorney General
(902)368-5280
Provincial Treasury
(902)368-4070
Transportation and Public Works
(902)368-5100

Prince Edward Island Representation in Federal Government
House of Commons: 4 members
Senate: 4 members

Finances

A statement of Prince Edward Island's current revenue and expenditures for the years 1992/93 and 1991/92 is shown below in thousands of dollars. The financial year runs from April 1 to March 31 of the year following.

	Actual 1992/93	*Actual 1991/92*
Revenue		
Taxation	226,889	231,385
Other	145,739	149,490
Government of Canada	306,884	299,615
Total revenue for the year	679,511	680,491
Expenditures		
Health and social services	261,447	247,568
Education	166,074	161,252
Transportation and public works	54,541	50,890
Industry	27,568	35,476
Interest on debt	113,165	103,446
Other	140,167	130,289
Total expenditures for the year	762,962	728,921
Deficit for the year	83,451	48,430

Economy

Prince Edward Island's moist, moderate climate and fertile, stone-free soils provide a favorable environment for farming. Almost 70% of the land is cultivated and 25% of all potatoes grown in Canada come from P.E.I. Its sandy beaches attract tourists and its proximity to the sea promotes a fishing industry. The lack of locally-produced hydroelectric power makes P.E.I.'s energy costs the highest in Canada. There are no mining activities and no large industries.

Major Industries Potatoes form P.E.I.'s most prominent resource industry, farming, followed in importance by fishing, especially lobster and shellfish. Tourism is of growing consequence. Secondary economic activity includes forestry, small manufacturing, tobacco production, and Irish moss.

Gross Domestic Product (1992) $1,936 million (in current dollars at factor cost); % of national G.D.P.: 0.3%; rank: 11th

Distribution of gross domestic product (1990)

Finance, insurance, real estate	15.4%
Government services	14.5%
Retail trade	7.9%
Educational services	7.8%
Manufacturing	7.5%
Construction	7.3%
Health services	6.8%
Agriculture	6.1%
Transportation, storage	4.7%

Wholesale trade	3.2%
Fishing and trapping	1.9%
Other utilities	1.9%
Logging	0.3%

Value of Manufacturing Shipments $449 million

Farm Cash Receipts $240 million

Employment (seasonally adjusted) 52,000; participation rate: 65.1%

Unemployment (seasonally adjusted) 11,000; per capita: 16.9%

Minimum Wage (1993) $4.75, general minimum

Fish Landings and Value (1992) 100.2 million pounds; $78.3 million

Number of Tourist Parties Via Auto and Air (1992) 120,344; amount expended by tourists: $57.5 million

Exports Prince Edward Island's exports in 1992 amounted to $175.4 million; 0.1% of total Canadian exports; *rank:* 10th
Largest trading partner: United States, 58% of P.E.I.'s exports
Major export commodities: potatoes 38%; lobster 25%; other fish 18%

History

ca. 10,000 B.C.	Paleo-Indians arrive.
ca. 3500 B.C.	Evidence of Shellfish People.
ca. 1st century A.D.	Micmac Indians supplant Shellfish People.
1500s–1650	French and Basque fishermen visit regularly.
1497	*June 24* John Cabot sights present-day Prince Edward Island.
1534	*July 1* Jacques Cartier lands at Cape Kildare and claims area for France.
1600s	French make land grants to various people who fail to establish settlements.
1710	Acadians who wish to remain French arrive (abandon Island in 1716).
1713	*April 11* France retains the Island in the Treaty of Utrecht.
1719	*August* Île Saint-Jean is granted to Louis-Hyacinthe Castel, Comte de Saint-Pierre.
1720	*August 23* Colonists from France led by Sieur de Gotteville de Bellisle arrive at Port La Joie.
1730	Saint-Pierre's grant is annulled and the Island is united to the Royal Domain as a dependency of Louisbourg.

1732–1744	Île Saint-Jean becomes a French colony. Acadians and other French settlers arrive.
1745	English capture the Island.
1748	*October 18* Island is restored to France in the Treaty of Aix-La-Chapelle.
1749–1755	Acadians immigrate from British territories.
1758	*August 17* French governor surrenders to the British. Many inhabitants are transported to France.
1763	*February 10* Treaty of Paris: France formally cedes its North American possessions to Britain.
	October 7 Island is annexed to Nova Scotia.
1765	*October 6* Samuel Holland completes a survey of the Island and divides it into 67 townships.
1767	*July 23* British government awards lands on the Island by lottery to military officers, lords, merchants, and others who become absentee landlords.
1768	Charles Morgan lays out townsite for Charlottetown.
1769	*June 28* Island of Saint John, formerly part of Nova Scotia, becomes a separate British colony with a governor, lieutenant-governor, council, and assembly.
	July 14 Walter Patterson is appointed the colony's first governor.
1770	*September* Regulation of the "sea cow" (walrus) industry is the colony's first legislative act.
	The Falmouth settlers arrive at Stanhope and the Annabella settlers at Malpeque, the first significant Scottish immigrants.
1771	First recorded incidence of potatoes grown on the Island.
1771–1772	Scottish Catholic settlers, sponsored by John MacDonald, Laird of Glenaladale, arrive at Scotchfort (*1771*) and Tracadie (*1772*).
1773	*July 4* First Assembly meets in Charlottetown.
1773–1774	Robert Clark and Robert Campbell bring ca. 200 Protestants to New London area.
1774	*October 17* Quit Rent Act passes imposing penalties on landholders who have not paid rent to the Crown. This has little effect.
1775	*November 17* American privateers plunder Charlottetown.
1780–1784	Five hundred to six hundred loyalists arrive.
1781	*November* Lots with unpaid quit rents are auctioned.
1783	*September 3* Treaty of Paris: formal end of British-United States conflict.
1784	Governor Patterson brings Loyalist settlers to Charlottetown.
1791	*Royal Gazette* is founded at Charlottetown.
1799	*June 3* Name "Island of Saint John" is officially changed to "Prince Edward Island" (P.E.I.)
1803	Scottish Highland settlers arrive at Orwell Bay on land purchased for their benefit by Thomas Douglas, 5th Earl of Selkirk.
1815	Arrival of many immigrants from Newfoundland and southeast Ireland begins.
1827	*March* Governor John Ready establishes the Central Agricultural Society.
1830	*April 28* Catholic Emancipation Act gives Catholics the right to vote in P.E.I.
1832	*August 1* British government confirms Land Assessment Act, previously passed by the P.E.I. legislature, which provides revenue for the operation of the P.E.I. government.
1834	Prince of Wales College is established.
1836	Law is passed that excludes a franchise for women.
1840–1890	P.E.I.'s prosperous era includes a shipbuilding boom in the 1850s and 1860s with construction at 176 locations.

1845	*December 4* P.E.I.'s first lighthouse at Point Prim goes into operation.
1847	*January* P.E.I. legislative building opens.
1851	*April 24* P.E.I. achieves responsible government when the Lieutenant-Governor asks George Coles, leader of the Reform Party, to form a government.
1852	Free Education Act establishes autonomous local school boards and disallows religious instruction; Bible readings are permitted but explanations forbidden.
1853	Land Purchase Act allows the P.E.I. government to buy out landowners and make land available for purchase by tenants.
1854	Island Telegraph System is established.
	June 4 Reciprocity Treaty with the United States increases export of agricultural products, adding to general prosperity.
	August 13 First locally-owned bank, the Bank of Prince Edward Island, opens.
1855	*January 17* St. Dunstan's College opens offering higher education for Catholic clergy and lay readers.
1859	*July* P.E.I.'s streets are lighted by gas for first time.
1864	*Spring* P.E.I. passes a resolution to discuss a Maritime union with Nova Scotia and New Brunswick.
	May 19 Tenant's League is formed and pledges to withhold rents until their lands are made freehold. British troops check ensuing violence by *August 1865.*
	September 1–9 Charlottetown Conference, originally called to discuss Maritime Union, changes course as visiting representatives from Canada promote a larger union.
1865	*February 18* In order to pressure P.E.I. into Confederation, the British government announces it will stop funding the Lieutenant-Governor's salary.
	April 3 Legislative committee has a negative reaction to Confederation.
1866	*July 15* Great Fire of Charlottetown.
	March 16 United States abrogates the Reciprocity Treaty.
	December P.E.I. withdraws from discussions about Confederation.
1870	*January 7* P.E.I. Executive Council turns down Canada's terms for inclusion in Confederation.
1873	*July 1* British government pressure and Canadian promises of absorbing the railroad building debt, year-round communication with the mainland, and funds for landlord buy-outs result in P.E.I. joining Canada.
1875	Land Purchase Act compels absentee landlords to sell estates.
	May 12 Prince Edward Island Railroad opens.
1879	Prince of Wales College admits women as students.
	October 23 First hospital in P.E.I., the Charlottetown Hospital, is established by Roman Catholic Bishop Peter McIntyre.
1885	Telephone Company of Prince Edward Island is established.
1890–1930s	P.E.I. becomes the centre of a silver fox pelt industry.
1890	*February 7* First hockey game in P.E.I. is played in Charlottetown.
1893	*April 20* Legislative Council is incorporated into the Legislative Assembly. In each constituency a property owner votes for a councillor and an assemblyman, each male for an assemblyman. Owners can vote in each constituency in which they hold property.
1894	*May 15* P.E.I. imposes 1% income tax on yearly incomes above $350.00.
1897	Lobsters become leading fishery product.
1899	Women are eligible to sit on school boards.
1900	*June 9* P.E.I. becomes the first province to adopt Prohibition. The Prohibition

	Act comes into effect in each county when a majority of the residents approve it. This is finally achieved in *1906*.
1901	*June 5* Provincial act bans the sale of alcohol, the first province to do so.
1906	*October 13* Summerside is devasted by fire with 155 buildings burned.
1908	*March 26* Legislative Assembly votes to ban all motor vehicles from P.E.I.
1913	Secret ballot is introduced.
	April 24 Ban on motor vehicles is lifted; cars are allowed to operate Mondays, Wednesdays, and Fridays.
1916	Full rail-ferry service to mainland opens.
1917	Prohibition Committee is established consisting of three Catholic and three Protestant clergy to administer the importation of liquor. This is primarily designed to curb the prescription of medicinal liquor by physicians and druggists.
1920s	Maritime Rights Movement, a regional protest against the Maritimes declining influence since Confederation, climaxes.
1922	*May 3* Women are given the same voting privileges as men in provincial elections.
1925	First fisherman's union is formed in Tignish.
1929	*July 18* Voters retain Prohibition in a plebescite.
1932	*May 1* Royal Canadian Mounted Police absorbs the provincial police force.
1935	*April 4* Public Libraries Act receives assent.
	July 23 Liberal Party wins all seats in the P.E.I. legislature, the first Commonwealth parliament ever elected without any sitting opposition.
	September Prohibition Committee is abolished and its functions are assumed by the Attorney General.
1936	Credit Union Societies Act is the first official recognition of cooperatives on P.E.I.
1948	P.E.I. ends Prohibition, the last province to do so.
	Labour unions are prohibited on P.E.I.
1953	Potato Marketing Board is established by the P.E.I. Potato Growers Association.
1959	*October 1* Federal-provincial hospital plan comes into effect.
1963	Ability to vote in each riding in which property held is abolished.
1969	Prince of Wales College and St. Dunstan's University are amalgamated into the University of Prince Edward Island.
1970	Many small school districts are replaced by five regional boards resulting in school closings and consolidated institutions.
1972	*August 14* Royal commission to look into land use and ownership on P.E.I. is appointed.
1973	Council of Maritime Premiers is formed to deal with cooperation in internal development and external influence.
1975	*June 26* Supreme Court of Canada upholds P.E.I. law forbidding nonresidents from owning more than 4 ha. (10 acres) of land in P.E.I.
1977	*February 1* Federal-provincial agreement gives P.E.I. 100% of royalties from offshore mineral discoveries within 5 km. (3 mi.) of the coast and 75% from resources beyond.
	Federal government declares 200 mi. (322 km.) sovereignty off Canada's coasts.
1980	*July 17* Heavy rains black out Charlottetown for several hours.
1982	*February 22* Blizzard creates snowdrifts 5–7 m. (16–23 ft.) high causing a state of emergency as Islanders are marooned for 5 days.
1987	*November 29* Federal government stops all shipments of P.E.I. mussels after

toxin kills two people and makes 100 ill in Montreal, Quebec, and Moncton, New Brunswick.

November P.E.I. and federal government sign a three-year Water Management Agreement.

1988   *January 18* In a plebescite voters are 59.4% in favor of a land connection across the Northumberland Strait to New Brunswick.

1989   *July 12* National Transport Agency approves the Canadian National Railways' plan to abandon seven lines on P.E.I.

1990   *August 6* Marion Loretta Reid becomes P.E.I.'s first woman lieutenant-governor.

1992   *January 30* Proposals for construction of a bridge across the Northumberland Strait pass environmental reviews.

1993   *March 19* Federal Court of Canada orders a halt to the P.E.I./New Brunswick bridge project until its potential impact on the surrounding environment can be studied in detail and because cessation of the ferry service, entrenched in the P.E.I. Confederation agreement, is unconstitutional.

March 29 Catherine Sophia Callbeck becomes the first woman in Canada to be elected as premier of a province.

Culture and Education

Performing Arts Prince Edward Island has five performing companies, several theatres and festivals. A selection follows.

Charlottetown Festival, Charlottetown (June to September) (Canadian musical theatre) (Maritimes)	(902)566-1267 or 800-565-0278
Charlottetown Winter Carnival, Charlottetown (February)	(902)892-5708
Eptek Centre, Summerside	(902)888-8373
King's Playhouse, Georgetown (summer theatre)	(902)628-2216
Prince Edward Island Festival of the Arts, province-wide (September)	(902)369-4418
Prince Edward Island Island Symphony Orchestra, Charlottetown	(902)894-3566
Theatre P.E.I., Charlottetown	(902)628-6102
Victoria Playhouse, Victoria	(902)658-2525

Provincial Museums and Galleries The following are major Prince Edward Island institutions.

Basin Head Fisheries Museum, Basin Head

Confederation Centre of the Arts Gallery, Charlottetown

Green Gables House, Cavendish

Green Park Shipbuilding Museum, Port Hill

Musée acadien de l'île-du-Prince Edouard, Miscouche

Prince Edward Island Museum and Heritage Foundation, Charlottetown

Universities and Colleges

University of Prince Edward Island, Charlottetown

Holland College, Charlottetown, and additional campuses in other centres

Motor Vehicle Use

Motor Vehicles Registered for Use on Prince Edward Island (1993): 77,092. Minimum driving age: 16

Drivers Licenced by Prince Edward Island (1993): ca. 80,000

Roads Paved: 3,794 km. (2,358 mi.); un-paved 1,504 km. (935 mi.); bridges maintained by the province: 148 piled bridges from 14 ft. to 450 ft. span

Speed Limits 80 kph (50 mph) unless otherwise posted

First, Biggest, and Best

World's first demonstration of kerosene: Charlottetown, 1846, by the inventor, Dr. Abraham Gesner

America's first undersea telegraph cable: laid November 22, 1852 between Carleton Head, P.E.I. and Cape Tormentine, New Brunswick, by Frederick Newton Gisbourne

Sources of Information About Prince Edward Island

Visitor Services Division, Department of Tourism and Parks: P.O. Box 940, Charlottetown, P.E.I. C1A 7M5 (902)368-4444, 800-565-7421 (Maritime provinces), 800-565-0267 (Canada and United States)

Island Information Service: P.O. Box 2000, Charlottetown, P.E.I. C1A 7N8 (902)368-4000

P.E.I. Government Publications may be purchased from Government House: P.O. Box 846, Charlottetown, P.E.I. C1A 7L9

Books About Prince Edward Island: A Selected List

Reference Guides

Atlantic Provinces Economic Council. *Atlantic Canada Today* (1987).

Atlas of the Province of Prince Edward Island (1927, rpt. with minor changes 1990).

Baglole, Harry (ed.). *Exploring Island History: A Guide to the Historical Resources of Prince Edward Island* (1977).

Barrett, John I. (ed.). *Who's Who on Prince Edward Island* (1986).

Bishop, Olga B. *Publications of the Governments of Nova Scotia, Prince Edward Island, New Brunswick, 1758–1952* (1957).

Blanchard, J.-Henri. *The Acadians of Prince Edward Island, 1720–1964* (1964, rpt. 1976).

Burrows, Roger. *A Birdwatcher's Guide to Atlantic Canada. Vol. 3: New Brunswick, Prince Edward Island, Maritime Quebec* (1982).

Canada. Atmospheric Environment Service. *Canadian Climate Normals, 1961–1990: Atlantic Provinces* (1993).

Canada. Energy, Mines and Resources Canada. *Gazetteer of Canada: Prince Edward Island* (3rd ed. 1990).

Clark, Andrew Hill. *Three Centuries and the Is-land: A Historical Geography of Settlement and Agriculture in Prince Edward Island, Canada* (1959).

Erskine, Anthony J. *Atlas of Breeding Birds of the Maritime Provinces* (1992).

Erskine, D.S. *The Plants of Prince Edward Island* (2nd ed. 1985).

Fleming, Patricia Lockhart. *Atlantic Canadian Imprints, 1801–1820: A Bibliography* (1991).

Illustrated Historical Atlas of the Province of Prince Edward Island (1880, rpt. 1973).

Jones, Orlo (comp.). *Family History in Prince Edward Island: A Genealogical Research Guide* (1981).

—— and Doris Haslam (eds.). *An Island Refuge: Loyalists and Disbanded Troops on the Island of Saint John* (1983).

Laugher, Charles T. *Atlantic Province Authors of the Twentieth Century: A Bio-bibliographical Checklist* (1982).

Macqueen, Malcolm. *Hebridean Pioneers* (1957).

McCalla, Robert J. *The Maritime Provinces Atlas* (new ed. 1991).

Morley, William F.E. *The Atlantic Provinces: Newfoundland, Nova Scotia, New Brunswick, Prince Edward Island* (1967). A bibliography.

Norton, Judith Ann (comp.). *New England Planters of the Maritime Provinces of Canada, 1759–1800: Bibliography of Sources* (1993).

Novack, Jack. *A Guide to Local Government in Prince Edward Island* (2nd ed. 1987).

Pratt, T.K. (ed.). *Dictionary of Prince Edward Island English* (1988).

Rayburn, Alan. *Geographical Names of Prince Edward Island* (1975).

Scott, W.B. and M.G. Scott. *Atlantic Fishes of Canada* (1988).

Smith, H.M. Scott. *The Historic Houses of Prince Edward Island* (1990).

Nonfiction Sources

*denotes a winner of a Governor General's Literary Award.

Alexander, David G. *Atlantic Canada and Confederation: Essays in Canadian Political Economy* (1983).

Arsenault, Georges. *The Island Acadians, 1720–1980* (1989).

Baldwin, Douglas. *Land of the Red Soil: A Popular History of Prince Edward Island* (1990).

—— and Thomas Spira (eds.). *Gaslights, Epidemics, and Vagabond Cows: Charlottetown in the Victorian Era* (1987).

Begley, Lorraine (ed.). *Crossing That Bridge: A Critical Look at the P.E.I. Fixed Link* (1993).

Bolger, Francis W.P. *Memories of the Old Home Place, Prince Edward Island* (1984).

——. *Prince Edward Island and Confederation, 1863–1873* (1964).

—— (ed.). *Canada's Smallest Province: A History of P.E.I.* (1973, rpt. 1993).

Brehaut, Mary C. (ed.). *Historic Highlights of Prince Edward Island* (1964).

Bruce, Harry. *Down Home: Notes of a Maritime Son* (1988).

Brym, Robert J. and R. James Sacouman (eds.). *Underdevelopment and Social Movements in Atlantic Canada* (1979).

Buckner, Phillip A. and David Frank (eds.). *Atlantic Canada Before Confederation* (2nd ed. 1990).

Buckner, Phillip A. and John G. Reid (eds.). *The Atlantic Region to Confederation: A History* (1994).

Bumstead, J.M. *Land, Settlement, and Politics on Eighteenth-Century Prince Edward Island* (1987).

Burrill, Gary and Ian McKay (eds.). *People, Resources, and Power: [Critical Perspectives on Underdevelopment and Primary Industries in the Atlantic Region]* (1987).

Callbeck, Lorne Clayton. *The Cradle of Confederation: A Brief History of Prince Edward Island From Its Discovery in 1534 to the Present Time* (1964).

Campbell, Duncan. *History of Prince Edward Island* (1875, rpt. 1990).

Carleton University. History Collaborative. *Urban and Community Development in Atlantic Canada, 1867–1991* (1993).

Clark, Andrew Hill. *Three Centuries and the Island: A Historical Geography of Settlement and Agriculture in Prince Edward Island, Canada* (1959).

Clarke, George Frederick. *Someone Before Us: Our Maritime Indians* (3rd ed. 1974).

Daigle, Jean (ed.). *Acadians of the Maritimes: Thematic Studies* (1982).

Davies, Gwendolyn. *Studies in Maritime Literary History, 1760–1930* (1991).

—— (ed.). *Myth and Milieu: Atlantic Literature and Culture 1918–1939* (1993).

Forbes, Ernest R. *The Maritime Rights Movement, 1919–1927: A Study in Canadian Regionalism* (1979).

——. *Challenging the Regional Stereotypes: Essays on the 20th Century Maritimes* (1989).

—— and D.A. Mulse (eds.). *The Atlantic Provinces in Confederation* (1993).

Greenhill, Basil and Ann Giffard. *Westcountrymen in Prince Edward's Isle: A Fragment of a Great Migration* (1967).

Harvey, Daniel Cobb. *The French Regime on Prince Edward Island* (1926, rpt. 1970).

—— (ed.). *Journeys to the Island of St. John or Prince Edward Island, 1775–1832* (1955).

Hornby, Jim. *Black Islanders: Prince Edward Island's Historical Black Community* (1991).

House, J. D. *Fish Versus Oil: Resources and Rural Development in North Atlantic Societies* (1986).

Howell, Colin and Richard Twomey (eds.). *Jack Tar in History: Essays in the History of Maritime Life and Labour* (1991).

Lord, Margaret Gray. *One Woman's Charlottetown: Diaries of Margaret Gray Lord 1863, 1876, 1890* (ed. by Evelyn J. MacLeod, 1988).

MacKinnon, Frank. *The Government of Prince Edward Island* (1951, rpt. 1974).

MacKinnon, Wayne E. J. *Walter Jones, the Farmer Premier* (1974).

MacNutt, W.S. *The Atlantic Provinces: The Emergence of a Colonial Society, 1712–1857* (1965).

The Maritimes: Tradition, Challenge and Change (1987).

McCann, Larry (ed.). *People and Place: Studies of Small Town Life in the Maritimes* (1987).

—— and Carrie MacMillan (eds.). *The Sea and*

Culture of Atlantic Canada: A Multidisciplinary Sampler (1992).

McGee, Harold Franklin (ed.). *The Native Peoples of Atlantic Canada: A History of Indian-European Relations* (1972, rpt. 1983).

McKenna, M. Olga. *Micmac By Choice: Elsie Stark, an Island Legend* (1990).

Medjuck, Sheva. *The Jews of Atlantic Canada* (1986).

Montgomery, L.M. *Spirit of Place: Lucy Maud Montgomery and Prince Edward Island* (1982).

Murphy, J. Elmer. *A Newspaper Man Remembers: Tales of Three to Five Years of Newspaper Work and Other Remembrances* (1980?).

Parratte, Henri-Dominique. *Acadia* (1991).

Paul, Daniel N. *We Are Not the Savages: A Micmac Perspective on the Collision of European and Aboriginal Civilizations* (1993).

Power, Thomas P. (ed.). *The Irish in Atlantic Canada, 1780–1900* (1991).

Rankin, Robert Allan. *Down at the Shore: A History of Summerside, Prince Edward Island (1752–1945)* (1980).

Rawlyk, George A. (ed.). *Historical Essays on the Atlantic Provinces* (1967).

Robertson, Ian (ed.). *The Prince Edward Island Land Commission of 1860* (1988).

Robinson, Gillian (comp.). *Island Memories: Photographs of Prince Edward Island, 1890–1920* (1982).

Rogers, Irene L. *Charlottetown, the Life in Its Buildings* (1983).

Sager, Eric W. with Gerald E. Panting. *Maritime Capital: The Shipping Industry in Atlantic Canada, 1820–1914* (1990).

Saunders, S.A. *The Economic History of the Maritime Provinces* (1939, rpt. 1984).

Selleck, Lester B. *My Island Home* (1973).

Sharpe, Errol. *A People's History of Prince Edward Island* (1976).

Shaw, Walter. *Tell Me the Tales* (1975).

Smitheran, Verner, David Milne, and Satadal Gupta (eds.). *The Garden Transformed: Prince Edward Island, 1945–1980* (1982).

Stewart, John. *An Account of Prince Edward Island in the Gulf of St. Lawrence, North America: Containing Its Geography, a Description of Its Different Divisions, Soil, Climate, Seasons, Natural Productions, Cultivation, Discovery, Conquest, Progress and Present State of the Settlement, Government, Constitution, Laws and Religion* (1806, rpt. 1964).

Sylvester, John. *From Red Clay & Salt Water: Prince Edward Island & Its People* (1994).

Tuck, James A. *Maritime Provinces Prehistory* (1984).

Tuck, Robert Critchlow (ed.). *The Island Family Harris: Letters of an Immigrant Family in British North America, 1856–1866* (1983).

Upton, Leslie F.S. *Micmacs and Colonists: Indian-White Relations in the Maritimes, 1713–1869* (1979).

Watson, Julie. *Ghost Stories & Legends of Prince Edward Island* (1988).

——. *A Prince Edward Island Album: Glimpses of the Way We Were* (1987).

——. *Shipwrecks & Seafaring Tales of Prince Edward Island* (1994).

Weale, David. *Them Times* (1992).

—— and Harry Baglole. *The Island and Confederation: The End of an Era* (1973).

Wells, Kennedy. *The Fishery of Prince Edward Island* (1986).

Whitehead, Ruth Holmes. *The Old Man Told Us: Excerpts From Micmac History 1500–1950* (1991).

Prince Edward Island in Literature

Bird, Will R. *An Earl Must Have a Wife* (1969). Historical fiction about Joseph Des Barres, Lieutenant-Governor of P.E.I., 1804–1812.

Brehaut, L. and others. *Island Women: Our Prose & Poetry* (1982).

Choyce, Lesley (ed.). *Chezzetcook: An Anthology of Contemporary Poetry and Fiction From Atlantic Canada* (1977).

Creighton, Helen. *A Folk Tale Journey Through the Maritimes* (1993).

Dalziel, Marjorie Hooper. *On Rustico Shore* (1982). Historical fiction.

Fraser, Raymond, Clyde Rose, and Jim Stewart (eds.). *East of Canada: An Atlantic Anthology* (1976).

Gallant, Antoinette. *Little Jack an' de Tax-Man and Other Stories from Prince Edward Island* (1979). Twenty-eight stories about Islanders of Acadian heritage.

Hennessey, Michael. *An Arch for the King and Other Stories* (1984).

Laviolette, Emily A. *The Oyster and the Mermaid and Other Island Stories* (1975).

Montgomery, L.M. *Anne of Green Gables* (1908, rpt. 1992); *Anne of Avonlea* (1909); *Anne of the Island* (1915); *Anne's House of Dreams* (1917); *Rainbow Valley* (1919); *Rilla of Ingleside* (1921); *Anne of Windy Poplars* (1936); *Anne of Ingleside* (1939). Rural P.E.I. is the setting for the story of a spirited orphan who grows to womanhood.

——. *Along the Shore: Tales By the Sea* (1989). Short stories originally published in magazines and newspaper, 1897–1930.

Morrison, Allan with Michael MacKenzie. *A Giant Among Friends* (1980). A romantic comedy set in north shore P.E.I. in Spring 1930.

Thompson, Kent. *Stories From Atlantic Canada: A Selection* (1973).

Walker, Diana. *The Thousand Dollar Farm* (1977). A story about a close-knit farm family, the arrival of a young loner, and the offer of a small fortune for the farm.

QUEBEC

Quebec, located in central Canada, is Canada's largest province in area and includes islands in the Gulf of St. Lawrence. It is bordered on the west by the province of Ontario, James Bay, and Hudson Bay; on the north by Hudson Strait and Ungava Bay; on the east by the Labrador portion of the province of Newfoundland and Labrador; and on the south by the province of New Brunswick and the states of New York, Vermont, New Hampshire, and Maine.

Name Province of Quebec. "Quebec" is adapted from an Algonquin Indian word meaning "where the river narrows". *Previous names:* New France (1663–1763); Province of Quebec (1763–1791); Lower Canada (1791–1841), Canada East (1841–1867). (NOTE: Quebec is the name of both the province and the provincial capital. In order to avoid confusion "Quebec" is used to indicate the province, "Quebec City" the capital.)

Flag A white cross on a sky-blue background with a white fleur-de-lis in the centre of each of the quarters formed by the cross. It was adopted by provincial order-in-council on January 21, 1948, and given royal assent on March 9, 1950.

Coat of Arms Shield is surmounted by a royal crown with a scroll containing the provincial motto beneath. The upper third of the shield has three golden fleur-de-lis on a blue background; the middle third, a golden leopard on a red background; the lower third, a sugar maple tree sprig with three green leaves on a gold background. It was originally granted by Queen Victoria in 1868; a modification was adopted by provincial order-in-council on December 9, 1939.

Motto *Je Me Souviens* (I remember).

Emblems
Bird snowy owl (*Nyctea scandiaca*)
Flower madonna lily (*Lilium candidum*)
Tree yellow birch (*Betula alleghianensis Britton*)

Date of Entry into Confederation July 1, 1867; one of the four original provinces in Confederation.

Official Language French.

Capital City Quebec City, situated in southern Quebec on the north shore of the St. Lawrence River at the mouth of the St.-Charles River; an important seaport; population 167,517, CMA population 645,550. Founded and named by Samuel de Champlain on July 3, 1608, on the site of Stadacona, a previously inhabited Indian village, Quebec City has continuously been a capital city—of New France, of the British colony called Province of Quebec, of Lower Canada, of Canada East, and of the present Province of Quebec. It was first incorporated as a city on June 5, 1832. The Communauté urbaine de Quebec, a federation of thirteen municipalities, was created December 23, 1969.

Provincial Statutory Holidays In addition to national statutory holidays (see page 2), Quebec residents celebrate Fête nationale or Quebec Day (June 24).

Geography and Climate

Geography Most of northern Quebec and 80% of the total land mass of the province is covered by the Canadian Shield, among the oldest rocks in the world, rich in mineral deposits, with only 5% suitable for agriculture. Most agricultural activity takes place in the fertile soils of the St. Lawrence Lowlands. The northern extension of the Appalachian Mountains are found south of the St. Lawrence River. The landscape changes from arctic tundra in the far north to taiga, boreal forest, and temperate forest in southern Quebec.

Area Total 1,540,680 sq. km. (594,857 sq. mi.). 15.5% of Canada. Rank: 1st among the provinces, 2nd among the provinces and territories.

Inland Water 183,889 sq. km. (71,000 sq. mi.), includes more than one million lakes. Largest lake: Lac Mistassini 2,335 sq. km. (902 sq. mi.).

Elevations Highest point: Mount D'Iberville, 1,652 m. (5,420 ft.). Lowest point: St. Lawrence shore, sea level.

Major Rivers (* indicates a designated Canadian Heritage River): Aux feuilles, Aux outardes, Grande rivière de la baleine, Eastmain, George, Grande, Harricana, *Jacques Cartier, Koksoak, Manicouagan, Nottaway, Ottawa, Romaine, Saguenay, St. Lawrence, St. Maurice.

Climate The great latitudinal extent of Quebec causes a large range in temperature from north to south. Northern Quebec has a subarctic climate, central Quebec long, cold winters and short hot summers, and southern Quebec brisk winters and warm summers with occasional spells of hot, humid weather. The average daily mean temperature in January in Kuujjuaq is −24.5°C (−12.1°F); in Montreal −8.7°C (17.3°F); in July in Kuujjuaq 9.1°C (48.4°F); in Montreal 21.8°C (71.2°F). The lowest recorded temperature in Quebec: −54.4°C (−65.9°F) at Doucet on February 5, 1923; the highest recorded temperature: 40.0°C (104°F) at Témiscamique on July 6, 1921.

Average annual snowfall in Montreal, 242.8 cm. (95.6 in.); in Schefferville, 386.5 cm. (152.2 in.). Greatest recorded Quebec annual snowfall: 1,281 cm. (504.3 in.) at Mine Madeleine in 1980. The greatest recorded Quebec annual precipitation: 3,125 mm. (123 in.) at Mine Madeleine in 1981.

Quebec holds several Canadian climate records: greatest recorded snowfall in over five consecutive days, 2,489 cm. (979.9 in.) at Pointe-des-Monts on March 16, 1885; snowiest city in Canada, Sept-Îles with an annual average snowfall of 415 cm. (163.4 in.); city with the greatest annual number of days of blowing snow, Chicoutimi, 37 days; highest recorded wind speed for one hour, Quaqtaq, 201.1 kph (125 mph) on November 18, 1931; the most damaging ice storm, with 120 kph (75 mph) winds causing $7 million damage and a week's electric power loss in some areas in Montreal on February 25, 1961.

Time Zones Most of the province is in the eastern time zone; the area east of the 63rd meridian is in the Atlantic time zone.

Parks and Historic Sites

In this section * indicates that the area is, or part of it is, a UNESCO World Heritage Site.

National Parks Located in Quebec

Park	Location	Size
Forillon	Gaspé Peninsula	245 sq. km. (95 sq. mi.)
La Mauricie	near Shawinigan	544 sq. km. (210 sq. mi.)
Mingan Archipelago	Gulf of St. Lawrence	151 sq. km. (58 sq. mi.)

Provincial Parks There are 37 provincial parks and reserves in Quebec covering 71,330 sq. km. (27,541 sq. mi.) and 350 km. (218 mi.) along river reserves: 21 wildlife reserves, 10 conservation parks, and 6 recreation parks. The largest parks are:

Park	Region	Type	Size
Albanel-Mistassuni-et-Waconichi	Nouveau-Québec	wildlife	16,400 sq. km. (6,332 sq. mi.)
La Vérendrye	Outaouais	wildlife	13,610 sq. km. (5,255 sq. mi.)
Assinica	Nouveau-Québec	wildlife	8,885 sq. km. (3,430 sq. mi.)
Laurentides	Québec	wildlife	7,934 sq. km. (3,063 sq. mi.)
Sept-Îles/Port Cartier	Côte-Nord	wildlife	6,423 sq. km. (2,480 sq. mi.)
Ashuapmushuan	Saguenay-Lac-St. Jean	wildlife	4,487 sq. km. (1,732 sq. mi.)
Papineau-Labelle	Outaouais	wildlife	1,667 sq. km. (664 sq. mi.)
Mastigouche	Trois-Rivières	wildlife	1,574 sq. km. (608 sq. mi.)
Mont-Tremblant	Montréal	recreation	1,490 sq. km. (575 sq. mi.)
Rouge-Matawin	Montréal	wildlife	1,394 sq. km. (538 sq. mi.)

Quebec also has 32 national bird sanctuaries (plus one shared with Northwest Territories) and 8 national wildlife areas. There are 3 Ramsar sites.

Major National Historic Sites and Parks in Quebec

Battle of Restigouche, Pointe-à-la-Croix
Fort Chambly, Chambly
Fort Lennox, Île-aux-Noix
Fur Trade in Lachine, Lachine
Grosse-Île, Grosse-Île
Louis St. Laurent, Compton
Pointe-au-Père Lighthouse, near Rimouski
*Quebec Historic District, Quebec City
Saint Maurice Forges, Saint-Maurice
Sir Wilfred Laurier, Ville des Laurentides

In addition, there are a number of historic sites in Quebec administered by the province, municipalities, or organizations. The following are a selection of such sites:

Pointe-au-Moulin Historic Park, Île Perrot
Village minier de Bourlamaque, Val-d'Or
Village québécois d'Antan, Drummondville

Demography

All figures relating to Quebec population and dwellings are 1991 data and do not include the population on 5 Indian reserves which did not cooperate in the 1991 census.

Quebec population: 6,895,963; 25.3% of national; *rank:* 2nd

Historical population data

1981	6,438,405
1971	6,027,765
1961	5,259,211
1951	4,055,681
1941	3,331,882
1921	2,360,510
1901	1,648,898
1881	1,359,027
1861	1,111,566

Population density: 5.1 persons per sq. km. (13.2 per sq. mi.)

Number of dwellings: 2,650,111

Indian reserves and settlements: 39

Population characteristics:
urban: 5,351,211; 77.6%
rural: 1,544,752; 22.4%
19 and under: 1,829,405; 26.5%
65 and over: 770,925; 11.2%
average income for full-time employment 15 years and over (1990): $31,705; men $36,079; women $24,801
average life expectancy at birth (1987): men 71.98 years (lowest in Canada); women 79.39 years
live birth rate: 97,310; 14.1 per 1000
deaths: 49,121; 7.2 per 1000
marriages: 28,922; 4.2 per 1000
divorces: 20,277; 2.94 per 1000

Largest Cities (for definitions of CMA and CA see page viii),

Name	Population	Dwellings	National Pop. Rank
Montreal	3,127,242 (CMA)	1,242,469	2
Quebec City	645,550 (CMA)	255,052	8
Hull (smaller part of the National Capital Region; see Ontario)	226,957 (CMA)	84,615	
Chicoutimi-Jonquière	160,928 (CMA)	57,805	20
Sherbrooke	139,194 (CMA)	139,194	22
Trois-Rivières	136,303 (CMA)	54,730	23
Saint-Jean-sur Richelieu	68,378 (CA)	26,314	41
Shawinigan	61,672 (CA)	25,089	44
Saint-Jérôme	51,986 (CA)	20,776	53
Saint-Hyacinthe	50,193 (CA)	19,979	54

Government and Politics, 1867–

A description of the division of powers between the federal and provincial governments will be found on page 4.

Lieutenant-Governor The Lieutenant-Governor is the nominal head of the Quebec government, and is appointed by the Governor General of Canada on the recommendation of the Prime Minister of Canada. (A description of the duties of lieutenant-governors is found on page 7.)

Lieutenant-Governors of Quebec	*Term*
Narcisse-Fortunat Belleau	1867–1873
René Édouard Caron	1873–1876
Luc Letellier de Saint-Just	1876–1879
Théodore Robitaille	1879–1884
Louis François-Rodrigue Masson	1884–1887
Auguste-Réal Angers	1887–1892
Joseph-Adolphe Chapleau	1892–1898
Louis-Amable Jetté	1898–1908
Charles-Alphonse-Pantaléon Pelletier	1908–1911
François-Charles-Stanislas Langelier	1911–1915
Pierre-Laurent-Damase-Evariste LeBlanc	1915–1918
Charles Fitzpatrick	1918–1923
Louis-Philippe Brodeur	1923–1924
Narcisse Perodeau	1924–1929
Jean-Lomer Gouin	1929

Henry George Carroll 1929–1934
Esioff-Léon Patenaude 1934–1939
Eugène-Marie-Joseph Fiset 1939–1950
Gaspard Fauteux 1950–1958
J. Onésime Gagnon 1958–1961
Paul Comtois 1961–1966
Hugues Lapointe 1966–1978
Jean-Pierre Côté 1978–1984
Giles Lamontagne 1984–1990
Martial Asselin 1990–

National Assembly (Assemblée nation-ale) The National Assembly of Quebec consists of 125 members elected by pop-ular vote, each member represents a con-stituency; term of office: up to 5 years or less if the party in power maintains the confidence of the National Assembly; re-muneration (1993): $63,475 + $11,203 ex-pense allowance, additional amounts for special appointments; qualifications for members: Canadian citizen, 18 years or older, resident in Quebec for the six pre-vious months, and not subject to any le-gal disqualifications. (A description of the duties of provincial legislatures are found on page 7.)

Qualifications for Voters in Provincial Elections Canadian citizen, 18 years or older, resident in Quebec for the six pre-vious months, and not subject to any le-gal disqualifications.

Premier Nominally appointed by the Lieutenant-Governor of Quebec, the Premier is generally the leader of the par-ty with the majority of seats in the Na-tional Assembly. (A description of the re-sponsibilities of provincial premiers is found on page 7.)

Premiers of Quebec/Party/Term
Pierre-Joseph-Olivier Chauveau
  (Conservative, 1867–1873)
Gèdèon Ouimet
  (Conservative, 1873–1874)
Charles-Eugène Boucher de Boucherville
  (Conservative, 1874–1878)
Henri-Gustav Joly de Lotbinière
  (Liberal, 1878–1879)
Joseph-Adolphe Chapleau
  (Conservative, 1879–1882)

Joseph-Alfred Mousseau
  (Conservative, 1882–1884)
John Jones Ross
  (Conservative, 1884–1887)
Louis-Olivier Taillon
  (Conservative, 1887)
Honoré Mercier
  (Liberal, 1887–1891)
Charles-Eugène Boucher de Boucherville
  (Conservative, 1891–1892)
Louis-Olivier Taillon
  (Conservative, 1892–1896)
Edmund James Flynn
  (Conservative, 1896–1897)
Félix-Gabriel Marchand
  (Liberal, 1897–1900)
Simon-Napoléon Parent
  (Liberal, 1900–1905)
Jean-Lomer Gouin
  (Liberal, 1905–1920)
Louis-Alexandre Taschereau
  (Liberal, 1920–1936)
Joseph-Adélard Godbout
  (Liberal, 1936)
Maurice Duplessis
  (Union nationale, 1936–1939)
Joseph-Adélard Godbout
  (Liberal, 1939–1944)
Maurice Duplessis
  (Union nationale, 1944–1959)
Paul Sauvé
  (Union nationale, 1959–1960)
J. Antonio Barrette
  (Union nationale, 1960)
Jean Lesage
  (Liberal, 1960–1966)
Daniel Johnson
  (Union nationale, 1966–1968)
Jean-Jacques Bertrand
  (Union nationale, 1968–1970)
Robert Bourassa
  (Liberal, 1970–1976)
René Lévesque
  (Parti québécois, 1976–1985)
Pierre-Marc Johnson
  (Parti québécois, 1985)
Robert Bourassa
  (Liberal, 1985–1994)
Daniel Johnson
  (Liberal, 1994)
Jacques Parizeau
  (Parti québécois, 1994–)

Cabinet The Cabinet consists of ministers appointed by the Premier, usually from elected members of the majority party in the National Assembly. Cabinet ministers serve at the Premier's pleasure; each member usually heads a government ministry.

Government Ministries The telephone numbers for general information are listed with the ministries.

Affaires internationales, immigration, et communautés culturelles
(418)649-2300
Affaires municipales
(418)691-2015
Agriculture, pêcheries et alimentation
(418)643-2673
Conseil du trésor
(418)643-5743
Culture et communications
(418)643-2183
Éducation
(418)643-7095
Emploi
(418)643-4817   800-265-1414
Environnement et faune
(418)643-6071

Finance
(418)691-2233
Industrie, commerce, science et technologie
(418)691-5950
Justice
(418)643-5140
Ressources naturelles
(418)646-2727
Revenu
(418)659-6500 800-567-4692
Santé et services sociaux
(418)643-3380
Sécurité du revenu
(418)643-6875   800-361-4743
Sécurité publique
(418)644-6826
Services gouvernementaux
(418)643-1529
Tourisme
(418)643-5959 800-363-7777
Transports
(418)643-6864

Quebec Representation in Federal Government
House of Commons: 75 members
Senate: 24 members

Finances

A statement of revenue and expenditures for the years 1992/93 and 1991/92 are shown below in millions of dollars. The financial year runs from April 1 to March 31 of the year following.

	Actual 1992/93	*Actual 1991/92*
Revenue		
Taxation	23,751	24,269
Other	3,877	3,410
Government of Canada	7,794	6,772
Total revenue for the year	35,423	34,451
Expenditures		
Health and social services	9,824	9,531
Education	9,359	9,035
Finance	4,864	4,777
Income security	3,863	3,365
Health insurance	2,711	2,670
Transport	2,026	2,054
Municipal affairs	1,235	1,147
Other	6,473	6,074
Total expenditures for the year	40,355	38,653
Deficit for the year	4,932	4,202

The Economy

Quebec is highly industrialized with the majority of its plants located in the Montreal area. It is Canada's largest producer of hydroelectric power, pulp and paper, and asbestos; second in sawmill production and newsprint export; and Canada's only producer of columbium and titanium. There is a significant shipping industry from its 33 ports. Farming, concentrated in the St. Lawrence lowlands, consists primarily of small dairy farms. Tourism constitutes an important industrial sector.

Major Industries Principal industries include mining, forestry, and agriculture and their associated manufacturing industries, clothing and textiles manufacturing, and service industries.

Gross Domestic Product (1992) $136,847 million (in current dollars at factor cost); % of national G.D.P.: 22.8%; *rank:* 2nd

Distribution of gross domestic product (1990)

Manufacturing	21.1%
Finance, insurance, real estate	13.5%
Construction	7.1%
Government services	6.8%
Retail trade	6.6%
Educational services	5.9%

Wholesale trade	5.1%
Health services	4.7%
Other utilities	3.9%
Transportation, storage	3.6%
Agriculture	1.6%
Mining	0.9%
Logging	0.6%

Value of Manufacturing Shipments $66,888 million

Farm Cash Receipts $3,693 million

Employment (seasonally adjusted) 2,967,000; participation rate: 62.6%

Unemployment (seasonally adjusted) 400,000; per capita: 11.9%

Minimum wage (1994) $5.85 general minimum; $5.13 alcohol servers

Exports Quebec's merchandising exports in goods in 1992 amounted to $27,249 million, 17% of total Canadian merchandising exports; *rank:* 2nd
Largest trading partner: United States; more than 73% of Quebec's export is shipped to the United States
Major export commodities: telecommunication equipment and materials 12%; newsprint 10%; aluminum and alloys 9%

History

ca. 9,000 B.C.	Paleo-Indians arrive.
ca. 2000 to 0 B.C.	Pre-Dorset Paleo-Inuit are the first inhabitants in present-day northwestern Quebec.
ca. 800 B.C.– ca. 1000 A.D.	Dorset people are in northern Hudson Bay and Hudson Strait areas.
ca. 1000 B.C.	Norse settlements are in Ungava.
875 A.D.	Irish monks may have landed on the Magdalen Islands.
900 A.D.	Algonkian people move along north shore of St. Lawrence River.
ca. 1500	Algonquin, Cree, Huron, Iroquois, Malecite, Micmac, Montagnais, and Naskapi tribes inhabit present-day Quebec with Inuit in far north.
1534	*July 24* Jacques Cartier raises a cross at Penouille Point, Gaspé, and claims land for France.

1535	*August 10* Cartier becomes the first known European to enter the St. Lawrence River.
	September 7 Cartier arrives in Stadacona (present-day Quebec City) where he winters.
	October 2 Cartier visits Hochelaga (present-day Montreal) for one day and names the mountain Mount Réal.
1541	*January 15* Jean-François de la Rocque de Roberval is appointed the first viceroy of Canada.
	August 23 Cartier arrives at Stadacona and builds Charles-bourg-Royal.
1542	*July* Michel Gaillon is hanged for theft at Cap-Rouge, the first instance of capital punishment in Canada.
	September 19 Oldest Canadian official document pardons Aussillon de Sauverterre accused of murder.
1542–1543	Roberval and colonists winter at Cap Rouge.
1544	Basques establish fisheries at Tadoussac.
1599	Pierre Chauvin establishes a colony at Tadoussac; most settlers do not survive the winter.
1600	King Henri IV of France grants a group of French merchants a fur-trading monopoly on the Gulf of St. Lawrence. The first fur trading post in Canada is built at Tadoussac by Francois Gravé du Pont and Pierre Chauvin de Tonnetuit.
1603	Samuel de Champlain explores the Saguenay River, Stadacona, Hochelaga, and Gaspé.
1608	*July 3* Champlain founds Quebec City, the first permanent settlement in Quebec.
1610	Henry Hudson explores Hudson and Ungava Bays and winters at Rupert River.
1612	Champlain is named the first governor of New France.
1615	Earliest recorded Catholic mass in New France is celebrated on the island of Montreal.
1616	*June 15* Recollet Brothers establish the first schools in New France for Indians at Trois-Rivières and Tadoussac.
1617	*June 14* Louis and Marie Hebert and their children arrive in Tadoussac, the first European settlers to farm land in New France.
1620	Champlain builds Fort Saint-Louis on Cap-aux-Diamants.
1621	*September 21* Code of Laws is issued, the first legislation in New France.
1625	*June* First Jesuit missionaries arrive in New France.
1628	*May 6* King Louis XIII grants to the Company of One Hundred Associates a fur trade monopoly and land in New France, Acadia, and Newfoundland to establish a French empire in North America, the start of New France's seigneurial system.
1629	*July 19* David and Lewis Kirke capture Quebec City.
1632	*March 29* Treaty of Saint-Germain-en-Laye returns Quebec to France.
1634	*July 4* Sieur de Laviolette establishes a fur trading post at Trois-Rivières.
1638	*June 11* First recorded earthquake in Canada occurs.
1639	Hotel-Dieu, the first hospital in New France, is established in Quebec City.
1642	*May 18* Paul de Chomeday, Sieur de Maisonneuve, founds Ville Marie (Montreal).
1643	*January 6* Maisonneuve places a cross on the top of Mont Royal.
1647	*July 16* Father Jean de Quen discovers Lac Saint-Jean and the route leading into the interior of the Saguenay.
1648	*March 5* Council of Quebec is reorganized as a seven-member ruling body.

1649	Iroquois Indians begin raids on New France.
	Laurent Berman becomes the first notary in Canada.
1658	Marguerite Bourgeoys opens a school for girls in Ville Marie.
1660	*April* Adam Dollard des Ormeaux and 17 men hold off 800 Iroquois for a week at Long Sault diverting them from attacking Montreal.
1663–1673	Ca. 800 *filles du roi* arrive as brides for settlers and soldiers with a dowry provided by the French King.
1663	*February 5* Great Quebec Earthquake which causes many deaths is the first recorded Canadian disaster.
	February 24 King Louis XIV declares New France a royal province with a council consisting of governor, bishop, five councillors, attorney general, and secretary; and an intendant to control finance and trading.
1665	Carignan-Salières Regiment builds Fort Sorel, Fort Saint-Louis, Fort Sainte-Thérèse, and Fort Saint-Jean.
1667	*February 5* Mining of iron ore begins at Trois-Rivières.
	April 2 Louis XIV issues a civil code for New France and establishes courts.
1668	*September 29* Zachariah Gillam in the *Nonsuch* reaches the Rupert River, builds Fort Charles, and purchases the Rupert River area from the Indians.
	Quebec Seminary (later Laval University), the first Quebec institution of higher education, is founded.
1670	*May 2* Hudson's Bay Company is formed and granted trade rights over all territory draining into Hudson Bay.
	September Fort Charles becomes the Hudson's Bay Company's first permanent trading post.
1672	Father Albanel travels overland to the mouth of the Rupert River and claims the territory for France.
1674	François de Laval becomes New France's first bishop.
1675	Abenaki Indians move from New England to Quebec.
1685	Michel Sarrazin establishes the first medical practice in New France.
	Louis XIV prohibits Jews and Huguenots (Protestants) from settling in New France.
1686	*July 3* Pierre LeMoyne d'Iberville captures Fort Charles and renames it Rupert House.
1688	*April* Council authorizes the establishment of an office for the poor in urban areas, the first form of public assistance in New France.
1690	*September 4* English militia and Iroquois Indians attack Montreal; they are defeated on *October 16.*
1692	*October* Marie-Madeleine Jarret de Verchères, 14, leads the defence of the seigneury against Iroquois attack for 8 days until soldiers arrive from Montreal.
1693	In the first recorded mail delivery in Canada Pedro da Silva is hired to carry letters between Montreal and Quebec City.
1697	*October 30* Treaty of Ryswick restores the status quo by returning all territory captured in North America during King William's War.
1700	*October* First elementary school opens in Quebec City.
	First Masonic Lodge in Canada is established in Montreal.
1711	*August 23* British fleet sailing to attack Quebec is shipwrecked off Île-aux-Oeufs; 950 dead.
1713	*April 11* France returns the Hudson Bay drainage basin to the British in the Treaty of Utrecht.
1717	Lamp that has never since been extinguished is lit in the Ursuline Convent in Quebec City.

1720	Montreal merchants re-establish the trading post at Fort Témiscamigue.
1730	Discovery of an iron ore deposit at Saint-Maurice leads to the establishment of the first iron works industry in Canada.
1732	Establishment of a shipyard on the St.-Charles River provides an impetus to a shipbuilding industry.
1734	Very destructive fire is set in Montreal by slave Marie-Joseph-Angélique.
1737	First important highway, Le Chemin du roi, is completed between Quebec City and Montreal.
1750	Primary textiles industry is established in Quebec.
1759	*June 29* British troops land at Point Lévis.
	July 9 British troops occupy the left bank of the Montmorency River.
	July 31 British forces are driven back in the Battle of Montmorency.
	September 12–13 Quebec City falls to the British in the Battle of the Plains of Abraham.
	October 12 James Murray is appointed governor of Quebec.
	November 12 English civil law is established in Quebec.
	Abraham Franks and Aleazar Levy become the first Jewish settlers in Quebec City.
1760	*April 28* French defeat the British at the Battle of Sainte-Foy.
	July 8 British ships defeat the French relief force at the Battle of Restigouche ending France's last mission to save its colonies in North America.
	September 8 Jeffery Amherst captures Montreal.
1763	*February 10* Treaty of Paris: France formally cedes its North American possessions to Britain including all of Canada east of the Rocky Mountains.
	Benjamin Franklin sets up a postal system in Canada with offices in Quebec City, Montreal, and Trois-Rivières.
	October 7 Royal proclamation gives Labrador to Newfoundland.
1765	Fire destroys one-quarter of Montreal.
1769	First novel written in Canada, *The History of Emily Montague* by Frances Brooke while resident in Quebec City, is published.
1774	*June 22* Quebec Act passed by the British Parliament extends the borders of Quebec to Labrador, Antocosti Island, Îles-de-la-Madeleine, west to the Great Lakes and Ohio country; establishes English criminal law; restores French civil law; grants religious freedom for Catholic Canadians; and establishes government by appointed council, effective *May 1, 1775.*
1775	*August 17* First legislative council meets at Quebec City.
	November 13 American forces occupy Montreal, retreat *May 7, 1776.*
	December 31 American forces attack Quebec City and keep it under siege until *May 9, 1776.*
1776	*June* British and Canadian forces repulse the American invasion of Trois-Rivières.
	July 23 Civil jurisdiction is re-established in the District of Quebec.
1777	First permanent synagogue in Canada, Shearith Israel Congregation, opens in Montreal.
1779	First canal lock in Canada is built at Coteau-du-Lac.
1783	*September 3* Treaty of Paris: formal end of the British-United States conflict sets a line running through the middle of the Great Lakes thus giving the Ohio country to the Americans.
1784–1786	Fifteen thousand United Empire Loyalists from the United States arrive in the Eastern Townships.
1784	Montreal fur traders form the North West Company to compete with the Hudson's Bay Company.
	Habeas corpus is established in Quebec.

1791	*June 10* Constitutional Act or Canada Act (British Parliament) divides Quebec into Upper and Lower Canada; establishes a system of government which includes an elected legislative assembly and an appointed lieutenant-governor, legislative council, and executive council; and guarantees continuity of the seigneurial system of land ownership in Lower Canada.
1792	*August* André Michaux becomes the first naturalist to explore interior of the Quebec-Labrador peninsula.
	December 17 First legislature of Lower Canada meets at Quebec City.
1796	*August 23* Emmanuel Allen is sold at public auction in Montreal, the last slave transaction in Canada.
1798	Floods in Montreal and Trois-Rivières are described as the worst in living memory.
1800	Philemon Wright founds Hull and develops a forestry industry.
1803	First paper mill in Canada is established near Lachute with paper made from cloth rags.
1806	Napoleon's blockade closes Baltic ports; English turn to British North America for timber supplies where the timber trade flourishes; preferential tariffs continue after Napoleon's defeat.
1807	Ezekiel Hart becomes the first Jew to be elected to the Quebec legislative assembly.
1809	*March 30* Labrador Act transfers the coast of Labrador from the Saint-Jean River to Hudson Strait and Anticosti Island from Quebec to Newfoundland.
	August 19 First steamboat built in Canada, *Accommodation*, is launched in Montreal for service between Montreal and Quebec City.
1812	*June 18* United States declares war on Britain.
	October 23 American victory at St.-Regis.
	November 20 Canadian victory at Odelltown.
1813	*October 26* Canadian victory at the Battle of Chateauguay.
1814	*December 24* Treaty of Ghent ends the conflict and both sides return what has been captured.
1815	*November 23* First street lights in Canada are installed in Montreal and fuelled by whale oil.
1816	*May–September* Series of cold waves cause near famine; Quebec City is covered by ca. 30 cm (1 ft.) of snow, *June 6–10*.
1817	*November 3* Canada's oldest chartered bank still operating, the Bank of Montreal, opens; charter is received in 1822.
	Road between Toronto and Montreal is completed.
1821	McGill university is founded.
1824	*March 9* Fabrique Act is passed empowering the priest in every parish to provide a school for every 100 families.
	First medical school in Canada, the Montreal Medical Institution, opens.
1825	Lachine Canal is completed allowing ships to bypass the Lachine Rapids and navigate the St. Lawrence River.
	British Parliament restores Anticosti Island and part of the southwest coast of Labrador to Newfoundland.
1827	Canada's earliest recorded trade union, a printer's union, is organized in Quebec City.
1829	*February 7* Act authorizes a Jewish religious corporation with power for its officials to enact marriages and other ceremonies.
1830	First steam railway line in British North America, carrying materials from Cape Diamond to the Citadel, opens.
	First Hudson's Bay Company post designed to trade with the Inuit is established at present-day Kuujjuaq.

1831	*Royal William*, the first Canadian ship to cross the Atlantic under steam power, is launched at Quebec City.
1832	Cholera epidemic brought by Irish immigrants claims thousands of lives in Quebec.
	Grosse-Île is designated as the major Canadian quarantine station for immigrants and continues in this capacity to *1937*.
	Montreal is incorporated as a city.
	June 15 Jews are given the same rights as other British subjects.
1833	Canada's first daily newspaper, the *Daily Advertiser*, is published in Montreal.
1836	*July 21* First passenger railway in Canada, the Champlain and St. Lawrence Railroad, opens; it runs from La Prairie to St.-Jean.
1837	*November 23* Patriote rebel forces defeat government troops at the Battle of St.-Denis.
	November 25 Government troops defeat Patriotes at the Battle of St.-Charles.
	December 14 Government troops capture St.-Eustache ending the rebellion.
1838	*February 10* British government suspends Lower Canada's constitution as of *March 27*, and appoints Lord Durham as Governor General with orders to investigate Canadian problems.
	Some members of Hunter's Lodges from the United States occupy Bois Blanc Island; others join with Patriotes in crossing the Vermont/Quebec border and proclaiming a republic with Robert Nelson as president.
	December 10 Canadian militia defeats Patriotes at Beauharnois ending the second rebellion.
1839	*February 4* Lord Durham recommends union of Upper and Lower Canada and the establishment of responsible government for local and regional affairs.
1840–1850	Economic crisis causes 40,000 French Canadians to immigrate to the United States.
1841	*February 10* Act of Union (British Parliament) creates the Province of Canada; Lower Canada becomes Canada East.
	May 17 Landslide from Cap Diamant leaves 32 dead in Quebec City.
1842	*August 9* Ashburton-Webster Treaty defines the southern boundary of Quebec.
1844	*May 10* Capital of the Province of Canada is moved to Montreal from Kingston.
	November 29 Second parliament of the Province of Canada meets in Montreal.
1845	*May 28* Fires demolish two-thirds of Quebec City.
	Beauharnois Canal opens.
1846	School Act provides for common schools in every parish.
1847	Anesthesia (ether) is first used in Canada by Dr. Edward Dagge Worthington during an operation in Sherbrooke.
1848	*March 11* Reformers Robert Lafontaine (Canada East) and Robert Baldwin (Canada West) are elected and achieve responsible government.
1849	*April 25* Lord Elgin assents to the Rebellion Losses Bill to compensate for property damage during the Rebellions of 1837; mobs attack Elgin and the Parliament Building in Montreal is burned.
	Parliament of Canada adopts both English and French as official languages.
	Imprisonment for debt is abolished.
	October 10 Three hundred twenty-five prominent Montreal citizens sign the Annexation Manifesto calling for union with the United States.
1849–1865	Capital of the Province of Canada alternates every four years between Toronto and Quebec City.
1850–1900	Five hundred thousand Quebec residents immigrate to the United States.
1852	*July 8* Fire in east end Montreal leaves more than 10,000 homeless.

1854	*February 1* Fire destroys the Parliament Buildings in Quebec City.
	June 6 Reciprocity Treaty with the United States, together with other factors, brings economic boom to Quebec.
	November 23 Seigneurial system is abolished officially.
1856	*April 30* Montmorency suspension bridge collapses.
1857	*March 12* Desjardin Canal bridge collapses sending a train into the water; 70 dead.
	June 26 Steamer *Montreal* burns near Quebec City killing 253.
1860	Asbestos is discovered for the first time in North America in the Des Plantes River region.
1861	*August 14* St. Lawrence floods one-quarter of Montreal.
	Lower Canada Education Act creates denominational schools and boards.
1864	*June 29* Ninety-nine are killed and 100 injured as a train plunges from an open Richelieu River swing bridge in Canada's deadliest train accident.
1866	*March 16* United States abrogates the Reciprocity Treaty.
	June 7 Fenians from the United States raid across the border at Missisquoi Bay.
1867	*July 1* Canada East, renamed Quebec, joins three other British North American colonies in Confederation.
	September Henry Seth Taylor demonstrates the first Canadian-built automobile, a steam-powered car, at Stanstead.
1869	*November 19* Canada purchases Rupert's Land from the Hudson's Bay Company; the transfer goes into effect *July 15, 1870*.
	Windsor Mills, the first chemical wood-pulp mill in Canada, opens near Sherbrooke.
1870	*May 24* Fire in Quebec City leaves 5,000 homeless.
	Fenians from the United States are involved in 2 raids across the Quebec border.
1874	Montreal Stock Exchange is founded, the oldest in Canada.
1875	*September 28* Sabotage may be the cause of a train derailment at Yamaska; 10 dead.
1877	Montreal Harbour Commission uses electricity for the first time in Canada to light the waterfront.
1878	*June 24* First recorded tennis tournament in Canada takes place at the Montreal Lacrosse Club.
	First Canadian production of asbestos begins at Thetford Mines.
1885	*March 8* Factories Act, Quebec's first labour law, limits hours of work and provides for safety measures.
1885–1886	Last smallpox epidemic to sweep a Western city claims nearly 6,000 victims in Montreal and 20,000 in the province.
1886	Parliament Building in Quebec City is completed.
	March 25 First Workman's Compensation Act in Canada.
1888	*August 16* Tornado moving from St.-Zotique to Valleyfield kills 9 and injures 14.
1889	*September 19* Massive rock slide in Quebec City kills 45.
1894	*January 4* Factories Act is replaced by the Industrial Establishments Act which incorporates the principle of the civil responsibility of employers.
1895	*October 2* Federal government establishes the Provisional District of Ungava as part of the North-West Territories.
	Laurentide Park becomes the first federal or provincial government-administered park in Canada.
1896	*July 6* Boundaries of Quebec are extended to the Hudson Bay shoreline enlarging the province by 306,765 sq. km. (118,450 sq. mi.).
1897	George Foote Foss builds Canada's first gas-driven car in Sherbrooke.

	Albert Peter Low surveys northern Quebec and reports large iron deposits north of the Manicougan River.
1898	Federal government transfers lands to Quebec, increasing Quebec's boundary northward to the Eastmain and Hamilton rivers.
	Emma Casgrain becomes Canada's first woman dentist when she graduates from the Quebec College of Dentistry.
1899	*September 19* Rock slide in Quebec City kills 45.
1900	Great Fire destroys three-quarters of Hull.
	December 6 Alphonse Desjardins founds the first Caisse populaire in Levis.
1902	*November 28* Oldest currently active orchestra in Canada, Orchestre symphonique de Québec, gives its first concert in Quebec City.
1907	*August 29* Seventy-five are killed when a section of the Quebec Bridge falls into the St. Lawrence River in Canada's worst bridge disaster.
1908	*August 26* Land slide partly destroys Notre-Dame-de-la-Salette and kills 37.
	Ernest Rutherford wins the Nobel Prize for chemistry for work done while at McGill University.
1909	More than 10,000 Quebec residents leave for the United States looking for work.
1911–1912	Robert Flaherty surveys the Ungava Peninsula.
1913	*October 8* W. Robinson makes the first commercial inter-city flight, Montreal to Ottawa.
1912	Quebec's boundaries are enlarged northward to their present size.
1914	*May 29* *Empress of Ireland* collides with *Sorestad* in the St. Lawrence River near Rimouski causing 1,014 deaths in Canada's worst marine disaster.
1915	*January 15* Canadian Northern Railroad between Quebec and Vancouver is completed.
1916	*September 11* Centre span of the Quebec Bridge, rebuilt after the 1907 disaster, collapses causing 13 deaths.
1917	*May* French Canadians riot in Montreal about the introduction of conscription by the federal government.
	November 26 National Hockey League is formed in Montreal.
1918	*March 28* Anti-conscription riots in Quebec City lead to the federal government's imposition of martial law on Quebec in *April*.
1921	*May 1* Quebec government takes control of liquor sales in the province.
	September 24 Canadian Catholic Federation of Labour is founded, a joining of two Quebec unions (later renamed Confederation of National Trade Unions in 1960).
1922	First French-language radio station, CKAC, is established in Montreal.
1924	*May 23* First Canadian scheduled air service begins between Angliers, Lake Fortune, and Rouyn.
	September First Canadian regular airmail service begins between Rouyn and Haileybury, Ontario.
	December 24 Cross on Mont Royal, Montreal, is lit for the first time.
1927	*January 9* Fire and panic in the Laurier Palace Theatre, Montreal, causes the death of 76 children, resulting in a law prohibiting children under 16 from attending movie theatres.
	March 1 Judicial Committee of the British Privy Council settles a long-standing dispute between Quebec and Newfoundland by giving Labrador to Newfoundland; it establishes the boundary between Canada and Labrador.
1930	*February 19* Quebec legislature votes against allowing women to practise law in Quebec.
	February 20 Cairine Reay Wilson of Montreal becomes the first woman senator in Canada.

	August 1 Imperial airship R-100 arrives at St.-Hubert airport and is moored at the only dirigible mooring tower in the world built outside Britain, the only time the tower is ever used.
1936	*November 2* Federal government establishes the Canadian Broadcasting Corporation as a crown corporation with French-language services based in Montreal.
1937	Quebec's Padlock Law allows the closing for one year of any building suspected of being used by Communists, the destruction of Communist materials, and the imprisonment without appeal of those involved.
1939	*April 5* Supreme Court of Canada declares the Inuit a federal responsibility.
1940	*April 25* Women are allowed to vote and hold provincial office.
1942	*April 27* Quebec is the only province to reject conscription in a national plebiscite.
	May–October German submarines in the Gulf of St. Lawrence sink 23 ships; 258 dead. The Gulf is closed to ocean shipping until 1944.
1943	*May 26* Quebec law requires free, compulsory education.
	August 10–24 Anglo-American war conference is held in Quebec City.
	Fred Rose, the only Communist ever to sit in the House of Commons, is elected in the Montreal-Cartier riding.
1944	*September 11–16* Second Anglo-American war conference is held in Quebec City.
1946	*October 16* Food and Agricultural Organization is founded in Montreal by a meeting of United Nations member countries.
1949	*February 14* Start of a four-month strike at Quebec's major asbestos mines introduces an era of bitter labour conflict and eventually leads to Quebec's Quiet Revolution.
1952	*September 6* Canada's first television station, CBFT, begins operation in Montreal.
1953	*December 7* First foreign-owned bank in Canada, the Mercantile Bank of Canada, is incorporated with head offices in Montreal.
1957	*March 6* Supreme Court of Canada nullifies Quebec's Padlock Law.
1959	*June 26* St. Lawrence Seaway is opened officially at St. Lambert Lock.
	Free Libraries Act is passed.
1960	Social changes and a new government herald the start of the Quiet Revolution.
	December 2 First conference of provincial premiers is held in Quebec City.
1961	*January 1* Federal-provincial hospital plan goes into effect in Quebec, the last province to join.
1963	*March* Front de liberation du Québec (FLQ) is formed in Montreal.
	April–May FLQ explodes a series of bombs in Montreal; a night watchman is killed.
	May 1 Quebec nationalizes 11 private electric power companies to form Hydro-Québec.
	November 29 Airplane crash at Ste.-Thérèse-de-Blainville kills 118 in Canada's worst air disaster involving Canadian aircraft.
1964	*January 1* Minimum voting age in Quebec is lowered to 18.
	July 1 Married women in Quebec are given the same rights as men.
1965	*May 1* United States Consulate in Montreal is bombed.
1966	*October 6* Agreement is reached between Hydro-Québec and British Newfoundland Corporation that Quebec will subsidize the development of Churchill Falls and buy all surplus power at a fixed rate for 40 years (negotiations between Newfoundland and Quebec are not completed until 1969).
	October 16 Montreal's subway begins operation.

1967   *April 27–October 29* Expo '67, Montreal's world fair, attracts more than 50 million visitors.

July 24 Charles de Gaulle, president of France, shouts "Vive le Québec libre" from Montreal's City Hall.

October 15 René Lévesque resigns from the Quebec Liberal Party when it rejects the idea of separation from Canada.

1968   *May 31* Dr. Pierre Grondin performs Canada's first heart transplant operation on Albert Murphy at the Montreal Heart Institute.

June 24 St.-Jean-de-Baptiste Day riots in Montreal injure 130; 290 arrested.

Lévesque founds the Parti quebecois with the policy of making Quebec a sovereign state associated with Canada.

December 31 Quebec abolishes the Legislative Council and changes the name of the Legislative Assembly to the National Assembly.

1969   *February 11* Students destroy the main computer and set fire to the data centre at Sir George Williams University; 96 arrested.

February 21 Réjane Laberge-Colas is appointed to the Quebec Supreme Court, the first woman in Canada to be named to the bench of a supreme court.

February–March FLQ sets 64 bombs in the Montreal area; many people are injured.

April 1 Quebec legalizes civil marriages.

October Canadian forces are called to Montreal to stop lawlessness caused by a strike by police and firemen.

December 28 Seventy cm. (28 in.) of snow falls on Montreal causing 15 deaths.

1970   *May 31* FLQ places five bombs in Westmount (Montreal) homes and offices.

October 5 FLQ kidnaps James Cross, British consular official, in Montreal; he is released *December 3.*

October 10 FLQ kidnaps Pierre Laporte, Quebec Minister of Labour, who is found dead on *October 17.*

October 17 Federal government declares War Measures Act; bans FLQ; and sends armed forces to Quebec to arrest and detain known and suspected separatist sympathizers.

December 28 Three suspects in Laporte's murder are arrested.

1971–1991 Giant hydroelectric power complex is built in northern Quebec.

1971   *January 18* Quebec requires English-language schools to teach French as a second language.

March 2 Quebec government announces compensation for those arrested but not charged in the October Crisis and destruction of their files and fingerprints.

March 4 In its worst snowstorm Montreal receives 47 cm. (19 in.) of snow with winds of 110 kph (68 mph) creating huge drifts and paralyzing the city.

May 4 Prolonged rainstorm at St.-Jean-Vianney causes a giant hole that swallows 36 houses, several cars, and a bus; 31 dead.

1972   *April 11–24* Two hundred thousand Quebec employees go on strike, the largest civil service strike in Canadian history.

May 5 Quebec Indian Association files legal action to stop the James Bay Power Project.

May 29 Quebec bans commercial salmon fishing in Gaspé Peninsula waters due to depleted fish stocks.

November 24 Quebec introduces legislation to create electoral districts in northern Quebec.

1974   *July 30* Official Languages Act makes French the official language of the province and requires linguistic aptitude tests for children whose parents want to enroll them in English schools.

1975 Cree Indians, Inuit, and the federal and Quebec governments sign the James Bay and Northern Quebec Agreement giving the aboriginal peoples some rights in the administration of their lands and monetary compensation for land lost to hydroelectric development.

1976 *April 6* Quebec Supreme Court rules against the Protestant School Boards' challenge that the Official Languages Act is unconstitutional.

July 17–August 1 Summer Olympics are held in Montreal; 250,000 spectators.

1977 *August 26* Bill 101 makes French the official language of the province and courts and restricts schooling in English to children whose mothers or fathers have attended English language primary schools in Quebec.

October 6 Quebec Superior Court rules that requiring court documents in French only is unconstitutional. In 1980 the Supreme Court of Canada agrees.

1978 *January 6* Sun Life Assurance Company announces its head office move from Montreal to Toronto because of the Quebec language laws and political instability; many other firms make similar moves.

February 20 Agreement with the federal government gives Quebec greater control over immigration to Quebec.

August 4 Forty-one are killed in Canada's worst bus accident when a bus plunges into a lake near Eastman.

Agricultural Land Protection Act protects Quebec's best farmland.

1980 *April 14* Jeanne-Mathilde Sauvé of Montreal becomes the first woman speaker of the House of Commons.

May 22 Referendum on a mandate to negotiate sovereignty-association is rejected by 60% of Quebec voters.

1981 *July 19–21* Seven-nation economic summit is held at Chateau Montebello.

September Law prohibiting signs in languages other than French goes into effect.

October 30 Child of a family residing in Quebec for less than three years may attend English-language schools.

1982 *April 7* Quebec Court of Appeal rejects the Quebec government's claim to veto power over constitutional change; this is supported by the Supreme Court of Canada on *December 6*.

1983 *June 9* Quebec Court of Appeals rules that people who were educated in English anywhere in Canada can send children to English-language schools in Quebec.

1984 *May 8* Denis Lortie sprays the Quebec National Assembly with a submachine gun killing 3 and wounding 13.

May 14 Jeanne-Mathilde Sauvé of Montreal becomes the first woman Governor General of Canada.

September 3 Bomb blast at Montreal's Central Station leaves 3 dead and 21 injured.

October 5 Marc Garneau of Quebec becomes the first Canadian in space on the United States space shuttle *Challenger*.

1985 *June 25* Quebec Superior Court rules unconstitutional a law realigning Quebec schools along linguistic rather than religious lines.

1986 *May 29* Hailstones up to 8 cm. (3 in.) in diameter cause $65 million damage on Montreal's south shore.

1987 *September* Thirty-three countries sign the Montreal Protocol stipulating that CFC production must end by 2000.

1988 *December 21* Quebec invokes the "notwithstanding" clause in the Charter of

	Rights and Freedoms to reinstate the French-only sign law struck down by the Supreme Court.
1989	*June* Federal and Quebec governments sign an agreement to coordinate efforts to protect and restore the St. Lawrence River.
	December 6 Marc Lepine kills 14 women and himself at the Université de Montreal Engineering Faculty as protest against feminists.
	December 25 Because of the sparse population, no damage occurs when an earthquake, measuring 6.2 on the Richter scale, hits the Ungava Peninsula and part of Northwest Territories.
1990	*Summer* Land dispute causes a 78-day armed confrontation between the Canadian Army and Mohawk Indians at Kanesatake; problems also erupt at the Akwesasne and Kahnawake reserves.
	December 27 Quebec gains exclusive responsibility for the selection of independent immigrants to Quebec.
1993	*June 16* Law permits bilingual signs as long as French is predominant.
	November 26 Raymonde Verreault becomes Chief Justice of the Montreal Municipal Court, the first woman to be appointed chief justice of any judicial court in Quebec.

Culture and Education

Performing Arts Quebec has about 500 professional music, theatre, dance, and multi-disciplinary organizations which present annually more than 2,500 performances and activities, almost 1,000 of these in the Montreal region. The major organizations are listed below. Many perform as well in other provinces and countries.

Carbone 14 [theatre company], Montreal	(514)521-4198
Carnaval, Quebec City (February) (festival of winter)	(418)626-3716
Carrefour international de théâtre de Québec, Quebec City (international theatre festival)	(418)692-3131
Centaur Theatre, Montreal	(514)288-3161
Cirque du soleil, Montreal (acrobatic dance performance)	(514)522-2324
Festival d'été international de Québec, Quebec City (July)	(514)692-4540
Festival de théâtre des Ameriques, Montreal (biennial, May/June, odd-numbered years)	(514)842-0704
Festival international de jazz de Montréal, Montreal (July)	(514)790-1245 or 800-361-4595
Festival international de Lanaudière, Joliette (international classical music festival)	(514)759-7636
Festival international de nouvelle danse, Montreal (biennial, September, odd-numbered years) (avant-garde dance)	(514)287-1423
Festival mondial de folklore de Drummondville, Drummondville	(819)472-1184
Grands ballets canadiens, Montreal	(514)849-8681
I Musici, Montreal	(514)982-6038
Just for Laughs International Comedy Festival, Montreal (world's largest comedy festival)	(416)872-2262
La La La Human Steps, Montreal	(514)288-8266
McGill Chamber Orchestra, Montreal	(514)487-5190
Montreal Symphony Orchestra, Montreal	(514)842-3402
O Vertigo Danse, Montreal	(514)251-9177
Orchestre symphonique de Québec, Quebec City	(514)643-5598
Opera de Montréal, Montreal	(514)985-2222

Opera de Québec, Quebec City	(514)529-4142
Théâtre d'aujourd'hui, Montreal	(514)282-7516
Théâtre de quat'sous, Montreal (Quebec plays)	(514)845-7277
Théâtre du nouveau monde, Montreal	(514)861-0563
Théâtre du rideau vert, Montreal	(514)844-1793
Théâtre du Trident, Quebec City	(418)643-5873
Théâtre les deux mondes, Montreal	(514)593-4417
Violons du Roy, Quebec City (chamber music orchestra)	(418)643-5598
World Film Festival, Montreal (August/September)	(514)848-3883

Provincial Museums and Galleries The following are major Quebec institutions.

Canadian Centre for Architecture, Montreal
Canadian Museum of Civilization, Hull
McCord Museum of Canadian History, Montreal
Museum of Fine Arts, Montreal (Canada's oldest art museum)
Musée d'art contemporain, Montreal
Musée de la civilisation, Quebec City
Musée des religions, Nicolet
Musée du Québec, Quebec City
Pointe-à-Callière Museum of Archaeology and History, Montreal
Village historique de Val-Jalbert, Chambord
Village québécois d'Antan, Drummondville

Universities and Colleges (* indicates additional campuses in other centres)
Bishop's University, Lennoxville
Concordia University, Montreal
McGill University, Montreal
Université Laval, Ste.-Foy
Université de Montréal, Montreal
Université de Québec, Quebec City*
Université de Sherbrooke, Sherbrooke

Collèges d'enseignement general et professionnel
de l'Abitibi-Témiscaminique, Rouyn*
Ahuntsic, Montreal
d'Alma, Alma
André Laurendeau, LaSalle
de Baie-Comeau, Baie-Comeau
Beauce-Appalaches, Ville de Saint-Georges
de Bois-de-Boulogne, Montreal
Champlain Regional College, Lennoxville*
de Chicoutimi, Chicoutimi
Dawson College, Montreal
de Drummondville, Drummondville
Edouard-Montpetit, Longueuil*

Francois-Xavier-Garneau, Quebec City
de la Gaspésie et des îles, Gaspé*
de Granby, Granby
Heritage College, Hull
John Abbott College, Ste-Anne-de-Bellevue
de Joliette-de-Lanaudière, Joliette
de Jonquière, Jonquière
de Lévis-Lauzon, Lauzon
de Limoilou, Quebec City
Lionel-Groulx, Ste.-Therese
de Maisonneuve, Montreal
de Matane, Matane
Montmorency, Laval
de l'Outaouais, Hull
de la Pocatière, Comte de Kamouraska
de la Region de l'Amiante, Thetford-Mines
de Rimouski, Rimouski
de Rivière-du-Loup, Rivière-du-Loup
de Rosemount, Montreal
de St.-Félicien, St.-Félicien
de Ste.-Foy, Ste.-Foy
de St.-Hyacinthe, St.-Hyacinthe
St.-Jean-sur-Richelieu, St.-Jean-sur-Richelieu
de St.-Jérôme, St.-Jérôme
de St.-Laurent, Ville St.-Laurent
de Sept-Îles, Sept-Îles
de Shawinigan, Shawinigan
de Sherbrooke, Sherbrooke
de Sorel-Tracy, Tracy
de Trois-Rivières, Trois-Rivières
de Valleyfield, Valleyfield
Vanier College, Ville St.-Laurent
de Victoriaville, Victoriaville
du Vieux-Montréal, Montreal

Miscellaneous Educational Institutions
Centre d'arts Orford, Magog
Institut de technologie agro-alimentaire, St.-Hyacinthe*
National Circus School, Montreal
National Theatre School of Canada, Montreal

Motor Vehicle Use

Motor vehicles registered for use in Quebec (1990): 3,580,765

Drivers licensed by Quebec (1987): 3,848,521. Minimum driving age: 16 with driver training, 18 without driver training

Roads Autoroutes: 2,958 km. (1,838 mi.); main highways: 9,744 km. (6,055 mi.); regional roads: 8,584 km. (5,334 mi.); municipal roads: 36,714 km. (22,814 mi.); bridges and viaducts maintained by the province: 8,600

Speed Limits Autoroutes: 100 kph (62 mph); hard-surfaced roads outside urban areas: 90 kph (56 mph); gravel roads outside urban areas: 70 kph (43 mph); urban areas unless otherwise posted and school zones: 50 kph (31 mph)

First, Biggest, and Best

World's second largest French-speaking city: Montreal
North America's largest French-speaking cultural event: Festival d'été international de Québec, Quebec City
North America's only existing walled city: Quebec City
World's longest cantilevered truss span: Pierre Laporte Suspension Bridge, 549 m. (1,800 ft.) between piers
World's largest underground walkway: 4.8 km. (3 mi.) containing 240 stores, 36 restaurants, 4 cinemas, and 10 office buildings in Montreal
World's largest French-language broadcasting production centre: Maison de Radio-Canada
World's largest area airport: Mirabel International Airport, northwest of Montreal
World's tallest inclined tower: Olympic Stadium Tower, Montreal, 175 m. (574 ft.)
World's largest underground power plant: La Grande 2, James Bay
World's only collection devoted to architecture: Canadian Centre for Architecture, Montreal
North America's first Unesco World Heritage Site: Quebec City historic district
World's first mechanical device for washing clothes: patented by Noah Cushing, 1824
North America's first water-driven mill: built by Jean de Biencourt, Sieur de Poutrincourt on Allains River, 1607
North America's first lock canal: built by William Truss at Coteau du Lac, 1781
North America's first hospital north of Mexico: Hotel-Dieu, Quebec City, 1639
World's highest multiple-arch dam: Daniel Johnson Dam at Manicougan-Outardes hydroelectric power project, centre arch 214 m. (702 ft.) high
North America's first successful steamboat built entirely in North America: *Accommodation* launched August 1809 at Montreal
World's first ship to cross the Atlantic Ocean from west to east under steam power: *Royal William* launched at Cape Cove, April 27, 1831
World's first international railway: St. Lawrence and Atlantic Railroad from Montreal to Portland, Maine, inaugurated July 18, 1853
North America's first commercial pulp mill: built by Alex Buntin at Valleyfield, 1869
North America's first plant to produce chemical pulp by the sulphate process: Brompton Pulp and Paper Company, East Angus, 1907
North America's first plant to manufacture kraft paper: Brompton Pulp and Paper Company, East Angus, 1907
World's first snowmobile: invented by Joseph-Armand Bombardier in 1922, but not produced commercially until 1959
North America's first wood-grinder: built by Alex Buntin in Valleyfield, 1866

North America's first permanent bank: Bank of Montreal established 1817

North America's first credit union: La Caisse populaire de Lévis founded December 16, 1900

World's first use of aircraft for forest fire control: St.-Maurice Valley, 1919

World's first specially-designed bush aircraft: *The Norseman* built in Montreal by Robert Noorduyn and first flown November 1935

North America's first scheduled radio broadcast: musical program on XWA, Montreal, May 20, 1920

North America's first operatic work with music written in North America: Colas et Colinette composed by Joseph Quesnel and staged in 1790

World's first documentary film: *Nanook of the North* filmed in northern Ungava, 1920–1921

World's first public ice hockey game: Montreal, March 3, 1875

World's first ice hockey game using a flat puck: played by McGill University students in Montreal, 1879

North America's oldest golf club: Royal Montreal Golf Club established November 4, 1873

North America's first YMCA chapter: Montreal established November 25, 1851

North America's first curling club: Montreal Curling Club established 1807

World's largest producer of maple syrup: two-thirds of world's production

World's greatest large-city snow removal: Montreal's annually averages 42 million tonnes of snow removed from 1,700 km. (1,056 mi.) of streets

World's only women's English-language film studio: National Film Board of Canada's Studio D, Montreal

North America's oldest French-language institution of higher learning: Université Laval established in Quebec City, December 8, 1852

World's largest French-language educational institution outside France: Université de Montreal

World's only continuous series of birth records stretching over three centuries: register of births begun in New France 1621

North America's oldest day-care centre: Montreal Day Nursery established 1888

Sources of Information About Quebec

Communication Québec: 1037, rue de la Chevrotiere, Québec, Qué. G1R 4Y7 (418) 643–1430

Tourisme Québec: C.P. 20,000, Québec, Qué. G1K 7X2 (514) 873–2015 or 800-363-7777

Les Publications du Québec: C.P. 1005, Québec, Qué. G1K 7B5 (418) 643–5150 or 800-463-2100

Books About Quebec: A Selected List

Reference Guides

Aubin, Paul with Paul André Linteau. *Bibliography of the History of Quebec and Canada, 1966–1975*, 2 vols. (1981).

Aubin, Paul and Louis-Marie Côté. *Bibliography of the History of Quebec and Canada, 1946–1965*, 2 vols. (1987).

——. *Bibliography of the History of Quebec and Canada, 1976–1980*, 2 vols. (1985).

——. *Bibliography of the History of Quebec and Canada, 1981–1985*, 2 vols. (1990).

Bergeron, Léandre. *The Quebecois Dictionary* (1982).

Burrows, Roger. *A Birdwatchers Guide to Atlantic Canada. Vol. 3, New Brunswick, Prince Edward Island, Maritime Quebec* (1982).

Canada. Atmospheric Environment Service. *Canadian Climate Normals, 1961–1990: Quebec* (1993).

Canada. Atmospheric Environment Service. *The Climate of Montreal* (1987).

Cardinal, Claudette. *The History of Quebec: A Bibliography of Works in English* (1981).

Cooke, Alan and Fabien Caron (comps.). *Bibliography of the Quebec-Labrador Peninsula*, 2 vols. (1968).

Cotnam, Jacques. *Contemporary Quebec: An Analytical Bibliography* (1973).

Crowe, R.B. *The Climate of Ottawa-Hull* (1984).

Franklin, Martin and David Franklin with Renée Des Rosiers de Lanauze. *Introduction to Quebec Law* (3rd ed. 1984).

Garigue, Philip. *A Bibliographical Introduction to the Study of French Canada* (1956).

Illustrated Atlas of the Eastern Townships and South Western Quebec (1881, rpt. 1972).

Kandiuk, Mary. *French-Canadian Authors: A Bibliography of Their Works and of English-Language Criticism* (1990).

Krueger, Donald R. *Quebec Politics in Historical and Cultural Perspective: A Selected Bibliography*, 2 vols. (1981).

Lambert, Ronald D. *The Sociology of Contemporary Quebec Nationalism: An Annotated Bibliography and Review* (1981).

O'Donnell, Brendan. *Printed Sources for the Study of English-Speaking Quebec: An Annotated Bibliography of Works Published Before 1980* (1985).

——. *Sources for the Study of English-Speaking Quebec: An Annotated Bibliography of Works Published between 1980 and 1990* (1992).

Orkin, Mark M. *Speaking Canadian French: An Informal Account of the French Language in Canada* (rev. ed. 1971).

Robeson, Virgina R. (ed.). *Lower Canada in the 1830s* (1977). Documents.

Robinson, Sinclair and Donald Smith. *Dictionary of Canadian French* (rev. ed. 1990; published in the United States as *NTC's Dictionary of Canadian French*; 1st ed. published as *Practical Handbook of Quebec and Acadian French*).

Sénécal, André. *A Reader's Guide to Quebec Studies* (rev. ed. 1988; 1st ed. published as *Quebec Studies: A Selected Annotated Bibliography*).

Tougas, Gérard (comp.). *A Checklist of Printed Materials Relating to French-Canadian Literature, 1763–1968* (2nd ed. 1973).

Trudel, Marcel. *An Atlas of New France* (2nd ed. 1973).

Vachon, André with Victorin Chabot and André Desrosiers. *Dreams of Empire: Canada Before 1700* (1982). Facsimile documents.

Walker, Douglas C. *Pronunciation of Canadian French* (1984).

Nonfiction Sources

*denotes a winner of a Governor General's Literary Award; **a winner of a Governor General's Literary Award for the title in its original French-language version.

Ames, Herbert Brown. *The City Below: A Sociological Study of a Portion of the City of Montreal, Canada* (1897, rpt. 1972).

Anderson, William Ashley. *Angel of Hudson Bay: The True Story of Maud Watt* (1961).

Armstrong, Elizabeth. *The Crisis of Quebec, 1914–1918* (1937, rpt. 1974).

Arnopoulos, Sheila McLeod and Dominique Clift. *The English Fact in Quebec* (2nd ed. 1984) **1st ed.

Behiels, Michael D. *Prelude to Quebec's Quiet Revolution: Liberalism vs Neo-nationalism, 1945–1960* (1985).

—— (ed.). *Quebec Since 1945: Selected Readings* (1987).

Black, Conrad. *Duplessis* (1977).

Bliss, Michael. *Plague: A Story of Smallpox in Montreal* (1991).

Bosworth, Newton. *Hochelaga Depicta: The Early History and Present State of the City and Island of Montreal* (1839, rpt. 1974).

Bradbury, Bettina. *Working Families: Age, Gender and Daily Survival in Industrializing Montreal* (1993).

Brown, Michael. *Jew or Juif?: Jews, French Canadians, and Anglo-Canadians, 1759–1914* (1986).

Burt, Alfred Leroy. *The Old Province of Quebec*, 2 vols. (1944, rpt. 1968).

Cagnon, Maurice. *The French Novel of Quebec* (1986).

Caldwell, Garry and Eric Waddell. *The English of Quebec: From Majority to Minority Status* (1982).

Chantraine, Pol. *The Living Ice: The Story of the Seals and the Men Who Hunt Them in the Gulf of St. Lawrence* (1980).

Charbonneau, André, Yvon Desloges, and Marc Lafrance. *Quebec, the Fortified City: From the 17th to the 19th Century* (1982).

Chenier, Rémi. *Québec, a French Colonial Town in North America, 1660 to 1690* (1991).

Chodos, Robert. *Quebec and the American Dream* (1991).

Clift, Dominique. *Quebec Nationalism in Crisis* (1982, rpt. 1989).

Coleman, William D. *Independence Movement in Quebec, 1945–1980* (1984).

Collard, Edgar Andrew. *All Our Yesterdays: A Collection of 100 Stories of People, Landmarks and Events From Montreal's Past* (1988).

——. *100 More Tales From All Our Yesterdays* (1990).

——. *Montreal: The Days that Are No More* (1976).

——. *Montreal: 350 Years in Vignettes* (1991).

——. *Montreal Yesterdays: More Stories From All Our Yesterdays* (1989).

Connell, Brian. *The Plains of Abraham* (1959; published in the United States as *The Savage Years*).

Conway, John F. *Debts to Pay: English Canada and Quebec From the Conquest to the Referendum* (1992).

Cook, Ramsay. *Canada and the French Canadian Question* (1966, rpt. 1986).

——. *Canada, Quebec, and the Uses of Nationalism* (1986).

—— (comp.). *French-Canadian Nationalism: An Anthology* (1969).

Copp, Terry. *The Anatomy of Poverty: The Condition of the Working Class in Montreal, 1897–1929* (1974).

Cross, Michael S. and Gregory S. Kealey (eds.). *Economy and Society During the French Regime to 1759* (1983).

Dechêne, Louise. ****Habitants and Merchants in Seventeenth Century Montreal* (1992).

Dejean, Paul. *The Haitians in Quebec: A Sociological Profile* (1980).

Delisle, Esther. *The Traitor and the Jew: Antisemitism and Extremist Right-Wing Nationalism in Quebec From 1929–1939* (1993).

Demchinsky, Bryan (comp.). *Montreal Then and Now: The Photographic Record of a Changing City* (1985).

Desbarais, Peter. *René: A Canadian in Search of a Country* (1976).

Desloges, Yvon. *A Tenant's Town: Québec in the 18th Century* (1991).

Dessaulles, Henriette. *Hopes and Dreams: The Diary of Henriette Dessaulles, 1874–1881* (1986). The daughter of a prominent St.-Hyacinthe family who kept a diary from age 14 to 21.

De Visser, John. *Montreal, a Portrait* (1988).

DeVolpi, Charles P. *Quebec, a Pictorial Record: Historical Prints* (1981).

Dickinson, John A. *Diverse Pasts: A History of Quebec and Canada* (1986).

—— and Brian Young. *A Short History of Quebec: A Socio-economic Prospective* (2nd ed. 1993).

Dodge, William (ed.). *The Boundaries of Identity: A Quebec Reader* (1992).

Dominigue, Richard-Philippe. *Choices on the Horizon: An Economic Analysis of the Political Status of Quebec* (1991).

Dubé, Philippe. *Charlevoix: Two Centuries at Murray Bay* (1990).

Dumas, Evelyn. *The Bitter Thirties in Québec* (1975).

Eccles, W.J. *Canada Under Louis XIV, 1663–1701* (1964, rpt. 1978).

——. *The Canadian Frontier, 1534–1760* (rev. ed. 1983).

——. *Canadian Society During the French Regime* (1968).

——. *Essays on New France* (1987).

——. *France in America* (rev. ed. 1990).

——. *Frontenac, the Courtier Governor* (1959, rpt. 1968).

Finnigan, Joan. *Some of the Stories I Told You Were True* (1981). Ottawa Valley in the past two centuries.

Fitzmaurice, John. *Québec and Canada: Past, Present, and Future* (1985).

Fournier, Louis. *F.L.Q., the Anatomy of an Underground Movement* (1983).

Fraser, Graham. *P.Q.: Rene Levesque and the Parti Quebecois in Power* (1984).

Fraser, Matthew. *Quebec Inc.: French-Canadian Entrepreneurs and the New Business Elite* (1987).

Frost, David B. (ed.). *Montréal Geographical Essays* (1981).

Gagnon, Alain-G. (ed.). *Quebec: State and Society* (2nd ed. 1993).

—— and Mary Beth Montcalm. *Quebec: Beyond the Quiet Revolution* (1990).

Gagnon, Serge. *Quebec and Its Historians, 1840 to 1920* (1982).

——. *Quebec and Its Historians, the Twentieth Century* (1985).

Gauvin, Lise. *Letters From an Other* (1989). A newcomer's reflections and impressions of life in Quebec.

Gougeon, Gilles (ed.). *A History of Quebec Nationalism* (1994).

Gould, Karen. *Writing in the Feminine: Feminism and Experimental Writing in Quebec* (1990).

Grady, Patrick. *The Economic Consequences of Quebec Sovereignty* (1991).

Graham, Conrad. *Mont Royal: Early Plans and Views of Montreal* (1992).

Graham, Ron. *The French Quarter* (1992).

Gratton, Michel. *French Canadians: An Outsider's Inside Look at Quebec* (1992).

Greenwood, F. Murray. *Legacies of Fear: Law and Politics in Quebec in the Era of the French Revolution* (1993).

Greer, Allan. *Peasant, Lord, and Merchant: Rural Society in Three Quebec Parishes, 1740–1840* (1985).

Gubbay, Aline. *Montreal, the Mountain and the River* (1981).

Guindon, Hubert. *Quebec Society: Tradition, Modernity, and Nationhood* (1988).

Haggart, Ron and Aubrey E. Golden. *Rumors of War* (1971).

Handler, Richard. *Nationalism and the Politics of Culture in Quebec* (1988).

Harris, Richard Colebrook. *The Seigneurial System in Early Canada: A Geographical Study* (1966, rpt. 1984).

Hatch, Robert McConnell. *Thrust for Quebec: The American Attempt on Quebec in 1775–1776* (1979).

Hébert, Jean-Claude (ed.). *The Siege of Quebec in 1759: Three Eye-Witness Accounts* (1974).

Higgins, Benjamin. *The Rise and Fall? of Montreal: A Case Study of Urban Growth, Regional Economic Expansion and National Development* (1986).

Hood, Hugh. *Around the Mountain: Scenes of Montreal Life* (1967).

Hopkins, J. Castell. *French Canada and the St. Lawrence: Historic, Picturesque and Descriptive* (1913, rpt. 1974).

Hornung, Rick. *One Nation Under the Gun* (1991).

Jacobs, Jane. *The Question of Separation: Quebec and the Struggle Over Sovereignty* (1980).

Jaenen, Cornelius J. *Friend and Foe: Aspect of French-Amerindian Cultural Contact in the Sixteenth and Seventeenth Centuries* (1976).

———. *The Role of the Church in New France* (1976).

Jauvin, Serge. *Aitnanu: The Lives of Hélène and William-Mathieu Mark* (1993). Innu living on the north shore of the St. Lawrence River.

Jones, Elizabeth. *Gentlemen and Jesuits: Quests for Glory and Adventure in the Early Days of New France* (1986).

Jones, George Stephen. *A Love Story From Nineteenth Century Quebec: The Diary of George Stephen Jones* (ed. by W. Peter Ward, 1989).

Kaplan, Harold. *Reform, Planning, and City Politics, Montreal, Winnipeg, Toronto* (1982).

Kenyon, W.A. *The History of James Bay 1610–1686: A Study in Historical Archaeology* (1986).

Knox, John. *The Siege of Quebec: And the Campaigns in North America, 1757–1760* (1769, ed. by Brian Connell, 1976; first published as *An Historical Journal of the Campaigns in North-America, For the Years 1757, 1758, 1758 and 1760;* subsequently published as *The Journals of John Knox.*)

Langlais, Jacques and David Rome. *Jews and French Quebecers: Two Hundred Years of Shared History* (1991).

Langlois, Simon and others. *Recent Social Trends in Québec, 1960–1990* (1992).

Le Moyne, Jean. **Convergence: Essays From Quebec* (1966).

Lévesque, René. *Memoirs* (1986).

———. *My Quebec* (1979).

———. *An Option For Quebec* (1968).

Levine, Marc V. *The Reconquest of Montreal: Language Policy and Social Change in a Bilingual City* (1990).

Levitt, Joseph. *Henri Bourassa and the Golden Calf: The Social Program of the Nationalists of Quebec, 1900–1914* (1969).

Linteau, Paul-André, René Durocher, and Jean-Claude Robert. *Quebec, a History, 1867–1929* (1983).

Linteau, Paul-André and others. *Quebec Since 1930* (1991).

Little, J.I. *Crofters and Habitants: Settler Society, Economy, and Culture in a Quebec Township, 1848–1881* (1991).

———. *Nationalism, Capitalism, and Colonization in Nineteenth Century Quebec: The Upper St. Francis District* (1989).

MacDonald, L. Ian. *From Bourassa to Bourassa: A Pivotal Decade in Canadian History* (1984).

MacKay, Donald. *The Square Mile: The Merchant Princes of Montreal* (1987).

Magnuson, Roger. *A Brief History of Quebec Education: From New France to Parti-Québécois* (1980).

———. *Education in New France* (1992).

Marie de l'Incarnation. *Word From New France: The Selected Letters of Marie de l'Incarnation* (ed. by Joyce Marshall, 1967).

Mathieu, Jacques. *Plains of Abraham: The Search For the Ideal* (1992).

McCallum, John. *Unequal Beginnings: Agriculture and Economic Development in Quebec and Ontario Until 1870* (1980).

McLean, Eric. *The Living Past of Montreal* (3rd rev. ed. 1993).

McRoberts, Kenneth. *Quebec, Social Change and Political Crisis* (3rd ed. with a postscript 1993).

McWhinney, Edward. *Quebec and the Constitution, 1960–1978* (1979).

Miquelon, Dale. *New France, 1701–1744: A Supplement to Europe* (1987).

——— (ed.). *Society and Conquest: The Debate on the Bourgeoisie and Social Change in French Canada, 1700–1850* (1977).

Mitchell, Elaine Allan. *Fort Timiskaming and the Fur Trade* (1977).

Miville-Deschenes, François. *The Soldier Off Duty: Domestic Aspects of Military Life at Fort Chambly Under the French Regime as Revealed by Archeological Objects* (1987).

Monet, Jacques. *The Last Cannon Shot: A Study of French Canadian Nationalism, 1837–1850* (1969, rpt. 1976).

Monière, Denis. **Ideologies in Quebec: The Historical Development* (1981).

Munro, Kenneth J. *The Political Career of Sir Adolphe Chapleau, Premier of Quebec, 1879–1882* (1992).

Naves, Elaine Kalman. *The Writers of Montreal* (1993).

Neatby, H. Blair. *Laurier and a Liberal Quebec: A Study in Political Management* (1973).

Neatby, Hilda. *The Quebec Act: Protest and Policy* (1972).

——. *Quebec, the Revolutionary Age, 1760–1791* (1966).

Noël, Françoise. *The Christie Seigneuries: Estate Management and Settlement in the Upper Richelieu Valley, 1760–1854* (1992).

Noppen, Luc and Gaston Deschenes. *Québec's Parliament Building: Witness to History* (1986).

Oliver, Michael. *The Passionate Debate: The Social and Political Ideas of Quebec Nationalism, 1920–1945* (1991).

Ouellet, Fernand. *Economic and Social History of Quebec, 1760–1850* (1980).

——. **Lower Canada, 1791–1840: Social Change and Nationalism* (1980).

—— (ed.). *Economy, Class, and Nation in Quebec: Interpretive Essays* (1991).

Peate, Mary. *Girl in a Red River Coat* (1970); *Girl in a Sloppy Joe Sweater* (1988). Memories of growing up in Montreal during the 1930s and 1940s.

Pelletier, Gerard. *The October Crisis* (1971, rpt. 1984).

Prevost, Robert. *Montreal, a History* (1993).

Price, Lynda. *Introduction to the Social History of Scots in Quebec, 1780–1840* (1981).

Provencher, Jean. *René Lévesque: Portrait of a Québécois* (1975).

Quebec. Department of Intergovernmental Affairs. *Life in Quebec*, 4 vols. (1980).

Quinn, Herbert F. *The Union Nationale: Quebec Nationalism From Duplessis to Lévesque* (2nd ed. 1979).

Raboy, Marc (ed.). *Old Passions, New Visions: Social Movements and Political Activism in Quebec* (1986).

Resnick, Philip. *Letters to a Québécois Friend, With a Reply From Daniel Latouche* (1990).

Richardson, Boyce. *Strangers Devour the Land: The Cree Hunters of the James Bay Area Versus Premier Bourassa and the James Bay Development Corporation* (1975, rpt. 1991).

Rioux, Marcel and Yves Martin (ed.). *French-Canadian Society* (1964, rpt. 1978).

Richler, Mordecai. *Oh Canada! Oh Quebec!: Requiem For a Divided Country* (1992).

Rome, David (comp.). *On the Jews of Lower Canada and 1837–38*, 3 vols. (1983).

Ross, Eric. *Full of Hope and Promise: The Canadas in 1841* (1991).

Ruddel, David-Thiery. *Quebec City, 1765–1832: The Evolution of a Colonial Town* (1987).

Rudin, Ronald. *The Forgotten Quebecers: A History of English-Speaking Quebec, 1759–1980* (1985).

Salisbury, Richard F. *A Homeland For the Cree: Regional Development in James Bay, 1971–1981* (1986).

Sancton, Andrew. *Governing the Island of Montreal: Language Differences and Metropolitan Politics* (1985).

Saywell, John. *The Rise of the Parti Québécois, 1967–1976* (1977).

Scowen, Reed. *A Different Vision: The English in Quebec in the 1990s* (1991).

See, Katherine O'Sullivan. *First World Nationalisms: Class and Ethnic Politics in Northern Ireland and Quebec* (1986).

Sellar, Robert. *The Tragedy of Quebec: The Expulsion of Its Protestant Farmers* (1907, rpt. 1974).

Shek, Ben-Zion. *French-Canadian & Québécois Novels* (1991).

Silliman, Benjamin. *A Tour to Quebec in the Autumn of 1819* (1820, rpt. 1968; originally published as *Remarks, Made on a Short Tour, Between Hartford and Quebec*).

Silver, A.I. *The French Canadian Idea of Confederation, 1864–1900* (1982).

Stacey, C.P. *Quebec 1759, the Siege and the Battle* (1959, rpt. 1984).

Stanley, George F.G. *Canada Invaded, 1775–1776* (1973, rpt. 1977).

——. *New France, The Last Phase, 1744–1760* (1968).

Stein, Michael B. *The Dynamics of Right-Wing Protest: A Political Analysis of Social Credit in Quebec* (1973).

Trofimenkoff, Susan Mann. *The Dream of Nation: A Social and Intellectual History of Quebec* (1982).

Trudeau, Pierre Elliott. *Federalism and the French Canadians* (1968, rpt. 1977).

—— (ed.). *The Asbestos Strike* (1974).

Trudel, Marcel. *The Beginnings of New France, 1524–1663* (1973).

Vastel, Michel. *Bourassa* (1992).

Vigod, Bernard L. *Quebec Before Duplessis: The Political Career of Louis-Alexandre Taschereau* (1986).

Wade, Mason. *The French Canadians, 1760–1967*, 2 vols. (rev. ed. 1968, rpt. 1975–1976).

——. *Mason Wade, Acadia and Quebec: The Perceptions of an Outsider* (ed. by N.E.S. Griffiths and G.A. Rawlyk, 1991).

Wallen, Thelma J. *Multiculturalism and Quebec: A Province in Crisis* (1991).

Williams, Dorothy W. *Blacks in Montreal, 1628–1986: An Urban Demography* (1989).

Wright, J.V. *Quebec Prehistory* (1979).

Yelin, Shulamis. *Shulamis: Stories From a Montreal Childhood* (1983).

York, Geoffrey and Loreen Pindera. *People of the Pines: The Warriors and the Legacy of Oka* (1991).

Young, Brian. *Georges-Etienne Cartier: Montreal Bourgeois* (1981).

Zoltvany, Yves. *Philippe de Rigaud de Vaudreuil, Governor of New France, 1703–1725* (1974).

Quebec in Literature

*denotes a winner of a Governor General's Literary Award; **a winner of a Governor General's Literary Award for the title in its original French-language version.

Aquin, Hubert. *Writing Quebec: Selected Essays* (ed. by Anthony Purdy, 1988).

Archambault, Gilles. *One For the Road: A Novel* (1982). A Montreal clerk faces a mid-life crisis.

——. *The Umbrella Pines* (1980). The conflicts and misunderstandings of a Quebec family's three generations.

Aubert de Gaspé, Philippe. *Canadians of Old* (1890, rpt. 1974). Two friends are separated in the aftermath of the British conquest of Quebec.

Bacque, James. *Big Lonely* (1969, rpt. 1978; originally published as *The Lonely Ones*). Four people are caught in Quebec's political conflicts.

Beauchemin, Yves. *The Alley Cat: A Novel* (1986). A comic novel set in Montreal.

——. *Juliette: A Novel* (1993). A woman searches for her niece through the streets of Montreal.

Bell, Donald. *Saturday Night at the Bagel Factory and Other Montreal Stories* (1972).

Benazon, Michael. *Montreal Mon Amour: Short Stories From Montreal* (1989).

Bessette, Gérard. *Not For Every Eye: A Novel* (1962, rpt. 1984). A bookseller sells forbidden works during the Duplessis regime.

Bissonnette, Lise. *Following the Summer: A Novel* (1993). Two young women learn from each other in a small Quebec mining town.

Blais, Marie-Claire. **Deaf to the City* (1981). A dark view of the city seen through the eyes of inhabitants of Old Montreal.

——. **The Manuscripts of Pauline Archange* (1970, rpt. 1982). A young girl's poverty-stricken childhood in a small Quebec town.

——. *A Season in the Life of Emmanuel* (1966, rpt. 1992). A novel about the sixteenth child in a Quebec farm family.

Bosco, Monique. **Lot's Wife* (1975). A despairing woman examines her past.

Boyarsky, Abraham. *A Pyramid of Time* (1978). Short stories about a young German concentration camp survivor in Montreal.

Brooke, Frances. *The History of Emily Montague* (1769, rpt. 1985). A novel in the form of a series of letters describes the social and political milieu of Quebec in the 1760s.

Buell, John. *Playground* (1976, rpt. 1991). An urban man spends over two weeks lost in the northern Quebec bush.

Buller, Herman. *Days of Rage* (1974). A novel of political protest.

——. *One Man Alone* (rev. ed. 1980). A novel about Montreal Jewish families and small-town French Canadians in the 1930s.

——. *Quebec in Revolt: The Guibord Affair* (1972). Based on a nineteenth-century incident in Quebec.

Callaghan, Morley. **The Loved and the Lost: A Novel* (1951, rpt. 1989). A Montreal woman is destroyed by her desire to be accepted by the black community.

——. *The Many Colored Coat* (1960, rpt. 1988). The Montreal business world is set against a background of racial and class tensions.

——. *Such is My Beloved* (1934, rpt. 1991). A Montreal priest tries to redeem two prostitutes.

Campbell, Wanda Blynn. *The Promise* (1983). Twelve short stories set in northern Quebec.

Carrier, Roch. *Floralie, Where Are You?* (1971); *The Garden of Delights* (1978); *Is It the Sun, Philibert?* (1972); *The Man in the Closet* (1993); *No Country Without Grandfathers* (1981); *Prayers of a Very Wise Child* (1991); *They Won't Demolish Me* (1974). A selection of the delightful books by this author set in Quebec.

Cather, Willa. *Shadows on the Rock* (1931, rpt. 1973). A novel of Quebec during the last days of Frontenac, 1689–1697.

Chabot, Denys. *Eldorado on Ice* (1981). A novel based on memories of the Abitibi region.

Cohen, Leonard. *Beautiful Losers* (1966, rpt. 1991); *The Favourite Game* (1963, rpt. 1986). Two novels set in Montreal.

Conan, Laure. *Angéline de Montbrun* (1884, rpt. 1975). This novel unfolds against the religious, political, and social climate of nineteenth-century French Canada.

Costain, Thomas B. *High Towers* (1949). Historical novel about Charles Le Moyne (1626–1685).

Dandurand, Anne, Claire Dé, and Hélène Rioux. *Three By Three* (1992). Short stories set in Montreal by three Quebec women.

Daymond, Douglas and Leslie Monkman (eds.). *Stories of Quebec* (1980).

Diamond, Ann. *Snakebite: Short Stories* (1989). Stories set in contemporary Montreal.

Donovan, Rita. *Daisy Circus: A Novel* (1991). Tears and laughter in the Montreal of the 1950s.

Drache, Sharon. *Ritual Slaughter* (1989). A Hasidic community north of Montreal comes into conflict with the French Canadians who surround them.

Ducharme, Réjean. ***Wild to Mild: A Tale* (1980). A satire of the culture and politics of Montreal in the 1970s.

Epps, Bernard. *Pilgarlic the Death: A Novel* (1967, rpt. 1980). Depiction of a small town in the Eastern Townships.

Ewert, Charles. *A Cross of Fire* (1981). A man in seventeenth-century New France leaves the Jesuits to marry a Huron Indian woman.

Ferron, Jacques. *The Cart: A Novel* (1980); *Dr. Cotnoir* (1973); *Quince Jam* (1977, rpt. 1992); *The Penniless Redeemer* (1984); *The Saint Elias* (1975); *Wild Roses: A Story Followed by a Love Letter* (1976); ***Tales For the Uncertain Country* (1972). The author slashes at legal, religious, and social power in these novels set in Quebec in various periods.

Gallant, Mavis. *Across the Bridge: Stories* (1993). Short stories with a Montreal milieu.

Girard, Rodolphe. *Marie Calumet* (1904, rpt. 1976). A humourous novel of life in rural Quebec in the 1860s.

Godbout, Jacques. ***Hail Galarneau!* (1970). A young would-be writer runs a hot dog stand.

Graham, Gwenthalyn. **Earth and High Heaven* (1944, rpt. 1969). A young Montreal journalist falls in love with a Jewish lawyer.

Gravel, François. *Felicity's Fool: A Novel* (1992). A quest for the physical nature of happiness set against the background of the early years of Montreal's first psychiatric hospital.

Grey, Francis William. *The Cure of St. Philippe: A Story of French-Canadian Politics* (1899, rpt. 1970). A comic novel of French-English relations in a small Quebec town.

Guèvremont, Germane. **The Outlander (1950, rpt. 1978). A stranger changes the life of a rural French Canadian family.

Harrison, Keith. *After Six Days* (1985). A week in the lives of two Montreal yuppie couples.

Hart, Matthew. *The Male of the Species: A Novel* (1993). Two young boys confront adolescence in a small Anglo community near Montreal.

Harvey, Jean-Charles. *Fear's Folly* (1982). This novel attacking the forces that kept Quebec from modernization was banned when it was published in the original French version in 1934.

Hébert, Anne. ***Children of the Black Sabbath* (1977). The practices described in this novel about demonic possession and exorcism in a Quebec convent are based on research.

——. *The First Garden* (1990). A famous Parisian actress returns to her native Quebec City.

——. *In the Shadow of the Wind* (1983). In 1936 a teenager's disappearance shatters a Gaspé village.

—— *Kamouraska: A Novel* (1973, rpt. 1982). Based on a nineteenth-century murder in Quebec.

Hemon, Louis. *Maria Chapdelaine: A Tale of the Lake St. John Country* (1921, rpt. 1992). Set in nineteenth-century Quebec.

Henderson, Keith. *The Restoration: The Referendum Years* (1987). An Anglo-Quebecer moves back to Montreal just prior to the Referendum.

Holden, Helene. *Snow* (1990). A snowstorm in Montreal forces the people in a building together.

Hood, Hugh and Peter O'Brien (eds.). *Fatal Recurrences: New Fiction in English From Montreal* (1984).

Kirby, William. *The Golden Dog: A Romance of Old Quebec* (1877, rpt. 1969). Political intrigue in eighteenth-century New France.

Laberge, Albert. *Bitter Bread* (1977). Two generations of a Quebec peasant family.

Laing, Bonnie. *Marble Season* (1992). An Anglophone girl grows up in working-class Montreal where tensions between English and French are aggravated by poverty.

Langevin, André. *Dust Over the City* (1955, rpt. 1977). Pollution from a Quebec asbestos mine complicates a doctor's troubled marriage.

Lawrence, P. Scott (ed.). *Souvenirs: New English Fiction From Quebec* (1987).

Leith, Linda (ed.). *Telling Differences: New English Fiction From Quebec* (1989).

Lemelin, Roger. *In Quest of Splendour* (1955); *The Plouffe Family* (1950); *The Town Below* (1948, rpt. 1969). Novels about the urban working class in Quebec City from the depression to after World War II.

MacLennan, Hugh. *Return of the Sphinx* (1967, rpt. 1986). Conflict between father and son, patriot vs separatist.

——. *Two Solitudes (1945, rpt. 1993). Tensions and misunderstandings in French-English relations between the two world wars.

——. **The Watch That Ends the Night: A Novel*

(1958, rpt. 1991). A doctor presumed dead returns to Montreal.

McFee, Oonah. *Sandbars* (1977, rpt. 1982). Family life in the Gatineau region of the 1930s.

McLachlan, Ian. *Helen in Exile* (1980). Three generations of women in a family portrayed against the backdrop of the October crisis.

Metcalf, John. *General Ludd* (1980). A satire about a writer-in-residence at a Montreal university who cracks under the strain of bureaucracy and declining standards.

——. *Going Down Slow* (1972). Humourous tale of a British teacher who challenges a Montreal high school's established system.

Moore, Brian. *The Luck of Ginger Coffey (1960, rpt. 1988). Irish immigrant in Montreal faces many problems.

——. *The Revolution Script* (1971). Documentary novel based on the events of the October Crisis.

Notar, Stephen. *The St. James Quest* (1976). A middle-aged orphan searches for his past in Montreal and rural Quebec.

Nugent, Jacqueline. *The Glass Treehouse* (1990). Two families from different backgrounds interact in rural Quebec.

Parker, Gilbert. *The Seats of the Mighty: Being the Memoirs of Captain John Moray, Sometime Officer in the Virginia Regiment, and Afterwards of Amherst's Regiment* (1896, rpt. 1981). A historical romance in a Quebec setting between 1757 and 1759.

Poulin, Gabrielle. *All the Way Home* (1984). A Quebec nun experiences doubt.

Poulin, Jacques. *The 'Jimmy' Trilogy* (1979). Three stories about a young Quebec writer.

——. **Spring Tides* (1986). Outsiders disrupt a reclusive Quebec translator.

——. *Volkswagen Blues* (1988). A man, a woman, and a cat retrace the canoe routes of the voyageurs and the paths of early settlers.

Purcell, Donald. *The Lucky Ones* (1985). A courtship between a middle-aged couple in rural Quebec in the late 1930s.

Renaud, Jacques. *Broke City* (1984). A story about the "shady" side of Montreal in the 1950s and 1960s.

Richler, Mordecai. *The Apprenticeship of Duddy Kravitz* (1959, rpt. 1989); *Son of a Smaller Hero* (1955, rpt. 1989); *The Street* (1969, rpt. 1985). Explorations of Jewishness in Montreal.

Ringuet. *Thirty Acres* (1940, rpt. 1970). The clash of rural French Canadian culture with twentieth-century progress.

Roberts, Kenneth. *Arundel: A Chronicle of the Province of Maine and of the Secret Expedition Against Quebec* (1929, rpt. 1956). Historical fiction about the invasion of Quebec, 1775–1776.

Roy, Gabrielle. *Enchanted Summer* (1976). Nineteen short stories set in the Charlevoix area.

——. *The Cashier* (1955, rpt. 1990); *The Tin Flute* (1947, rpt. 1989). Novels about the lives of humble people in Montreal.

Saint-Pierre, Gaston (ed.). *The French Canadian Experience* (1979). Poetry and prose from New France to the present.

Savard, Felix-Antoine. *Master of the River* (1976). The struggle of French Canadian loggers in the Charlevoix region is depicted.

Scott, Duncan Campbell. *In the Village of the Viger and Other Stories* (1896, rpt. 1973). A nineteenth-century Quebec village feels the forces of urbanization and industrialization.

Scott, Gail. *Heroine: A Novel* (1987). The tenth anniversary of the October Crisis forces a woman to deal with her passage from the 1970s to the 1980s.

——. *Main Brides: Against Ochre Pediment and Azure Skies* (1993). A woman sitting in a Montreal bar tries to guess the stories of other women she sees and remembers her own life.

Stratford, Philip (comp.). *Stories From Quebec* (1974).

Tefs, Wayne. *The Cartier Street Contract* (1985). Fiction about the October Crisis.

Telesky, Richard (ed.). *The Oxford Book of French Canadian Short Stories* (1983).

Thériault, Yves. *Agaguk* (1958, rpt. 1963); *Agoak: The Legacy of Agaguk* (1979). The stark reality of Arctic life in northern Quebec is depicted.

——. **Ashini: A Novel* (1971); *N'Ysuk: A Novel* (1972). Fictionalized biographies of Montagnais Indians.

Tremblay, Michel. *The Fat Woman Next Door is Pregnant: A Novel* (1981). A humourous look at one day in a 1942 east end Montreal neighbourhood.

——. *The Heart Laid Bare* (1986). A gay Montreal professor learns to accept his lover's young son as part of his life.

——. *Therese and Pierrette and the Little Hanging Angel: A Novel* (1984). This story centres around the annual Corpus Christie Day ceremony in a 1942 Montreal working class parish.

Verne, Jules. *Family Without a Name: A Romance of the Rebellion of 1837 in Quebec* (1889, rpt. 1982).

Weintraub, William. *The Underdogs* (1979). Political satire set in Montreal.

Werbowski, Tecia. *Bitter Sweet Taste of Maple* (1984). A short novel about twelve women employed in a Montreal social work agency.

Wexler, Jerry. *The Bequest and Other Stories* (1984). Ten short stories set in Montreal.

SASKATCHEWAN

Saskatchewan, the middle Prairie Province, is the only province or territory to have no natural borders. It is bordered on the west by the province of Alberta; on the north by the Northwest Territories; on the east by the province of Manitoba; and on the south by the states of Montana and North Dakota.

Name Province of Saskatchewan. "Saskatchewan" is derived from the Plains Cree word "Kisiskatchewan" meaning "river that flows swiftly". *Previous names:* part of Rupert's Land (1670–1870); part of the North-West Territories (1870–1905), divided from 1882–1905 into the provisional district of Assiniboia in the south and the provisional district of Saskatchewan farther north.

Flag Divided horizontally with a green upper half and a gold lower half; the provincial shield is found in the upper half near the staff, the provincial floral emblem covering both parts in the area farthest from the staff. Dedicated on September 22, 1969.

Coat of Arms The top portion of the shield has a red lion on a gold background; in the bottom portion are three golden sheaves of wheat on a green background. The shield is supported on the left by a royal lion and on the right by a white-tailed deer, both wearing collars of Prairie Indian beadwork with badges; on the lion's badge a maple leaf, on the deer's the provincial flower. Above the shield is a helm with red and white man-

tling upon which rests a wreath supporting a beaver holding the provincial flower and with a royal crown on its back. Beneath the shield is a scroll entwined with the provincial flower and inscribed with the provincial motto. The coat of arms was granted by King Edward VII on August 25, 1906, the crest, supporters, and motto by Queen Elizabeth II on September 16, 1986.

Motto *Multis E Gentibus Vires* (From many peoples strength).

Emblems
Bird sharp-tailed grouse (*Pedioecetes phasianellus jamesi*)
Flower western red lily (*Lilium phildelphicum L. var. andinum*)
Tartan gold, brown, green, red, yellow, white, and black
Tree white birch (*Betula papyrifera*)

Date of Entry into Confederation September 1, 1905.

Official Language English.

Capital City Regina, situated on a wide alluvial plain in south central Saskatchewan; the commercial and financial centre of the province; population 179,178, CMA population 191,692. Originally called Wascana, the Cree word for "pile of bones", it was first settled on August 23, 1882, and named "Regina" by Princess Louise, wife of the Governor General, to honour her mother, Queen Victoria. Regina was chosen as the capital of the North-West Territories in 1883. It was in-corporated as a city on June 19, 1903, and designated as the capital of the Province of Saskatchewan in 1905.

Provincial Holidays In addition to national statutory holidays (see page 2), Saskatchewan residents celebrate Saskatchewan Day (the first Monday in August).

Geography and Climate

Geography The Canadian Shield underlies the northern third of Saskatchewan, an area of muskeg, swamp, forests, and rock. The rest is a vast, fertile plain sloping gradually to the east and north. The subarctic forest in northern Saskatchewan gives way to coniferous forest, to mixed woods, to aspen parkland, to mid-grass prairie, and to short-grass prairie in the south. Minor upland areas are found in the southwest.

Area 651,900 sq. km. (251,700 sq. mi.); 6.5% of Canada. *Rank:* 5th among the provinces, 6th among the provinces and territories.

Inland Water 81,630 sq. km. (31,517.5 sq. mi.), includes nearly 100,000 lakes. Largest lake wholly in Saskatchewan: Wollaston Lake 2,681 sq. km. (1,035 sq. mi.). Big Quill Lake is Canada's largest inland saltwater lake, 18,000 ha. (44,000 acres).

Elevations Highest point: Cypress Hills 1,468 m. (4,816 ft.). Lowest point: Lake Athabasca shoreline 65 m. (213 ft.).

Major Rivers (* indicates a designated Canadian Heritage River): Assiniboine, Battle, Churchill, *Clearwater, Fond du Lac, *North Saskatchewan, Qu'Appelle, Saskatchewan, Souris, South Saskatchewan.

Climate Saskatchewan has a continental climate with short, warm, dry summers and long, cold winters. It has the largest daily and the largest annual ranges of temperatures in the ten provinces and is the driest province. The daily mean temperature in January in Regina is −17.9°C (−0.2°F); in Prince Arthur −21.5°C (−6.7°F); in July in Regina 18.9°C (66°F); in Prince Arthur 17.4°C (64.3°F). The lowest recorded temperature in Saskatchewan, −56.7°C (−70.1°F) at Prince Albert on February 1, 1893.

Average annual precipitation in Regina is 384 mm. (15.1 in.); in Prince Arthur, 398.4 mm. (15.7 in.). Average annual snowfall in Regina, 115.7 cm. (45.6 in.); in Prince Arthur, 121.7 cm. (47.9 in.). Greatest recorded snowfall over five consecutive days: 97 cm. (38.2 in.) at Cypress Hills, May 28, 1982. The longest dry period in Saskatchewan without measurable precipitation, 141 days at Kisbey starting August 11, 1976.

Saskatchewan holds several additional Canadian weather records: the highest recorded temperature 45°C (113°F) at Midale and Yellow Grass on July 5, 1937; average sunniest place, 2,537 hours at Estevan; sunniest major city, 2,450 hours average at Saskatoon; longest cold spell, below −18°C (−0.4°F) for 58 consecutive days January 3–March 1, 1936.

Time Zones Eastern and most of southern Saskatchewan: Central; western and northwestern Saskatchewan: Mountain. Saskatchewan is the only province to legislate the use of standard time all year.

Parks and Historic Sites

In this section * indicates the area is, or part of it is, a Ramsar site.

National Parks Located in Saskatchewan

Park	Location	Size
Grasslands	Val Marie	902 sq. km. (348 sq. mi.)
Prince Albert	Waskesiu Lake	3,875 sq. km. (1,496 sq. mi.)

Provincial Parks There are 31 provincial parks in Saskatchewan covering 9,080 sq. km. (3,506 sq. mi.): 11 natural environment parks, 3 wilderness parks, 10 recreation parks, and 6 historic parks. The largest parks are:

Park	Location	Type	Size
Lac La Ronge	La Ronge	natural	344,470 ha. (1,330 sq. mi.)
*Clearwater River	near La Loche	wilderness	224,035 ha. (865 sq. mi.)
Athabasca Sand Dunes	Lake Athabasca	wilderness	192,500 ha. (743 sq. mi.)
Meadow Lake	near Goodsoil	natural environment	165,893 ha. (640 sq. mi.)
Narrow Hills	near Smeaton	natural environment	53,610 ha. (207 sq. mi.)
Moose Mountain	near Carlyle	natural environment	40,600 ha. (157 sq. mi.)
Duck Mountain	near Kamsack	natural environment	26,160 ha. (101 sq. mi.)
Wildcat Hill	near Hudson Bay, Sask.	wilderness	21,772 ha. (84 sq. mi.)
Greenwater Lake	near Kelvington	natural environment	20,720 ha. (80 sq. mi.)
Cypress Hills	near Maple Creek	natural environment	18,140 ha. (70 sq. mi.)

Saskatchewan also has 15 national bird sanctuaries, 7 national wildlife areas, and 2 Ramsar sites.

Major National Historic Sites and Parks in Saskatchewan

Batoche, Batoche
Fort Battleford, Battleford
Fort Walsh, Maple Creek
Motherwell Homestead, near Abernethy

In addition, there are a large number of historic sites in Saskatchewan administered by the province, municipalities, or organizations. The major sites are:

Cannington Manor Provincial Historic Park, near Manor
Fort Carlton Provincial Historic Park, Duck Lake
Last Mountain House Provincial Historic Park, near Craven
National Doukhobour Heritage Village, Veregin
St. Victor's Petroglyphs Provincial Historic Park, near St. Victor
Wanuskewin Heritage Park, near Saskatoon
Wood Mountain Post Provincial Historic Park, near Wood Mountain

Demography

All figures relating to Saskatchewan population and dwellings are 1991 data and do not include the population on 1 Indian reserve that did not cooperate in the 1991 census.

Saskatchewan Population: 988,928; 3.6% of national; *rank* 6th
Historical population data
1981   968,310
1971   926,245

1961	925,181
1951	831,728
1941	895,992
1921	757,510
1901	91,279

Population Density: 1.7 persons per sq. km. (4.5 per sq. mi.)

Number of Dwellings: 366,075

Indian Reserves: 70 Indian bands on 149 reserves

Population Characteristics:
urban: 623,397; 63%
rural: 365,531; 37%

19 and under: 310,605; 31.4%
65 and over: 139,925; 14.1% (highest in Canada)
average income for full-time employment 15 years and over (1990): $27,868 (lowest in Canada); men $31,386; women $21,989
average life expectancy at birth (1987): men 73.66 years; women 80.47 years (highest in Canada)
live birth rate: 15,304; 15.4 per 1000
deaths: 8,098; 8.1 per 1000
marriages: 5,923; 6.0 per 1000
divorces: 2,240; 2.27 per 1000

Largest Cities *(for definitions of CMA and CA, see page viii)*

Name	Population	Dwellings	National Pop. Rank
Saskatoon	210,023 (CMA)	79,867	17
Regina	191,692 (CMA)	71,961	18
Prince Albert	41,259 (CA)	14,516	64
Moose Jaw	35,552 (CA)	14,073	75
North Battleford	18,457 (CA)	6,971	103
Yorkton	18,023 (CA)	7,084	105
Swift Current	14,815	6,207	120
Estevan	11,379 (CA)	4,450	132

Government and Politics, 1905–

A description of the division of powers between the federal and provincial governments will be found on page 4.

Lieutenant-Governor The Lieutenant-Governor is the nominal head of the Saskatchewan government, and is appointed by the Governor General of Canada on the recommendation of the Prime Minister of Canada. (A description of the duties of lieutenant-governors is found on page 7.)

Lieutenant-Governors of Saskatchewan	Term
Amédée Emmanuel Forget	1905–1910
George William Brown	1910–1915
Richard Stuart Lake	1915–1921
Henry William Newlands	1921–1931
Hugh Edwin Munroe	1931–1936
Archibald Peter McNab	1936–1945
Thomas Miller	1945
Reginal John Marsden Parker	1945–1948
John Michael Uhrich	1948–1951
William John Patterson	1951–1958
Frank Lindsay Bastedo	1958–1963
Robert Leith Hanbidge	1963–1970
Stephen Worobetz	1970–1976
George Porteous	1976–1978
Cameron Irwin McIntosh	1978–1983
Frederick William Johnson	1983–1988
Sylvia Olga Fedoruk	1988–

Legislative Assembly The Legislative Assembly of Saskatchewan consists of 66 members elected by popular vote, each member representing a constituency; term of office: up to 5 years as long as the party in power maintains the confidence of the Legislative Assembly; remuneration: (1994) $38,546 + $7,622 expense allowance, additional amounts for special appointments; qualifications for members: Canadian citizen or British subject, 18 years of age or older, ordinarily resident in Saskatchewan, not legally disqualified. (A description of the duties of provincial legislatures are found on page 7.)

Qualification for Saskatchewan Voters in Provincial Elections Canadian citizen on polling day or British subject qualified as a voter on June 23, 1971, 18 years of age or older on polling day, ordinarily resident in Saskatchewan for at least six months immediately preceding the day

the writ is issued, ordinarily resident in the constituency on the day the writ is issued.

Premier Nominally appointed by the Lieutenant-Governor of Saskatchewan, the Premier is generally the leader of the party with the majority of seats in the Legislative Assembly. (A description of the responsibilities of provincial premiers is found on page 7.)

Premiers of Saskatchewan/Party/Term
Thomas Walter Scott
   (Liberal, 1905–1916)
William Melville Martin
   (Liberal, 1916–1922)
Charles Avery Dunning
   (Liberal, 1922–1926)
James Garfield Gardiner
   (Liberal, 1926–1929)
James Thomas Milton Anderson
   (Conservative, 1929–1934)
James Garfield Gardiner
   (Liberal, 1934–1935)

William John Patterson
   (Liberal, 1935–1944)
Thomas Clement Douglas
   (CCF, 1944–1961)
Woodrow Stanley Lloyd
   (CCF, 1961–1964)
William Ross Thatcher
   (Liberal, 1964–1971)
Allan Emrys Blakeney
   (New Democratic, 1971–1982)
Donald Grant Devine
   (Conservative, 1982–1991)
Roy John Romanow
   (New Democratic, 1991–)

Cabinet The Cabinet consists of ministers appointed by the Premier, usually from elected members of the majority party in the Legislative Assembly. Cabinet ministers serve at the Premier's pleasure; each member usually heads a government department.

Agriculture and Food
   (306)787-5140
Community Services
   (306)787-2635
Economic Development
   (306)787-2232
Education
   (306)787-6030
Energy and Mines
   (306)787-2526
Environment and Public Safety
   (306)787-6113
Finance
   (306)787-6768

Government Departments The general information about the work of government departments can be obtained from the Provincial Inquiry Centre (306)787-0222 or 800-667-0666 (Saskatchewan only) or (306)787-1776 (French).

Health
   (306)787-0222
Highways and Transportation
   (306)787-4800
Justice
   (306)787-8971
Labour
   (306)787-2431
Natural Resources
   (306)787-2700
Provincial Secretary
   (306)787-1643
Rural Development
   (306)787-2727
Social Services
   (306)787-3700

Saskatchewan Representation in Federal Government
House of Commons: 14 members
Senate: 6 members

Finances

A statement of Saskatchewan's revenue and expenditures for the years 1992/93 and 1991/92 are shown below in thousands of dollars. The financial year runs from April 1 to March 31 of the year following.

	Actual 1992/93	Actual 1991/92
Revenue		
Taxation	2,296,275	2,159,749
Other	775,480	629,557
Government of Canada	1,304,323	1,259,842
Total revenue for the year	4,376,078	4,049,148
Expenditures		
Health	1,548,477	1,581,268
Education	904,496	908,313
Social services	424,900	389,821
Agriculture and food	263,859	344,661
Interest on debt	739,916	502,072
Other	1,086,533	1,165,422
Total expenditures for the year	4,968,181	4,891,557
Deficit for the year	592,103	842,409

Economy

Saskatchewan has 44% of Canada's farmland and produces 60% of Canada's wheat crop together with other grains and cattle ranching. The Saskatchewan Wheat Pool is one of the world's largest marketing cooperatives. Saskatchewan has Canada's second largest crude oil production, second largest uranium supply, Canada's only known natural supply of sodium sulfate, and more than 40% of the known recoverable potash in the world.

Major Industries Principal industries include agriculture, mining, oil and petroleum production and refining. The manufacturing sector is small and varied.

Gross Domestic Product (1992) $18,221 million (in current dollars at factor cost); % of national G.D.P.: 3.1%; *rank:* 6th

Distribution of gross domestic product (1992)

Services	21.5%
Finance, insurance, and real estate	21.2%
Mining	5.6%
Trade	10.8%
Public administration	8.6%
Transportation, communication, and storage	8.9%
Manufacturing	7.5%
Agriculture	6.7%
Construction	3.9%
Utilities	3.2%
Forestry	0.3%

Value of Manufacturing Shipments $3,651 million

Farm Cash Receipts $4,058 million

Employment (seasonally adjusted) 446,000; Participation rate: 66.8%

Unemployment (seasonally adjusted) 35,000; per capita: 7.3%

Minimum Wage $5.35

Exports Saskatchewan's total exports in 1992 amounted to $7,925 million; 3.8% of total Canadian merchandising exports; *rank:* 5th

Largest trading partner: United States, 35% of Saskatchewan's merchandising exports

Other important markets: China 9%, former USSR and Japan about 8%. Wheat made up the major portion of export to the former USSR and to China.

Major export commodities: grain 31%, crude oil 17%, potash and manufactured goods each about 10%

History

ca. 10,000 B.C.	Paleo-Indians arrive.
ca. 8,000 B.C.	Evidence of Clovis Culture.
ca. 4,000 B.C.	Northern Plains Indians are in northern Saskatchewan.
300 A.D.	Evidence of Plains Village culture.
ca. 17th century	Assiniboine, Beaver, Blackfoot, Cree, Gros Ventre, Slavey peoples inhabit present-day Saskatchewan.
1670	*May 2* Hudson's Bay Company is formed and granted trade rights over all territory draining into Hudson Bay; names territory Rupert's Land.
1690	Henry Kelsey becomes the first white man to see "Saskatchewan".
1730s	Pierre Gaultier de Varennes et de la Verendrye and sons build a trading post on the Saskatchewan River.
1753	Louis François de la Corne builds Fort St. Louis below the forks of the Saskatchewan River.
1754	De la Corne plants in Carrot River Valley the first wheat grown in the Prairies.
1774	Samuel Hearne establishes the first Hudson's Bay Company inland post, Cumberland House, the first permanent settlement in Saskatchewan.
1776	*April 12* Thomas and Joseph Frobisher and Alexander Henry build a trading post at Île à la Crosse.
	Peter Pond establishes a trading post west of present-day Prince Albert.
1778	Roderick Mackenzie establishes Fort Chipewyan on Lake Athabasca for the North West Company.
	Peter Pond discovers the Methy Portage.
1790	David Thompson, fur trader and explorer, surveys the Saskatchewan River.
1796	Thompson explores area north of Churchill River to Lake Athabasca.
1800	Peter Fidler crosses Saskatchewan on the South Saskatchewan River and establishes Chesterfield House.
1810	Hudson's Bay Company establishes Carlton House (later called Fort Carlton).
1814	Division of the Northern Department of Rupert's Land includes Saskatchewan Inland.
1818	*October 20* Convention of 1818 between the United States and Britain sets the southern boundary of the Hudson's Bay Company territory at the 49th parallel from the Lake of the Woods to the Rocky Mountains.
1821	*March 21* Hudson's Bay Company takes over the North West Company ending strife in the fur trade industry.
1857	Palliser Expedition sent to assess Rupert's Land's potential reports a fertile belt and deposits of coal and minerals.
1866	*August* James Nisbet with 10 settlers found Prince Albert.

1868	Plague of grasshoppers causes Prairie crop failure.
1869	*November 19* Hudson's Bay Company transfers Rupert's Land to British Crown.
1870s	Permanent settlements slowly develop outside Fort Edmonton.
1870	*Fall* Battle between the Cree and Assiniboine Indians and the Peigan Indians near Fort Whoop-Up leaves ca. 300 dead.
	December 1 British Crown gives Rupert's Land to Canada, which compensates the Hudson's Bay Company in land and money. The transfer takes effect *July 15, 1870.*
1872	Dominion Lands Act (federal government) grants 65 ha. (161 acres) of free land to settlers.
1873	Government of Canada appoints a North-West Territories provisional government with a council of 11 members headed by the Lieutenant-Governor of Manitoba.
1874	*September 15* Cree and Chippewa Indians sign a treaty at Fort Qu'Appelle surrendering land for money and reserves.
1875	North-West Territories Act provides for a lieutenant-governor and legislature operating from the territorial capital in Battleford.
	North-West Mounted Police establish Fort Walsh.
1876	First shipment of Saskatchewan grain is made to Great Britain.
	First post office in North-West Territories opens in Battleford.
	August 23 Federal government signs a treaty with Plains and Wood Cree Indians at Fort Carlton.
	December Sitting Bull and 5,000 Dakota Sioux Indians fleeing across the Saskatchewan border after the Battle of Little Big Horn are met by James Morrow Walsh, North-West Mounted Police, who allows them to live peacefully in Canada for the next five years.
1878	*August 11 Saskatchewan Herald*, first newspaper in the North-West Territories, is published in Battleford.
1879	North-West Mounted Police headquarters move from Fort Macleod to Fort Walsh.
	Because of the depletion of buffalo herds 7,000 Indians are fed at Fort Macleod during the winter.
1882	*May 8* North-West Territories (Prairie section) is divided into four provisional districts: Saskatchewan in the middle part of present-day Saskatchewan, Assiniboia in the southern part, and two in Alberta.
	August 18 John Lake names the site for a temperance settlement "Saskatoon"; settlers arrive in 1883.
	August 30 Canadian Pacific Railway reaches Regina opening up area for settlement.
	December 6 North-West Territories government is moved to Regina.
1883	*August 20* First session of the North-West Territories Council is held at Regina.
1884	North-West Territories School Ordinance establishes a dual Protestant-Catholic system.
1885	*March 8* At the urging of Louis Riel a meeting of Métis in St. Laurent passes the "Revolutionary Bill of Rights" which asserts Métis rights to land grants, responsible government, and other rights.
	March 19 Métis at Batoche proclaim a provisional government with Riel as President and declare that the District of Saskatchewan is seceded from Canada.
	March 26 Métis and Indians ambush North-West Mounted Police and volunteers at Duck Lake killing 12; 5 Métis and 1 Indian are also killed.

March 30 Chief Poundmaker and 200 Cree attack Battleford.
April 2 Crees kill 9 white settlers at Frog Lake.
April 14 Crees besiege Fort Pitt.
April 24 William Dillon Otter and 500 men from Swift Current relieve Battleford.
April 24 Frederick Dobson Middleton with 800 militiamen from Fort Qu'Appelle battle Métis at Fish Creek ending in a stalemate.
May 2 Cree and Assiniboine Indians force Otter's retreat at Cut Knife Hill.
May 12 Middleton defeats Métis at Batoche; Riel surrenders.
May 26 Chief Poundmaker surrenders to Middleton at Battleford.
May 28 Thomas Bland Strange and the Alberta Field Force attack Big Bear at Frenchman's Butte; both sides retreat.
June 3 In the last military engagement in Canada Big Bear and the North-West Mounted Police commanded by Samuel Benfield Steele skirmish at Loon Lake; 4 Indians killed.
July 2 Big Bear surrenders to North-West Mounted Police at Fort Carlton.
September 18 Riel is sentenced to death and hanged in Regina on *November 16*.

1886	*July 17* Prince Albert stage is held up, the first mail stage robbery in Saskatchewan.
1887	Coal, the first mineral mined in Saskatchewan, is mined near Estevan.
1888	Federal government establishes a Territorial Assembly with 23 elected members and 3 nonvoting legal advisors with substantial federal control.
	October 31 First North-West Territories Legislative Assembly opens in Regina.
1890	Railroad is built between Regina and Saskatoon.
1891	Territorial legislature discards the official use of French.
	Legislative Assembly is made totally elective.
1896–1914	Large numbers of immigrants arrive from Ontario, the United States, Great Britain, and Europe.
1897	Responsible government is granted to North-West Territories, but without control of public lands and natural resources or a wide tax base.
1899	Doukhobors emigrate from Russia to Saskatchewan with money provided by Leo Tolstoy.
1903	*April 17* Colonists led by Rev. Isaac Barr arrive in Saskatoon and settle the area between Maidstone and the Alberta border.
	July Barr colonists found Lloydminster.
1904	*March* Three-day blizzard with 100 kph (62 mph) winds drops 30 cm. (11.8 in.) snow in the southern Prairies; 5 trains are snowbound between Winnipeg and Calgary.
1905	*September 1* Saskatchewan becomes a province of Canada.
1906	*March 29* First legislature of the Province of Saskatchewan opens in Regina.
	Chipewayan and Cree of Alberta and northern Saskatchewan sign a treaty covering 220,150 sq. km. (85,000 sq. mi.).
	Saskatoon, Nutana, and Riverdale are amalgamated as Saskatoon is incorporated as a city.
	Public Libraries Act passed.
1907	*August 3* Supreme Court of Saskatchewan and 8 district court regions each with its own judge are established.
	Marquis wheat, a fast-maturing variety well suited to the Prairies, is tested at Indian Hat.
	University of Saskatchewan is founded.
1908	Saskatchewan government buys a telephone company and sets up telephone service as a public utility.

1910	Most Doukhobors move from Saskatchewan to establish farming communities in the Kettle and Kootenay Valleys in British Columbia.
1911	Electric tram system opens in Regina.
	Saskatchewan farmers organize the Saskatchewan Co-operative Elevator Company.
1912	*June 30* Worst tornado in Canadian history strikes Regina leaving 28 dead, 200 injured, and 500 buildings destroyed.
	December 12 Act makes it illegal for a white woman to work for Chinese employers.
	Saskatchewan legislative building opens.
1913	Economic depression halts Regina's growth.
1915	Saskatchewan representation in the Canadian Senate is raised from 4 to 6 members.
1916	*March 14* Women are granted the right to vote in provincial elections.
	December 11 Saskatchewan votes to abolish liquor stores.
1917	Women in Saskatchewan who hold property are permitted to hold office.
1920	*February 1* Royal North-West Mounted Police becomes Royal Canadian Mounted Police; its headquarters are moved from Ottawa to Regina.
	October 25 Saskatchewan votes for Prohibition in a plebiscite.
1924	*July 16* Prohibition ends when Saskatchewan votes for government control of liquor.
1928	*June 1* Royal Canadian Mounted Police absorbs the Saskatchewan provincial police.
1929	*December 14* Federal government transfers control of natural resources to Saskatchewan.
1930s	Long agricultural depression is caused by low world wheat prices and periods of severe drought.
	Mass immigration stops because most arable land is occupied.
1931	*September 29* Striking coal miners clash with Royal Canadian Mounted Police at Estevan; 3 miners are dead.
	First provincial parks are established at Duck Mountain, Cypress Hills, and Moose Mountain.
1933	In its first convention the Co-operative Commonwealth Federation adopts the Regina Manifesto which advocates the nationalization of many institutions.
	Smallest Saskatchewan wheat crop since 1920 is caused by a grasshopper plague and drought.
1935	*July 1* Two thousand employed in the "On-To-Ottawa Trek" clash with police in Regina leaving 1 dead, 100 injured, and 130 arrested.
1943	Potash is discovered near Esterhazy while drilling for oil.
1944	*June 15* Co-operative Commonwealth Federation, the first socialist provincial government in Canada, is elected.
	Government Insurance Act makes property, fire, and car insurance a Saskatchewan government responsibility; car insurance is compulsory for the first time in Canada.
1946	First program of socialized medicine in Canada is introduced.
	Swift Current Regional Health Plan provides public health services to 53,000 people on an experimental basis.
1947	*January 1* Saskatchewan becomes the first province to provide hospital care for all its citizens.
	February Ten-day blizzard blocks all highways into Regina and buries one train in a snowdrift 1 km. (0.6 mi.) and 8 m. (26 ft.) deep.

April 1 Saskatchewan Bill of Rights, Canada's first, receives royal assent. Saskatchewan Research Council is established.

1948   *April* Extensive floods occur in Saskatchewan.

1949   Saskatchewan Power Corporation is established.

1954   Commercial airline crash at Moose Jaw kills 37.

1953   *October 15* Trans Mountain Oil Pipeline from Edmonton to Vancouver is completed.

1957   *August 23* Saskatchewan part of the TransCanada Highway opens making Saskatchewan the first province to complete its portion.

1958   *July 1* Federal-provincial hospital plan takes effect in Saskatchewan.

1961   *May 30* Buffalo Gap receives 250 mm. (9.8 in.) of rain in less than one hour, a Canadian record.

Worst drought year in the twentieth century for Prairie wheat.

1962   *August 2* Medical Care Insurance Act providing the first prepaid medical care plan in Canada comes into effect.

September 20 World's largest potash mine opens at Esterhazy.

1964   *December 15* Heavy snows, 90 kph (56 mph) winds, and −34°C (−29°F) cause the death of three people and 1,000 animals in the southern Prairies.

1965   *May 12* Courts uphold 1876 treaty with Saskatchewan Indian tribes requiring the federal government to provide free medical care.

1966   *September 8* Saskatchewan passes the Essential Services Act requiring compulsory arbitration without appeal in labour disputes that involve essential services.

1967   Extensive drought in the Prairies.

1969   *August 1* Saskatchewan government announces feed grain will be accepted as payment for the university tuition of Saskatchewan farm children.

1973   *August 27* Heaviest hailstone ever documented in Canada falls on Cedoux: 290 g. (10.2 oz.) in weight and 114 mm. (4.5 in.) in diameter.

Ernie Boychuck is appointed Saskatchewan's first ombudsman.

1974   *April 17* Saskatchewan government announces a plan to provide free prescriptions to residents for certain drugs and free dental care for children 3 to 12 years of age.

September 17 First female Royal Canadian Mounted Police recruits begin training at Regina.

1976   *June 28* Saskatchewan passes legislation authorizing the takeover of potash mines in the province.

1977   Western Saskatchewan experiences severe drought.

1978   *February 6* Snowdrifts reach Regina rooftops as Regina is snowbound for 4 days; many livestock perish.

1979–1980   Poor wheat and pasture years.

1984   Sask Water, a Crown corporation, is established to manage Saskatchewan water resources

1985   *May 4* Saskatchewan Métis elect an administration to negotiate rights with the federal government, the first Métis governing body since 1885.

1986   *January 31* Back-to-work law is passed ending 16-month rotating strikes by 12,500 members of the Saskatchewan Government Employees' Union.

First export sale of Saskatchewan natural gas is made.

1988   *February 25* Supreme Court of Canada rules that Saskatchewan must either translate its laws into French and allow French to be used in its courts or enact a law requiring English only.

Drought and low wheat prices affect the Saskatchewan economy.

Canada's first heavy oil upgrader begins operation in Regina.

1990	*December 21* Federal Court of Appeal rejects a bid to stop the construction of the Rafferty-Alameda dam project in southern Saskatchewan.
1992	*August 17* Saskatchewan government announces plans to decentralize health care to cut costs.
	November Saskatchewan Government Employees' Union launches a series of rotating strikes over wage freezes.
1993	*January 8* Janice MacKinnon becomes Saskatchewan Minister of Finance, the first woman finance minister in Canada.
	November 5 Saskatchewan government releases a white paper on agriculture that proposes a long-term plan to move away from grain crops.

Culture and Education

Performing Arts Saskatchewan has several professional performing arts companies and many festivals. Some significant organizations are:

Big Valley Jamboree, Craven (July) (Canada's largest country music festival)	(306)565-4500
Folkfest, Saskatoon (August)	(306)931-0100
Fringe on Broadway, Saskatoon (July/August)	(306)664-2239
Globe Theatre Productions, Regina	(306)525-9553
Nightcap Productions, Saskatoon	(306)653-2300
Opera Saskatchewan, Regina	(306)522-9008
Persephone Theatre, Saskatoon	(306)384-2126
Regina Folk Festival, Regina	(306)757-7684
Regina Symphony Orchestra, Regina	(306)586-9555
Saskatchewan Jazz Festival, Saskatoon (June/July)	(306)652-1421
Saskatoon Symphony Orchestra, Saskatoon	(306)665-6414
Shakespeare on the Saskatchewan, Saskatoon	(306)653-2300
25th Street Theatre, Saskatoon (plays by Saskatchewan writers)	(306)664-2239

Provincial Museums and Galleries Saskatchewan has over 250 museums and galleries. The following are major Saskatchewan institutions.

Dunlop Art Gallery, Regina
MacKenzie Art Gallery, Regina
Royal Canadian Centennial Museum, Regina
Royal Saskatchewan Museum, Regina
Saskatchewan Museum of Natural History, Regina
Saskatchewan Science Centre, Regina
Ukrainian Museum of Canada, Saskatoon
Western Development Museum, Moose Jaw, North Battleford, Saskatoon, and Yorkton

Universities and Colleges
University of Regina, Regina
University of Saskatchewan, Saskatoon

Colleges and Institutes (* indicates additional campuses in other centres)
Carlton Trail Regional College, Humboldt
Cumberland Regional College, Nipawin
Cypress Hills Regional College, Swift Current
Lakeland College, Lloydminster
Northlands College, Air Ronge*
North West Regional College, North Battleford
Olds College, Olds
Parkland Regional College, Melville
Prairie West Regional College, Biggar*
Saskatchewan Indian Community College, Asimakaniseekan Askij Reserve
Saskatchewan Institute of Applied Science and Technology, Saskatoon*
Southeast Regional College, Weyburn

Motor Vehicle Use

Motor Vehicles Registered for Use in Saskatchewan (1993): 698,429.

Drivers Licensed by Saskatchewan (1993): 643,995. Minimum driving age: 16

Roads Four-lane highways: 757 km. (470 mi.), two-lane highways: 18, 773 km. (11,655 mi.), gravel roads: 5,852 km.

(3,636 mi.); bridges maintained by the province: 896

Speed Limits Provincial highways: 90–100 kph (56–62 mph); other roads: 80 kph (50 mph) unless otherwise posted; 60 kph (37 mph) when passing highway construction and maintenance workers

First, Biggest, and Best

World's largest known recoverable potash reserves: Esterhazy, estimated to have two-thirds of the world's reserves

World's largest potash mine: Esterhazy

World's largest uranium mine: Key Lake

World's largest urban park: Wascana Centre, Regina, 930 ha. (3.6 sq. mi)

World's largest indoor agricultural showplace: Canadian Western Agribition, Regina, 7.3 ha. (18 acres) of indoor space attracting an annual average of more than 150,000 people

World's largest grain-handling cooperative: Saskatchewan Wheat Pool handles an annual average of 10 million tons

World's first official opening of a cobalt therapy unit: University of Saskatchewan, October 23, 1951

North America's largest uncultivated grasslands retaining pre-homesteader species: 259 sq. km. (100 sq. mi.) area in Grasslands National Park

North America's first bird sanctuary: Last Mountain Lake established June 8, 1887

World's largest population of piping plovers (endangered species): Lake Diefenbaker

World's largest complete tyrannosaurus skeleton: Frenchman River Valley, discovered by Robert Gebhardt in 1991

World's largest tomahawk: Cut Knife, 12 m. (39.4 ft.) high

North America's and the Commonwealth's first socialist government: election of Co-operative Commonwealth Federation, June 15, 1944

North America's first universal insurance for health care: implemented January 1, 1947

North America's first arts board: Saskatchewan Arts Board created by Order-in-Council, 1948

World record for deer with biggest known antlers: bask 6 x 6 with a 68.6 cm. (27 in.) inside spread scored at 214 4/8 net typical points, shot by Milo Hanson north of Biggar in November 1993

North America's reading capital (1993): two Saskatchewan cities are the only Canadian cities listed in the top ten out of 343 North American cities in a report on library use published in Places Rated Almanac; Saskatoon first, and Regina fourth

Sources of Information About Saskatchewan

Government of Saskatchewan Provincial Inquiry Service, 140 1st Street North, 2nd floor, Saskatoon, SK S7K 1W8 (306)787-0222 (Regina), (306)933- 5888 (Saskatoon), 800-667-0666 (Saskatchewan), (306)787-1776 (French)

Tourism Saskatchewan: 1919 Saskatchewan Drive, Regina, SK S4P 3V7 (306)787-2300, 800-667-7538 (Saskatchewan), 800-667-7191 (general)
Government publications can be obtained directly from pertinent government departments.

Books About Saskatchewan: A Selected List

Reference Guides

Arora, Ved (comp.). *Saskatchewan Bibliography* (1980 + supplement).

Artibise, Alan F.J. *Western Canada Since 1870: A Select Bibliography and Guide* (1978).

Bothwell, George and Ron Coulson (eds.). *Regina, the Street Where You Live: The Origins of Regina Street Names* (1988).

Budd, A.C. *Budd's Flora of the Canadian Prairie Provinces* (rev. and enl. by J. Looman and K.F. Best, 1987).

Callin, E. Murray. *Birds of the Qu'Appelle, 1857–1979* (1980).

Canada. Atmospheric Environment Service. *Canadian Climate Normals, 1961–1990: Prairie Provinces* (1993).

Canada. Energy, Mines and Resources Canada. *Gazetteer of Canada: Saskatchewan* (3rd ed. 1985).

Dibb, Sandra (ed.). *Northern Saskatchewan Bibliography* (1975).

Gilroy, Doug. *Prairie Birds in Color* (rev. and expanded ed. 1976).

Jones, Timothy E.H. (ed.). *Annotated Bibliography of Saskatchewan Archaeology and Prehistory* (1988).

Lapointe, Richard. *Saskatlas* (1990).

MacDonald, Christine (comp.). *Publications of the Governments of the North-West Territories, 1867–1905, and of the Province of Saskatchewan, 1905–1952* (1952).

Peel, Bruce (comp.). *A Bibliography of the Prairie Provinces to 1953, With Bibliographical Index* (2nd ed. 1973).

Richards, J. Howard (ed.). *Atlas of Saskatchewan* (1969).

Robinson, Jill M. (comp.). *Seas of the Earth: An Annotated Bibliography of Saskatchewan Literature As It Relates to the Environment* (1977).

Russell, Edmund T. *What's In a Name?: The Story Behind Saskatchewan Place Names* (3rd ed. 1980).

Smith, David E. (ed.). *Building a Province: A History of Saskatchewan in Documents* (1992).

——. *Saskatchewan Speaks: A History of the Province in Documents* (1990).

Symons, R.D. *Hours and the Birds: A Saskatchewan Record* (1967).

Thomas, Lewis G. (ed.). *The Prairie West to 1905: A Canadian Sourcebook* (1975).

Vance, Fenton R., J.R. Jowsey, and J.S. McLean. *Wildflowers Across the Prairies* (rev. and expanded 1984).

Warkentin, John (ed.). *The Western Interior of Canada: A Record of Geographical Discovery, 1612–1917* (1964).

Nonfiction Sources

*denotes a winner of a Governor General's Literary Award.

Angus, Terry (ed.). *The Prairie Experience* (1975).

Archer, John H. *Saskatchewan: A History* (1980).

Baron, Don and Paul Jackson. *Battleground: The Socialist Assault on Grant Devine's Dream* (1991).

Beal, Bob and Rod Macleod. *Prairie Fire: The 1885 North-West Rebellion* (1984, rpt. 1994).

Berton, Pierre. *The Promised Land: Settling the West, 1896–1914* (1984, rpt. 1990).

Biggs, Lesley and Mark Stobbe. *Devine Rule in Saskatchewan: A Decade of Hope and Hardship* (1991).

Bocking, D.H. (ed.). *Pages From the Past: Essays on Saskatchewan History* (1979).

——. *Saskatchewan, a Pictorial History* (1979).

Bowen, Lynne. *Muddling Through: The Remarkable Story of the Barr Colonists* (1992).

Braithwaite, Max. *Never Sleep Three in a Bed* (1969). Hilarious recollections of growing up as a member of a large family in small Saskatchewan towns in the first quarter of the twentieth century.

——. *Why Shoot the Teacher* (1975). A year's teaching in a rural Saskatchewan school in the 1930s.

Breen, David H. *The Canadian Prairie West and the Ranching Frontier, 1874–1924* (1983).

Brennan, J. William. *Regina: An Illustrated History* (1989).

Broadfoot, Barry. *The Pioneer Years, 1895–1914: Memories of the Settlers Who Opened the West* (1976).

Bryan, Liz. *The Buffalo People: Prehistoric Archaeology on the Canadian Plains* (1991).

Butala, Sharon. *The Perfection of the Morning: An Apprenticeship in Nature* (1994).

Campbell, Marjorie. **The Saskatchewan* (1950, rpt. 1982).

——. *The Silent Song of Mary Eleanor* (1983). Cultured English immigrant at the turn of the century.

Charette, Guillaume. *Vanishing Species: (Memoirs of a Prairie Métis)* (1976).

Christensen, Deana and Menno Fieguth. *Historic Saskatchewan* (1986).

Collins, Robert. *Butter Down the Well: Reflections of a Canadian Childhood* (1980, rpt. 1992).

Dale, Edmund H. (ed.). *The Future Saskatchewan Small Town* (1988).

——. *Regina, Regional Isolation and Innovative Development* (1980).

Delainey, William P., John D. Duerkop, and William A.S. Sarjeant. *Saskatoon: A Century in Pictures* (1982).

Douglas, T.C. *The Making of a Socialist: Recollections of T.C. Douglas* (ed. by Lewis H. Thomas, 1982).

——. *T.C. Douglas Speaks: Till Power is Brought to Pooling* (ed. by L.D. Lovick, 1979).

Dumont, Gabriel. *Gabriel Dumont Speaks* (1993).

Eager, Evelyn. *Saskatchewan Government: Politics and Pragmatism* (1980).

Eisler, Dale. *Rumors of Glory: Saskatchewan & the Thatcher Years* (1987).

Fairbairn, Garry Laurence. *From Prairie Roots: The Remarkable Story of the Saskatchewan Wheat Pool* (1984).

Fieguth, Menno. *Saskatchewan: A Celebration* (1991).

Flanagan, Thomas. *Riel and the Rebellion of 1885 Reconsidered* (1983).

Francis, R. Douglas and Howard Palmer (eds.). *The Prairie West: Historical Readings* (2nd ed. 1992).

Friesen, Gerald. *The Canadian Prairies: A History* (1984).

Gelder, Willem de. *A Dutch Homesteader on the Prairie: Letters of Willem de Gelder, 1910–1913* (1993).

Giscard, Gaston. *On the Prairie* (1982). Bilingual homesteader 1910–1913.

Gray, James H. *The Roar of the Twenties* (1975).

——. *The Winter Years: The Depression on the Prairies* (1966, rpt. 1976).

Gruending, Dennis. *Promises to Keep: A Political Biography of Allan Blakeney* (1990).

Harrison, Dick. *The Struggle for a Canadian Prairie Fiction* (1977).

Hiemstra, Mary. *Gully Farm* (1955, rpt. 1966).

Higginbotham, C.H. *Off the Record: The CCF in Saskatchewan* (1968).

Hildebrandt, Walter. *The Battle of Batoche: British Small Warfare and the Entrenched Métis* (1985).

Hillis, Doris. *Plainspeaking: Interviews With Saskatchewan Writers* (1988).

——. *Voices and Visions: Interviews With Saskatchewan Writers* (1985).

Howard, Victor. *We Are the Salt of the Earth!: A Narrative of the On-to-Ottawa Trek and the Regina Riot* (1985).

Hrynuik, Margaret. *"A Tower of Attraction": An Illustrated History of Government House, Regina, Saskatchewan* (1991).

Jaques, Edna. *Uphill All the Way: The Autobiography of Edna Jaques* (1977). A poet recalls homesteading in the Saskatchewan of the early twentieth century.

Karras, A.L. *Face the Wind* (1975).

——. *North to Cree Lake* (1970). A trapper in northern Saskatchewan in the 1930s.

Kerr, Don and Stan Hanson. *Saskatoon, the First Half Century* (1982).

Klimko, Olga. *The Archaeology and History of Fort Pelly I, 1824–1856* (1983).

—— and Michael Taft. *"Them Days": Memories of a Prairie Valley* (1993).

Lapointe, Richard. *The Francophones of Saskatchewan: A History* (1983).

Lipsett, S.M. *Agrarian Socialism: The Cooperative Commonwealth Federation in Saskatchewan: A Study in Political Sociology* (rev. ed. 1971).

Lloyd, Diane. *Woodrow: A Biography of W.S. Lloyd* (1979).

Loveridge, D.M. and Barry Potyondi. *From Wood Mountain to the Whitemud: A Historical Survey of Grasslands National Park Area* (1983).

MacGregor, James G. *Blankets and Beads: A History of the Saskatchewan River* (1949).

McConnell, Gail A. *Saskatoon, Hub City of the West: An Illustrated History* (1983).

McCourt, Edward. *Saskatchewan* (1968, rpt. 1977).

McCoy, Ingo D. *As I Remember* (1980).

McKervill, Hugh W. *The Sinbuster of Smoky Burn: The Memoirs of a Student Minister on the Prairie* (1993).

McLeod, David C. (ed.). *We'll All Be Buried Down Here: The Prairie Dryland Disaster, 1917–1926* (1986).

McLeod, Thomas H. *Tommy Douglas: The Road to Jerusalem* (1987).

Memories of Rural Saskatoon, 1890–1982 (1982).

Minifie, James H. *Homesteading: A Prairie Boyhood Recalled* (1972).

Mitchell, Elizabeth B. *In Western Canada Before the War: Impressions of Early Twentieth Century Prairie Communities* (1915, rpt. 1981).

Morton, Desmond. *The Last War Drum: The North-West Campaign of 1885* (1972).

Neatby, Leslie H. *Chronicle of a Pioneer Prairie Family* (1979).

Oppen, William A. *The Riel Rebellions: A Cartographic History* (1979).

Palmer, Howard and Don Smith (eds.). *The New Provinces: Alberta and Saskatchewan, 1905–1980* (1980).

Patterson, G. James. *The Romanians of Saskatchewan: Four Generations of Adaptation* (1977).

Pawson, Alice (ed.). *Memories of Shand: History of a Saskatchewan Coal Mining Community* (1992).

Peel, Bruce. *Steamboats on the Saskatchewan* (1972).

Pitsula, James M. and Kenneth A. Rasmussen. *Privatizing a Province: The New Right in Saskatchewan* (1990).

Richards, John and Larry Pratt. *Prairie Capitalism: Power and Influence in the New West* (1979).

Richards, John Howard. *Saskatchewan, a Geographical Appraisal* (1981).

Riddell, W.A. *Regina, From Pile O'Bones to Queen City of the Plains: An Illustrated History* (1981).

Ring, Dan. *The Urban Prairie* (1993).

Russell, R.C. *The Carlton Trail: The Broad Highway into the Saskatchewan Country From the Red River Settlement, 1840–1880* (2nd ed. 1971).

Schmalz, Wayne. *On Air: Radio in Saskatchewan* (1990).

Shackleton, Doris French. *Tommy Douglas* (1975, rpt. 1983).

Sharp, Paul F. *Whoop-Up Country: The Canadian-American West, 1865–1885* (1955, rpt. 1973).

Shillington, C. Howard. *Historic Land Track of Saskatchewan* (1985).

Smith, David E. *Prairie Liberalism: The Liberal Party in Saskatchewan, 1905–71* (1975).

——. *The Regional Decline of a National Party: Liberals on the Prairies* (1981).

Stanley, George F.G. *The Birth of Western Canada: Red River Rebellion 1869–70* (new ed. 1992).

Stegner, Wallace. *Wolf Willow: A History, A Story and A Memory of the Last Plains Frontier* (1962, rpt. 1980).

Story, Gertrude. *The Last House on Main Street* (1988); *How to Saw Wood With an Angel* (1992). Personal reflections on life in her native village, Vanscoy.

Symons, R.D. *Silton Seasons: From the Diary of a Countryman* (1975).

Taft, Michael. *Discovering Saskatchewan Folklore: Three Case Studies* (1983).

Thatcher, Colin. *Backrooms: A Story of Politics* (1985).

Thompson, Robert H. *Penny Candy, Bobskates and Frozen Apples: Growing Up in the 1930s and 1940s* (1990).

Tyman, James. *Inside Out: An Autobiography By a Canadian Indian* (1989).

Tyman, John Langton. *By Sector, Township and Range: Studies in Prairie Settlement* (1972).

Tyre, Robert. *Douglas in Saskatchewan: The Story of a Socialist Experiment* (1962).

Walker, Ernest G. *The Gowen Site: Cultural Responses to Climactic Warming on the Northern Plains (7500–5000 B.P.)* (1992).

Ward, Norman and David Smith. *Jimmy Gardiner: Relentless Liberal* (1990).

—— and Duff Spafford (eds.). *Politics in Saskatchewan* (1968).

Wiebe, Rudy and Bob Beal (comps.). *War in the West: Voices of the 1885 Rebellion* (1985).

Wilson, Barry. *Politics of Defeat: The Decline of the Liberal Party in Saskatchewan* (1980).

Woodcock, George. *Gabriel Dumont: The Métis Chief and His Lost World* (1975).

Saskatchewan in Literature

*denotes a winner of a Governor General's Literary Award.

Barclay, Byra. *The Summer of the Hungry Pup* (1981). Historical fiction about the Rebellion of 1885.

Begamudre, Ven (ed.). *Lodestone: Stories by Regina Writers* (1993).

Brady, Carolee. *Winter Lily: A Novel* (1980). Two lonely people, a widowed farmer and a young woman, develop a relationship in rural Saskatchewan.

Braithwaite, Max. *All the Way Home* (1986). After an absence of 43 years a famous playwright returns to Saskatoon.

——. *The Commodore's Barge is Alongside* (1979). Humourous story of a naval recruit aboard a stone frigate in Saskatchewan.

——. *The Night We Stole the Mountie's Car* (1971, rpt. 1984). Humourous tale of the vice-principal of a small Saskatchewan school in the last years of the depression.

Butala, Sharon. *Country of the Heart* (1984). The daughter of a wealthy Saskatchewan farmer falls in love with an old rancher.

——. *Upstream: "Le Pays en Haut"* (1991). A Saskatchewan woman struggles with her half-French, half-English heritage.

Cormack, Barbara Villy. *Westward Ho!: 1903* (1967). Manchester millworker's family survives through hard work in Lloydminster.

Currie, Bob, Gary Hyland, and Jim McLean (eds.). *100% Cracked Wheat* (1983). Humourous poetry and short stories by Saskatchewan writers.

Currie, Robert. *Night Games* (1983). Adolescence to manhood from the 1950s to the 1980s in Moose Jaw.

Dagg, Mel. *The Women on the Bridge* (1992). The Frog Lake Massacre links these short stories.

Fisher, Chris. *Sun Angel* (1992). Fifteen linked stories explore life in small-town Saskatchewan.

Forrie, Allan, Patrick O'Rourke, and Glen Sorestad. *The Last Map Is the Heart: An Anthology of Western Canadian Fiction* (1989).

Ghan, Linda. *A Gift of Sky* (1988). A Jewish girl grows up on a Saskatchewan farm after World War I.

Heath, Caroline (ed.). *Double Bond: An Anthology of Prairie Women's Fiction* (1984).

Heath, Terrence. *The Last Hiding Place* (1982). Part Indian, part European, a man struggles to reconcile his dual heritage.

Hiebert, Paul. *Sarah Binks* (1947, rpt. 1964); *Willows Revisited* (1967); *For the Birds* (1980). Tongue-in-cheek satires of Saskatchewan life styles, social pretensions, and western Canadian literature.

Kroetsch, Robert (ed.). *Sundogs: Stories From Saskatchewan* (1980).

MacLeod, Jack. *Zinger and Me* (1979). A comic novel of letters between a Prince Albert newspaper man and a Toronto academic.

McBain, Daniel. *Art Roebuck Comes to Born With a Tooth* (1991). Man comatose in a Saskatchewan town for fourteen years revives as someone else.

McNamee, James. *Them Damn Canadians Hanged Louis Riel* (1971). A twelve-year old describes life at the time of the Riel Rebellion of 1885.

Mitchell, Ken. *Con Man: A Novel* (1979). Comic story of a half-breed Indian who gets in and out of trouble in Saskatchewan during the 1960s.

—— *Everybody Gets Something Here: Stories* (1977). Fourteen stories about rogues and hustlers in rural Saskatchewan.

—— (ed.). *Horizon: Writings of the Canadian Prairies* (1977).

Mitchell, W.O. *Who Has Seen the Wind* (1947, rpt. 1991); *Jake and the Kid* (1962, rpt. 1991); *According to Jake and the Kid: A Collection of New Stories* (1989). Humourous stories about a farmhand and a boy living near "Crocus" (Weyburn).

Rigelhof, T.F. *The Education of J.J. Pass: A Novel* (1983). Memories of an Ukrainian immigrant to Saskatchewan reveal conflicts between old and new world views.

Ross, Sinclair. *As For Me and My House: A Novel* (1941, rpt. 1989). The diary of a minister's wife's reveals her husband as a frustrated artist struggling to express himself in rural Saskatchewan.

——. *Sawbones Memorial* (1974). A novel about a retirement party for a Saskatchewan town's doctor in 1948.

——. *The Well* (1958). Montreal boy with criminal tendencies finds his humanity in a summer spent on a Saskatchewan farm.

Sapergia, Barbara. *Foreigners* (1984, rpt. 1990). A family of Romanian immigrants struggles to find a new life in the badlands of southern Saskatchewan.

Schroeder, Andreas. *Dustship Glory* (1986). Based on the true story of a Finnish immigrant who built a cargo boat near Many Bones, a thousand miles from the sea.

Seitz, Mary Ann. *Shelterbelt* (1979). In the 1930s and 1940s an Ukrainian girl grows up on a large Saskatchewan farm.

Silver, Alfred. *Lord of the Plains* (1990). Historical fiction about Gabriel Dumont.

Story, Gertrude. *The Way to Always Dance* (1983); *It Never Pays to Laugh Too Much* (1984); *This Need of Always Wanting* (1985); *After Sixty: Going Home* (1991). Stories about people of German heritage in Saskatchewan.

Symons, R.D. *Still the Wind Blows: A Historical Novel of the Canadian Northwest, 1860–1916* (1971).

Ursell, Geoffrey. *Perdue; or, How the West Was Lost* (1984). A novel about a town in central Saskatchewan.

—— (ed.). *Saskatchewan Gold* (1982); *More Saskatchewan Gold* (1984); *Sky High: Stories From Saskatchewan* (1988). Short stories.

Vanderhaeghe, Guy. *Homesick: A Novel* (1989). A woman returns to a small Saskatchewan town with her son and resumes a difficult relationship with her father.

Wiebe, Rudy. *Peace Shall Destroy the Many* (1962, rpt. 1972). Conflict arises in a small Saskatchewan Mennonite community during World War II.

——. **The Temptations of Big Bear* (1976, rpt.

1984). Indian resistance from the Indian point of view at the time of the 1885 rebellion.

Williams, David. *The Burning Wood* (1975). A clash between a northern Saskatchewan white community and an Indian reserve.

——. *The River Horsemen* (1981). Four men make a river journey to Saskatoon.

NORTHWEST TERRITORIES

Northwest Territories occupies ca. one-third of Canada, stretching from 60°N to the North Pole, including the islands of the Arctic Archipelago. It is bordered on the west by Yukon Territory; on the north by the Arctic Ocean; on the east by the Robeson Channel, Smith Sound, Baffin Bay, Davis Strait, and Hudson Bay; and on the south by the provinces of Quebec, Manitoba, Saskatchewan, Alberta, and British Columbia. Cape Columbia on Ellesmere Island is the northernmost land in Canada; Baker Lake is the geographic centre of Canada.

Name Northwest Territories. This name is an adaptation of the phrase "Rupert's Land and the North-Western Territories" in the 1670 Hudson's Bay Company charter. *Previous names:* Rupert's Land (1670–1868), North-West Territories (1868–1905); until 1905 the territory included most of western Canada and parts of Labrador and Quebec.

Flag The provincial shield in a white middle panel with blue panels on either side. Adopted by Territorial Council on January 1, 1969.

Coat of Arms A blue wavy line on a white background in the top third of the shield; the bottom two-thirds divided diagonally, the upper right part the head of a fox on a red background, the lower left part gold ingots on a green background. Above the shield, two golden narwhales guard a compass rose. Authorized by Queen Elizabeth II on February 24, 1956.

Motto None.

Emblems
Bird gyrfalcon (*Falco rusticolus*)
Flower mountain avens (*Dryas integrifolia*)
Mineral gold
Tartan blue, green, brown, and shades of red
Tree jack pine (*Pinus banksiana*)

Date of Entry into Confederation July 15, 1870; reconstituted in present form on September 1, 1905.

Official Languages Chipewyan, Cree, Dogrib, English, French, Gwich'in, Inuktitut (including Inuinnaqtun and Inuvialuktun), Slavey (North and South).

Capital City Yellowknife, the most northerly and the coldest city in Canada, situated on the north shore of Great Slave Lake; population 15,179. The name is derived from the term fur traders gave to Athapaskan Indians who carried copper-bladed knives. The first settlement was a trading post established by

Alexander Mackenzie in 1789. Gold was first discovered at Yellowknife Bay in 1895, but a permanent settlement was not established until 1934. Incorporated as a city on January 1, 1970; Yellowknife became the major administrative centre and capital of Northwest Territories on January 18, 1967 (previous capital, Fort Smith). The administrative functions were transferred from the federal government on September 17, 1967.

Territorial Holidays In addition to national statutory holidays (see page 2), Northwest Territories residents celebrate Civic Holiday (the first Monday in August).

Geography and Climate

Geography The land west of the Mackenzie River is part of North America's western cordillera. Rugged mountains are also found on the islands of the eastern Arctic Archipelago, many of which have permanent ice caps. The Canadian shield underlies most of the mainland and together with the western islands forms a lowland studded with many lakes. The tree line stretches from the Mackenzie River Delta to the Hudson Bay shore near Manitoba. North and east of this line is a treeless tundra, south and west of the line taiga forests. Only the southern part of Northwest Territories is outside the permafrost region.

Area 3,426,320 sq. km. (1,322,902 sq. mi.); 34.4% of Canada. *Rank:* 1st.

Inland Water 133,300 sq. km. (51,467 sq. mi.) includes very many lakes. Largest lake: Great Bear Lake 31,328 sq. km. (12,096 sq. mi.), the largest lake wholly in Canada. Great Slave Lake is the deepest lake in Canada, 614 m. (2,014 ft.).

Elevations Highest point: Unnamed peak, Mackenzie Mountains (N62° 7' W127° 41'), 2,762 m. (9,062 ft.). Lowest point: shoreline, sea level.

Major Rivers (* indicates a designated Canadian Heritage River; ** indicates a Ramsar site): Anderson, *Arctic Red, Back, Coppermine, Dubawnt, Horton, */**Kazan, Liard, Mackenzie (Canada's longest river), */**Seal, *Soper, */**South Nahanni, */**Thelon.

Climate Northwest Territories (N.W.T.) experiences long, cold winters and cool, dry summers, the latter ranging from three months in the southwest to three weeks in the far north. The average daily mean temperature in January in Fort Simpson is -28.2°C (−18.8°F); in Baker Lake −33°C (−27.4°F); in Resolute −32.1°C (−25.8°F); in July in Fort Simpson 16.6°C (61.9°F); in Baker Lake 11°C (51.8°F); in Resolute 4.1°C (39.4°F). The lowest recorded temperature in N.W.T.: −61.7°C (−79.1°F) at Fort Good Hope on December 31, 1910; the highest recorded temperature 39.4°C (102.9°F) at Fort Smith on July 18, 1941.

While precipitation varies in this vast territory, many parts of N.W.T. are among the driest in Canada and the world, creating an Arctic desert. Average precipitation in Fort Simpson is 355.1 mm. (14 in.), in Resolute 131.4 mm. (5.2 in.). Greatest recorded annual precipitation in N.W.T. is 1,071 mm. (42.2 in.) in 1979 at Cape Dyer. The average annual snowfall at Eureka is 44 cm. (17.3 in.); in Yellowknife 135 cm. (53.1 in.). Greatest recorded snowfall over five consecutive days: 153.7 cm. (60.5 in.) at Fort Resolution on November 19, 1947. Greatest recorded annual snowfall: 977 cm. (384.6 in.) at Cape Dyer winter of 1978/79.

Because of its position near and above the Arctic circle, N.W.T. holds several Canadian records for sunshine; the greatest annual number of possible hours of sunshine, 4,580 hours at Alert;

the average sunniest summer, 1,065 hours (June, July, August) at Yellowknife; the sunniest month, 621 hours in May 1973 at Eureka. Other Canadian records are: the coldest month, −47.9°C (−54.2°F) in February 1979 at Eureka on Ellesmere Island; the coldest year, −21.7°C (−7.1°F) in 1972 at Eureka; the coldest wind chill day, −92°C (-133.6°F) on January 13, 1975 at Pelly Bay; the lowest average annual precipitation, 64 mm. (2.5 in.) per year at Eureka; the lowest precipitation in a single year, 12.7 mm. (0.5 in.) at Arctic Bay in 1949; the longest period without measurable precipitation, 218 days at Rea Point.

Time Zones East of the 68th meridian: Atlantic; between the 68th and the 85th meridians including all of Southampton Island: Eastern; between the 85th and the 102nd meridians: Central; west of the 102nd meridian: Mountain.

Parks and Historic Sites

In this section, the following designations are used: *indicates the area is, or part of it is, a Unesco World Heritage Site; ** indicates the area is, or part of it is, a Ramsar site.

National Parks Located in Northwest Territories

Park	Location	Size
Aulavik	Banks Island	12,275 sq. km. (4,739 sq. mi.)
Auyuittuq	near Pangnirtung, Baffin Island	21,471 sq. km. (8,290 sq. mi.)
Ellesmere Island	northern Ellesmere Island	37,775 sq. km. (14,585 sq. mi.)
*Nahanni	southwest N.W.T.	4,766 sq. km. (1,840 sq. mi.)
*/**Wood Buffalo	N.W.T./Alberta border one-third in N.W.T.	44,807 sq. km. (17,300 sq. mi.)

Territorial Parks There are 50 territorial parks in N.W.T.: 12 community parks, 28 wayside parks, 2 outdoor recreation parks, and 8 historic parks. The largest parks are:

Park	Region	Type	Size
Hidden Lake	North Slave	outdoor recreation	2,300 ha. (9 sq. mi.)
Powder Point	North Slave	wayside	1,700 ha. (7 sq. mi.)
Blackstone	Deh Cho	outdoor recreation	1,430 ha. (6 sq. mi.)
Lady Evelyn Falls	Fort Smith	wayside	1,354ha. (5 sq. mi.)
Saamba Deh	Deh Cho	wayside	575 ha. (2 sq. mi.)

N.W.T. has 14 national bird sanctuaries plus one shared with Ontario and one with Quebec, 1 national wildlife area, and 5 Ramsar sites plus one shared with Alberta.

National Historic Sites and Parks in Northwest Territories

Our Lady of Good Hope Church, Fort Good Hope

Pingo Canadian Landmark, near Coppermine

In addition, there are a number of historic sites in Northwest Territories administered by the Territories, municipalities, or organizations. The major sites are:

Fort Smith Mission Historic Park, Fort Smith

Ijiraliq Archaeological Site, near Rankin Inlet

Kekerten Historic Park, Cumberland Sound

Nadlok Archaeological Site, Burnside River

Northwest Passage Historic Park, Gjoa Haven

Qaummaarviit Historic Park, near Iqaluit

Demography

Native peoples comprise 58% of the population. Generally, Inuit inhabit the Arctic Islands and coast, Dene the subarctic Mackenzie Valley, and Métis the Mackenzie Valley and the Slave River region.

Northwest Territories Population: 57,649; 0.2% of national; *rank* 11th

Historical population data
1981	45,740
1971	34,805
1961	22,998
1951	16,004
1941	12,028
1921	8,143

Population Density: 0.02 persons per sq. km.; 0.05 per sq. mi. (lowest in Canada)

Number of Dwellings: 16,349

Indian Reserves: 2 reserves and 23 bands (most not on reserves)

Population Characteristics:
urban: 21,157; 36.7%
rural: 36,492; 63.3%
19 and under: 23,650; 41.0% (highest in Canada)
65 and over: 1,605; 2.8% (lowest in Canada)
average income for full-time employment 15 years and over (1990): $42,268 (highest in Canada); men $47,061; women $35,071
average life expectancy at birth: not available
live birth rate: 1,634; 28.3 per 1000 (highest in Canada)
deaths: 237; 4.3 per 1000
marriages: 215; 3.7 per 1000 (lowest in Canada)
divorces: 87; 1.51 per 1000 (lowest in Canada)

Cities and Towns *(for definitions of CA and CSD, see page viii)*

Name	Population	Dwellings	National Pop. Rank
Yellowknife	15,179	5,020	113 (CA)
Iqaluit	3,552	1,091	966 (CSD)
Inuvik	3,206	1,119	1,045 (CSD)
Hay River	3,206	1,100	1,045 (CSD)
Fort Smith	2,480	791	1,274 (CSD)

Government and Politics, 1905–

A description of the division of powers between the federal and territorial governments will be found on page 4.

Commissioner The Commissioner is the chief executive officer of the Northwest Territories (N.W.T.) government, and is appointed by the federal government. Under the direction of the federal Minister of Northern Affairs and Northern Development, the Commissioner is responsible for the administration of N.W.T.

Commissioners of Northwest Territories

	Term
Frederick D. White	1905–1919
William Wallace Cory	1919–1931
Hugh Howard Rowatt	1931–1934
Charles Camsell	1936–1946
Hugh Llewellyn Keenleyside	1947–1950
Hugh Andrew Young	1950–1953
Robert Gordon Robertson	1953–1963
Bent Gestur Sivertz	1963–1967
Stuart Milton Hodgson	1967–1979
John Havelock Parker	1979–1989
Daniel Leonard Norris	1989–

Legislative Assembly The Legislative Assembly of Northwest Territories has powers similar to those of a provincial legislative assembly, except the federal government is responsible for forestry, fire suppression, and natural resources other than game and the federal government can disallow any act within one year. The Assembly consists of 24 members elected by popular vote, each member represents a constituency; term of office: 4 years. It does not operate on a party system, but rather by consensus; remuneration (1994): $39,514 + $20,032 constituency indemnity; additional amounts for special appointments; qualifications for members: Canadian citizen, 19 years of age or older, ordinarily resident in N.W.T. for at least twelve months immediately prior to polling day, not legally disqualified, e.g., government employee.

Qualifications for Northwest Territories Voters in Territorial Elections Canadian citizen, 19 years of age or older, ordinarily resident in N.W.T. for at least twelve months immediately prior to polling day, not legally disqualified, e.g., prisoner in penal institutions, returning officer.

Government Leader The Government Leader is chosen by members of the Legislative Assembly from one of the 8 members of the Executive Council and serves as chairperson of the Council.

Northwest Territories Representation in Federal Government
House of Commons: 2 members
Senate: 1 member

Government Leaders of Northwest Territories	Term
George Braden	1980–1984
Richard Nerysoo	1984–1985
Nick Gordon Sibbeston	1985–1987
Dennis Glen Patterson	1987–1991
Nellie Joy Cournoyea	1991–

Executive Council The Executive Council consists of a maximum of 8 members of the Legislative Assembly who are chosen by the Assembly. Council members are responsible for one or more Territorial government departments.

Government Departments All departments may be contacted through the general switchboard at (403)873-7110 or 800-661-0884 for service in French.

Economic Development and Tourism
Education, Culture and Employment Programs
Energy, Mines and Petroleum Resources
Finance
Health
Intergovernmental and Aboriginal Affairs
Justice
Municipal and Community Affairs
Public Works and Services
Renewable Resources
Safety and Public Services
Social Services
Transportation

Finances

A schedule of Northwest Territories' revenue and expenditures for the years 1992/93 and 1991/92 are shown below in thousands of dollars. The financial year runs from April 1 to March 31 of the year following.

	Actual 1992/93	Actual 1991/92
Revenue		
Taxation	145,306	136,472
General revenue	36,040	34,295
Other revenue	26,645	33,331
Government of Canada	911,048	899,198

Capital	7,122	3,050
Total revenue for the year	1,119,039	1,106,346
Operating and maintenance expenditures		
Health	183,193	199,763
Education	181,519	174,121
Public works	116,319	110,656
Social services	74,196	90,517
Municipal and community services	59,246	59,112
N.W.T. housing corporation	55,732	55,125
Renewable resources	42,631	46,804
Transportation	39,775	39,938
Economic development and tourism	34,521	37,054
Other	172,427	157,369
Total operating and maint. expenditures	959,559	970,459
Capital expenditures for the year	167,833	173,794

Economy

Immense transportation distances, isolated communities, small markets, and heavy reliance on imported goods and services make the likelihood of a modern industrial economy difficult, even improbable. Climate, the short growing season, and poor soil conditions limit agriculture to a few market gardens in the Hay River region. N.W.T.'s economy is based primarily on natural resources; reserves are not easily exploited because of the expense involved in doing so. Forestry is limited due to slow growth and distance from markets. Tourism, small business development, and native arts and crafts are making increasing contributions to N.W.T.'s economy.

Major Industries Primary resource extraction, including oil and gas exploration, and mining for gold, lead-zinc, silver, tungsten, etc., is N.W.T.'s principal industry. Hunting, fishing, trapping, and arts and crafts occupy many native people and they are increasingly involved in tourism.

Gross Domestic Product (1992) $2,173 million (in current dollars at factor cost); % of national G.D.P.: 0.4%; *rank:* 10th

Distribution of gross domestic product (1990)

Mining	24.0%
Government services	19.3%
Finance, insurance, real estate	10.5%
Construction	9.2%
Educational services	6.6%
Transportation, storage	4.0%
Retail trade	3.8%
Other utilities	2.5%
Health services	2.4%
Manufacturing	0.7%
Wholesale trade	0.7%
Fishing and trapping	0.2%
Agriculture	0.1%
Logging	0.1%

Employment 20,342

Unemployment Insurance Recipients 2,353

Fur Production (1991/92) number of pelts produced: 38,906; value: $2.4 million

Fish Harvest Value and Landings (1991/92) $1.9 million; 1,780 tonnes

Value of Mineral Shipments $703.2 million

Minimum Wage along N.W.T. highway system: $6.50, and $6.00 under 16 years of age; elsewhere: $7.00, and $6.50 under 16

Exports (1992) combined merchandising exports for Northwest Territories and Yukon Territory amounted to $366 million

History

ca. 10,000 B.C.	Paleo-Indians arrive.
ca. 7000 B.C.	Archaic Boreal culture is found in the Canadian Arctic mainland. Small bands of Dene follow migrating caribou herds north from the southern plains.
ca. 2000–0 B.C.	Pre-Dorset Paleo-Inuit are the first inhabitants in high and eastern Arctic.
ca. 800 B.C.– ca. 1000 A.D.	Dorset people are in the high and eastern Arctic.
ca. 1000	First Inuit, the Thule people, arrive and overwhelm the Dorset culture. Thorstein, son of Leif Ericsson, lands at Cumberland Peninsula, Baffin Island.
1476	Johannes Scolvas, Danish explorer, winters in Hudson Bay.
1500s	Many explorers and fur traders seek a northwest passage to the Orient.
1576	*July* Martin Frobisher reaches Frobisher Strait and Frobisher Bay and claims land for England.
1578	Frobisher attempts to found a settlement at present-day Iqaluit.
1585	*July–August* John Davis explores the Baffin Island coastline.
1610	Henry Hudson explores Hudson Bay and tries to find a northwest passage.
1616	Robert Bylot and William Baffin map Baffin Bay and discover Lancaster Sound.
1631	Luke Foxe sails into Foxe Channel as far as Cape Dorchester, establishing that this is not part of the northwest passage.
1670	*May 2* Hudson's Bay Company is formed and granted trade rights over all territory draining into Hudson Bay.
1670–1713	French and English struggle over control of Hudson Bay.
1713	*April 11* France returns Hudson Bay drainage basin to British in the Treaty of Utrecht.
1719	Commercial whaling on a regular basis begins.
1742	Christopher Middleton commands the first official British expedition to search for a northwest passage, and in 1743 produces the first map showing the northwestern coast of Hudson Bay.
1761–1762	William Christopher discovers Chesterfield Inlet.
1763	*February 10* Treaty of Paris: France formally cedes its North American possessions to Britain including all of Canada east of the Rocky Mountains.
1770–1772	Samuel Hearne makes the first significant land exploration including the Coppermine and Slave Rivers and Great Slave Lake.
1771	*July 18* Samuel Hearne reaches the mouth of the Coppermine River, becoming the first European to reach the Arctic Ocean overland.
1789	*June 29* Alexander Mackenzie discovers and enters the Mackenzie River and reaches the Arctic Delta on *July 10*. Mackenzie discovers liquid seepage at Norman Wells, but oil is not tapped for another 130 years.
1804	Hudson's Bay Company establishes Fort Simpson, the oldest continuously occupied trading post in the Mackenzie River Valley.
1807	North West Company builds a post near present-day Fort Liard.
1810	North West Company constructs a post at Fort Norman.
1819	William Parry commands the first ships to cross 110°W and discovers ca. 20 Arctic islands, including Banks, Beachy, Cornwallis, Devon, Melville, and Somerset.

1819–1827	John Franklin commands expeditions that explore the N.W.T. interior and Arctic coast.
1820–1840	Peak of whaling activity in the Canadian Arctic.
1831	*June 1* British expedition headed by James Clark Ross locates the magnetic north pole at Cape Adelaide on the west coast of Boothia Peninsula and plants the British flag.
1833–1835	George Back explores the Back River to the Arctic coast and north and west of Great Slave Lake.
1837	Thomas Simpson surveys the Arctic coast from the Mackenzie River to Alaska.
1839	*September* William Parry, accompanied by Inuit, explores Exeter Sound.
1840	James Evans, a Methodist minister, invents a nine-character syllabic alphabet for Cree and Inuktitut.
1848	Disappearance of the Franklin expedition leads to expanded exploration of N.W.T.
1853	John Rae completes a survey of the north coast of North America.
1857	*August* Mathias Warmow, the first Christian missionary in Baffin area, lands at Kekerten.
1867	*November 6* Federal government adopts a resolution for the admission of Rupert's Land into Canada.
1868	Hudson's Bay Company establishes a trading post at Hay River.
1869	*November 19* Canada purchases Rupert's Land from the Hudson's Bay Company; the transfer in effect *July 15, 1870*. This does not include the Arctic Archipelago.
1880	*July 31* Britain transfers Arctic Archipelago to Canada.
1884	*June 21* Seven survivors of the American scientific expedition led by Adolphus Greely are rescued at Cape Sabine, Ellesmere Island.
1886	*May 14* Federal government passes an act to allow N.W.T. representation in the federal parliament.
1893	James Williams Tyrrell, an engineer, and Joseph Burr Tyrrell, a geologist, travel through N.W.T. and produce the first accurate description of the interior of the Barren Lands.
1895	*October 2* Federal government establishes the Provisional Districts of Mackenzie and Franklin and the boundary between N.W.T. and Yukon Territory.
1897	Federal government alters the N.W.T. boundaries.
1898–1902	Otto Sverdrup explores and claims several Arctic islands for Norway.
Early 1900s	Inuvaluit move from Yukon Territory to the Mackenzie River delta area because of the demise of the whaling industry.
1900	*March 13* J.W. Tyrrell begins a journey to survey the area from Great Slave Lake to Chesterfield Inlet.
1903–1906	Roald Amundsen in the *Gjoa* is the first to find a Northwest Passage.
1903	By exploring and patrolling the islands and waters of Hudson Bay and the north *Neptune* establishes Canadian authority in these regions. First North-West Mounted Police post north of the Arctic Circle is established at Fort McPherson.
1904	Albert Peter Low maps and claims Ellesmere Island for Canada.
1905	*July 25* Northwest Territories Act creates new boundaries for N.W.T. and sets up N.W.T. government by appointed commissioner and council, composed of civil servants based in Ottawa.
1909	*July 1* Joseph-Elzear Bernier places a plaque on Melville Island claiming it for Canada.
1912	N.W.T.'s present boundaries are established.

1913–1918	Vilhjalmur Stefansson explores the last large blank on the map of Canada, establishing the nature and position of all lands in the western part of the Arctic Archipelago.
1915	Commercial whaling is halted.
1918	Hudson's Bay Company founds Aklavik in the Mackenzie Delta.
1919	Imperial Oil Ltd. drills the first well at Norman Wells.
1920s	Popularity of white fox fur brings many trappers and traders to N.W.T.
1920	*January 1* Federal government divides N.W.T. into three provisional districts: Mackenzie, Keewatin, and Franklin.
	July 13 Federal government asks the Danish government to stop Greenlanders hunting on Ellesmere Island.
1921	Dene sign a treaty granting the federal government an interest in their lands in exchange for services such as health care and education.
1922	Royal Canadian Mounted Police (RCMP) posts are established at Craig Harbour, Ellesmere Island, and Pond Inlet, Baffin Island.
1923	Hudson's Bay Company establishes a post at Clyde River, RCMP at Pangnirtung, Baffin Island.
1924	RCMP establishes a post at Dundas Harbour, Devon Island.
1926	RCMP establishes a post on the east coast of Ellesmere Island.
1927	*August 31* N.W.T. Commissioner is given responsibility for welfare of the Inuit.
1928	*August 28* Clennell Haggerston Dickins and C.D.H. MacAlpine are the first to fly across the Barren Lands.
	Fisheries Act prohibits walrus hunting in Baffin Island and Hudson Bay except by Inuit for food.
1929	*July 1* Dickins flies to Aklavik, the first person to reach the Arctic coast by air.
1930	Norway abandons its claim to the Sverdrup Islands.
	May 16 Prospector Gilbert LaBine discovers silver mixed with pitchblende (radium) near Great Bear Lake.
1931	Amended Fisheries Act sets walrus hunting quotas for Inuit and prohibits export of walrus hides.
1933	*August 20* Two thousand one hundred reindeer, purchased by the federal government to be used as food and clothing for the Inuit, arrive at Kotzebue.
1939	*April 5* Supreme Court of Canada declares the Inuit a federal responsibility.
1940–1942	*St. Roch*, captained by Henry Asbjorn Larsen, becomes the first ship to travel through the Northwest Passage from west to east.
1940	*January 1* First municipal government in N.W.T. is inaugurated in Yellowknife.
1941	Military base is built at Coral Harbour, Southampton Island.
1942–1944	United States government constructs the Canol Pipeline from Norman Wells across the Mackenzie River to Whitehorse, Yukon Territory; it is abandoned *March 1945*.
1944	*St. Roch*, captained by Larsen, travels the Northwest Passage from east to west becoming the first ship to make this trip both ways.
1945	Because the Inuit have only one name, frequently changed, the federal government issues each a number on a tag to be worn around the neck from birth.
1947	*April 15* First public meeting of N.W.T. Council heralds the beginning of local autonomy.
1948	Mackenzie Highway opens from Hay River to Grimshaw, Alberta.
	Northern Canada Power Commission is established.
1949	N.W.T. Game Ordinance requires every hunter be licensed.
1950	Inuit are given the right to vote in federal elections.

1951	*June 15* Northwest Territories Act is amended to provide for a partially elected Council.
	September 17 First election for N.W.T. Council is held.
1953	*August* Fifty-three Inuit are moved to the high Arctic partly to establish Canadian sovereignty.
1954–1957	Distant Early Warning Line, a joint Canadian-American project with 22 stations from Alaska to Baffin Island, is built.
1954	Founding of Inuvik to replace Aklavik as the administrative centre of the western Arctic region, the first settlement designed for permanent residence in the far north.
1955	*January 27* N.W.T. passes a liquor control law prohibiting Inuit from having liquor except in certain circumstances.
	September 30 Operation Franklin, a geological survey of Canada's Arctic islands, is completed.
	North Rankin Mines Ltd. establishes Rankin Inlet.
1956	Canadian Forces Station Alert is established.
1957	*February 26* Baker Lake Council is organized composed of 14 Inuit under the guidance of a federal official.
1959	Caribou Inuit move from Ennadai to establish Whale Cove on Hudson Bay.
1961	First oil-drilling rig in Arctic arrives on Melville Island.
1962	*April 2* Microwave system between Hay River and Peace River, Alberta, built by Alberta Government Telephones and CN Telecommunications, opens.
1963	*May 3–4* Severe floods in Hay River and Fort Simpson cause the evacuation of ca. 1,900 people.
	July 12 Bent Gestur Sivertz becomes the first full-time commissioner.
	December 10 First permanent research laboratory north of the Arctic Circle is completed in Inuvik.
1964	Great Slave Lake Railway is completed.
1965	*October 18* Federal government appoints Abraham Allen Okpik as the first Inuit N.W.T. Council member.
1966	*January 6* *The Drum,* the first newspaper in the Arctic issued in English, Inuktituk, and Loucheux, is published.
	November 10 N.W.T. legislation is passed to establish a system of free public libraries.
1967	Canada signs the International Agreement on the Conservation of Polar Bears.
1968	Federal government imposes hunting quotas on polar bears and divides these between native settlements.
1970	Federal government appoints Abraham Okpik to journey through the north to help Inuit select surnames and record them.
	Northwest Territories Act amendment provides for an executive, legislative, and judicial structure.
	April 1 Federal Department of Indian Affairs and Northern Development transfers responsibility for governing the eastern and upper Arctic to N.W.T.
	April 17 Announcement is made that Yellowknife will become the permanent headquarters for Canadian military activities in the north.
	First Northern Games, competitive events held every two years for people who live north of 60° (Canada, Alaska, Greenland), is held in summer at Inuvik, in winter at Yellowknife.
1971	*January 20* Radio Tuktoyaktuk begins broadcasting in English and Inuktituk.
1972	*February 24* Panarctic Oils Ltd. announces an oil discovery on Ellesmere Island.

1972	*March 7* Yukon Territory gives 13 sq. km. (5 sq. mi.) on Mount Logan to N.W.T. as compensation for a surveying error.

1972   *March 7* Yukon Territory gives 13 sq. km. (5 sq. mi.) on Mount Logan to N.W.T. as compensation for a surveying error.

August 2 Federal government proclaims the Arctic Waters Pollution Prevention Act to protect the Arctic from pollution by foreign supertankers.

Federal government bans commercial whaling.

1974   *October 30* Crash of Pan-Arctic Oils airplane at Rea Point causes 32 deaths, the worst Canadian accident involving a noncommercial aircraft.

1975   *February 28* Federal government passes legislation giving N.W.T. a second seat in Parliament.

May 30 Federal government passes legislation providing one N.W.T. Senate seat.

N.W.T. Council members are chosen by the elected Assembly with the exception of the Commissioner and two assistants.

1976   *April 15* Dome Petroleum Ltd. receives government approval to drill offshore wells in the Beaufort Sea.

Inuit Tapirisat of Canada proposes an Inuit homeland.

1977   *April 5* Willy Adams is appointed to the Senate and becomes the first Inuit to sit in Parliament.

May 8 Berger Commission report recommends a ten-year moratorium on a Mackenzie Valley pipeline until native land claims are settled.

1978   *January 24* Soviet nuclear-powered observation satellite breaks up spreading debris across 46,000 sq. km. (28,584 sq. mi.) north of Great Slave Lake.

July 30 Land claims agreement with 2,500 Inuit in the western Arctic: $4.5 million to be paid between 1981–1994 in exchange for the release of aboriginal rights to 270,480 sq. km. (160,073 sq. mi.).

1979   *February 6–18* −40°C (−40°F), 100 kph (62 mph) winds, and snow keep Iqaluit residents indoors for 10 days.

August 18 Dempster Highway from Inuvik to Dawson City, Yukon Territory, opens.

Hunting of bowhead whales in Canadian waters is prohibited except under special permit by the Minister of Fisheries and Oceans.

1980   *December 1* Inuit-run TV network broadcasting in Inuktituk to eastern Arctic begins.

1981   *November 3* Dome Petroleum Ltd. announces huge new oil deposits found in the Beaufort Sea.

1982   In a plebiscite 56.5% of N.W.T. voters support the principle of the division of N.W.T. into two separate territories.

December 21 N.W.T. and federal governments sign a $21 million economic development agreement.

1984   *April 25* Canadian and Soviet Union governments sign an agreement for cooperation in Arctic scientific research.

September 17 Agnes Semmler is the first aboriginal Canadian to be appointed deputy commissioner of N.W.T.

Liard Highway from near Fort Nelson to south of Fort Simpson is completed.

1985   Federal government endorses the plan to divide N.W.T. into Nunavut in the east, inhabited primarily by Inuit, and Denendeh in the west, inhabited primarily by Dene and Métis.

1987   N.W.T. government establishes Arctic College.

1988   *January 11* Canadian/American Arctic Cooperation Agreement is signed in which the United States agrees to ask permission from Canada before sending ice breakers into Arctic straits.

September 5 Federal government and Dene and Métis sign land claims agreement for payment of $500 million over 20 years and certain land rights. Federal government cedes responsibility for health care to N.W.T.

1989 *March 2* First test over Canada of a United States Cruise missile using Stealth technology flies from Beaufort Sea to Primrose Lake weapons testing range, Alberta.

December 25 Powerful earthquake, 6.2 on the Richter scale, in Baffin Island and eastern N.W.T. causes no damage because of sparse population.

National Energy Board grants 20-year licences, beginning in 1997, for the export of natural gas from the Beaufort Sea and Mackenzie Delta to the United States.

1991 *April* Announcement is made of the Arctic Environment Strategy spreading $100 million over 6 years to preserve and enhance Arctic ecosystems.

November 1 Announcement by Charles Fipke of the discovery of diamond-bearing rock in the Lac de Gras area sets off a diamond rush in Yellowknife.

1992 *April 22* Federal government signs a land claim granting Gwich'in Indians from N.W.T. and Yukon Territory title to 14,806 sq. km. (9,200 sq. mi.) and $75 million over 15 years.

May Fifty-four percent of N.W.T. residents vote in favour of the proposed division of N.W.T.

November 3–5 Referendum is approved by 69% eligible Inuit voters on the land claim settlement leading to the creation of Nunavut on *April 1, 1999*; the settlement is signed with federal government *May 25, 1993*.

1993 *March 4* Land claim agreement is signed with the Dene of Colville Lake, Fort Franklin, Fort Good Hope, and Fort Norman and the Métis of Fort Good Hope, Fort Franklin, and Norman Wells.

June 10 Bill to create Nunavut receives royal assent.

November 17 First meeting is held in new legislature building in Yellowknife.

Culture and Education

Performing Arts N.W.T. has several professional or semi-professional performing companies. Some of these are:

Lunch Pail Theatre Company, Yellowknife	(403)873-3156
Northern Arts and Cultural Centre	(403)873-4950
Tunooniq Theatre Company, Pond Inlet	(819)899-8934
Xaesade Native Theatre Group, Yellowknife	(403)873-6996
Yellowknife Theatre Group, Yellowknife	(403)873-3156

In addition, there are many local festivals, especially at the winter and summer solstices. Some of the most prominent are:

Caribou Carnival, Yellowknife (March) (winter sports contests)	(403)873-9698
Folk on the Rocks, Yellowknife (July)	(403)920-7806
Great Northern Arts Festival, Inuvik (July)	(403)979-3536
Toonik Tyme Carnival, Iqaluit (April) (traditional Inuit games, dog sled and snowmobile races)	(819)979-4095

Territorial Museums and Galleries The following are a representative selection of N.W.T. museums.

Angmarlik Visitor Centre, Pangnirtung
Kingnait Centre, Cape Dorset

Norman Wells Historical Centre, Norman Wells

Northern Life Museum, Fort Smith

Nunatta Sunaqutangit (Things of the Land Museum), Iqaluit

Prince of Wales Northern Heritage Centre, Yellowknife

College (* indicates additional campuses in other centres)

Arctic College, Yellowknife* (will be divided into two colleges, one serving the Nunavut region and one western N.W.T., by July 1, 1994)

Motor Vehicle Use

Motor Vehicles Registered for Use in N.W.T. (1993): 31,959.

Drivers Licensed by N.W.T. (1993): 27,535. Minimum driving age: 16

Roads 2,215 km. (1,376 mi.) all-weather roads including 570 km. (354 mi.) of paved roads, 125 km. (78 mi.) of treated gravel roads, and 620 km. (385 mi.) untreated gravel roads; 1,325 km. (823 mi.) of winter roads; bridges: 29. Since aircraft is the only practical method of travel through most N.W.T., there are 184 airfields.

Speed Limits Highways: 90 kph (56 mph); populated areas: 50 kph (31 mph)

First, Biggest, and Best

World's oldest scientifically-dated rocks: Acasta gneisses, 962 million years found 320 km. (199 mi.) north of Yellowknife

World's biggest canyon system north of 60°: in Nahanni National Park

World's largest group of islands: Arctic Archipelago, 1.3 million sq. km. (501,933 sq. mi.) including intervening waters

Western hemisphere's largest park: Wood Buffalo National Park 44,800 sq. km. (17,297 sq. mi.), one third of which is in N.W.T.

World's farthest north continuously inhabited place: Canadian-U.S. weather station at Alert on northern tip of Ellesmere Island

North America's most northern community: Grise Fiord on the south shore of Ellesmere Island

World's first park established above the Arctic Circle: Auyuittuq National Park, 1972

North America's most northern park: Ellesmere Island National Park Reserve

North America's most northern place that can be reached on a public highway: Inuvik

North America's only public Highway above the Arctic Circle: Dempster Highway from Inuvik to Dawson City, Yukon Territory

World's richest musk-ox habitat: Aulavik National Park, Banks Island

World's largest free-roaming herd of wood bison: Wood Buffalo National Park; bison are the largest terrestrial animals in North America

North America's largest variety of geese in any single area: Queen Maud Gulf Migratory Bird Sanctuary

World's only natural breeding habitat of whooping cranes: Wood Buffalo National Park

World's largest lake trout: 30.2 kg. (66 lb., 8 oz.) caught by Rodney Harbeck, Great Bear Lake, July 19, 1991

World's largest arctic char: 14.9kg. (32 lb., 9 oz.) caught by Jeffrey Lee Ward on July 19, 1981, in Tree River

World's most northerly marathon: Nanisivik, Baffin Island, June 25, 1979, 42.2 km. (26.2 mi.)

Sources of Information About Northwest Territories

Economic Development and Tourism, Government of Northwest Territories: Box 1320, Yellowknife, N.W.T. X1A 2L9 (403)873-7200, 800-661-0788
N.W.T. Government publications may be obtained from Artisan Press Ltd.: Box 1566, Yellowknife, N.W.T. X1A 2P2 (403)920-2794

Books About Northwest Territories: A Selected List

Reference Guides

Agreement Between the Inuit of the Nunavut Settlement and Her Majesty the Queen in Right of Canada (1993).
Arctic Bibliography, 16 vols. (1953–1975).
Biographies of Inuit Artists, 3 vols. (2nd ed. 1984).
Brown, M.P. Sharon (comp.). *Eastern Arctic Study: Annotated Bibliography* (1984).
Bruemmer, Fred. *Arctic Animals: A Celebration of Survival* (1986).
Burt, Page. *Barrenland Beauties: Showy Plants of the Arctic Coast* (1991).
Canada. Atmospheric Environment Service. *Canadian Climate Normals: Yukon and Northwest Territories* (1993).
Canada. Energy, Mines and Resources Canada. *Gazetteer of Canada: Northwest Territories* (1980).
Canada. Indian and Northern Affairs Canada. *Canada's North: The Reference Manual* (rev. ed. 1990).
———. *Inuit Art Bibliography* (2nd ed. 1992).
Cooke, Alan and Clive Holland. *The Exploration of Northern Canada, 500 to 1920: A Chronology* (1978).
Gedalof, Robin. *An Annotated Bibliography of Canadian Inuit Literature* (1979).
Goodwin, C. Ross and Lynda M. Howard. *The Beaufort Sea, Mackenzie Delta, Mackenzie Valley, and Northern Yukon: A Bibliographical Essay* (1984).
Haley, Delphine (ed.). *Marine Mammals of the North Pacific and Arctic Waters* (2nd ed. rev. 1986).
———. *Seabirds of the North Pacific and Arctic Waters* (1984).
Herrington, Clyde. *Atlas of the Canadian Arctic Islands* (1969).
Holmes, Douglas. *Northerners: Profiles of People in the Northwest Territories* (1989).
Hoyt, Erich. *The Whales of Canada* (1984).
Mackenzie Valley Pipeline Inquiry. *Northern Frontier, Northern Homeland: Report of the Mackenzie Valley Pipeline Inquiry*, 3 vols. (1977).
Markham, W.E. *Ice Atlas: Canadian Arctic Waterways* (1981).
———. *Ice Atlas: Hudson Bay and Approaches* (1988).
Maxwell, J.B. *The Climate of the Canadian Arctic Islands and Adjacent Waters*, 2 vols. (1980–1982).
Morley, William F.E. *Ontario and the Canadian North* (1978). The second part of this bibliography is devoted largely to local histories of N.W.T. and Yukon Territory.
N.W.T. Data Book: A Complete Information Guide to the Northwest Territories and Its Communities (annual).
Porsild, A.E. *Illustrated Flora of the Canadian Arctic Archipelago* (2nd ed. rev. 1964).
——— and W.J. Cody. *Vascular Plants of Continental Northwest Territories, Canada* (1980).
Riewe, Rick (ed.). *Nunavut Atlas* (1992).
Trettin, H.P. (ed.). *Geology of the Innuitian Orogen and Arctic Platform of Canada and Greenland* (1991).
Usher, Peter J. *Historical Statistics Approximating Fur, Fish and Game Harvests Within Inuit Lands of the N.W.T. and Yukon, 1915–1974, With Text* (1975).

Nonfiction Sources

*denotes a winner of a Governor General's Literary Award; **a winner for the title in its original French-language version.

Abel, Kerry. *Drum Songs: Glimpses of Dene History* (1993).
Aquilina, Alfred P. *The Mackenzie, Yesterday and Beyond* (1981).
Beattie, Owen and John Geiger. *Frozen in Time: Unlocking the Secrets of the Franklin Expedition* (1992).
Berton, Pierre. *The Arctic Grail: The Quest for the Northwest Passage and the North Pole, 1818–1909* (1988).
———. *The Mysterious North* (1956, rpt. 1989).

Blondin, George. *When the World Was New: Stories of the Sahtu Dene* (1990).

Bockstoce, John. *Arctic Passages: A Unique Small-Boat Journey Through the Great Northern Waterway* (1991).

Bonnycastle, R.H.G. *A Gentleman Adventurer: The Arctic Diaries of R.H.G. Bonnycastle* (1984).

Bray, Emile-Frédéric de. *A Frenchman in Search of Franklin: De Bray's Journal, 1852–1854* (ed. by William Barr 1992).

Briggs, Jean L. *Never in Anger: Portrait of an Eskimo Family* (1970).

Brody, Hugh. *The People's Land: Inuit, Whites and the Eastern Arctic* (1975, rpt. 1991).

Bruemmer, Fred. *The Arctic* (1974, rpt. 1982).

——. *Arctic Memories: Living With the Inuit* (1993).

—— and others. *The Arctic World* (1985).

Buerschaper, Peter. *Arctic Journey: Paintings, Sketches, and Reminiscences of a Vanishing World* (1977).

Burnford, Sheila. *One Woman's Arctic* (1973).

Buliard, Roger P. *Inuk* (2nd ed. rev. 1956).

Calef, George. **Caribou and the Barren Lands* (1981).

Chappel, Bernice M. *Lure of the Arctic, or, Lost on the Tundra* (1986).

Clark, Donald W. *Western Subarctic Prehistory* (1991).

Coates, Kenneth S. *Canada's Colonies: A History of the Yukon and Northwest Territories* (1985).

—— and William R. Morrison (eds.). *Interpreting Canada's North: Selected Readings* (1989).

Comer, George. *An Arctic Whaling Diary: The Journal of Captain George Comer in Hudson Bay, 1903–1905* (ed. by W. Gillies Ross, 1984).

Crnkovich, Mary (ed.). *"Gossip": A Spoken History of Women in the North* (1990).

Dacks, Gurston (ed.). *Devolution and Constitutional Development in the Canadian North* (1990).

Davids, Richard C. *Lords of the Arctic: A Journey Among the Polar Bears* (1982).

Dickerson, Mark O. *Whose North?: Political Change, Political Development, and Self-Government in the Northwest Territories* (1992).

Diubaldo, Richard. *Stefansson and the Canadian Arctic* (1978).

Dosman, Edgar J. *The National Interest: The Politics of Northern Development, 1968–75* (1975).

Duffy, R. Quinn. *The Road to Nunavut: The Progress of the Eastern Arctic Inuit Since the Second World War* (1988).

Dumond, Don E. *The Eskimos and Aleuts* (rev. ed. 1987).

Francis, Daniel. *Arctic Chase: A History of Whaling in Canada's North* (1984).

Freeman, Minnie Aodla. *Life Among the Qallunaat* (1978). A young Inuit woman grapples with the white world.

Freeman, Milton M.R., Eleanor E. Wein, and Darren E. Keith. *Recovering Rights: Bowhead Whales and Inuvialuit Subsistence in the Western Canadian Arctic* (1992).

French, Alice. *My Name is Masak* (1976).

Fumoleau, Rene. *Denendeh: A Dene Celebration* (1984).

Georgia. *Georgia: An Arctic Diary* (1982).

Graham, Katherine A. *Local and Regional Government in the Northwest Territories* (1980).

—— and others. *A Climate for Change: Alternatives for the Central and Eastern Arctic* (1984).

Griffiths, Franklyn (ed.). *Politics of the Northwest Passage* (1987).

Hall, Ed (ed.). *People and Caribou in the Northwest Territories* (1989).

——. *A Way of Life* (1986).

Hall, Sam. *The Fourth World: The Heritage of the Arctic and Its Destruction* (1987).

Hamelin, Louis-Edmond. ***Canadian Nordicity: It's Your North, Too* (1979).

Hamilton, John David. *Arctic Revolution: Social Change in the Northwest Territories, 1935–1994* (1994).

——. *Bob Friday's Other Eye and More Outrageous True Tales of Canada's Northern Frontier* (1986).

Hearne, Samuel. *Coppermine Journey: An Account of a Great Adventure* (ed. by Farley Mowat, 1958).

Hood, Robert. *To the Arctic by Canoe, 1819–1821: The Journal and Paintings of Robert Hood, Midshipman With Franklin* (1974, rpt. 1994).

Hunt, L.A.C.O. *Rebels, Rascals & Royalty: The Colourful North of L.A.C.O. Hunt* (1983).

Hunter, Archie. *Northern Traders: Caribou Hair in the Stew* (1983).

Iglauer, Edith. *Denison's Ice Road* (1974, rpt. 1982).

——. *Inuit Journey* (1979).

Hoare, W.H.B. *Journal of a Barrenlander: W.H.B. Hoare, 1928–1929* (1990).

Jackson, Susan (ed.). *Yellowknife, N.W.T.: An Illustrated History* (1990).

James, Thomas. *The Strange and Dangerous Voyage of Captain Thomas James* (1633, ed. by W.A. Kenyon, 1975).

Klein, Clayton. *Cold Summer Wind* (1983).

Klutschak, Heinrich. *Overland to Starvation Cove: With the Inuit in Search of Franklin, 1878–1880* (1987, rpt. 1993).

Lauritzen, Philip. *Oil and Amulets: Inuit, a People United at the Top of the World* (1983).

Lee, Betty. *Lutiapik: The Little One Who Cares for Us* (1975, rpt. 1982).

Levere, Trevor H. *Science and the Canadian Arctic: A Century of Exploration 1818–1918* (1993).

Livingston, John. *Arctic Oil* (1981).

Lopez, Barry. *Arctic Dreams: Imagination and Desire in a Northern Landscape* (1986).

Lyall, Ernie. *An Arctic Man: Sixty-Five Years in Canada's North* (1979, rpt. 1983).

Macduff, Alistair. *Lords of Stone: An Anthology of Eskimo Sculpture* (1982).

Mackenzie, Alexander. *The Journals and Letters of Sir Alexander Mackenzie* (ed. by W. Kaye Lamb, 1970).

Macpherson, Norman John. *Dreams & Visions: Education in the Northwest Territories From Early Days to 1984* (1991).

Matthiasson, John S. *Living on the Land: Change Among the Inuit of Northern Baffin Island* (1992).

Maxwell, A.E. and Ivar Rudd. *The Year-Long Day: One Man's Arctic* (1976).

McGhee, Robert. *Canadian Arctic Prehistory* (1978).

McKay, John W. *Arctic Adventure, a Kazan River Journal: Being a Narrative, Day by Day, of a Group of Intrepid Adventures on the Kazan River, N.W.T. in the Summer of 1982* (1983).

Mead, Robert Douglas. *Ultimate North: Canoeing Mackenzie's Great River* (1976).

Merritt, John and others. *Nunavut: Political Choices and Manifest Destiny* (1989).

Mowat, Farley. *The Desperate People* (1959, rpt. 1980).

———. *Ordeal by Ice: The Search for the Northwest Passage* (rev ed. 1973, rpt. 1989).

———. *People of the Deer* (rev. ed. 1975, rpt. 1980).

———. *Tundra: Selections From the Great Accounts of Arctic Land Voyages* (1973, rpt. 1989).

Nanton, Paul. *Arctic Breakthrough: Franklin's Expeditions, 1819–1847* (1970, rpt. 1981).

North, Dick. *Arctic Exodus: The Last Great Trail Drive* (1991).

———. *The Lost Patrol* (1978).

O'Malley, Martin. *The Past and Future Land: An Account of the Berger Inquiry Into the Mackenzie Valley Pipeline* (1976).

Paine, Robert (ed.). *Patrons and Brokers in the East Arctic* (1971).

———. *The White Arctic: Anthropological Essays on Tutelage and Ethnicity* (1977).

Patterson, Mary Jean, Charles D. Arnold, and Robert R. Jane (eds.). *Collected Papers on the Human History of the Northwest Territories* (1985).

Pelly, David F. *Expedition: An Arctic Journey Through History on George Back's River* (1981).

——— and Christopher C. Hanks (eds.). *The Kazan: Journey Into an Emerging Land* (1991).

Perkins, Robert. *Into the Great Solitude: An Arctic Journey* (1991).

Petrone, Penny (ed.). *Northern Voices: Inuit Writing in English* (1988).

Pitseolak, Peter. *People From Our Side: A Life Story With Photographs and Oral Biography* (new ed. with Dorothy Harley Eber, 1993).

Pryde, Duncan. *Nunaga: My Land, My Country* (1971).

Purich, Donald. *The Inuit and Their Land: The Story of Nunavut* (1992).

Rasky, Frank. *The Polar Voyagers: Explorers of the North* (1976).

Rea, K.J. *The Political Economy of the Canadian North: An Interpretation of the Course of Development in the Northern Territories of Canada to the Early 1960s* (1968).

Richardson, John. *Arctic Ordeal: The Journal of John Richardson, Surgeon-Naturalist with Franklin, 1820–1822* (1984).

Roberts, Leslie. *The Mackenzie* (1949, rpt. 1974).

Seidelman, Harold and James Turner. *The Inuit Imagination: Myth and Sculpture in the Canadian North* (1993).

Shapiro, Jane Ann (ed.). *Voices From the Eastern Arctic* (1987).

Smith, David M. *Moose-Deer Island House People: A History of Native People in Fort Resolution* (1982).

Smith, James K. *The Mackenzie River: Yesterday's Fur Frontier, Tomorrow's Energy Battleground* (1977).

Soper, J. Dewey. *Canadian Arctic Recollections: Baffin Island, 1923–1951* (1981).

Stoneman-McNichol, Jane. *On Blue Ice: The Inuvik Adventure* (1983).

Struzick, Edward. *Northwest Passage: The Quest For an Arctic Route to the East* (1991).

Tetso, John. *Trapping Is My Life* (new enl. ed. 1970, rpt. 1977).

Thomas, Lewis H. *The Struggle for Responsible Government in the North-West Territories, 1870–97* (2nd ed. 1978).

Turner, Dick. *Nahanni* (1975).

———. *Sunrise on the Mackenzie* (1977).

———. *Wings of the North* (1976).

Valentine, Victor F. and Frank G. Vallee (eds.). *Eskimo of the Canadian Arctic* (1968, rpt. 1978).

Van Steensel, Maja (ed.). *People of Light and Dark* (1966, rpt. 1974).

VanderZwaag, David L. and Cynthia Lamson (eds.). *The Challenge of Arctic Shipping: Science, Environmental Assessment, and Human Values* (1990).

Watt, Erik. *Yellowknife: How a City Grew* (1990).

Watt, Frederick B. *Great Bear, a Journey Remembered* (1980).

Wiebe, Rudy. *Playing Dead: A Contemplation Concerning the Arctic* (1989).

Wilkinson, Douglas. *Arctic Fever: The Search for the Northwest Passage* (1971).

——. *Land of the Long Day* (1955, rpt. 1967).

Wilson, Ian and Sally Wilson. *Arctic Adventures: Exploring Canada's North by Canoe and Dog Team* (1992).

Woodman, David C. *Unravelling the Franklin Mystery: Inuit Testimony* (1991).

Zaslow, Morris. *The Opening of the Canadian North, 1870–1914* (1971).

Northwest Territories in Literature

Ballem, John. *The Moon Pool* (1978). A foreign power plots to use the native peoples as pawns.

Buchan, John. *Sick Heart River* (1941, rpt. 1981). A dying man searches the Arctic for a missing man.

Clark, Larry. *Doomsday Minus Four: Nuclear Brinksmanship and Beyond in the Canadian Arctic* (1981). An espionage thriller.

Edmonds, Yvette. *Beyond the Snowstorm* (1992). A novel about Inuit.

Gedalof, Robin (ed.). *Paper Stays Put: A Collection of Inuit Writing* (1980).

Henighan, Tom. *The Well of Time* (1988). Historical fiction about a Viking settlement.

Houston, James. *Spirit Wrestler* (1980). An Inuit shaman's power conflicts with white culture.

——. *The White Dawn: An Eskimo Saga* (1971, rpt. 1983). The story, based on fact, about three white marooned whalers who disrupt an isolated Inuit community.

——. *Whiteout* (1988). A rebellious youth is sent north to an isolated settlement on Baffin Island.

Ipellie, Alootook. *Arctic Dreams and Nightmares* (1993). Inuit fiction.

Knox, Alexander. *Night of the White Bear* (1971). Three Inuit strive to survive the elements and a waiting bear.

Markoosie. *Harpoon of the Hunter* (1970). The first piece of Inuit fiction tells the story of a young Inuit hunter coming into manhood in a brutal environment.

Mowat, Farley. *The Snow Walker* (1975). Eleven stories about Inuit and their lives.

Nicol, Clive. *The White Shaman* (1979). A man on an Arctic expedition comes to understand the land and the Inuit.

Nungak, Zebedee and Eugene Arima. *Inuit Stories: Povungnituk* (rev. ed. 1988).

Perrault, E.G. *Spoil!: A Novel* (1975). An oil rig blow-out impacts both the Arctic environment and the people involved.

Schroeder, Andreas and Rudy Wiebe (eds.). *Stories From Pacific & Arctic Canada: A Selection* (1974).

Schultz-Lorentzen, Finn. *Arctic* (1976). A series of vignettes set in a fictional village on the Keewatin coast.

Stories From Pangnirtung (1976).

Walker, David. *Where the High Winds Blow* (1960). A romantic adventure about the opening of the north.

Whitaker, Muriel (ed.). *Stories From the Canadian North* (1980).

Wiebe, Rudy. *A Discovery of Strangers* (1994). Based on the 1819–1822 Franklin expedition.

——. *The Mad Trapper: A Novel* (1980). Based on the true story of the RCMP's tracking through N.W.T. of Albert Johnson, a man wanted for murder.

York, Thomas. *The Musk Ox Passion* (1978). A satire about the Canadian north.

——. *Snowman: A Novel* (1976). Partly based on fact, this is a story of survival in the savage north.

——. *Trapper* (1981). Historical fiction about Albert Johnson, the Mad Trapper.

YUKON TERRITORY

Yukon Territory is situated in the northwest corner of Canada's continental mainland. It is bordered on the west by the state of Alaska; on the north by the Beaufort Sea; on the east by Northwest Territories; and on the south by the province of British Columbia. Beaver Creek is Canada's most westerly community.

Name Yukon Territory. "Yukon" is adapted from the Loucheux Indian word "yu-kun-ah" meaning "great river". *Previous names:* Rupert's Land (1670–1868); North-West Territories (1868–1895); North-West Territories, District of Yukon (1895–1898).

Flag The flag is divided vertically in three equal parts, green, white, and blue panels with the arms of the Yukon above a wreath of fireweed on the white field. Adopted by the Territorial Council on March 1, 1968.

Coat of Arms A red cross on a white background with a centred blue and white roundel occupies the top third of the shield. The blue background in the bottom two-thirds is divided vertically by two wavy white lines; each bisected half contains a red wedge enclosing two gold discs. Above the shield is a black and white malamute dog standing on a mound of snow and a gold and red wreath. Authorized by Queen Elizabeth II on February 24, 1956.

Motto None.

Emblems
Bird common raven (*Corvus corax*)
Flower fireweed (*Epilobium angustifolium*)
Gemstone lazulite
Tartan green, dark blue, magenta, yellow, and white on a light blue background

Date of Entry into Confederation June 13, 1898.

Official Languages English, French, and Yukon aboriginal languages; the latter may be used in the Legislature and where the Commissioner in Executive Council makes regulations for their use.

Capital City Whitehorse, situated mainly on the west side of the Yukon River ca. 105 km. (65 mi.) north of the British Columbia border; the transportation, business, and service centre of Yukon Territory; population 17,925. Whitehorse takes its name from the nearby Whitehorse Rapids. In 1898 it became a temporary stopping point for prospectors because of its location at the head of navigation on the Yukon River. A permanent

233

settlement was established in 1900. Incorporated 1950; Whitehorse replaced Dawson City as the capital of Yukon Territory in 1953.

Territorial Holidays In addition to national statutory holidays (see page 2), Yukon Territory residents celebrate Discovery Day (the third Monday in August).

Geography and Climate

Geography Yukon Territory, roughly triangular in shape, is mostly rugged mountain terrain with high plateaus, a few lowland river valleys, and a tundra plain along the Arctic coast. There are permanent icecaps on many mountains and permafrost, while found in many areas, is continuous north of the Porcupine River. Forests cover about half the territory, particularly in the area south of Dawson City where well-forested river valleys are found.

Area 483,450 sq. km. (186,661 sq. mi.); 4.8% of Canada. *Rank:* 8th.

Inland Water 4,481 sq. km. (1,730 sq. mi.); number of lakes not available. Largest lake: Teslin Lake, 381 sq. km. (147 sq. mi.).

Elevations Highest point: Mount Logan, 5,959 m. (19,550 ft.), highest point in Canada, second highest in North America. Lowest point: Beaufort Sea shoreline, sea level.

Major Rivers (* indicates a designated Canadian Heritage River or a part has been designated): *Alsek, *Bonnet Plume, Donjek, Klondike, Liard, MacMillan, McQuesten, Nisutlin, Peel, Pelly, Porcupine, Ross, Snake, White, Wind, *Yukon.

Climate Yukon Territory experiences long, cold winters and short, warm, dry summers and has enormous annual temperature ranges, averaging ca. 40°C (104°F). The greatest recorded absolute range is 98.3°C (208.9°F) at Mayo. The average daily mean temperature in January in southern Yukon is −20°C (−4°F); in northern Yukon −30°C (−22°F); in July in Yukon as a whole, 15°C (59°F). The lowest recorded temperature in Yukon Territory: −63°C (−81.4°F) at Snag on February 3, 1947, the coldest recorded temperature in North America; the highest recorded temperature in Yukon Territory: 36.1°C (97°F) at Mayo on June 14, 1969.

Annual precipitation varies widely averaging 200 mm. (0.8 in.) along the Beaufort Sea coast to 2,000 mm. (7.9 in.) in the southwest corner of the Territory. Average annual snowfall ranges from 60 cm. (23.6 in.) on the Beaufort Sea coast to 250 cm. (98.4 in.) in mountain areas. Greatest recorded snowfall over five consecutive days: 86.4 cm. (34 in.) at Carcross on February 18, 1923.

Time Zone Pacific.

Parks and Historic Sites

In this section, * indicates the area is, or part of it is, a Unesco World Heritage Site.

National Parks Located in Yukon Territory

Park	Location	Size
Ivvavik	northwest corner	10,168 sq. km. (3,926 sq. mi.)
*Kluane	Haines Junction	22,013 sq. km. (8,499 sq. mi.)
Vuntut	north of Old Crow	4,400 sq. km. (1,699 sq. mi.)

Territorial Parks

Park	Location	Size
Coal River Springs	east of Watson Lake	16 sq. km. (6 sq. mi.)
Herschel Island	off Arctic coast	101 sq. km. (39 sq. mi.)

Yukon Territory has 2 wildlife sanctuaries and 1 Ramsar site.

National Historic Sites and Parks in Yukon Territory
Canol Road, Ross River
Chilkoot, access Bennett Lake
Klondike, Dawson City
S.S. Klondike, Whitehorse

International Historic Park in Yukon Territory
Klondike Gold Rush (shared with Alaska)

In addition, there are a number of historic sites in the Yukon Territory administered by the Territory, municipalities, or organizations. The major sites are:

Dalton Post Heritage Site, Dalton Post
Fort Selkirk, Fort Selkirk
Old Log Church Museum Territorial Historic Site, Whitehorse

Demography

Native peoples comprise 12% of the population. Most of these are Indians and Métis; there are less than 100 Inuit. All figures relating to Yukon Territory population do not include the population on two incompletely enumerated aboriginal communities. Staff at the Government of Yukon Bureau of Statistics estimate that ca. 450 live in these communities.

Yukon Territory Population: 27,797; 0.1% of national; *rank* 12th

Historical population data

1981	23,155
1971	18,390
1961	14,628
1951	9,096
1941	4,914
1921	4,157

Population Density: 0.06 persons per sq. km. (0.14 per sq. mi.)

Number of Dwellings: 10,071

Indian Bands: 16

Population characteristics:
urban: 16,335; 58.8%
rural: 11,462; 41.2%
19 and under: 8,700; 31.3%
65 and over: 1,095; 3.9%
average income for full-time employment 15 years and over (1990): $37,287; men $41,353; women $31,806
average life expectancy at birth (1989): (lowest in Canada)
  non-native men: 68.3 years
  native men: 65.7 years
  non-native women: 75.2 years
  native women: 74.0 years
live birth rate: 568; 20.4 per 1000
deaths: 114; 4.2 per 1000 (lowest in Canada)
marriages: 196; 7.1 per 1000
divorces: 67; 2.41 per 1000

Cities and Towns (for definitions of CA and CSD, see page viii)

Name	Population	Dwellings	National Pop. Rank
Whitehorse	17,925	6,241	106 (CA)
Faro	1,221	476	2,133 (CSD)
Dawson City	972	416	2,522 (CSD)
Watson Lake	912	303	2,630 (CSD)

Government and Politics, 1898–

A description of the division of powers between the federal and territorial governments will be found on page 4.

Commissioner The Commissioner fulfills a function similar to that of a lieutenant-governor in the provinces but reports to the Minister of Indian Affairs and Northern Development. (A description of the duties of lieutenant-governors is found on page 7.)

Commissioners of Yukon Territory/Title/Term

James Morrow Walsh
(Commissioner, 1897–1898)
William Ogilvie
(Commissioner, 1898)
Thomas Fawcett
(Gold Commissioner, 1898)
Gordon Hunter
(Gold Commissioner, 1898)
Edmund Cumming Senkler
(Gold Commissioner, 1898–1901)
James Hamilton Ross
(Commissioner, 1901–1902)
Zachary Taylor Wood
(Acting Commissioner, 1902–1903)
Frederick Tennyson Congdon)
(Commissioner, 1903–1905)
William Wallace Burns McInnes
(Commissioner, 1905–1907)
Alexander Henderson
(Commissioner, 1907–1912)
F.X. Gosselin
(Gold Commissioner, 1907–1913)
George Black
(Commissioner, 1912–1916)
George Patton MacKenzie
(Gold Commissioner, 1913–1918)
George Norris Williams
(Administrator, 1916–1918)
George Patton MacKenzie
(Gold Commissioner, 1918–1925)
Percy Reid
(Gold Commissioner, 1925–1928)
George Ian MacLean
(Gold Commissioner, 1928–1932)
George Allan Jeckell
(Comptroller, 1932–1936)
George Allan Jeckell
(Controller, 1936–1947)
John Edward Gibben
(Controller, 1947–1948)
John Edward Gibben
(Commissioner, 1948–1950)

Andrew Harold Gibson
(Commissioner, 1950–1951)
Wilfred George Brown
(Commissioner, 1952–1955)
Frederick Howard Collins
(Commissioner, 1955–1962)
Gordon Robertson Cameron
(Commissioner, 1962–1966)
James Smith
(Commissioner, 1966–1976)
Arthur MacDonald Pearson
(Commissioner, 1976–1978)
Frank B. Fingland
(Commissioner, 1978–1979)
Ione Jean Christensen
(Commissioner, 1979)
Douglas Leslie Dewey Bell
(Administrator, 1979–1980)
Douglas Leslie Dewey Bell
(Commissioner, 1980–1986)
John Kenneth McKinnon
(Commissioner, 1986–   )

Legislative Assembly The Legislative Assembly of Yukon Territory has powers similar to those of a provincial assembly, except the federal government is responsible for forestry, fire suppression, and natural resources other than game and the federal government can disallow any act within one year. The Assembly consists of 17 members elected by popular vote, each member representing a constituency; term of office: up to 4 years. Remuneration (1994/5): $32,133 + $15,263 expense allowance for members from outside Whitehorse and $13,327 for Whitehorse member; additional amounts for special appointments; qualifications for members: Canadian citizen, 18 years of age or older, ordinarily resident in Yukon Territory for twelve months.

Qualifications for Yukon Territory Voters in Territorial Elections Canadian citizen, 18 years of age or older, ordinarily resident in Yukon Territory for twelve months.

Government Leaders of Yukon Territory/Party/Term
Christopher William Pearson
(Conservative, 1978–1985)
Williard Phelps
(Conservative, 1985)
Anthony Penikett
(New Democratic, 1985–1992)
John L. Ostashek
(Yukon, 1992–)

Executive Council The Executive Council consists of a maximum of 8 members of the Legislative Assembly who are chosen by the Assembly. Council members are responsible for one or more Territorial government departments.

Government Leader The Government Leader is chosen by members of the Legislative Assembly from one of the members of the Executive Council and serves as chairperson of the Council.

Government Departments All departments may be contacted through the Inquiry Centre at (403)667-5811 or 667–5812.

Community and Transportation Services
Economic Development
Education
Finance
Government Services
Health and Social Services
Justice
Renewable Resources
Tourism

Yukon Territory Representation in Federal Government
House of Commons: 1 member
Senate: 1 member

Finances

Consolidated schedules of Yukon Territory's revenue and expenditures for the years 1992/93 and 1991/92 are shown below in thousands of dollars. The financial year runs from April 1 to March 31 of the year following.

	Actual 1992/93	*Actual 1991/92*
Revenue		
Taxation and general revenue	40,717	45,276
Other	12,916	16,552
Investment income	11,306	15,110
Government of Canada	255,753	235,371
Total revenue for the year	320,692	312,309
Expenditures		
Health and social services	77,781	68,999
Education	73,958	66,705
Community transportation services	67,034	62,621
Justice	29,551	26,888
Government services	23,891	21,659
Renewable resources	13,163	11,782
Other	49,091	41,374
Interest on debt	805	893
Total expenditures for the year	335,274	300,921
Surplus for the year	(14,582)	11,388

Economy

Rugged terrain and difficult access make the likelihood of a modern industrial economy improbable. Limited agriculture with cool season vegetables and forage crops is only possible along some river valleys. Primary extraction of natural resources is the basis of Yukon's economy. Only 12% of Yukon Territory is suitable for a productive forest industry. There is a large potential hydroelectric resource. Aboriginal peoples are involved in the provision of fur and are part of the growing tourism industry.

Major Industries Primary resource extraction, principally mining for gold, lead-zinc, silver, etc., is Yukon Territory's principal industry. Tourism has become second in importance. There are some small manufacturing industries.

Gross Domestic Product (1992) $962 million (in current dollars at factor cost); % of national: 0.2%; *rank:* 12th

Distribution of gross domestic product (1990)

Mining	36.0%
Government services	14.5%
Construction	11.3%
Finance, insurance, real estate	8.2%
Educational services	5.1%
Transportation, storage	5.0%
Retail trade	4.4%
Other utilities	2.3%
Manufacturing	1.7%
Health services	1.5%
Wholesale trade	1.3%
Logging	0.2%
Agriculture	0.1%
Fishing and trapping	0.1%

Employment 13,336

Unemployment Rate (December 1993) 12.0%

Fur Production Value $429,836

Value of Mineral Production $340.7 million

Minimum Wage $6.24

Exports (1992) Combined merchandising export for Yukon Territory and Northwest Territories amounted to $366 million.

History

ca. 150,000 B.C.	Some evidence that Homo Erectus may have been in Old Crow Flats.
ca. 28,000 B.C.–8,000 B.C.	Paleo-Indians arrive; Yukon Territory is the only part of Canada's surface exposed during last ice age.
ca. 17th century	Gwich'in, Han, Inuit, Kaska, Tagish, Tutchone, Upper Tanana live in present-day Yukon Territory.
1825	*February 25* Britain and Russia sign a treaty establishing the inland boundaries of Alaska at the first mountain range and the 141st meridian. John Franklin maps the Arctic coastline from the mouth of the Mackenzie River to the Alaskan north slope.
1826	Franklin names Herschel Island.
1837	Thomas Simpson surveys the Arctic coast from the Mackenzie River to Alaska.
1842	Hudson's Bay Company establishes Fort Frances.
1845	Robert Campbell becomes the first white man to explore the Yukon region. John Bell reaches the junction of the Yukon and Porcupine Rivers, the first white man to do so. Hudson's Bay Company establishes Pelly Banks post.

1847	*Summer* Hudson's Bay Company establishes Fort Yukon at mouth of the Porcupine River.
1848	Campbell establishes Fort Selkirk on the Pelly River.
1852	Tlingit Indians ransack Fort Selkirk.
1863	First significant report of gold in Yukon Territory is made. In the next few years small parties of prospectors arrive.
1867	*March* Russia sells Alaska to the United States.
	Because Fort Yukon is deemed to be in United States territory, the Hudson's Bay Company builds a new post, Rampart House.
	November 6 Federal government adopts a resolution for the admission of Rupert's Land into Canada.
1869	*November 19* Canada purchases Rupert's Land from the Hudson's Bay Company; the transfer in effect *July 15, 1870.*
1886	*May 14* Federal government passes an act to allow North-West Territories representation in the federal parliament.
	First important gold discovery is made at the junction of the Forty Mile and Yukon rivers.
	First permanent mining camp is established at Forty Mile River.
1887	George Richard McConnell surveys Yukon Territory.
1889	Arthur Harper establishes a trading post in the Selkirk area.
1892–1895	American whalers winter on Herschel Island.
1894	*May* North-West Mounted Police arrive at Forty Mile Creek to begin policing Yukon Territory.
1895	*July 24* Charles Constantine arrives at the junction of Forty Mile Creek and Yukon River where he builds Fort Constantine for the North-West Mounted Police.
	October 2 Federal government establishes the Provisional District of Yukon Territory and the boundary between Yukon and the North-West Territories.
1896	*August 17* George Washington Carmack and companions discover gold in the Klondike, starting a gold rush that brings 100,000 people to Yukon Territory.
	August Joseph Ladue founds Dawson City.
1897	*August 16* Privy Council establishes the Yukon Judicial District.
	August 17 James Morrow Walsh is appointed commissioner of the Provisional District of Yukon.
1898	*May 27 Klondike Nugget*, Yukon's first newspaper, is published in Dawson City.
	June 13 Yukon Territory is separated from North-West Territories with Dawson City as its capital. Provision is made for government by a territorial commissioner and a partly appointed, partly elected, four-member council.
	July 4 William Ogilvie is appointed the first commissioner of Yukon Territory.
	September 11 Yukon Field Force, sent by the federal government to help the North-West Mounted Police preserve order and bolster Canada's claims to the Alaska-Yukon border, arrives in Dawson City.
	Frank Watson, a trapper, settles at Watson Lake.
1899	*August 11* Yukon Act is amended to add two elected members to the Territorial Council.
Early 1900s	Inuvaluit move from Yukon Territory to the Mackenzie River delta area because of the demise of the whaling industry.
	Easily extracted placer gold is depleted in the Klondike ending the boom.
1900	*July* White Pass and Yukon Railway built from Skagway, Alaska, to Whitehorse, 177 km. (110 mi.), is opened.
	October 17 First Yukon Territory Council election is held.

1901	Yukon Territory's first museum, Dawson City Museum, is established.
1902	*May 15* Yukon Act amendment raises the number of elected members on the Territorial Council to 5 and allows 1 Yukon representative to sit in the federal House of Commons.
	Dawson City is incorporated.
1903	*August 7* North-West Mounted Police post placed on Herschel Island establishes Canadian sovereignty, the first permanent police post north of the Canadian Arctic coast.
	October 20 International Joint High Commission settles the Alaska panhandle boundary dispute cutting off Yukon's access to the Pacific Ocean; Canada is enraged by British betrayal of Canadian interests.
	Permanent settlement at Teslin begins with the founding of a trading post serving the Tlingit Indians.
1906	Silver/lead deposit is discovered near Mayo.
1907	*July 20* Yukon Act amendment provides for a wholly elected Council of 10 members for a 3-year term.
	September 23 North-West Mounted Police complete a 2.4 m. (7.9 ft.) wide trail from Edmonton to Dawson City, the first access to Yukon Territory entirely on Canadian soil.
	Whaling market collapses.
1909	*June 28* First sitting of the wholly elected Council.
1913	First hardrock mine producing silver and lead opens at Keno Hill.
1918	*March 28* Decline in population since 1898 causes the federal government to cut the Territory's budget in half and amend the Yukon Act to abolish the Territorial Council; Gold Commissioner assumes the powers previously invested in the Commissioner and the Administrator.
1919	*April 3* Yukon Act amendment reinstates the elected Territorial Council with 3 members and allows women to vote in elections for Council.
1920	World War I Prohibition is reversed allowing alcoholic beverages to be sold legally through government stores.
1930s	High prices for furs make trapping an important activity.
1932	*June 30* Federal government transfers the powers of the gold commissioner to the office of comptroller.
1934	*February 20* Office of gold commissioner is abolished retroactive to March 20, 1932.
1936	*December 3* Name of Yukon's chief executive officer is changed from comptroller to controller.
1937	*April 27* Yukon Council protests the proposed federal plan to annex Yukon Territory to British Columbia.
1938	Hudson's Bay Company re-establishes a trading post at Fort Selkirk.
1942–1944	United States government constructs the Canol Pipeline from Norman Wells, Northwest Territories, across the Mackenzie River to Whitehorse; it is abandoned *March 1945*.
1942–1945	Whitehorse becomes a centre of the United States Army Corps of Engineers construction activity in response to the Japanese occupation of the Aleutian Islands.
1942	Watson Lake booms as a major centre for the construction of the Alaska Highway.
	November 20 First long distance land route in Yukon Territory, the Alaska Highway, built by the United States Army from Dawson Creek, British Columbia, to Delta Junction near Fairbanks, Alaska, opens officially.

1946	*April 3* Canada buys the Canadian section of the Alaska Highway from the United States for $108,000,000.
1948	Commissioner becomes the chief executive officer of the Yukon Territory replacing the Comptroller. Several other territorial officers are also appointed.
1949	Canadian and American armed forces build Atlin Road from Atlin, British Columbia, to Whitehorse.
1951	*May 31* Territorial Council is increased to 5 elected members.
1952	Northern Power Commission, a federal crown corporation, becomes the principal electric utility in Yukon Territory.
1953	Dawson City and Whitehorse are linked by an all-weather road.
1957	Major hydroelectric plant is built in Whitehorse.
1959	*August 17* Federal Department of Northern Affairs announces discovery of oil in Yukon Territory.
1960	*July 1* Yukon Hospital Insurance Service comes into effect.
1961	*July 22* Northwest Telecommunications System, the largest single microwave project in Canada, is inaugurated at Whitehorse.
	September Yukon Regional Library is established.
1964	Last non-native residents leave Herschel Island when the Royal Canadian Mounted Police post is abandoned.
1966	Yukon Act amendment provides for a Commissioner as head of government and for a legislative body.
	Government Organization Act makes the federal Minister of Northern Affairs responsible for directing the Commissioner in the administration of Yukon Territory.
1967	*September 11* Jean Gordon becomes the first woman to be elected to the Territorial Council.
1969	Cyprus Anvil Mines Company opens a major lead-zinc mine and founds Faro to provide housing for workers.
1970	*June 17* Federal government directs the Commissioner to establish an Executive Committee headed by the Commissioner with four members (two from the elected Council) responsible for advising the Commissioner in the administration of Yukon Territory.
1972	*March 7* Yukon Territory gives 13 sq. km. (5 sq. mi.) on Mount Logan to Northwest Territories as compensation for a surveying error.
	April 1 Yukon government takes responsibility for maintaining the Alaska Highway.
	August 2 Federal government proclaims the Arctic Waters Pollution Prevention Act to protect the Arctic from pollution by foreign supertankers.
1974	*April 1* Yukon Act amendment increases to 12 the number of members in the Territorial Council.
	July 15–16 Floods close many sections of the Alaska Highway and damage bridges.
1975	*May 30* Federal legislation provides for a seat in the Senate of Canada for a Yukon representative.
	October 23 Paul Lucier is appointed as the first senator from Yukon Territory.
	November 14 Federal government announces that the Yukon government will be fully involved in land claims negotiations.
1976	*April 15* Dome Petroleum receives government approval to drill offshore wells in the Beaufort Sea.
1977	*May 8* Berger Commission report recommends a permanent ban on any pipeline from Alaska across northern Yukon.

1978   *July 6* Federal government prohibits all new development from Porcupine and Bell rivers to Beaufort Sea in preparation for a national wilderness area.

September Hilda Watson is elected leader of the Yukon Territorial Progressive Conservative Party becoming the first woman to lead a political party in Canada.

November Territorial Council of 3 appointed and 12 elected members is replaced by a 16 member elected legislature.

November 20 First Yukon election to be fought on party lines, the first election since 1958 to be run entirely by the Yukon government, and the first natives, Grafton Njootli and Maurice Byblow, are elected to the Yukon Legislative Assembly.

Completion of Haines Road from Carcross to Whitehorse gives Yukon its first access to the Pacific Ocean at Skagway.

1979   *January 20* Ione Jean Christensen becomes Yukon's first woman commissioner.

May 3 Ice jam on the Yukon River causes severe flooding in Dawson City damaging 80% of the buildings.

August 18 Dempster Highway from Dawson City to Inuvik, Northwest Territories, opens.

October 19 Yukon Territory achieves responsible government when the federal government reduces the powers of the Commissioner who is removed from the Executive Committee (renamed the Executive Council) and must accept advice from the Executive Council, composed of 5 members of the Yukon Legislative Assembly, on matters under Yukon Territory jurisdiction.

1981   *November 3* Dome Petroleum Ltd. announces huge new oil deposits found in the Beaufort Sea.

1982   *October* White Pass and Yukon Railway closes.

Depressed world markets result in closure of all major Yukon mines.

1984   *January 26* Federal government and Yukon Indians sign a tentative land claims agreement including $620 million to be paid over 20 years and aboriginal title to 20,000 sq. km. (7,722 sq. mi.).

1985   Federal and Yukon governments sign an agreement to manage the Porcupine caribou herd.

1986   Many major Yukon mines reopen as world demand increases.

1987   *July* First territorial park, Herschel Island, is established.

Canada and the United States sign a treaty for the conservation of the Porcupine caribou herd.

Yukon assets in the Northern Canada Power Commission are transferred to the Yukon Energy Corporation.

1988   *May 18* Yukon Territories government passes the Languages Act concerning the official use of English, French, and Yukon aboriginal languages.

1989   *December 2* Audrey McLaughlin, Whitehorse, is elected leader of the federal New Democratic Party, becoming the first female leader of a federal party.

Federal government transfers to Yukon Territory responsibility for freshwater fisheries and mine safety.

1990   Federal government transfers to Yukon Territory responsibility for interterritorial roads.

1991   *April* Announcement is made of the Arctic Environment Strategy spreading $100 million over 6 years to preserve and enhance Arctic ecosystems.

1992   *April 22* Federal government signs a land claim granting Gwich'in Indians from Yukon Territory and Northwest Territories title to 14,805.6 sq.km. (9,200 sq. mi.) and $75 million over 15 years.

Culture and Education

Performing Arts Yukon Territory has 4 amateur theatre companies, 1 dance organization, 1 major performing arts centre, and several annual festivals. The following is a selection of events.

Dawson City Music Festival (July) (contemporary music of the Yukon and Canada)	(403)993-5584
Discovery Days, Dawson City (August)	(403)993-5434
Frostbite Music Festival, Whitehorse (February)	(403)668-4921
Nakai Theatre Ensemble, Whitehorse (northern cultural expression)	(403)667-2646
Yukon International Festival of Storytelling, Whitehorse (June) (storytelling, dance, and music from the circumpolar north and other exotic parts of the world)	(403)633-7550
Yukon Sourdough Rendezvous, Whitehorse (February)	(403)667-2148

Territorial Museums and Galleries The following are representative of the museums and art galleries in Yukon Territory.

Dawson City Museum, Dawson City
George Johnston [Tlingit Indian] Museum, Teslin
Keno City Mining Museum, Keno City
Kluane Museum of Natural History, Burwash Landing

McBride Centennial Museum/Museum of the Yukon, Whitehorse
Yukon Permanent Art Collection, Whitehorse
Yukon Transportation Museum, Whitehorse

College (* indicates additional campuses in other centres)
Yukon College, Whitehorse*

Motor Vehicle Use

Motor Vehicles Registered for Use in Yukon Territory (1994): 32,762

Drivers Licenced by Yukon Territory (1994): 17,923. Minimum driving age: 16

Roads Paved: 1,924 km. (1,196 mi.); gravel surface: 2,808 km. (1,745 mi.); bridges maintained by the province: 120

Speed Limits Highways: 90 kph (56 mph); communities: 50 kph (31 mph); school zones 30 kph (19 mph)

First, Biggest, and Best

World's largest nonpolar icefield ranges: Kluane National Park
World's largest tungsten reserve: Mae Pass
North America's largest accumulation of high peaks: Elias Mountains in Kluane National Park has more than 20 summits of more than 4,200 m. (13,779.5 ft.)
North America's most northern lock: Marsh Lake Lock 24 km. (14.9 mi.) south of Whitehorse
America's earliest undisputed evidence of human activity: stone tools and animal bones probably 20,000 years old in caves on the Bluefish River in northern Yukon
North America's only public highway to cross the Arctic Circle: Dempster Highway crosses north of Eagle Plain
World's record for largest hot air balloon flown, for duration in air, for distance: Richard

Branson and Per Lindstrand flew 7,673 km. (4,768 mi.) in 46 hrs., 15 min. in a balloon with 73,620 cu. m. (2.6 million cu. ft.) capacity from Japan to Lac la Matre, January 17, 1991

World's largest recorded deer: Alaskan Moose bull shot on Yukon River, September 1897, had a standing height of 2.34 m. (7 ft., 8 in.) and an estimated weight of 1,180 kg (2,600 lbs)

World's largest recorded moose antler spread: 199.4 cm. (78.5 in.) from a moose killed near the Stewart River, October 1897

World's largest population of Dall sheep: Kluane National Park

World's highest concentration of grizzly bears: Kluane National Park

North America's lowest recorded temperature: −63°C (−81.4°F) at Snag, February 3, 1947

Sources of Information About Yukon Territory

Yukon Department of Tourism: Box 2703, Whitehorse, YT Y1A 2C6 (403)667-5811

Inquiry Centre, Yukon Executive Council Office: Box 2703, Whitehorse, YT Y1A 2C6 (403)667-5812

Yukon Government publications are available from individual government departments. Most publications, with the exception of legislation, are available free of charge.

Books About Yukon Territory: A Selected List

Reference Guides

The Alaska Highway, 1942–1991: A Comprehensive Bibliography of Material Available in the Yukon Archives & McBride Museum (1993).

Arctic Bibliography, 16 vols. (1953–1975).

Barker, Mary. *The Natural Resources of British Columbia and the Yukon* (1977).

Bruemmer, Fred. *Arctic Animals: A Celebration of Survival* (1986).

Burt, Page. *Barrenland Beauties: Show Plants of the Arctic Coast* (1991).

Cameron, Kirk and Graham Gomme. *A Compendium of Documents Relating to The Constitutional Development of the Yukon Territory* (1991).

Canada. Atmospheric Environment Service. *Canadian Climate Normals: Yukon and Northwest Territories* (1993).

Canada. Energy, Mines and Resources Canada. *Gazetteer of Canada: Yukon Territory* (5th ed. 1988).

Canada. Indian and Northern Affairs Canada. *Canada's North: The Reference Manual* (rev. ed. 1990).

Clark, Donald W. *Western Subarctic Prehistory* (1991).

Cooke, Alan and Clive Holland. *The Exploration of Northern Canada, 500 to 1920: A Chronology* (1978).

Coutts, R.C. *Yukon Places & Names* (1980).

Drazan, Joseph Gerald. *The Pacific Northwest: An Index to People and Places in Books* (1979). Includes Yukon Territory.

Goodwin, C. Ross and Lynda M. Howard. *The Beaufort Sea, Mackenzie Delta, Mackenzie Valley, and Northern Yukon: A Bibliographical Essay* (1984).

Haley, Delphine (ed.). *Marine Mammals of the North Pacific and Arctic Waters* (2nd ed. rev. 1986).

———. *Seabirds of the North Pacific and Arctic Waters* (1984).

Herrington, Clyde. *Atlas of the Canadian Arctic Islands* (1969).

Hoyt, Erich. *The Whales of Canada* (1984).

Maxwell, J.B. *The Climate of the Canadian Arctic Islands and Adjacent Waters*, 2 vols. (1980–1982).

Morley, William F.E. *Ontario and the Canadian North* (1978). The second part of this bibliography is devoted largely to local histories of Yukon Territory and Northwest Territories.

Philips, James W. *Alaska-Yukon Place Names* (1973).

Porsild, E.A. *Botany of South Eastern Yukon Adjacent to the Canol Road* (1951).

Smyth, Steven. *The Yukon Chronology* (1991).

Usher, Peter J. *Historical Statistics Approximating Fur, Fish and Game Harvests Within Inuit Lands of the N.W.T. and Yukon, 1915–1974, With Text* (1975).

Wahl, H.E. and others. *Climate of Yukon* (1987).

Youngman, Phillip M. *Mammals of the Yukon Territory* (1975).

Yukon Data Book (annual).

Yukon Bibliography (1964 + supplements).

Nonfiction Sources

*denotes a winner of a Governor General's Literary Award; **a winner for the title in its original French-language version.

Anderson, Barry C. *Lifeline to the Yukon: A History of Yukon River Navigation* (1983).

Anderson, Doris. *Ways Harsh & Wild* (1973).

Baird, Andrew. *Sixty Years on the Klondike* (1965).

Basque, Garnet (ed.). *Frontier Days in the Yukon* (1991).

Bennett, Gordon. *Yukon Transportation: A History* (1978).

Berton, Laura Beatrice. *I Married the Yukon* (1954, rpt. 1982).

Berton, Pierre. *The Arctic Grail: The Quest for the Northwest Passage and the North Pole, 1818–1909* (1988).

——. *Drifting Home* (1973, rpt. 1993).

——. **Klondike: The Last Great Gold Rush, 1896–1899* (rev. ed. 1986; published in the United States as *The Klondike Fever: The Life and Death of the Last Great Gold Rush*).

——. *The Klondike Quest: A Photographic Essay, 1897–1899* (1983).

——. **The Mysterious North* (1956, rpt. 1989).

Black, Martha Louise. *My Ninety Years* (rev. ed. by Flo Whyard 1980; originally published as *My Seventy Years*, 1938).

Bolotin, Norm. *Klondike Lost: A Decade of Photographs by Kinsey & Kinsey* (1980).

Brennan, Ann. *The Real Klondike Kate* (1990).

Bruemmer, Fred. *The Arctic* (1974, rpt. 1982).

—— and others. *The Arctic World* (1985).

Buerschaper, Peter. *Arctic Journey: Paintings, Sketches, and Reminiscences of a Vanishing World* (1977).

Calef, George. **Caribou and the Barren Lands* (1981).

Cantin, Eugene. *Yukon Summer* (1973).

Coates, Kenneth S. *Best Left as Indians: Native-White Relations in the Yukon Territory, 1840–1973* (1991).

——. *Canada's Colonies: A History of the Yukon and Northwest Territories* (1985).

—— and William R. Morrison. *Alaska Highway in World War II: The U.S. Army of Occupation in Canada's Northwest* (1992).

——. *Land of the Midnight Sun: A History of the Yukon* (1988).

—— (eds.). *Interpreting Canada's North: Selected Readings* (1989).

Crnkovich, Mary (ed.). *"Gossip": A Spoken History of Women in the North* (1990).

Cruikshank, Julie. *Reading Voices: Oral and Written Interpretations of the Yukon's Past* (1991).

—— with Angela Sidney, Kitty Smith, and Annie Ned. *Life Lived Like a Story: Life Stories of Three Yukon Elders.* (1990).

Cruikshank Lunny, June. *Spirit of the Yukon* (1992). Biography of a bush pilot.

Dacks, Gurston (ed.). *Devolution and Constitutional Development in the Canadian North* (1990).

Davids, Richard C. *Lords of the Arctic: A Journey Among the Polar Bears* (1982).

Dawson, George M. *Report on an Exploration in the Yukon District, N.W.T., and Adjacent Northern Portion of British Columbia, 1887* (1887, rpt. 1987).

Dosman, Edgar J. *The National Interest: The Politics of Northern Development, 1968–75* (1975).

Dumond, Don E. *The Eskimos and Aleuts* (rev. ed. 1987).

Duncan, Allan. *Medicine, Madams and Mounties: Stories of a Yukon Doctor* (1989).

Francis, Daniel. *Arctic Chase: A History of Whaling in Canada's North* (1984).

Freeman, Milton M.R., Eleanor E. Wein, and Darren E. Keith. *Recovering Rights: Bowhead Whales and Inuvialuit Subsistence in the Western Canadian Arctic* (1992).

Gordon-Cooper, H. *Yukoners: True Tales of the Yukon* (1978, rept. 1990).

Green, Lewis. *The Gold Hustlers* (rev. ed. 1994).

Hall, Sam. *The Fourth World: The Heritage of the Arctic and Its Destruction* (1987).

Hamelin, Louis-Edmond. ***Canadian Nordicity: It's Your North, Too* (1979).

Hamilton, John David. *Bob Friday's Other Eye and More Outrageous True Tales of Canada's Northern Frontier* (1986).

Hamilton, Walter R. *The Yukon Story: A Sourdough's Record of Gold Rush Days and Yukon Progress From the Earliest Times to the Present Day* (3rd ed. 1972).

Hildebrand, John. *Reading the River: A Voyage Down the Yukon* (1988).

Hines, Harold R. *Yukon Antics* (1987). Memoirs of a flying lawyer.

Hunt, William R. *North of 53'80: The Wild Days of the Alaska-Yukon Mining Frontier, 1870–1914* (1974).

Ingersoll, Ernest. *Gold Fields of the Klondike* (1897, rpt. 1981).

Laurence, Guy. *40 Years on the Yukon Telegraph* (1965, rpt. 1990).

Leonoff, Cyril Edward. *Pioneers, Pedlars, and Prayer Shawls: The Jewish Community in British Columbia and the Yukon* (1978).

Lester, Edward. *Guarding the Goldfields: The Story of the Yukon Field Force* (1987).

Livingston, John. *Arctic Oil* (1981).

MacGowan, Michael. *The Hard Road to Klondike* (1962).

McAdam, Ebenezer. *From Duck Lake to Dawson City: The Diary of Ebenezer McAdam's Journey to the Klondike, 1898–1899* (ed. by Robert G. Moyles, 1977).

McClellan, Catharine and others. *Part of the Land, Part of the Water: A Study of the Yukon Indians* (1987).

McGhee, Robert. *Canadian Arctic Prehistory* (1978).

Mercier, Francois Xavier. *Recollections of the Youkon: Memoirs From the Years 1868–1885* (1986).

Michael, Janet Moodie. *From Sissons to Meyer: The Administrative Development of the Yukon Government, 1948–1979* (1987).

Minter, Roy. *The White Pass: Gateway to the Klondike* (1987).

Morrison, David R. *The Politics of the Yukon Territory, 1898–1909* (1968).

Morritt, Hope. *Land of Fireweed: A Young Woman's Story of Alaska Highway Construction Days* (1985).

North, Dick. *The Lost Patrol* (1978).

Ogilvie, William. *Early Days on the Yukon* (1913, rpt. 1974).

Paine, Robert (ed.). *The White Arctic: Anthropological Essays on Tutelage and Ethnicity* (1977).

Paterson, T.W. *Ghost Towns of the Yukon* (1977).

Pohl, William L. (comp.). *Down North: Profiles From Alaska and the Yukon* (1986).

Satterfield, Archie. *After the Gold Rush* (1976).

——. *Chilkoot Pass, the Most Famous Trail in the North* (rev. ed. 1980).

——. *Klondike Park: From Seattle to Dawson City* (1993).

Shand, Margaret Clark and Ora M. Shand. *The Summit and Beyond* (1959).

Sinclair James M. *Mission Klondike* (1978).

Smythe, Emma B. with Hugh D. Maclean. *Yukon Lady: A Tale of Loyalty and Courage* (1985).

Taylor, Leonard W. *The Sourdough and the Queen: The Many Lives of Klondike Joe Boyle* (1983).

Therberge, John B. (ed.). *Kluane: Pinnacle of the Yukon* (1980).

Tryck, Keith. *Yukon Passage: Rafting 2000 Miles to the Bering Sea* (1980).

Watson, Jack B. with Gray Campbell. *Yukon Memories: A Mountie's Story* (1993).

Webb, Melody. *The Last Frontier: A History of the Yukon Basin of Canada and Alaska* (1985, rpt. 1993 as *Yukon, the Last Frontier*).

Wells, E. Hazard. *Magnificence and Misery: A Firsthand Account of the 1897 Klondike Gold Rush* (ed. by Randell M. Dodd, 1984).

White, Elmer J. *Tales of a Klondike Newsman* (1969).

Wilson, Amy V. *No Man Stands Alone* (1965). District nurse to the Yukon Indians.

Wright, Allen A. *Prelude to Bonanza: The Discovery and Exploration of the Yukon* (1976).

Yardley, Joyce. *Crazy Cooks and Gold Miners* (1992).

Zaslow, Morris. *The Opening of the Canadian North, 1870–1914* (1971).

Yukon Territory in Literature

Cameron, Anne. *South of an Unnamed Creek* (1989). Six young women find their separate ways from despair to a common purpose in the Klondike gold rush.

Edmonds, Jane. *Rivers of Gold* (1990). A novel set against the background of the Klondike gold rush.

Fry, Alan. *Come a Long Journey: A Novel* (1971). On a journey down the Yukon River a white man learns from his Indian guide the necessity of friendship.

London, Jack. *Call of the Wild* (1903, rpt. 1991). A dog is forcibly taken to the Klondike gold fields where he eventually becomes the leader of a wolf pack.

Lotz, Jim. *Death in Dawson* (1978). A crime story that includes the history of the Yukon.

Morritt, Hope. *Bohunk Road* (1987). A novel set in Whitehorse and Edmonton.

Service, Robert. *Songs of a Sourdough* (1907, rpt. many times); *The Spell of the Yukon* (1907, rpt. many times). Ballads celebrating the Klondike gold rush.

Van Herk, Aritha. *The Tent Peg: A Novel* (1981). A woman disguised as a man cooks for an all-male group prospecting in the Yukon.

Wiebe, Rudy. *The Mad Trapper: A Novel* (1980). Based on the true story of the RCMP's tracking of Albert Johnson, a man wanted for murder, through the Arctic to his final shooting at Rat River, Yukon Territory.

York, Thomas. *Trapper* (1981). Historical fiction about Albert Johnson, the Mad Trapper.